Darfur Genocide

Darfur Genocide

THE ESSENTIAL REFERENCE GUIDE

Alexis Herr, Editor

An Imprint of ABC-CLIO, LLC

Santa Barbara, California • Denver, Colorado

Library of Congress Cataloging-in-Publication Data

Names: Herr, Alexis, editor.
Title: Darfur genocide : the essential reference guide / Alexis Herr, editor.
Description: Santa Barbara : ABC-CLIO, 2020. | Includes bibliographical references and index.
Identifiers: LCCN 2019037092 (print) | LCCN 2019037093 (ebook) |
    ISBN 9781440865503 (cloth) | ISBN 9781440865510 (ebook)
Subjects: LCSH: Sudan—History—Darfur Conflict, 2003– | Sudan—Politics and
    government—1985– | Genocide—Sudan—Darfur. | Darfur (Sudan)—Ethnic relations. |
    Ethnic conflict—Sudan—Darfur.
Classification: LCC DT159.6.D27 D376 2020 (print) | LCC DT159.6.D27 (ebook) |
    DDC 962.404/3—dc23
LC record available at https://lccn.loc.gov/2019037092
LC ebook record available at https://lccn.loc.gov/2019037093

ISBN: 978-1-4408-6550-3 (print)
    978-1-4408-6551-0 (ebook)

24 23 22 21 20   1 2 3 4 5

This book is also available as an eBook.

ABC-CLIO
An Imprint of ABC-CLIO, LLC

ABC-CLIO, LLC
147 Castilian Drive
Santa Barbara, California 93117
www.abc-clio.com

This book is printed on acid-free paper ∞

Manufactured in the United States of America

I dedicate this book to all the genocide survivors who have shared their experiences with me, and to all the victims of the Darfur Genocide whose stories have never been heard.

Contents

List of Entries, ix

List of Primary Documents, xi

Preface, xiii

Introduction, xvii
    Overview, xvii
    Causes, xx
    Consequences, xxii
    Perpetrators, xxiv
    Victims, xxvii
    Bystanders, xxix
    International Reaction, xxxi

A–Z Entries, 1

Primary Documents, 165

Perspective Essays, 211
    What Was the Primary Cause of the Darfur Genocide?, 211
    Is the Conflict in Darfur an Example of a Just Case for Intervention?, 218

Chronology, 229

Abbreviations, 235

Bibliography, 237

List of Contributors, 243

Index, 245

List of Entries

Abdel Shafi, Ahmad
African Union
African Union Mission in Sudan
African Union–United Nations Mission in
    Darfur
Amnesty International
Annan, Kofi
Anyidoho, Henry Kwami
Banda, Abdallah
Bashir, Omar Hassan Ahmed al-
Bassolé, Djibril
Black Book, The
British Involvement in Darfur
Cheadle, Don
Child Soldiers
Clooney, George
Coalition for International Justice
Comprehensive Peace Agreement
Damon, Matt
Darfur
Darfur Atrocities Documentation Project
Darfur Development Front
Denial of the Darfur Genocide
Dinka
Diraige, Ahmed Ibrahim
Doha Document for Peace in Darfur
Egeland, Jan
Egyptian Involvement in Darfur
Enough Project
Famine of 1984–1985
Farrow, Mia
Fur

Gambari, Ibrahim
Garang, John
Gosh, Salah Abdallah
Harun, Ahmad
Hilal, Musa
Hussein, Abdel Raheem Muhammad
Ibrahim, Khalil
Itno, Idriss Déby
Janjaweed
Jihad
Jolie, Angelina
Justice and Equality Movement
Kapila, Mukesh
Khartoum
Kiir, Salva
Kristof, Nicholas
Kushayb, Ali
Liberation and Justice Movement
Lost Boys and Girls of Sudan
Massalit
McGrady, Tracy
Minawi, Minni
National Islamic Front
Nuba
Power, Samantha
Prendergast, John
Prosper, Pierre-Richard
Rape
Reeves, Eric
Religion
Satellite Sentinel Project
Save Darfur Coalition

South Sudan
Steidle, Brian
Sudan
Sudanese Civil Wars
Sudan Liberation Army
Sudan People's Liberation Movement/
　Army
Talisman Energy Corporation
Turabi, Hassan al-
United Nations Commission of Inquiry on
　Darfur
United Nations Convention on the Preven-
　tion and Punishment of the Crime of
　Genocide
United Nations Mission in the Sudan
United States Involvement in Darfur
Wahid, Abdel
Wallace, Gretchen Steidle
Weintraub, Jerry
What Is the What
Wiesel, Elie
Zaghawa

List of Primary Documents

1. U.S. Department of State Describes the Janjaweed Militia (March 6, 2004)
2. U.S. Department of State Memo on Genocide in Darfur (June 25, 2004)
3. U.S. Government Calls for International Resolve to Combat Darfur Genocide (July 2, 2004)
4. John Garang: Speech at Signing of Comprehensive Peace Agreement (January 10, 2005)
5. Excerpts from the United Nations Commission of Inquiry on Darfur (January 25, 2005)
   A. Establishment of the Commission
   B. Do Crimes Perpetrated in Darfur Constitute Genocide?
   C. Justice and Equality Movement
   D. Sudan Liberation Movement/Army
   E. The 'Janjaweed'
   F. The Commission's Recommendations Concerning Measures Designed to Ensure that Those Responsible are Held Accountable
6. "Sudan: Accountability for War Crimes," U.S. Department of State Press Guidance (January 28, 2005)
7. John Garang: Speech on "Social Contract" for Sudan (March 5, 2005)
8. Darfur Peace and Accountability Act (2006)

Preface

All genocides have a past, present, and future. In our quest to learn about the Darfur Genocide, it is imperative to remember this simple truth in order to avoid the common error of mistaking dates as definitive, statistics as representative, and accumulated knowledge as understanding. Ultimately, any true study of genocide requires its students, myself included, to grapple with a reality that is too tangled to unwind and too dark to fully illuminate.

When Western media outlets first reported on the eruption of violence in the Darfur region of Western Sudan in 2003, they attempted to simply describe the seed of the conflict as racial violence so that their readers could comprehend the confrontation that U.S. secretary of state Colin Powell would later call a genocide. Journalists reported that "Arabs" were killing "Africans," thus framing the violence as racially driven.

The explanation of racial hatred was not a foreign concept for Westerners, even if Darfur and Sudan required an internet search to locate. Ever since images of the Holocaust (1939–1945) entered into our collective consciousness through print and visual media, the notion of genocide has had a strong association with the attempted annihilation of an entire people. The killing of the Tutsis by the Hutus in Rwanda (1994) reinforced this image of racially or ethnically motivated genocide. So, the explanation of Darfur as a genocide motivated by racial hatred brought familiar clarity for those in the West about an otherwise distant conflict.

But this oversimplification allowed for uninformed assumptions about a people and a place, due in part to the broader global context. The world had been forever changed just two years before the genocide began in Darfur, when al-Qaeda terrorists launched an attack on the West on September 11, 2001, murdering nearly 3,000 people from more than fifty-seven countries in a single day. For many years, Osama bin Laden, the mastermind of the September 11 attacks, was painted as the poster child for Islamic extremism and the so-called Arab world was depicted as the greatest enemy of Western Christianity and democracy.

Western confusion about Sudan was made worse by the fact that bin Laden had a history in the country, having spent years nurturing his nascent terrorist group there. Sudanese president Hassan al-Turabi had welcomed bin Laden to the country in December 1991, and as he set up terrorist training camps, Turabi intensified his own Islamic extremism through his party, the National Islamic Front (NIF). As one scholar has aptly explained, "if al-Qaeda was not actually born in Sudan, it certainly developed its modus operandi in the bosom of al-Turabi's

Islamic revolution" (Crockett 2010: 122–123). Thus, when reporters wrote in 2003 that Sudanese "Arabs" were murdering "Africans," many saw the conflict through the lens of Western Islamophobia.

For some, the category of "Arab" was interpreted as "Muslim" and violence against "Africans" as religiously motivated. Thus, despite the fact that nearly all the perpetrators and the victims of the Darfur Genocide practice Islam, some well-meaning people reading about violence in Darfur assumed the conflict was a religiously motivated genocide. Such assumptions expose one of the weaknesses of studying violent acts within the temporal vacuum in which we live. In our rush to understand that which defies simple explanation, we take shortcuts. This approach, however, ultimately limits our ability to gain the understanding needed to effectively upend and prevent genocide.

In reality, the Darfur Genocide is complex and multifaceted. Studying Darfur, like all genocides, requires us to continually question our assumptions because, ultimately, we should never accept the answer that hatred alone is the root of all genocides. Such a conclusion is far too simplistic and in overreaching it ignores the steps that transform difference into division and neighbors into enemies. Nearly all the victims and perpetrators of the Darfur Genocide were born in Africa and nearly all involved practice Islam. To claim that the Darfur Genocide is motivated by Arabs killing Africans, or even more erroneous, Muslims killing Christians, belies Sudan's rich and long history of identity, tradition, and culture.

The Darfur Genocide is far more than a seventeen-year conflict driven by racial hatred. Curated to avoid such tropes, this volume includes entries that help us widen our gaze,

take into consideration historical events that inform identity politics in Sudan, and debate key questions about the genocide. In the Introduction, readers will gain a thoughtful overview of the history, conflict, and outcomes of the genocide and in so doing develop the intellectual toolset to study the Darfur Genocide in greater detail. To conclude this volume, we have reproduced nine primary source documents that allow readers to explore what the international community knew when the killings began, how the United Nations and its member states responded, and read speeches from John Garang, who championed the fight for South Sudan's independence and advocated for peace in Darfur. Lastly, this volume includes articles from five leading genocide scholars who take different positions when answering the following questions: Is the conflict in Darfur a just case for intervention? What was the primary cause of the Darfur Genocide?

The wealth of entries, arranged in alphabetical order for ease of use, go even deeper into the history to enhance a learner's comprehension of the genocide. For example, in addition to perceived ethnic divisions (see Dinka; Fur; Massalit; Zaghawa), it is helpful to consider environmental (see Famine of 1984–1985), colonial (see British Involvement in Darfur; Egyptian Involvement in Darfur; Religion), and political developments (see Bashir, Omar Hassan Ahmed al-; Darfur Development Front; Justice and Equality Movement; Khartoum; National Islamic Front; South Sudan; Sudanese Civil Wars) that stratified tribal and regional identities. Likewise, any effort to study the Darfur Genocide is significantly enriched when contemplated in conjunction with the Sudanese Civil Wars, which help to explain, in part, why most of the international community and the United Nations did not refer to the killings in Darfur as genocide even when the United States did (see Annan, Kofi; Comprehensive Peace Agreement; Denial of the Darfur Genocide; Garang, John; Kiir, Salva; Nuba; Religion; South Sudan; Sudanese Civil Wars).

This work also highlights the many efforts of African and international governments, coalitions, celebrities, and grassroot organizations to stop the killing of Darfurians and alleviate the suffering of refugees. The international community experimented with new peacekeeping efforts (see African Union Mission in Sudan; Lost Boys and Girls of the Sudan; United Nations–African Union Mission in Darfur; United Nations Mission in the Sudan) and endeavored to gather accurate information about the killings despite Sudanese president Omar Hassan Ahmed al-Bashir's best attempts to block humanitarian access (see Amnesty International; Coalition for International Justice; Darfur Atrocities Documentation Project; Enough Project; Satellite Sentinel Project; Save Darfur Coalition). Celebrities also used their fame to shine a spotlight on the killing, and in so doing helped the Darfur Genocide get more attention than any other modern atrocity (see Cheadle, Don; Clooney, George; Damon, Matt; Farrow, Mia; Jolie, Angelina; Kristof, Nicholas; McGrady, Tracy; Prendergast, John).

And yet, despite the press coverage, research, and international involvement in peace efforts, the killing in Darfur continues, which is why recent events in Sudan are all the more remarkable. When thousands of citizens gathered in Khartoum, the Sudanese capital, in 2018 to protest rising food prices, calls for food subsidies quickly changed into chants to remove Bashir from power. Since Bashir overthrew the Sudanese

government almost thirty years ago, the condition of human rights in Sudan has declined rapidly. Under his leadership, millions have died in conflicts described as genocide, civil war, war crimes, crimes against humanity, and terrorism. Millions more have abandoned their homes to escape the violence. Prior to South Sudan achieving independent statehood in 2011, Sudan held the somber distinction of having more internally displaced persons than any other country in the world with nearly 4.3 million Sudanese displaced by decades of conflict.

While foreign leaders, the United Nations, and celebrity clout could not remove this dictator from his throne, the manifest force of a civilian population unwilling to backdown has succeeded. The Sudanese Professional Association, an alliance of doctors, educators, scientists, lawyers, and other such lay leaders, has rallied a million people to peacefully assemble and demand a democratic Sudan. On April 14, 2019, Bashir was deposed and arrested. Currently, Sudanese civilians continue to gather in Khartoum to press the military powers that have assumed the role of government in the interim to create a power sharing agreement with the people. Though Sudan's past is full of pain, its present is one of resolve and hope. Its future is now up to the people of Sudan.

I am incredibly grateful to have worked on this project with ABC-CLIO, and I am thankful for its proven commitment to genocide education. In particular, Padraic (Pat) Carlin, a former managing editor at ABC-CLIO, has been a great supporter of this work and our shared frustration over the ongoing genocide in Darfur helped motivate the publication of this reference guide. I also want to express my appreciation for Nicole

Azze and Jitendra Kumar, both of whom worked hard to complete this project. Genocide activism can take many forms and there are endless ways to get involved in upending atrocity like that in Darfur. This is our contribution to the fight against genocide. It is our hope that in learning more about Darfur, we will be more prepared to prevent genocide and support its victims now and in the future.

And as always, I am thankful for the support of my husband, Shayle Kann, and my friends and family for encouraging me to keep learning and teaching about atrocities, even when it keeps me up late at night.

Alexis Herr

Introduction

Overview

In the first years of the twenty-first century, the Sudanese government initiated a campaign of genocide, terror, economic destruction, rape, and murder against Darfurians whom the perpetrators defined as "non-Arab" and "black Africans." The perpetrators viewed themselves as "Arab," and thus superior to their "black African" victims.

Darfur, a region roughly the size of France, is located in the western part of Sudan, bordering Libya, Chad, and the Central African Republic. Prior to the outbreak of violence in 2003, some 6.2 million people lived in Darfur of whom 80 percent resided in rural areas. An estimated forty to ninety different tribes or ethnic groups (depending on one's definition) inhabited the region, of whom 39 percent were considered Arab and 61 percent were considered "non-Arab." While the genocide was often described as a conflict between "non-Arab, black Africans" and "Arabs," these terms are misleading. Due to intermarriage, the distinction between "Arabs" and "non-Arabs" or "black Africans" owes more to lifestyle differences and cultural affiliation than "race." Arab Darfurians tend to lead nomadic lives, herding cattle and camels throughout the region, while non-Arabs are typically sedentary farmers. One exception is the Zaghawa, a non-Arab tribe that herds camels.

The outbreak of violence in 2003 is partly tied to environmental factors that disrupted the balance of life between the nomadic herders and the stationary farmers. After many years of drought, desertification, and a rise in population, a decisive lack of rainfall upset farming and water access throughout the region and resulted in widespread famine. This created competition for resources—nomadic herders directed their flocks to graze on the sedentary farmer's land and access to water often resulted in violent conflict. Sudan's central government, located hundreds of miles away in Khartoum, failed to act to help Darfurians, which sowed discontent throughout the Darfur region.

In late February 2003, two Darfurian rebel movements—the Sudan Liberation Army (SLA) and the Justice and Equality Movement (JEM)—attacked government military installations in Gulu, the capital of Jebel Marrah Province. SLA and JEM were rising up against the Sudanese government's economic, political, and social marginalization of populations living in the peripheries of Sudan and beyond the government center in Khartoum. In response, Sudan's armed forces, including the Popular Defense Force (PDF) and the intelligence services, and government-backed "Arab" militias, namely the Janjaweed (an Arabic colloquialism for "a man with a gun on horseback"), launched a brutal campaign targeting "non-Arab" Darfurian tribes accused of supporting SLA and JEM rebels.

Notably, while many scholars point to February 2003 as the beginning of the conflict that bore the genocide in Darfur, the region has a long history of conflict. Indeed, government attacks against "non-Arab" communities around Darfur were on the rise since 2001. In the late 1980s, a coalition of Arab nomads attacked Fur (a people of the Darfur region in western Sudan) farmers after the latter began fencing in land, hindering nomadic migrations. These early conflicts ruptured Darfur's population across tribal lines, pitting "Arab" nomads against "non-Arab" farmers. The Sudanese government capitalized on this division in its campaign to eradicate "African" Darfurian rebel groups during the genocide.

The victims of the Darfur genocide are primarily from three "non-Arab" tribal groups: the Fur, the Zaghawa, and the Massalit. Eyewitness accounts describe how Sudanese government forces and Janjaweed militias rode into Fur, Zaghawa, and Massalit villages on horses and camels, wielding automatic weapons (provided by the Sudanese government) and firing indiscriminately at civilians. Homes, grain stores, and crops were destroyed, while women, children, and the elderly were whipped, raped, tortured, and murdered. These tactics were designed to terrorize victims, forcing them to flee their homelands for displaced persons camps within Darfur or refugee camps in neighboring Chad. Once gone, "Arab" populations would resettle the land. The murderous intent behind the indiscriminate violence targeting all Darfurians, not just the Darfurian rebel groups, deviated from a pattern of violence that had plagued Darfur for decades.

At first, foreign governments like the United States and international coalitions such as the United Nations (UN) and European Union failed to take decisive action to save lives in Darfur. Their delayed response can be explained in part by their focus on a different conflict that predated the Darfur Genocide; namely, what some have described as a genocide waged by the Islamic Sudanese government in northern Sudan against the largely Christian south. When genocide erupted in Darfur in 2003, Western governments were focused on negotiating a peace agreement between the government of Sudan and the south's Sudan People's Liberation Movement/Army (SPLM/A). By the time the United States and others finally took stock of the bloodshed in Darfur, tens of thousands of Darfurians had already died and even more had been displaced.

While governments in the western hemisphere stood by as genocide erupted in Darfur, other nations armed and funded the Sudanese government's attacks. Russia and China, for example, provided support to the Sudanese government in the form of arms sales, investment, and the purchase of Sudanese oil. Meanwhile, Darfurian rebel groups sought, and largely won, the support of Chadian president Idriss Déby Itno and the SPLM/A rebel group in southern Sudan.

The African Union (AU), a continental union of African countries established in 2001, launched a peacekeeping mission in Sudan known as the African Union Mission in Sudan, which operated from 2004 to 2007. In 2006, the United Nations prepared to deploy a joint UN and AU peacekeeping operation in Darfur. The African Union had never partnered with UN peacekeepers. The Security Council of the United Nations, one of six principal organs of the United Nations charged with the maintenance of international peace and security, established the unprecedented hybrid peacekeeping force on July 31, 2007, through the adoption of resolution 1769. Known by the acronym UNAMID (which stands for "United Nations–African Union Mission in Darfur"), the core mandate of the mission is the protection of civilians. On June 29, 2017, the Security Council adopted Resolution 2363, which renewed the mission's mandate and called for a sizing-down of UNAMID's troop and police force. As of April 2018, the UNAMID force was composed of 15,126 personnel.

Not all international bodies and countries agree on whether the violence in Darfur constitutes genocide. As defined by the United Nations, the crime of genocide is distinguished by other legally defined acts, such as crimes against humanity and war crimes, by the intent of the perpetrators. According to the UN Convention for the Prevention and Punishment of Genocide (1948), acts are considered genocide if they are intended "to destroy, in whole or in part, a national, ethnic, racial, or religious group." By 2004, some observers, most prominently American politicians, called the Sudanese government's violent and targeted campaign against "non-Arab" Darfurians a "genocide," while others, including the United Nations, have refrained from using that term. All parties agree that the Sudanese government has waged a campaign to murder, rape, and destroy the so-called non-Arab Darfurians, but not all parties agree on what motivated the government to commit mass murder and destruction. Regardless of what it is called, the conflict has had, and continues to have, devastating consequences for the Darfur people. By 2008, the United Nations estimated that between 200,000 and 300,000 people had died in Darfur, and 2.7 million more were displaced. In other words, since 2003, half of Darfur's population has either been murdered or fled their homes. As of late June 2012, 1.7 million people lived in internally displaced persons (IDP) camps in Darfur and an additional 264,000 resided in refugee camps in Chad. The United Nations High Commission for Refugees (UNHCR) reports that the majority of these refugees are reluctant to return home due to continued instability in the region. Additionally, owing to the perpetrators' scorched earth campaign, refugees and IDPs have little or nothing to return to.

The suffering of the Darfur people, coupled with the United State government's declaration of genocide in September 2004, galvanized U.S.-based advocacy groups. For example, the Save Darfur network and the Enough Project, cofounded by John Prendergast, initiated vociferous and largely effective campaigns designed to raise awareness of the situation in Darfur and encourage individuals and corporations to divest their assets from Sudan. Activist groups also called for the U.S. government to enhance its existing sanctions against the government of Sudan—and it worked. In May 2007, President George W. Bush imposed sanctions on Sudanese citizens implicated in the Darfur conflict and on companies owned or controlled by the Sudanese government.

The UN Security Council, in three successive resolutions passed between 2004 and 2010, has imposed a sanctions agenda that precludes UN member states from supplying arms, technical training, or assistance to any actor operating in Darfur. On March 31, 2005, the UN Security Council adopted Resolution 1593, which referred the situation in Darfur to the prosecutor of the International Criminal Court (ICC). The ICC is an intergovernmental organization and international tribunal that sits in The Hague, in the Netherlands. The referral permitted the ICC prosecutor to initiate investigations into whether Sudanese government officials, rebel leaders, and other actors had committed war crimes, crimes against humanity, crimes of aggression, and genocide.

Since June 2005, the ICC has issued arrest warrants for six current and former Sudanese government officials for their alleged involvement in crimes committed against the people of Darfur: Ahmad Muhammad Harun, Ali Muhammad Ali Abd-Al-Rahman (Ali Kushayb), Omar Hassan Ahmed al-Bashir, Abu Garda (case closed, charges not confirmed), Saleh Mohammed Jerbo Jamus (case terminated after his passing on October 4, 2013), and Abdel Raheem Muhammad Hussein. The suspects range from government officials, militia/Janjaweed leaders, and leaders of the Resistance Front and include charges for the crime of genocide, war crimes, and crimes against humanity. Notably, Bashir, Harun, and Hussein continued to hold prominent positions within the Sudanese government and are suspected of committing further atrocities against Sudanese civilians of the Nuba tribe in the Nuba Mountains within the context of an ongoing conflict with the Sudan Revolutionary Front (SRF), which began in June 2011.

While the fighting and atrocities committed against civilian populations reached their highest levels between 2003 to 2006, insecurity within Darfur continues to the present day, despite the presence of UNAMID and the conclusion of two, largely unimplemented, peace agreements.

Causes

The causes of the genocide in Darfur are complex and multifaceted. It is a common misconception that the underlying causes of the conflict relate exclusively to disputes over scarce natural resources. While

the government of Sudan capitalized on traditional tensions between nomads and sedentary farmers over land and water resources in Darfur, the underlying causes of the conflict are also related to the government's economic, political, and social marginalization of populations living in the peripheries of Sudan.

Tensions Over Natural Resources in Darfur

Traditionally, Darfur's population was roughly divided between nomadic herders, commonly referred to as "Arabs," and sedentary farmers, typically referred to as "non-Arabs" or "black Africans." Given centuries of intermarriage, the distinction between Arabs and non-Arabs or black Africans in this context speaks more to a difference in lifestyle and cultural affiliation rather than a difference in "race." However, the black African farmers tended to be from two tribal groups: the Fur and Massalit. A third group, the Zaghawa, identify as non-Arabs but, nonetheless, herd camels.

Until the late 1980s, the "Arab" nomads and "black African farmers" lived in relative peace, with the farmers tolerating the nomads as the latter traversed Darfur's farmland to graze their herds. However, climate change brought on by droughts in the 1970s and 1980s caused farmers to fence in their lands to protect them from passing herds who were forced to graze their animals closer to villages. The nomadic herders viewed this as a provocation by the farmers. In 1987, fighting broke out between the nomads and farmers, resulting in thousands of deaths and the destruction of property. During this period, the Sudanese government armed nomadic Arab tribes. Despite the introduction of a peace agreement in 1989, fighting flared again in the 1990s. The nomads banded together in an alliance known as the Arab

Gathering, while some of the Fur tribe in Darfur unified under the name African Belt. The banding together of Darfur's population largely along tribal lines, and Khartoum's explicit support of the Arabs, later contributed to the genocide.

Marginalization of Sudanese in the Borderlands

When the genocide erupted in 2003, Sudan was the largest country on the continent. Its capital city of Khartoum is located in the central northeast of the country, making it more than 1,000 kilometers (621 miles) from the Darfur region. During the famines and droughts that plagued Darfur in the 1980s and 1990s, it was easy for Khartoum to ignore the suffering of its citizens in an area that was time consuming to visit. When Darfurian rebel groups—the Darfur Liberation Front (DLF), later renamed the Sudan Liberation Army (SLA), and the Justice and Equality Movement (JEM)—attacked government buildings in Gulu in September 2003, they were hoping to provoke the government in Khartoum to pay attention to the suffering of Darfurians. The SLA and JEM cited the government of Sudan's political, social, and cultural marginalization of the people of Darfur and other periphery regions of Sudan as an underlying cause of their revolt. The SLA originally focused its grievances exclusively on the people of Darfur, but later declared it was fighting for all marginalized people throughout Sudan. JEM, on the other hand, in a manifesto known as *The Black Book*, noted as an underlying cause of its opposition to Khartoum the marginalization of populations throughout Darfur and other regions in Sudan, including the south, the Nuba Mountains, and the east.

The nomadic Arab tribes used by the Sudanese government to counter the Darfur rebellion were also affected by Khartoum's marginalization of the peripheries, even as the government continued to mobilize Arabs to protect its own power base. Climate change and escalating violence in the region left the nomadic Arab tribes increasingly reliant on the small compensation, mostly in the form of war loot plundered from their victims, that they received for their service as militia members. This perpetuated the conflict in Darfur and helps to explain, at least in part, why some Arab tribes instigated and participated in the killings. In addition, the promise of acquiring the land occupied by non-Arabs encouraged Darfurian Arab tribes to continue to fight on behalf of the government.

The Rise of Arab Supremacy

The formation of the Arab Gathering Alliance (Arabic: *Al Tajamu*; *Al Arabi*) in the late 1980s and early 1990s influenced Arab and non-Arab relations in Darfur. The Arab Gathering Alliance aimed to control the indigenous populations of Sudan (and later Chad, Cameroon, Central African Republic, Niger, and beyond). According to the group's rhetoric, those deemed Arab were superior to non-Arabs, a view that the nomadic Arab herders in Darfur adopted.

This notion of Arab supremacy was elucidated in a letter sent by twenty-three Darfurian intellectuals, tribal figures, and senior officials to Sudanese prime minister Sadiq al-Mahdi on October 5, 1987. The letter described the Arab "race" as the creators of Darfur's governance, religion, and language and the main source of Darfur's wealth. Furthermore, it bemoaned the underrepresentation of Arabs in government at all levels. Internal Arab Gathering memoranda from the late 1980s, which has since become public, reveals plans to forcibly remove non-Arabs from their homelands and replace them with Arabs. These plans became all too real during the Darfur genocide.

Proliferation of Small Arms and Porous Borders

In response to the government's arming of Arab nomads, Darfur's largely sedentary non-Arab tribes sought ways to arms themselves against Arab attacks. A thriving black market, small arms trade in Sudan, and smugglers from neighboring Chad and Libya all proved apt sources for weapons. The proliferation of weapons, mostly small arms, in Darfur from sources within Sudan and across its porous borders intensified violence in the region.

The Impact of the Sudanese Civil Wars on Darfur

While not a direct cause per se, the Sudanese Civil Wars certainly informed the timing and outcomes of the Darfur Genocide. The civil war was a conflict between the predominately Arab and Islamic north, represented by the government of Sudan in Khartoum, and the so-called non-Arab and Christian south, represented by the SPLM/A. Peace negotiations between Khartoum and the SPLM/A began in earnest in Kenya in 2002. Darfur's rebel groups, fearing that the future political composition of Sudan was being decided without them, began their operations in late 2002 and officially launched their own rebellion against Khartoum in 2003. Ultimately, the negotiations concluded in 2005 with the government of Sudan and the SPLM/A signing the Comprehensive Peace Agreement (CPA). The CPA did not reference the conflict in Darfur, nor did it incorporate the Darfurian people into the agreement's wealth-and power-sharing schemes. With their grievances unaddressed in the CPA, Darfur's rebel groups continued their insurrection against the Sudanese government.

Consequences

The consequences of the Darfur Genocide, which began in 2003, reverberate into the present. Despite efforts to negotiate settlements between the government of Sudan and Darfurian rebel groups, such deals have proved largely unsuccessful. And in some respects, these failed negotiations have even hindered comprehensive democratic and constitutional reforms in Sudan.

Human Consequences

Since fighting broke out in 2003 between armed rebel groups and government of Sudan forces including the Janjaweed militia, the number of those impacted by the conflict steadily increased. In the first year of the conflict, the United Nations estimated that thousands of civilians were killed, 700,000 more were forcibly displaced within Darfur, and 130,000 fled to refugee camps in neighboring Chad. In 2004, UN officials called the conflict in Darfur the greatest humanitarian crisis in Africa, likening it to the Rwandan Genocide. By August of the same year, reports emerged that over half of Darfur's villages had been destroyed and 1.2 million people had been displaced. According to a UN report released in 2007, an estimated 200,000 had died in the conflict and at least 2 million were displaced. A year later, the United Nations stated that 4.7 million people were directly affected by the conflict out of Darfur's total population of approximately 6.2 million; between 200,000 and 300,000 people had died in Darfur, and 2.7 million more were displaced. As of late June 2012, 1.7 million people lived in IDP camps in Darfur and hundreds of thousands more resided in refugee camps bordering Sudan.

The perpetrators' policy of burning Darfurian villages to the ground has made returning home nearly impossible for those who escaped the killing. To make matters worse, helping refugees return to Darfur from neighboring countries is an expensive process. In December 2017, the United Nations High Commission on Refugees (UNHCR) flew 1,500 refugees from the Central African Republic to South Darfur. The UNHCR reported in April 2018 that it had facilitated the first of what it hoped would become a new series of voluntary returns of Sudanese refugees in Chad. The first group of fifty-three refugees were loaded onto buses at the Iridimi refugee camp in eastern Chad and four hours and 70 kilometers (43.5 miles) later arrived in north Darfur. Despite more refugees having indicated their desire to return home, the UNHCR is unable to organize largescale resettlement at this moment as they lack the funding to do so. And historically, many Darfurians have been unwilling to return owing to their fear that there is nothing stopping President Omar Hassan Ahmed al-Bashir from launching another offense. Now that President Bashir has been forcibly removed from office (2019), it remains to be seen how Darfurian refugees and IDPs will respond.

Despite claiming its commitment to grant unhindered humanitarian access throughout Darfur, the government of Sudan impeded the access of international relief organizations to the region from 2003 to 2009, mainly through delays in the issuance of visa and travel documents and an inability or unwillingness to ensure security. From early 2003 to September 2008, 225 humanitarian vehicles were hijacked or stolen, 32 humanitarian convoys were attacked, 144 humanitarian compounds were broken into, and 11 humanitarian workers were killed. Then, in 2009, the government summarily dismissed 13 aid organizations from Darfur. The timing coincided with the ICC's issuance of an arrest warrant against President Bashir. While some of these organizations were ultimately permitted back into Darfur, humanitarian access continues to be an issue.

Political Consequences

The genocide in Darfur has undoubtedly impacted politics in Sudan. However, the conflict has not inspired widespread democratic and constitutional reforms within the Sudanese government. As a result, Darfurians remain underrepresented in Sudanese economy, society, and government.

It is remarkable that the CPA, signed in 2005, made no mention of the fighting in Darfur. The signing of the CPA marked a significant event in Sudanese history and the decision to not include Darfur in the process speaks to national and international politics and priorities at that time. The CPA was a deal brokered between the National Congress Party (NCP) in the north—the governing party of the president and an Islamic and Arab movement—and the Sudan People's Liberation Movement/Army (SPLM/A), which represented the interests of the non-Arab south. This deal, mediated in part by the United Nations and Western governments, established a power-sharing agreement between the north and south and eventually led to a referendum in 2011 that created an independent South Sudan. After having worked toward a peace agreement between North and South Sudan since the early 1990s, the United Nations and Western governments did not want to jeopardize the peace deal by forcing Khartoum to address Sudan.

Passed in 2006, the Darfur Peace Agreement (DPA) promised that Darfur could choose its leaders (and not have ones appointed for them by the central Sudanese government in Khartoum), decide on whether to unite the region or maintain the status quo of three states, address power and wealth sharing among Arab and non-Arab Darfurians, enact a final cease-fire, and implement security arrangements. Both Abdel-Wahid al Nur's Sudan Liberation Army faction (SLA-AW) and the JEM opted not to sign the agreement. At the time, the Minni Minawi faction of the SLA (SLA-MM) did sign, but it represented less than 10 percent of Darfur's population, immediately calling into question the significance of the DPA vis-à-vis ongoing conflict involving the non-signatory rebel groups. Indeed, from June to September 2006, large numbers of SLA-MM forces defected, joining other non-signatory rebel groups or simply returning home. Paradoxically, the defections, and Minawi's unlikely military alliance with government forces, caused an upsurge in violence in the period following the DPA's conclusion.

The 2011 Doha Document for Peace in Darfur (DDPD) that followed the failed DPA was finalized in Doha, Qatar, and was the culmination of more than two years of negotiations with all major parties to the Darfur conflict, stakeholders, and international partners. It addressed power sharing, disbursement of wealth, human rights, justice and reconciliation, and the return of land. The agreement was signed by the government of Sudan and the Liberty and Justice Movement (LJM), a group of eleven rebel factions cobbled together by the international mediators in an effort to save the floundering talks. Notably, those rebel groups who were and continue to be militarily active in Darfur and elsewhere in Sudan (namely, JEM and the two factions of the SLA) refused to sign the agreement. At the time of writing this entry, the United Nations reports that disputes over land ownership exist and that "the implementation of the Doha Document for Peace in Darfur remains constrained" (United Nations Security Council Report 2018: 1).

Regional Dynamics and Proxy Wars

In December 2005, Chadian president Itno decided to support the Zaghawa Darfurian rebels. The president himself belonged to the Zaghawa people, a Central African Muslim ethnic group located in western Sudan and eastern Chad. This, in turn, prompted the government of Sudan to support Chadian rebels fighting against President Itno's government. The result was a de facto proxy war between Sudan and Chad, which occurred mostly in Darfur, adding to the violence that already engulfed the region. This proxy war continued until the passage of a Sudan-Chad peace deal in January 2010, in which both sides agreed to cease support of rebels in the other's territory.

In short, the consequences of the Darfur Genocide are ongoing. Until refugees are able (and willing) to return to Darfur and IDPs can leave camps and rebuild their homes, tensions in the area will continue to exist. Likewise, the failure to hold those responsible for the genocide accountable for the crimes makes returning home all that much harder for those who fled nearly two decades ago.

Perpetrators

The perpetrators of genocide in Darfur fall into two main categories: Sudan's regular armed forces, which include the Popular Defense Force (PDF) and the intelligence services; and government-backed militias, namely the Janjaweed. The Sudanese government coordinated the operations of its regular forces with the Janjaweed to perpetrate a scorched-earth campaign in Darfur designed to remove "non-Arabs" from their homelands. According to the government, "non-Arabs" formed the support base of Darfur's rebel movements and therefore needed to be eradicated. While Darfur's rebel movements are not widely charged with perpetrating genocide, it would be a mistake to not note here their role in perpetuating the conflict, too.

Sudan's Regular Armed Forces

Sudan's regular armed forces are comprised of ground forces, including the PDF, air forces, and intelligence services. The commander-in-chief of the armed forces is the president of Sudan, while the minister of defense oversees operations of the force. President Bashir, who assumed office following a coup d'état in 1989, was the commander-in-chief of the armed forces throughout the genocide. The ICC, an independent judicial body established by the Rome Statute (1998), has issued two arrest warrants for Bashir (2009 and 2010) for his involvement in the genocide.

The PDF is an auxiliary paramilitary force organized to support Sudan's standing armed forces. During the genocide, the PDF was comprised of four components: volunteers from the National Islamic Front, the precursor to Sudan's ruling National Congress Party; drafted students, civil servants, and professors; forcibly enlisted teenagers; and preexisting tribal militias. Primary responsibility for the PDF throughout the genocide rested with the interior minister. The ICC issued an arrest warrant for Ahmad Harun, state interior minister during the height of the conflict, in 2007. He remains at large.

Sudan's national security and intelligence services are notoriously powerful and wield expansive powers to detain individuals, without charge, for extensive periods of time. During the genocide, the government used the security services to gather information on suspected rebel activity, which, in turn, informed operational planning for military and paramilitary actions.

Sudan's air forces supported ground forces in their campaign to rid Darfur of non-Arabs. The air forces were comprised largely of helicopter gunships and modified Antonov cargo planes used to drop rudimentary bombs indiscriminately onto civilian areas.

Janjaweed

The Janjaweed, also referred to as the *fursan* (horseman or knights) or the *mujahideen* (the plural form of mujahid, one who is engaged in Jihad), is the term used to describe the Arab militia that operated with impunity and under the authority of the Khartoum regime in Darfur throughout the genocide. Translated, the term means "a man or a devil on a horse." The Janjaweed are generally described as Arab militias. However, this description does not imply that all perpetrators of the genocide were Arabs.

When fighting erupted in Darfur in 2003, Khartoum called on a number of aligned Arab tribes to organize into militia groups— the Janjaweed—and fight the rebels. The UN Commission of Inquiry on Darfur discovered evidence that Janjaweed forces were also comprised of Arab outlaws, convicted felons, and fighters from Chad and Libya. The Janjaweed did not have a uniform structure, but, rather, was comprised of different militias operating with various levels of affiliation with the government in Khartoum. While some Janjaweed members were also members of the Popular Defense Force (PDF), others were only loosely affiliated with the Sudanese armed forces.

Despite accounts from victims evidencing strong coordination between the Janjaweed and government security and military forces, Sudanese government officials repeatedly deny the government's affiliation with the Janjaweed.

Darfur's Rebel Groups

Darfur's rebel groups have seen a number of iterations since the early 2000s, as alliances have been made and broken while groups formed and disbanded. Some of this fracturing even led to fighting within and between rebel groups.

The origins of the SLA may be found in village self-defense committees established throughout the late 1980s and 1990s in Fur, Zaghawa, and Massalit villages to fend off government-backed Arab militias. Among the movement's earliest leaders was Abdel Wahid Mohammad Ahmad Nur, a Fur lawyer from central West Darfur. By November 2001, Abdel Wahid and his Fur comrades had established strategic alliances with Zaghawa and Massalit rebel groups, forming the DLF.

In early 2003, the DLF renamed itself the SLA and initiated a series of successful military attacks against government targets in Darfur, including an April 2003 takeover of the airport in el-Fasher. The SLA generally focused its attacks on government targets and not Arab nomads or Janjaweed, for fear of alienating Darfur's Arab community.

Early military successes invoked a harsh response from the Sudanese government and its forces. By early 2004, the SLA was forced to scatter throughout Darfur to avoid complete defeat by government and Janjaweed forces. This tactic proved to further split the rebel group down ethnic lines. By mid-2004, fighting had erupted between the Zaghawa and Fur SLA rebels in Jebel Marra in Darfur. Zaghawa forces reportedly harassed and killed Fur civilians in the area and even attempted to cut off supply lines to Abdel Wahid's forces.

The fighting between the Zaghawa and Fur elements of the SLA was fueled not only by differences between the two communities, but also by a power struggle between

its leaders, Minawi and Abdel Wahid. In late 2005, the SLA officially split into two different rebel groups: Abdel Wahid's Fur SLA, known as SLA–Abdel Wahid (SLA-AW) and Minawi's Zaghawa SLA, known as SLA-Minni Minawi (SLA-MM).

Established in 2001, JEM's first military operations occurred in March 2003. Led by Dr. Khalil Ibrahim, the movement's president, JEM distinguished itself from the SLA in terms of its developed political structure, which included a congress, assembly, and president. In addition, JEM's forces were much smaller than those of the SLA, it fought less frequently with government forces, and it controlled less territory. The movement's power base was centered on a small Zaghawa sub-clan, the Kobe.

Prior to emerging as JEM's leader, Ibrahim was a member of the National Islamic Front (NIF)—the precursor to President Bashir's National Congress Party (NCP)—and served in a number of government posts from 1989 until the late 1990s. At that time, tensions were mounting within the NIF between Hassan al-Turabi (a religious and Islamist political leader in Sudan) and President Bashir. Some speculate that this split contributed to Ibrahim's departure from the NIF.

By 2001, Ibrahim had established JEM and publicly proclaimed his opposition to the Islamist government in Khartoum. However, rumors persisted that there remained a link between the Islamists and JEM. This link, real or not, proved problematic for JEM in terms of its popularity among many Darfurians, who continued to dislike the Islamists for their overthrow of the popularly elected Sadiq al-Mahdi, a Sudanese political and religious figure who served as prime minister of Sudan between 1966 and 1967, and again from 1986 until he was overthrown in 1989.

While JEM fought alongside the SLA, most notably in the April 2003 attack on el-Fasher, it was, as well, the target of SLA aggression. In May 2005, SLA-MM attacked JEM forces in Gereida and Jughana. Shortly thereafter, in July 2005, SLA-MM and JEM leadership briefly considered unifying the two groups. The efforts were unsuccessful, though, given intra-Zaghawa rivalries, the SLA's distrust of JEM's rumored connections with the NIF, and JEM's unclear position on whether Sudan should be an Islamic state or a secular one. In 2011, JEM and both SLA factions allied with the Sudan People's Liberation Movement—North to form the Sudan Revolutionary Front, a coalition military force.

Victims

Victims of the Darfur Genocide, like the perpetrators of the violence, practice Islam. The perpetrators of the genocide perceived their victims as originating from different ethnic or racial origins. According to their killers, the tribal groups targeted for annihilation were "black African" and "non-Arab," whereas the perpetrators viewed themselves as "non-black Africans" and "Arabs." Despite their shared culture and religion, victims were killed by their countrymen and women, some of whom were their neighbors. And the sexual violence unleashed by the killers draws attention to the gendered experiences of torture and trauma during genocide.

Targeted Tribal Groups
The perpetrators of the Darfur genocide primarily targeted three tribal groups: the Fur, the Zaghawa, and the Massalit. It has been widely reported that the victims of the Darfur Genocide were Christian or animist "black Africans" targeted by Muslim "Arabs."

This description of the genocide in Darfur is, however, incorrect. In fact, 99 percent of Darfurians, perpetrators and victims alike, are Muslim. That said, there is a local distinction drawn between "black Africans" or "non-Arabs," often called *Zurga* ("blacks), and "Arabs." Due to intermarriage, the distinction owes more to lifestyle and cultural affiliation than ethnic or racial identity. In addition, historic accounts indicate that, at times, individuals voluntarily switched their tribal affiliations.

The Fur, Zaghawa, and Massalit are all considered "black African" or "non-Arab." The Fur and Massalit are sedentary farmers, while the Zaghawa herd camels. "Arabs" likewise lead nomadic lifestyles, herding camels and cattle throughout the region. The Fur is Darfur's largest tribal group. The traditional homelands of the Zaghawa, a Saharan people, stretch along the Sudan-Chad border.

Historically, Darfur's multitude of tribal groups occasionally clashed, mainly over the use of land, water resources, or the theft of livestock. These conflicts did not, however, assume an "Arab" versus "non-Arab" dimension until 1987–1989. By this time, the government of Sudan had begun arming "Arab" tribes in an effort to undermine the ability of SPLM/A to solidify a power base in central and northern Sudan. The government supported the "Arab" militias during these early conflicts in Darfur in order to forcibly displace "non-Arab" tribes (like the Fur) from their homes and replace them with Arab nomads who, presumably, supported the Sudanese government in its ongoing war with the SPLM/A.

During the genocide, this tactic was again employed, this time to eliminate the Darfurian rebels' "non-Arab" support base, replacing it with "Arab" nomads friendly to Khartoum. To achieve this, government forces and Janjaweed militias perpetrated crimes against humanity, ethnic cleansing, and genocide against the Fur, Zaghawa, and Massalit of Darfur. Survivors of Janjaweed attacks reported that "Arab" militias swept into villages on horse or camel back, wielding automatic weapons and firing indiscriminately at civilians. Homes, grain stores, and crops were destroyed, while women, children, and the elderly were whipped, raped, tortured, and, in some instances, murdered. The tactics were designed to terrorize victims, forcing them to flee their homelands for displaced persons camps within Darfur or refugee camps in neighboring countries.

Official accounts from the United Nations and other international observers of the genocide are numerous and horrific. For instance, the UN Darfur Task Force documented an attack on the town of Tweila in late February 2004, during which the Janjaweed and the Sudanese Army killed at least 67 people, displaced another 5,000, abducted 16 schoolgirls, and raped 93 more.

In its arrest warrant for Ali Kushayb, a senior Janjaweed commander, the ICC notes an incident during which seventy-one men, mostly Fur, were marched from their homes, lined up, forced to kneel, and shot in the back of the head. At the time, none of the men were actively involved in the conflict or belonged to the rebel groups the perpetrators claimed to be attacking.

A 2004 report by the UN interagency fact-finding and rapid-assessment mission indicates that in Kailek, in South Darfur State, Janjaweed and Sudanese police were holding IDPs hostage with the intent of purposely starving them. Countless more survivor testimony, primarily from the period 2003 to 2006, note similar atrocities committed against Fur, Zaghawa, and Masaliet noncombatants.

Female Victims

Rape is a weapon of war and genocide in Darfur. It is now well-known that Janjaweed and government forces used rape to torture and destroy Darfur's "non-Arab" populations. Janjaweed militia members and government soldiers intentionally and repeatedly raped girls and women with the goal of impregnating them. As tribal affiliation runs through the male line in Darfur, any offspring of these rapes would be considered "Arab," regardless of the mother's tribe. This plan was carried out with ruthless savagery throughout the region against Fur, Zaghawa, and Massalit women and girls.

Social mores have made determining the exact extent of sexually based violence in Darfur difficult, as women and girls are reluctant to come forward and admit that they were raped. However, it may be deduced from numerous victims' accounts that the incidence of gender-based violence during the Darfur Genocide was extensive. Indeed, Doctors Without Borders reportedly treated nearly 500 women and girls for rape between October 2004 and mid-February 2005. The organization believed that this figure likely reflected only a small fraction of the total number of Darfurian rape victims during that same period. Out of the nearly 500 women and girls treated, Doctors Without Borders reported that 28 percent had been gang raped.

Survivors report horrific attacks, often coupled with extreme physical abuse and torture. One account from the UN Task Force for Darfur described Janjaweed militia members' rape of 93 schoolgirls in the town of Tweila on February 27, 2004. Six girls were raped in front of their families. The Janjaweed branded the girls who they raped on the hand so that they would be ostracized from society for the remainder of their lives.

A 2015 Human Rights Watch report entitled *Mass Rape in North Darfur: Sudanese Army Attacks Against Civilians in Tabit,* documents a series of attacks over a 36-hour period in Tabit in North Darfur during which Sudanese soldiers raped women and girls. The Sudanese government has denied that its army committed such crimes and prevented the AU-UN Hybrid Operation in Darfur (UNAMID) from investigating the attack.

The ongoing nature of the Darfur Genocide has produced countless children born of rape, the extent of which is unknown.

Bystanders

Bystanders play a role in every genocide, Darfur included. While many scholars have proposed their own definition of the bystander category, the common consensus is that a bystander—unlike a victim or perpetrator—is an individual who was not targeted for annihilation, not a direct perpetrator or planner of a genocide, and either by choice or out of ignorance (willing or otherwise) did nothing to stop and/or intervene in the genocide. Some have argued that inaction or passivity during genocide becomes a form of agency as it works to encourage the perpetrators to go on killing without giving it a second thought. By some accounts, bystanders are the on-the-ground witnesses to genocide while for others international governments typify bystanders. In short, the definition of a bystander has many facets and its application is not always clear. Thus, true to form, when considering bystanders during the Darfur Genocide, it is not always easy to determine who was a bystander.

Depending on one's definition, bystanders to the Darfur Genocide include international and national actors. Despite having knowledge of the killings, foreign governments

and institutions such as the United States, United Nations, and the European Union prioritized other foreign policy goals over intervening in the escalating crisis in Darfur. It was not until late 2004 that the international community focused its attention on the government of Sudan. By that time, however, the genocide was in full swing.

Sudan's Civil Wars and Foreign Policy Priorities

The Darfur Genocide was not an immediate priority for foreign governments. Instead, the international community—which had the power and resources to stop the genocide—was focused on reaching a peace deal between the government of Sudan and the SPLM/A. The goal of this process was to negotiate an end to the Sudanese Civil Wars (1955 to 1972 and 1983 to 2005), a conflict that ultimately claimed the lives of some 2.5 million people and displaced over 4 million more. Mediated by the Intergovernmental Authority on Development (IGAD), the process formally began in June 2002, although representatives from both sides had met previously to lay the groundwork for the talks. The governments of the United States, Great Britain, and Norway, known collectively as the Sudan Troika, along with China, Ethiopia, and Kenya, as well as the United Nations, the African Union, and the European Union, were all involved in the negotiation process, providing various degrees of technical and financial support and exerting diplomatic pressure on both sides to ensure the conclusion of a viable and comprehensive peace agreement. Given their sustained investment in brokering peace, the foreign powers feared that any attempt to intervene in Darfur would cause the government of Sudan to withdraw from the peace process and thus fuel a continuation of the civil war between the north and south.

While many, including the United Nations, the United States, and the European Union, began, as early as late 2003 to publicly decry the humanitarian situation in Darfur and demand access for aid agencies to the region, these actors largely avoided comments or discussions of the underlying causes of the Darfur conflict, opting, instead to use what little diplomatic capital they had with Khartoum on the IGAD negotiation process. Aid operations began in earnest, albeit largely stymied by the Sudanese government's subversive tactics, including the slow issuance of visas and travel permits. And the aid operations did not halt or prevent the Sudanese government's killing and destruction campaign in Darfur. In addition, there was little public discourse concerning options for an intervention to stop the bloodshed, despite widespread reports of atrocities and the U.S. government's own recognition, in September 2004, that the government of Sudan had carried out genocide in Darfur.

Funding and Sourcing Genocide

During the genocide in Darfur, the Sudanese government received support from critical international allies in the form of arms sales, foreign investment, and loans. The most prominent allies of the Khartoum regime included the governments of China and Russia. China and Russia chose to favor Khartoum's role in the devastation of Darfur and Darfurians due to those nations' economic interests in Sudan as related to arms sales and oil.

During the height of the conflict in Darfur from 2003 to 2006, China sold over $55 million worth of small arms to the government, despite a 2004 UN-imposed embargo on arms transfers to Darfur. During the same period, Russia and China sold aircraft and other military hardware to the Sudanese government. Additionally, Chinese companies reportedly provided support to Khartoum so that the latter could open three weapons and ammunition assembly plants.

Throughout the conflict in Darfur, China remained Sudan's largest purchaser of oil. China bought 50 percent of Sudan's oil exports in 2005 and, in the following year, China exported $4.7 billion worth of oil, thus adding money to coffers of the Sudanese government that could then be spent buying weapons from China and Russia. The Chinese also extended loans to the government of Sudan throughout the Darfur Genocide, while maintaining large investments in Sudan's oil sector.

External Sources of Support for Darfur Rebel Factions

Throughout the conflict, Darfur's rebel groups sought funding and support from Chad's president Itno and the SPLM/A, the rebel group representing the interests of southern Sudan in its civil war with the north.

Itno's complicated relationship to the Darfur Genocide is framed by his ethnic identity and involvement in Chadian politics. Itno took refuge in Darfur following his failed plot to unseat Chadian president Hissène Habré in 1989. Many of Itno's followers, known first as the April 1 Movement and later as *Mouvement patriotique du salut* or MPS, belonged to the Zaghawa tribe, one of the three main tribes in Darfur. There are also a number of Chadian Zaghawa, including Itno himself. When he returned to Chad in 1990 and was sworn in as president shortly thereafter, he spent years (1992 to 2005) refusing requests for support from Zaghawa Darfurian rebels, including those from Dr. Khalil Ibrahim, president of the JEM. His refusal led one Zaghawa Darfurian group to support a

Zaghawa rival of Itno in Chad. In the face of mounting government attacks against Darfurian Zaghawa, Zaghawa in Chad began funneling increasing amounts of money, weapons, and other supplies to Darfur's rebels, despite the Chadian president's refusal to do the same. Itno's hand was finally tipped in December 2005, when Khartoum-backed Chadian rebels launched an attack on the Chadian border town of Adré. Thereafter, President Itno began openly supporting Darfur's rebel movements until the conclusion of a Sudan-Chad peace deal in January 2010, in which both sides agreed to cease support of rebels in the other's territory.

The SPLM/A, led by Dr. John Garang from 1983 to 2005, rebelled against the Sudanese government. The SPLM/A called for greater autonomy for southern Sudan and the extension of full rights and freedoms to all Sudanese people. The SPLM/A supplied Darfurian rebels with weapons and training to fight against their shared enemy, the government. In addition, Garang's emphasis on a united "New Sudan"—in which all Sudanese would have full rights and freedoms and whose interests the central government would represent—worked to focus the Darfurian rebels' aspirations nationally, and not just regionally.

Under pressure from the international community concerning the IGAD process, the SPLM/A's support to Darfur's rebel movements largely ceased in or around 2004. However, it is believed that some support may have continued well past the 2005 conclusion of the CPA.

International Reaction

International reactions to the conflict in Darfur varied and were informed by whether a nation or governing body viewed the conflict as a genocide. While some, including the United States, proclaimed that the Sudanese government's actions in Darfur amounted to genocide, others, including the United Nations, did not concur. Meanwhile, activist groups around the world lobbied for the international community to sanction the government of Sudan, intervene to protect the people of Darfur, and hold accountable those responsible for the genocide. And all agreed on the need to address the mounting humanitarian crisis in Darfur, while making varied, and oftentimes unsuccessful, attempts at addressing the underlying causes of the conflict.

Humanitarian Response

The government of Khartoum, the same body responsible for directing the violence in Darfur, determined whether Darfurians had access to international humanitarian aid within Sudan. Such aid included shelter for refugees, food, water, and medical treatment. When the conflict first erupted in early 2003, only five foreign relief agencies were permitted to conduct routine operations in Darfur. However, by February 2004, when Sudanese president Omar Hassan Ahmed al-Bashir announced an "end" to government military operations in Darfur and a partial opening of the region to international relief agencies, the World Food Programme (WFP), the United States Agency for International Development (USAID), European donors, and other international nongovernmental organizations (NGOs) began operations in the region. While the government's cessation of military operations was never fully realized, international aid continued to flow into Darfur, as permitted by Khartoum. During the same period, UN agencies and other organizations channeled additional resources to Darfurians displaced to refugee camps in neighboring Chad.

On March 9, 2009, the same day that the ICC issued its first arrest warrant against President Bashir, the government of Sudan expelled thirteen international aid organizations from Darfur. As a result, the number of aid workers in the region plummeted from 17,700 to roughly 6,850, 97 percent of whom were Sudanese nationals. The United Nations called the move "disastrous." Some were eventually permitted back into the region, while organizations that were not originally expelled expanded their operations in an effort to compensate for the shortfall. The Sudanese government has since threatened to and, at times, expelled or suspended the access of aid organizations while limiting the movements of others in Darfur.

According to the United Nations Office for the Coordination of Humanitarian Affairs, foreign aid groups unable to gain access to Darfur have skirted their banishment by empowering local Darfurians and Sudanese agencies to deliver their programs in Darfur.

Reactions in the United States

On September 9, 2004, before the Senate Foreign Relations Committee, U.S. secretary of state Colin Powell declared that the Sudanese government had committed genocide in Darfur and that genocide may be ongoing in the region. In so doing, Powell became the first sitting member of the U.S. government to use the term "genocide" to describe an ongoing conflict. Six weeks earlier, on July 22, the Senate and House, through a concurrent resolution, determined that the government of Sudan and its forces were committing genocide against non-Arab groups in Darfur and called on the United Nations to pass a resolution imposing sanctions on the perpetrators.

Despite Powell's declaration, other countries, including close U.S. allies, were reluctant to use the term *genocide*. The United Nations and the U.S. government's historic reluctance to apply the term to an ongoing conflict stemmed from a concern that doing so would require them to, in turn, intervene to prevent further atrocities. This requirement to prevent genocide is found in the 1948 UN Convention on the Prevention and Punishment of Genocide, to which the United States is a party.

Powell's declaration ultimately galvanized U.S.-based advocacy organizations, such as the Save Darfur network and the Enough Project, cofounded by John Prendergast, which initiated vociferous and largely effective campaigns designed to raise awareness of the situation in Darfur and encourage individuals and corporations to divest their assets from Sudan. In addition, there were calls for the U.S. government to expand its existing sanctions against the government of Sudan. In May 2007, President George W. Bush imposed additional sanctions on Sudanese citizens implicated in the Darfur conflict and Sudanese government–owned or controlled companies.

The Response of the United Nations and the African Union

Beginning in 2004, the United Nations and the African Union, a continental organization of African states, supported numerous processes designed to negotiate a cessation of hostilities between the rebels in Darfur and Khartoum. The first was a cease-fire agreement signed on April 8, 2004, in N'djamena, Chad. The agreement was, however, short-lived and failed to halt hostilities on the ground. Two further agreements signed on November 9, 2004, did little to calm tensions or forestall the government's brutal campaign. Later processes in Abuja, Nigeria, in 2006, and Doha, Qatar, in 2009, 2010, and 2011 resulted in additional agreements that stipulated a cessation of hostilities and provided for certain political and economic reforms for Darfur. To date, no agreement has been fully implemented.

The United Nations and African Union coupled these efforts with the establishment of two peacekeeping missions for Darfur. The first, the African Union Mission in Sudan (AMIS), was mandated to monitor compliance with the 2004 Humanitarian Ceasefire Agreement between the Sudanese government and two rebel groups in Darfur, the JEM and the SLM/A. The 2004 agreement endeavored to create an environment in which humanitarian aid was possible. AMIS enjoyed early success, but soon proved ineffective as fresh violence broke out shortly after the mission was launched.

The second mission, a hybrid UN-AU peacekeeping force, was formed following prolonged international pressure on the Sudanese government. UN Security Council Resolution 1769, passed on July 31, 2006, established UNAMID. UNAMID incorporated existing AMIS personnel but operates under a more robust mandate that includes, among other things, the protection of civilian populations under imminent threat of physical violence and the facilitation of full humanitarian access throughout Darfur. Today, UNAMID continues to operate in Darfur, although in March 2012, the United Nations and African Union announced that they would reduce the mission's force strength over the ensuing eighteen months, owing largely to changing security threats in Darfur and a desire to remove ineffective troops. At the time of writing, UNAMID is composed of 9,029 military personnel, 920 police advisers, 1,533 formed police unit officers, 666 international civilian staff, 122 United Nations volunteers, and 1,835 national civilian staff.

Furthermore, the UN Security Council passed a number of critical resolutions in response to the crisis in Darfur. Among them, Resolution 1564, adopted on September 18, 2004, established the UN International Commission of Inquiry on Darfur (International Commission). Following three months of investigations, on January 25, 2005, the International Commission issued its final report, in which it concluded that the government of Sudan's actions in Darfur, while widespread and systematic, did not amount to genocide. Instead, the International Commission asserted that the government and government-backed militia forces' indiscriminate killing of civilians, torture, enforced disappearances, destruction of property, pillage, rape and other forms of sexual violence, and forced displacements amounted to crimes against humanity. What was missing for the International Commission was the critical element of "genocidal intent," whereby it must be clear that the perpetrators intended their actions to amount to the destruction, in whole or in part, of an ethnic, racial, religious, or national group.

In three successive resolutions—Resolution 1556 (2004), Resolution 1591 (2005), and Resolution 1945 (2010)—the UN Security Council imposed sanctions that precluded UN member states from supplying arms, technical training, or assistance to any actor operating in Darfur. The resolutions further imposed travel bans and froze the assets of certain individuals suspected of involvement in the conflict in Darfur. Resolution 1591 further imposed a ban on offensive flights over Darfur. However, UN member states have not put into place effective mechanisms to ensure that the ban is enforced.

International Criminal Court

On March 31, 2005, the UN Security Council adopted Resolution 1593, which referred the situation in Darfur, since July 1, 2002, to the prosecutor of the ICC. The referral permitted the ICC prosecutor to initiate investigations into whether Sudanese government officials, rebel leaders, and other actors had committed war crimes, crimes against humanity, crimes of aggression, and genocide.

Since April 2007, the ICC has issued arrest warrants against six individuals for crimes committed in Darfur: Ahmad Harun; Ali Kushayb; President Bashir; Abu Garda; Abdallah Banda; Abdel Raheem Muhammad Hussein. Notably, three of these officials, Bashir, Harun, and Hussein, continued to hold prominent positions within the Sudanese government and are suspected of committing further atrocities against Sudanese civilians in the Nuba Mountains within the context of an ongoing conflict with the Sudan Revolutionary Front (SRF), which began in June 2011.

Jennifer Christian and Alexis Herr

Further Reading

Cheadle, Don, and John Prendergast. 2010. *The Enough Moment: Fighting to End Africa's Worst Human Rights Crimes*. New York: Three Rivers Press.

Doctors Without Borders/Médecins Sans Frontières. 2005. "The Crushing Burden of Rape, Sexual Violence in Darfur." Briefing Paper, March 8.

Flint, Julie, and Alex de Waal. 2006. *Darfur: A Short History of a Long War*. London: Zed Books.

Hamilton, Rebecca. 2011. *Fighting for Darfur: Public Action and the Struggle to Stop Genocide*. London: Palgrave Macmillan.

Human Rights Watch. 2015. "Mass Rape in North Darfur: Sudanese Army Attacks against Civilians in Tabit." February 11.

International Crisis Group. 2004. "Darfur Rising: Sudan's New Crisis." *Africa Report* 76. March 25.

International Crisis Group. 2007. "Darfur: Revitalizing the Peace Process." *Africa Report* 125. April 30.

Prunier, Gerard. 2005. *Darfur: The Ambiguous Genocide*. Ithaca, NY: Cornell University Press.

Tanner, Victor, and Jerome Tubiana. 2007. *Divided They Fall: The Fragmentation of Darfur's Rebel Groups*. Geneva, Switzerland: Small Arms Survey.

United Nations–African Union Mission in Darfur. 2018. "UNAMID Facts and Figures." https://unamid.unmissions.org/unamid-facts-and-figures.

United Nations High Commission on Refugees. 2018. "First Darfur Refugee Returns from Chad." April 20. https://www.unhcr.org/en-us/news/briefing/2018/4/5ad9a4604/first-darfur-refugee-returns-from-chad.html.

United Nations Peacekeeping. 2018. "UNAMID Fact Sheet." https://peacekeeping.un.org/en/mission/unamid.

United Nations Security Council Report. 2018. *Report of the Secretary-General on the African Union-United Nations Hybrid Operation in Darfur*, S/2018/389 .April 25.

Zissis, Carin. 2006. "Darfur. Crisis Continues." United States Council on Foreign Relations. May 4. https://www.cfr.org/backgrounder/darfur-crisis-continues.

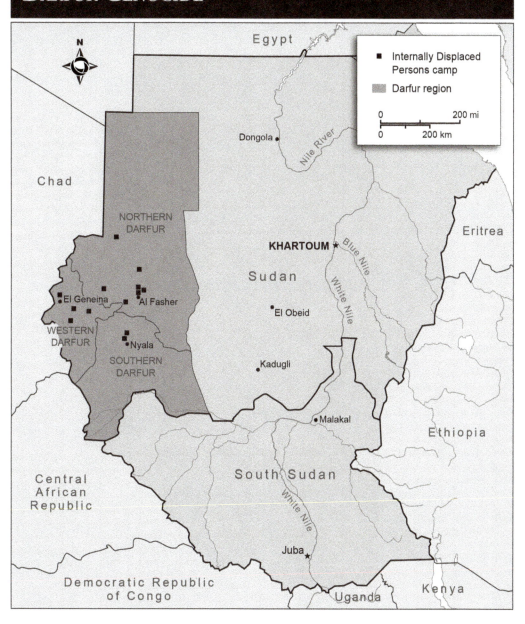

DARFUR GENOCIDE

Egypt

N

Chad

Dongola

Nile River

NORTHERN
DARFUR

KHARTOUM ★

Blue Nile

S u d a n

White Nile

Eritrea

El Geneina

Al Fasher

El Obeid

WESTERN
DARFUR

Nyala

SOUTHERN
DARFUR

Kadugli

Malakal

Ethiopia

Central
African
Republic

S o u t h   S u d a n

White Nile

Juba ★

Democratic Republic
of Congo

Uganda

Kenya

■ Internally Displaced
  Persons camp

  Darfur region

0   200 mi
0   200 km

A

Abdel Shafi, Ahmad

Ahmad Abdel Shafi, along with Abdel Wahid and Abdu Abdalla Ismail, was one of three young Darfur activists in the mid-1990s who would come to play a prominent role in the rebellion against the Sudanese government in Darfur. The three young Fur tribesmen, all of whom had little political experience, managed to assemble support for their cause across Darfur and Sudan. And it was their uprising in Darfur against the government that President Omar Hassan al-Bashir used to justify his genocidal attack in west Sudan.

Abdel Shafi's early involvement and long career in activism against the Sudanese government began in 1996. At that time, the Sudanese government was engaged in a brutal civil war with the south and actively arming Arab groups in the north to attack and kill those in the south whom they considered African and Christian. In an interview with Abdel Shafi a decade later, he claimed that the government had also set in motion a plan to "crush our people" (Flint and de Wall 2008: 75). Abdel Shafi feared that Arab-supremacist paramilitary forces would seize land and block water access that was critical to the survival of non-Arab ethnic groups in Darfur, including the Fur and the Zaghawa. In response, Abdel Shafi, along with Abdel Wahid and Abdalla, began raising money to buy weapons and ammunition from kinsmen in the army, which they then distributed to self-defense groups in Darfur.

The following year, Abdel Wahid and Abdel Shafi organized resistance cells across Darfur by recruiting village commanders to oppose the Khartoum government's sponsorship of paramilitary units. Abdel Shafi also sought to mobilize students, women, and political leaders in Sudan's capital, Khartoum. Abdel Wahid's and Abdel Shafi's mounting activism led to the creation of the Sudan Liberation Army (SLA) in 2002 and its political wing, the Sudan Liberation Movement (SLM), together known (until 2003) as the Darfur Liberation Front (DLF). The DLF launched its first attack on a police station in Golo in June 2002, eight months prior to their February 26, 2003, attack on Golo that scholars often point to as the reason for al-Bashir's genocidal attack on Darfurians. Shortly after their 2003 attack, the DLF announced on March 14 that the movement would now be called the Sudan Liberation Movement and the Sudan Liberation Army (SLM/A).

Disagreements between Abdel Shafi and Abdul Wahid in 2006 over peace talks resulted into the splintering of the SLM/A. Minni Minnawi, a former educator and secretary of the SLA, and Abdel Wahid each led their own faction of the Sudan Liberation Movement, and Abdel Shafi became the leader of the SLA. His assumption of power came at a price, however—it lost him the support of much of the Fur community and many SLA commanders. Although most Fur and SLA leaders had criticized Abdel Wahid's erratic tactics, they had wanted him removed by a democratic vote at a unity conference instead of being ousted by Shafi and other SLA leaders.

In his new role, Abdel Shafi reiterated the SLA's commitment to the cease-fire accords that Minnawi's faction had agreed to with Khartoum (but which Abdel Wahid had rejected), and he stressed the readiness of his group to hold peace talks with the government. Abdel Shafi's authority was augmented in November 2007, when he chaired a group of SLA commanders in Juba, the capital of southern Sudan, under the auspices of the Sudan People's Liberation Movement/Army (SPLM/A). However, his close associates came to resent his absence from Darfur and his connection to the SPLM/A and South Sudan.

As chair and commander in chief of the Juba faction of the splintered SLA, Abdel Shafi issued decrees in August 2009 establishing an executive council, an advisory body, representatives to regional and international organizations, and a political bureau (with himself as chair). The following year, the SLA-Juba was one of five rebel factions that united with the Liberation and Justice Movement (LJM)—an alliance of smaller Darfur rebel groups formed in 2010—leading to Abdel Shafi's appointment as vice president of the LJM.

The LJM and the Sudanese government signed the Doha Peace Agreement (DPA) on July 14, 2011. Abdel Shafi initially hailed the accord and led the LJM delegation to Khartoum to begin implementing it. However, he broke from the LJM in January 2012, citing the fighting in the states of South Kordofan and the Blue Nile as evidence that the government was not truly committed to peace in Darfur or anywhere else in Sudan. As of 2013, Abdel Shafi was leading the rebel group Sudan Liberation Movement–Juba Unity (SLM–Juba Unity). Abdel Shafi announced that SLM–Juba Unity had killed seventeen Sudanese soldiers in northern Darfur.

Karl A. Yambert and Alexis Herr

See also: Fur; Liberation and Justice Movement; Minnawi, Minni; Sudan Liberation Army; Sudan People's Liberation Movement/Army; Wahid, Abdel

Further Reading

Burr, J. Millard, and Robert O. Collins. 2006. *Darfur: The Long Road to Disaster*. Princeton, NJ: Markus Weiner.

Flint, Julie, and Alex de Waal. 2008. *Darfur: A New History of a Long War*. London: Zed Books.

African Union

The African Union (AU) is a coalition of African nations. During the Darfur Genocide, the AU became involved in staffing and running peacekeeping operations in Sudan.

The AU was created in 2002 to replace the Organization of African Unity (OAU). Thirty-two African states, which had recently gained independence from colonial powers, had formed the OAU on May 25, 1963, in Addis Ababa, Ethiopia. By the time the AU replaced the OAU on July 9, 2002, its membership included fifty-three nations—every country on the continent except Morocco, which had quit the OAU in 1985 after the group admitted the disputed territory of Western Sahara as a member. Following its break from Sudan, South Sudan joined the AU on July 9, 2011, as the organization's fifty-fourth member.

Modeled after the European Union, the AU aims to build economic and political stability on the African continent with a multinational peacekeeping force and a single African parliament, court of justice, and central bank. Unlike the OAU, the AU has the authority to intervene in wars that show signs of genocide or human rights abuses, to create a single African currency, and to negotiate for the spread of democracy and economic reform.

The AU is composed of ten organs: the Assembly, the Executive Council, the Commission, the Permanent Representatives' Committee, the Peace and Security Council (PSC), Pan-African Parliament, the Court of Justice, the Specialized Technical Committees, the Financial Institutions, and the Economic, Social, and Cultural Council (ECOSOCC). Each organ is intended to address and support the organization's goal to promote peace and stability in Africa. They accomplish this through various channels by addressing an array of issues, such as trade and customs (the Specialized Technical Committees), the African Monetary Fund (the Financial Institutions), legal matters (the Court of Justice), and continent-wide participation in AU affairs (Pan African Parliament).

An early criticism of the AU centered on its acceptance of the reelection of Zimbabwean president Robert Mugabe in March 2002, which many other nations of the world deemed undemocratic and corrupt. The organization has also been faulted for not condemning other African leaders who have seized power without elections or changed laws to tighten their grip on power. Critics question whether the AU can be effective if it continues to support autocratic governments in some of its member-states.

The AU is following a difficult road as it tries to bring together a continent plagued by poverty, economic trade barriers, soaring debt, poor infrastructure, and a number of armed conflicts. Its first order of business was establishing the PSC for the purpose of monitoring wars and putting together an armed peacekeeping force drawn from its member-states. The organization's goal is to create a permanent, continent-wide African Standby Force that would be capable of rapid deployment to restore or keep peace. While the AU has yet to fully establish this force, it has assembled special military missions on occasion to intervene in African conflicts, including in Darfur. The African Union Mission in Sudan (AMIS) was established in 2004 and operated until July 2007.

Economic integration (including the creation of a central bank) will take years, according to AU leaders. The implementation of a common African currency is expected to proceed very slowly; the 1991 treaty that set its creation as a goal allowed a transitional period of thirty-four years.

The AU established the Pan-African Parliament in March 2004. The parliament is an advisory body to the Assembly, the AU's governing body, composed of the heads of state and government of the AU member-states. The first parliament had 202 members from forty-one of the fifty-three member-states. The first president was Gertrude Mongella of Tanzania. The parliament met for a second time in September 2004 under the theme "One Africa, One Voice." Discussed at the session were topics such as security, the AU's mission, and the parliamentary rules concerning procedure and budget. In February 2004, the AU set up a continent-wide human rights court, which now is located in Arusha, Tanzania. Just thirty of its fifty-three member-states ratified the African Court on Human and Peoples' Rights, however, and therefore the body has jurisdiction only in those nations. Sudan is among the nations that have not ratified it.

Touted by leaders as more people-oriented than the OAU, the AU was the brainchild of Libyan leader Muammar Gaddafi, who wanted the group's headquarters to be in Libya. However, the Ethiopian capital, Addis Ababa, which hosted the OAU headquarters, was chosen instead.

The AU has received criticism in the past for not doing more to pressure the government of Sudan to end its killing of Darfurians. Eric Reeves, an American professor and activist, has gone so far as to claim that the AU's failure to act to secure the safety of Darfurians represented "deadly complicity in ongoing genocidal destruction" (Reeves 2005). Others, however, point to the AU's involvement in establishing a peacekeeping force in 2004 and its role in negotiating peace agreements between Darfur rebel factions and the government of Sudan as evidence of its attempt to rein in the violence and terror in Darfur.

Terri Nichols

See also: African Union Mission in Sudan; Reeves, Eric

Further Reading

Burr, J. Millard, and Robert O. Collins. 2003. *Revolutionary Sudan: Hasan al-Turabi and the Islamist State, 1989–2000*. Boston: Brill Academic Publishers.

Makinda, Samuel M. 2007. *The African Union: Challenges of Globalization, Security, and Governance*. New York: Routledge.

Reeves, Eric. 2005. "The Failure of the African Union in Darfur: A Global Failure to Protect Civilian Populations Facing Genocide." Global Policy Forum. September 7.

African Union Mission in Sudan

The African Union Mission in Sudan (AMIS) was a peacekeeping force established in 2004 by the African Union (a continental union of African countries established in 2001) that operated until 2007. Prior to the creation of the joint African Union–United Nations Mission in Darfur (UNAMID) in July 2007, AMIS was the sole external military force operating in Sudan's Darfur region.

The African Union (AU) formed its second peacekeeping mission in Darfur following the Abuja Peace Talks, the first foreign-led negotiations for peace in Darfur initiated by Chadian president Idriss Déby. The talks led to the signing of an agreement between the government of Sudan and the Sudan Liberation Movement/Army (SLM/A). In addition to calling for a forty-five-day cease-fire, the agreement committed both parties to further negotiations for comprehensive peace. The AU took over the subsequent discussions, which went seven rounds and were finally completed in May 2005 with the signing of the Darfur Peace Agreement (DPA).

The AU launched AMIS is 2004 as an observer mission, tasked with monitoring the cease-fire agreement between the government of Sudan and SLM/A and reporting on violence in the western Sudan region of Darfur. AMIS was the second peace operation established by the AU, the first being the African Mission in Burundi (AMIB). The government of Sudan and two Darfuri rebel groups, the SLM/A and the Justice and Equality Movement (JEM), agreed to the establishment of AMIS when they signed the Humanitarian Cease-Fire Agreement (HCFA) on April 8, 2004.

AMIS faced many challenges in its initial deployment, which its former officials have explained as symptomatic of a failure to plan and prepare adequately for its instillation. The initial group of AMIS soldiers numbered just 150 troops and was mandated only to monitor the cease-fire and to protect the monitors and themselves. By June 19, 2004, AMIS was up and running in Darfur. As the cease-fire was ultimately ignored by all parties involved in the conflict, AMIS sought to strengthen itself by sending in a protection force of 300 soldiers.

Realizing that AMIS was underfunded and unprepared for the task at hand, the AU launched what was known as AMIS II. Unlike its first rendition, AMIS II had a more robust force and slightly expanded mandate. AMIS II was to increase in size, introduce a civilian police force, and was tasked with an "enhanced observer mission" that allowed for them to send troops to more areas. Despite the stated goals of the AU, AMIS deployment lagged and as of April 2005, only 2,200 of the mandated 3,320 personnel had been disseminated. AMIS also found it difficult to staff a civilian police force (Human Rights Watch 2006, 16–17).

With the cease-fire violations continuing into 2005, the AU and United Nations (UN) elected to launch an assessment mission to Darfur with the goal of finding ways to increase the effectiveness of AMIS. The joint mission suggested an expansion of AMIS II, which eventually became known as AMIS IIE, and it began operating in July 2005. This iteration of the AU peace-keeping mission called for 6,171 troops, 1,560 civilian police, and an expansion of deployment sites from fifteen under AMIS II to twenty-nine under AMIS IIE. The force was comprised of troops from Nigeria, Rwanda, South Africa, Senegal, Kenya, and Gambia. Foreign governments (such as Great Britain, Canada, and the Netherlands) helped keep AMIS operational and mobile by supplying four-by-four vehicles, communication equipment such as satellite phones and data transfer systems, armored vehicles, and helicopters.

In an attempt to prevent civilian deaths, AMIS IIE attempted to gather intelligence in order to predict where an attack was likely to occur, and then it would dispatch troops to that area to deter massacres. This plan worked to a certain extent, but AMIS IIE was limited by meager intelligence support and had to contend with inadequate resources for communicating about and traveling to suspected conflict sites.

In 2005, AMIS IIE soldiers went from being observers to victims of the violence in Darfur. The first AMIS soldiers (two Nigerian nationals) were killed when they were ambushed in October 2005. Another eighteen AMIS troops were kidnapped on October 18 by members of a JEM faction. When AMIS launched a rescue mission, those soldiers were taken hostage, too. Eventually, the hostages were released, but the message was clear: stay out of JEM-controlled areas. In response to increasing attacks on its soldiers, of whom fifty-nine soldiers in total were killed, AMIS pursued a more passive approach, just observing and not preventing attacks on civilians (Ekengard 2008: 19–24).

As the killing in Darfur intensified, the size of AMIS IIE grew incrementally. As of April 30, 2006, its force on the ground had reached 7,271 personnel, which included military observers, protection force troops, and civilian police. Despite the increasing number of staff, the Janjaweed armed forces continued their killings (U.S. Government Accountability Office 2006: 18). AMIS operations came to an end when the UNAMID commanders took over peacekeeping operations on December 31, 2007.

Alexis Herr

See also: African Union; Justice and Equality Movement; Rape; Sudan People's Liberation Movement/Army; United Nations Mission in the Sudan

Further Reading

Ekengard, Arvid. 2008. *The African Union Mission in Sudan (AMIS): Experiences and*

Lessons Learned. Stockholm: FOI, Swedish Defense Research Agency.

Human Rights Watch. 2006. *Imperatives for Immediate Change: The African Mission in Sudan*. Human Rights Watch. Vol. 18, No. 1A, January 19. https://www.hrw.org /report/2006/01/19/sudan-imperatives -immediate-change/african-union-mission -sudan.

U.S. Government Accountability Office. 2006. *Darfur Crisis: Progress in Aid and Peace Monitoring Threatened by Ongoing Violence and Operational Challenges*. Report No. GAO-07-9. November 9.

African Union–United Nations Mission in Darfur

The African Union–United Nations Mission in Darfur, commonly referred to by its acronym UNAMID, was created on July 31, 2007, to protect civilians, facilitate humanitarian aid, and support the political forces in Darfur. While the United Nations has not officially recognized the violence in Darfur as genocide, they have acknowledged and continue to work to alleviate the immense suffering caused by the violence.

UNAMID was preceded by the African Union Mission in Sudan (AMIS). The African Union (AU; a continental union of African countries established in 2001) launched AMIS 2004 with urging from Western nations. The United States, embroiled with its armed forces in Afghanistan and Iraq, was unwilling to commit troops to Sudan; meanwhile, Britain and France did not want to get embroiled in a drawn-out fight in a remote area of Africa either. Therefore, both the United States and the European Union (a coalition of European nations) offered to provide logistical support (via the United Nations) and increase humanitarian aid, while urging the African Union to intervene militarily. By August 2004, the African Union commissioned 125 monitors under the Nigerian Brigadier General Chukwuemeka Okonkwo to support an AMIS force of 300 troops from Rwanda and Nigeria. The government of Sudan, however, attempted to undermine AMIS by refusing to accept peacekeepers with a mandate to use force to impose peace. As a result, AMIS could only protect AU personnel in Darfur who were stationed there to monitor violence, which soured their ability to protect civilians from government troops and government-backed militias like the Janjaweed.

UN secretary-general Kofi Annan reported to the Security Council on August 30, 2004, about the violent state of affairs in Darfur and urged it to approve a rapid expansion of AMIS. Meanwhile, the United Nations had pursued a diplomatic solution to the Darfur violence and by mid-July had established the Joint Implementation Mechanism. Its report to the United Nations echoed that of Annan and resulted in Security Council Resolution 1556, which demanded that the government of Sudan agree to a cease-fire and disarm the Janjaweed militia. But Khartoum, despite its many smoke-and-mirror tactics, was shown not to take the United Nations or the African Union seriously, and violence continued within the region.

The UN Department of Peacekeeping Operations decided to augment the existing AMIS force following a high-level meeting in Addis Ababa, Ethiopia, on November 16, 2006. The AU-UN hybrid operation was formally created six months later on July 31, 2007, through the adoption of Resolution 1769 under Chapter VII of the UN Charter. The freshly formed UNAMID force took over from AMIS on December 31, 2007. The government of Sudan, much like its approach to AMIS, has made it difficult for UNAMID to fulfill its mandate. A common tactic has been obstructing the delivery of any equipment from Port Sudan to Darfur.

UNAMID's mandate included the following actions: to protect civilians, without prejudice to the responsibility of the Sudanese government; to facilitate the delivery of humanitarian assistance and the safety and security of humanitarian personnel; to mediate between the government of Sudan and armed movements in accordance with the Doha Document for Peace in Darfur; and to support the mediation of community conflict. Its mandate has been complicated by numerous logistical and security issues, including unforgiving terrain; inadequate equipment, infrastructure, and aviation assets; and a hostile political environment. The mission's various headquarters are located in El Geneina (West Darfur), Nyala (South Darfur), Zalingei (Central Darfur), and El Daein (East Darfur). Furthermore, UNAMID had thirty-five deployment locations through the five states that make up Darfur.

Over the many years of conflict, the size of UNAMID's forces have increased and decreased. On July 31, 2007, for example, UNAMID had an authorized force of 25,987 uniformed peacekeepers, which included 19,555 troops, 360 military observers and liaison officers, 3,772 police advisers, and 2,660 Formed Police Units. By the beginning of 2009, however, the complement was up to barely 10,000, and by the start of 2010, UNAMID was still short some 6,000 policemen and soldiers. In July 2012, the mission had an authorized strength of 23,743 personnel.

Then on June 29, 2017, the UN Security Council adopted Resolution 2363, which, in addition to renewing UNAMID's mandate, called for a slow reduction of UNAMID troops and police over the next year. As of

March 2019, 10,683 personnel are currently deployed in Darfur, which includes 2,620 civilians, 5,469 contingent troops, 54 experts on the mission, 2,303 police, 132 staff officers, and 105 UN volunteers. This number is just half of the 19,248 number of personnel authorized by the United Nations to work in Darfur. According to its mandate, 15,845 military personnel (including contingent troops, experts on the mission, and staff officers), 1,583 police, and 13 Formed Police Units comprising 140 personnel each are approved for deployment. The budget of July 2018 to June 2019 totaled $385,678,500 (United Nations 2019). In a vote on June 27, 3019, the UN Security Council voted to extend its mandate.

Despite being one of the world's largest peacekeeping forces, UNAMID has faced allegations that it has not done enough to protect civilians, a shortcoming the United Nations has acknowledged as well.

Alexis Herr

See also: African Union; African Union Mission in Sudan; Amnesty International; Doha Document for Peace in Darfur; Janjaweed; United Nations Commission of Inquiry on Darfur

Further Reading

United Nations. 2019. "UNAMID Fact Sheet." Available at https://peacekeeping.un.org/en/mission/unamid.

Amnesty International

Amnesty International is a global human rights movement that works to free prisoners of conscience, assist political prisoners, abolish the death penalty, and end extrajudicial executions and disappearances through education, grassroots efforts, and letter-writing campaigns. Amnesty International has also been an outspoken critic of the Sudanese government's persecution of Darfurians. Up until his forcible removal from office in early 2019, President Omar Hassan Ahmed al-Bashir of Sudan had continued to imprison and torture his political opponents, which garnered the attention of the human rights group.

The organization was founded in May 1961, when Peter Benenson, a lawyer in London, read in the *London Observer* about a group of students in Portugal who had been jailed for proposing a toast to freedom in a public restaurant. Benenson launched a campaign called "Appeal for Amnesty 1961," which kept the issue in the columns of the *Observer* for a year and encouraged people to write letters to officials in all countries where people were imprisoned for their political beliefs. The campaign was a great success and spread to other countries besides Portugal. By the end of 1961, Benenson formed Amnesty International, a nongovernmental organization (NGO) to lead these efforts.

Amnesty International based its principles on the Universal Declaration of Human Rights by the United Nations (UN), which was adopted by the UN General Assembly in 1948. Defining "prisoners of conscience" as people unjustly jailed because of their beliefs, race, gender, or ethnic origin, the agency began by investigating the cases of individual prisoners. It would adopt the cause of anyone who indeed was a prisoner of conscience, and a letter-writing campaign would commence. When it was deemed safe, the families of these prisoners were also contacted and assistance offered. The early emphasis was on freeing individuals, not on changing entire political systems.

By the late 1960s, Amnesty International had expanded some of its efforts into education, grassroots fund-raising, and reaching out to churches, schools, businesses, and labor unions to spread awareness of its campaigns. After some trial and error, the agency adopted the rule that organization members could work only on cases outside their own country. This helped to preserve impartiality in the investigation of human rights abuses and thereby maintain the reputation of the organization. Despite growing international opposition by human rights abusers, Amnesty International was awarded the Nobel Peace Prize in 1977.

Many of the first members of Amnesty International were professors, but during the 1980s, the number of students in the organization grew rapidly. The student membership did not adopt prisoners; instead, they organized publicity about unjust political systems and helped to write letters for prisoners adopted by other groups. The tendency to call attention to particular injustices became even more pronounced as prominent musicians and artists adopted Amnesty International as a special cause. Concerts and other events not only provided a major boost to the organization's budget, they expanded the reach of its educational campaigns. Amnesty International benefit concerts in the 1980s included rock and folk legends such as Joan Baez, Tracy Chapman, Bono from the band U2, Peter Gabriel, and many others.

The organization remains independent of any government, political party, religious faction, or economic interest. Its emphasis on accuracy and impartiality has established its reputation as a credible source of information. A good part of the budget of the International Secretariat, in the central headquarters based in London, goes toward careful research into the situations of political prisoners.

Amnesty International has more than 7 million members, supporters, and subscribers in more than 150 countries and territories, and it has offices in more than 70 countries. The organization is headed by an International Council, which meets every two years and has representatives from each section (a section is a group of members in a given country). The International Executive Committee meets at least twice a year and includes the treasurer, a representative from the International Secretariat staff, and seven regular members. The International Executive Committee appoints the organization's secretary-general. The organization is funded by its membership, as well as by donations and fund-raising.

The group's Urgent Action Network conducts letter-writing campaigns on behalf of people who are in grave danger. The group issues an annual newsletter, as well as reports, studies, and audiovisual resources. Amnesty International has been successful in getting 50 percent of designated prisoners of conscience released within a short time.

Throughout the Darfur Genocide, Amnesty International has endeavored to draw attention to Khartoum's abuse of Darfurians and their allies. To date, the organization has disseminated some 613 articles and calls to action regarding violence and oppression in Sudan.

Alexis Herr

See also: Bashir, Omar Hassan Ahmed al-; Darfur

Further Reading

Clark, Ann Marie. 2001. *Diplomacy of Conscience: Amnesty International and Changing Human Rights Norms*. Princeton, NJ: Princeton University Press.

Desmond, Cosmas. 1983. *Persecution East and West: Human Rights, Political Prisoners, and Amnesty*. New York: Penguin Books.

Power, Jonathan. 1981. *Amnesty International: The Human Rights Story*. New York: Pergamon Press.

Annan, Kofi

From 1997 to 2006, Kofi Annan served as the seventh secretary-general (the chief administrative officer) of the United Nations (UN). During his tenure, he took on many complicated roles that influenced how the organization responded to genocide and atrocities.

Early Life and Career

Annan was born in Kumasi, in what was then the British Gold Coast colony (now Ghana), on April 8, 1938. He came from an upper-class merchant family that had descended from tribal chiefs. As a teenager, Annan attended a local boarding school, and in 1958, he entered the Kumasi University of Science and Technology (now Kwame Nkrumah University), where he studied economics. While there, he received a grant to complete his studies at Macalester College, in St. Paul, Minnesota. Between 1961 and 1962, he pursued and obtained a degree in international relations at the Graduate Institute of International and Development Studies in Geneva, Switzerland.

Annan spent the majority of his life employed by the United Nations. While pursuing his studies in Switzerland, he joined the World Health Organization (WHO) in Geneva in 1962, where he later also worked in the Office of the UN High Commissioner for Refugees in 1980. From 1971 to 1972, Annan took a sabbatical to attend the Massachusetts Institute of Technology on an Alfred Sloan fellowship, where he received a Master of Science in management. In May 1974, the United Nations assigned Annan to the UN Emergency Force in Egypt, where he served as chief personnel officer for civilians working with the peacekeeping mission there.

Six months later, Annan left the United Nations to become the managing director of the Ghana Tourist Agency, where he remained until September 1976, when he returned to the United Nations as a personnel officer in New York. For the next decade, Annan continued to work at the UN offices in New York, taking on new and increasing complex roles within the agency. By 1987, he had become a key bureaucrat with the United Nations, serving successively in senior positions in a diverse range of departments, including Human Resources Management (1987–1990), Budget and Finance (1990–1992), and Peacekeeping (February 1993–February 1994).

His considerable tenure and successful work at the United Nations brought him greater responsibility and opportunities. Before becoming the UN secretary general in 1997, Annan took on many complex roles and special assignments, such as going to Iraq in 1990 to negotiate the release of UN staff held as hostages, serving as undersecretary-general in charge of peacekeeping operations (1993–1994 and 1996–1997), and representing the office of the UN secretary-general in the former Yugoslavia (1995). While he found success in many of these positions, everything else during his tenure paled when measured against the organization's unproductive handling of the crisis in Rwanda prior to, during, and after the genocide that took place there in 1994.

Annan and the Rwandan Genocide

The UN efforts toward halting the Rwandan Genocide were thoroughly inadequate, a point subsequently acknowledged by Annan

on a number of occasions. In fact, he later apologized for the role that the United Nations played during the genocide, expressing "deep remorse" that he and the United Nations as a whole had not done more to stop it (United Nations 1999). Annan was criticized by many, both at the time and later, for adopting a passive approach to pleas for help from the commander of the UN Assistance Mission for Rwanda, Lieutenant General Roméo Dallaire, who argued that Annan wavered over whether to reinforce the mission or try to arrange a new mandate that would allow more effective action. Dallaire also claimed that Annan refused to respond to his repeated requests for authorization to use force on the ground. In this, some have asserted, Annan was restricted by the lines of demarcation within the UN bureaucracy and was overruled by his immediate superior, Iqbal Riza, and, further up the chain, the then-secretary-general, Boutros Boutros-Ghali.

The UN failure in Rwanda also raised the question of what role the organization should play in intervening in genocide. In 2004, on the occasion of the tenth anniversary of the genocide, Annan reflected on Rwanda, saying that he could and should have done more to stop it and acknowledging that he did not push hard enough for action to be taken by UN member-states or the Secretariat. The painful memory of this inaction was profound, and he became determined from that point on never to allow another such tragedy to occur on his watch again. Rwanda thus influenced many of Annan's later decisions once he became secretary-general.

On April 7, 2004, in a speech in Geneva commemorating the tenth anniversary of the genocide in Rwanda, Annan launched a five-point action plan to prevent genocide. This included (1) preventing armed conflict, which usually provides the context for genocide; (2) protecting civilians in armed conflicts, including a mandate to use UN peacekeepers for that purpose; (3) ending impunity through judicial action in both national and international courts; (4) gathering information and disseminating early warnings through a UN special adviser for genocide prevention, and making recommendations to the UN Security Council on actions to prevent or halt genocide; and (5) taking swift and decisive action along a continuum of steps, including military action.

The fourth point featured a pledge to designate an official who would collect data and monitor any serious violations of human rights or international law that have racial or ethnic dimensions that could lead to genocide. By July 14, 2004, the appointment was made. Juan E. Méndez, an Argentinean lawyer, took the position, charged with the task of acting in an early-warning capacity that would advise the secretary-general and the Security Council about potential genocidal situations. Once this determination was made, he would make recommendations to the Security Council about how the United Nations could prevent these events. After Méndez left the office in 2007, Francis Deng of Sudan held the position until 2012. Adama Dieng, a Senegalese jurist, was appointed secretary-general on the Prevention of Genocide on September 1, 2012, a position he still holds.

Appointment to Secretary-General

On December 13, 1996, Annan was recommended by the UN Security Council to be the next secretary-general. Replacing Boutros-Ghali, an Egyptian, he would be the second successive African to serve in the post, and the first from sub-Saharan Africa. He was also the first secretary-general to be elected from the ranks of the UN bureaucracy. His five-year term began on January 1, 1997, and it was renewed in June 2001 after the UN Security Council unanimously agreed to reappoint him for a second term that began on January 1, 2002.

As secretary-general, Annan negotiated or presided over a number of highly delicate situations, including an attempt in 1998 to gain Iraq's compliance with Security Council Resolution 687 and a mission that same year to promote the transition to civilian rule in Nigeria. In 1999, he helped to resolve a stalemate between Libya and the Security Council and to forge an international response to preindependence violence in East Timor.

Much of his work in the international arena focused on issues related to global health and he took a leading role in mobilizing the global community in the battle against the AIDS pandemic. In April 2001, he proposed a Global AIDS and Health Fund to help developing countries confront the crisis, and for this, both he and the United Nations were awarded the 2001 Nobel Peace Prize.

As secretary-general, Annan prioritized strengthening and revitalizing the organization's work and improving its image. This included strengthening the traditional work of the United Nations in the areas of development and the maintenance of international peace and security; advocating for human rights, the rule of law, and the universal values of equality, tolerance, and human dignity; and restoring public confidence in the United Nations by reaching out to new partners.

To help achieve this, he issued a report in April 2000 that considered what the role of the United Nations should be in the twenty-first century. The so-called Millennium Declarations that followed were adopted by many of the world's leaders attending the UN Millennium Summit that September.

These Millennium Development Goals set specific targets to end poverty and inequality, improve education, protect vulnerable groups from violence, combat HIV/AIDS, and protect the environment.

On December 31, 2006, Annan retired as secretary-general and was succeeded by the South Korean statesman Ban Ki-moon. Annan returned to Ghana, where he maintained an active role as one of Africa's senior statesmen. In 2012, he agreed to serve as a special envoy of the United Nations and the Arab League in an effort to end the ongoing Syrian civil war; however, after six months of largely fruitless efforts, he resigned the post in late August 2012. In September 2016, Annan was tapped to lead a UN commission charged with investigating the 2015 Rohingya crisis in Southeast Asia.

Annan and the Darfur Genocide

Annan was secretary-general during the first four years of the genocidal crisis in Darfur, Sudan, during which the United Nations did little that was effective in stopping the killings. When the violence first broke out, the organization failed to even classify the killings as a genocide, focusing instead on the refugee crisis that had been created. In December 2003, Annan voiced his first statement of alarm about the situation in Darfur, but according to him, the Security Council "had no desire to place the complicated and heavy demands of Darfur on its agenda, I could do little more than make verbal appeals and try and negotiate throughout this protracted period" (Annan 2012, 119).

In March 2004, when Western newspapers starting publishing articles calling the bloodshed in Darfur a genocide, public pressure mounted for decisive action. In the midst of the mounting social movement calling for the United Nations to stop the killing, Annan made a personal phone call to the president of Sudan, Omar al-Bashir, on March 29. According to Annan, he told the president that the situation in Darfur was unacceptable and urged him to protect Darfurians from the Janjaweed militias that were perpetrating the violence. For his part, al-Bashir thanked Annan for his concern, knowing full well that only the Security Council could approve military action.

During ceremonies in April 2004 marking the tenth anniversary of the Rwandan Genocide, Annan discussed the possibility of UN military action. That same month, the African Union (AU), a continental organization of African states, did what the United Nations had failed to do; it dispatched a small task force—the African Union Mission in Sudan (AMIS)—to monitor a recently drafted humanitarian cease-fire that collapsed shortly thereafter.

In 2005, Annan joined Colin Powell, the U.S. secretary of state, on a trip to Khartoum, Sudan's capital and seat of government, and the Darfur region. While Powell had publicly described the violence in Darfur as a genocide in 2004, Annan and the United Nations avoided the "g-word." Despite the difference of opinion and word choice, this trip helped generate action within the organization. The trip included visiting some of the internally displaced person (IDP) camps in Darfur and refugee camps in neighboring Chad, and meeting with President al-Bashir and other senior members of his government.

Following prolonged public pressure, the UN Security Council put its considerable weight behind AMIS and the AU when it passed Resolution 1769 on July 31, 2007. This resolution established the African Union–United Nations Mission in Darfur (UNAMID), a joint peacekeeping force. For his part, Annan supported the sending of a UN peacekeeping mission and worked with the government of Sudan to accept a transfer of power from an AU monitoring force to one under the authority of the United Nations.

In his 2012 book *Interventions: A Life in War and Peace*, Annan maintained that what happened in Darfur did not constitute genocide. This opinion was not much different from what he had said in 2006, when he described the bloodshed in Darfur as the "world's worst humanitarian crisis" at that time and stressed support for Darfurian refugees. This comment highlights the problematic reality of the legal definition of genocide. To establish that Bashir's government was committing genocide, it would be necessary to prove that it intended to exterminate Darfurians, in whole or in part.

After more than four decades of service at the United Nations and a lifetime dedicated to improving the situations of those most in need, Kofi Annan passed away at the age of eighty on August 18, 2018, in Switzerland, the same country where he first began his career at the United Nations.

Paul R. Bartrop and Alexis Herr

See also: African Union; Bashir, Omar Hassan Ahmed al-; Janjaweed; United Nations Commission of Inquiry on Darfur; United Nations Convention on the Prevention and Punishment of the Crime of Genocide; United Nations Mission in the Sudan

Further Reading

Annan, Kofi. 2012. *Interventions: A Life in War and Peace*. New York: Penguin Books.

Meisler, Stanley. 2008. *Kofi Annan: A Man of Peace in a World of War*. New York: Wiley.

Mills, Kurt. 2015. *International Responses to Mass Atrocities in Africa: Responsibility to Protect, Prosecute, and Palliate*. Philadelphia: University of Pennsylvania Press.

United Nations. 1999. "Kofi Annan Emphasizes Commitment to Enabling UN Never Again to Fail in Protecting Civilian Population from Genocide or Mass Slaughter." Press Release SG/SM/7263 AFR/196. December 16. Available at https://www.un.org/press/en/1999/19991216.sgsm7263.doc.html.

United Nations. 2008. *Atrocities and International Accountability: Beyond Transitional Justice*. New York: United Nations.

Anyidoho, Henry Kwami

Major General Henry Kwami Anyidoho is one of Ghana's most distinguished and well known military officers. He spent nearly forty-one years in the service of the Ghana Armed Forces and participated in international peacekeeping operations in Rwanda, Lebanon, Liberia, Cambodia, and Darfur.

Anyidoho was born in the rural village of Tanyigbe, in the Volta Region of Ghana, on July 13, 1940. A career soldier, he is a graduate of the Ghana Military Academy and the U.S. Marine Staff College in Quantico, Virginia. He received his commission with the Ghanaian army's Signal Corps in 1965 and served in various military capacities, including as the commanding officer of the Army Signal Regiment; commandant of the Ghana Military Academy and Training Schools; director general of logistics, joint operations, and plans at the general headquarters of the Ghana Armed Forces; and the general officer in charge of the Northern Command.

Anyidoho earned international recognition as a leader and participant in a number of important United Nations (UN) peacekeeping missions. Prior to his deployment to Sudan in 2005, he was involved in international peacekeeping operations such as the United Nations Emergency Force (UNEF) in

Sinai; the United Nations Interim Force in Lebanon; the Economic Community of West African States Monitoring Group in Liberia in 1990; and the United Nations Transitional Authority in Cambodia. He was appointed as the deputy force commander and chief of staff of the United Nations Assistance Mission for Rwanda (UNAMIR) in December 1994 and arrived in Kigali on January 15, 1994. While working under the command of Lieutenant General Roméo Dallaire, Anyidoho headed the Ghanaian contingent of some 850 troops within the UNAMIR forces. UNAMIR's mandate was to help administer peace accords between the Rwandan government, which was backed by the Hutu majority (the nationality of the perpetrators of the genocide), and the Rwandan Patriotic Front, composed of Tutsi rebels (the ethnicity targeted for annihilation by the Hutu perpetrators). By April 1994, any semblance of peace had evaporated, and the Rwandan government had launched a genocide against the Tutsi.

Anyidoho's experiences in previous peacekeeping missions did not provide him with a template of how to respond to the carnage that descended on Rwanda in April 1994, but he was quick to adapt as it developed. Organizing the Ghanaian troops under his command and liaising closely with Dallaire, he found himself pulled in a dozen directions at once, with calls to station soldiers at the homes of prominent moderate Hutu politicians (most of whom were targeted by Hutu perpetrators for not being anti-Tutsi or for not participating in the bloodletting), or to rescue Tutsis (a minority making up 15 percent of Rwanda's population) and bring them to safety. The forces under his command were very quickly overwhelmed, and yet they still endeavored to save lives.

As Rwanda descended into genocide, the UN headquarters in New York ordered that

UNAMIR be shut down. Nations that had originally contributed troops (like Ghana) recalled them, and on April 21, the UN Security Council passed Resolution 912, which called for a reduction of the UNAMIR force from 2,548 to just 270. Anyidoho was the first senior officer in Kigali to receive the news on the phone, as Dallaire was away from the office attempting to negotiate a cease-fire. His immediate reaction was to resist the reduction order and to defy the UN command to withdraw. He advised Dallaire along these lines; Dallaire, in turn, had received the news from his chief of staff, Major Brent Beardsley, and had already reached more or less the same conclusion.

Pleading with New York to keep the mission open, Dallaire achieved a reprieve of sorts that allowed UNAMIR to remain, but only with the reduced force of 270 troops. Ultimately, the number was settled at 456—78 percent of whom belonged to Anyidoho's Ghanaian battalion. The higher figure was not endorsed by the Security Council; it was simply adhered to by the personnel on the ground in Rwanda, who refused to leave.

Anyidoho's decision to stay in Rwanda to try to save lives was his alone. He communicated this to his government in Accra, and the government ultimately agreed. With this commitment forming the backbone of the remaining UN force still in Rwanda, Dallaire managed to lead his troops to protect as many Tutsis as he could. As a result, it has been estimated that up to 30,000 people were saved from the gruesome fate planned for them by the Hutu government and the militias acting in its name.

After the genocide, Anyidoho returned to Ghana. He then embarked on a number of appointments: as a member of the Organization of African Unity (OAU; later reconstituted as the African Union, AU) task force on the Mechanism for Conflict Prevention

Management and Resolution; as the UN expert who wrote the major discussion document at the initial meeting of the Heads of the Armed Forces of the OAU in Addis Ababa, Ethiopia, in June 1996; and, in 2004, as the team leader of UN observers for the Cameroon-Nigeria Mixed Commission. Soon after this, Anyidoho was made team leader of another UN mission, a Humanitarian Assistance Cell providing strategic advice to the AU on Darfur, following which he became coordinator of UN support to the AU Mission in Sudan (AMIS). This gave him a unique qualification for his next post; in 2005, he was appointed by the secretary-general of the AU and the UN secretary-general as the joint special representative for the African Union–United Nations Mission in Darfur (UNAMID).

In 1999, Anyidoho published *Guns over Kigali*, a memoir of his time in Rwanda during the genocide. Roméo Dallaire's own 2003 book on Rwanda, *Shake Hands with the Devil*, corroborated much of what Anyidoho had recalled. The conclusion to be drawn from both works is that the courage and resourcefulness of Anyidoho and his Ghanaian troops did much to keep the residual UNAMIR force in place in Rwanda, maintaining a UN presence in the country when the preference from New York City (where the United Nations has its headquarters) was otherwise. Anyidoho, who was later decorated with the Distinguished Service Order for Gallantry, thus must be considered a major force behind the protection of tens of thousands of Rwandan Tutsis and moderate Hutus, who, through his actions, were saved from certain death.

Paul R. Bartrop

See also: African Union; African Union Mission in Sudan; African Union–United Nations Mission in Darfur

Further Reading

Anyidoho, Henry Kwami. 2012. *Guns over Kigali: The Rwandese Civil War*. Accra, Ghana: Sub-Saharan Publishers.

Evans, Glynne. 1997. *Responding to Crises in the African Great Lakes*. Oxford: Oxford University Press.

Klinghoffer, Arthur Jay. 1998. *The International Dimension of Genocide in Rwanda*. New York: New York University Press.

B

Banda, Abdallah

Abdallah Banda Abakaer Nourain, commonly referred to as Banda, is one of six men wanted by the International Criminal Court (ICC) for his deadly involvement in Darfur. He is alleged to have committed war crimes while serving as a commander of the Justice and Equality Movement (JEM), a Darfur-based rebel group fighting government forces.

Banda was born in April 1963 in north Darfur to a Zaghawa family. Like many other members of the Zaghawa tribe, Banda joined JEM to fight the Janjaweed and Sudanese government forces in Darfur. He soon became a leader of the group. Darfurian members of the National Islamic Front (the group that formed after President Omar Hassan al-Bashir overthrew the Sudanese government in 1999), led by Dr. Khalil Ibrahim, founded JEM in 2000.

According to charges brought against him by the ICC, Banda led an attack of JEM forces on September 29, 2007, against the African Union Mission in Sudan (AMIS) stationed at the Haskanita Military Group Site (MGS Haskanita) in Umm Kadada in northern Darfur. AMIS was an African Union (AU) peacekeeping force founded in 2004 to monitor the situation in Darfur, which was ultimately replaced by the African Union–United Nations Mission in Darfur (UNAMID) on December 31, 2007. During the Banda-led attack on the AMIS mission in Haskanita that year, twelve peacekeepers were killed and another eight injured.

The ICC summoned Banda to its headquarters in The Hague in August 2009. The ICC alleged that during the 2007 Haskanita attack, Banda engaged in war crimes, including violence to life; intentionally attacking peacekeeping personnel, installations, materials, units, and vehicles; and pillaging. According to prosecution witnesses, Banda had been in command during the attack, planned the attack, and provided weapons and vehicles to rebel troops. Banda voluntarily appeared in front of The Hague in June 2010 and told the judges that he wanted to waive his rights to be present during a later confirmation of charges hearing. He also informed the court that during the hearing, his defense team did not intend to call witnesses or make any presentations. Thus, with Banda absent, the ICC held a confirmation of charges hearing in December 2010. In a pretrial chamber convened on March 7, 2011, the charges of war crimes against Banda were confirmed, and eighty-nine victims were authorized to participate in his hearing. The court issued a warrant for his arrest on September 11, 2014, which the government of Sudan has not enforced. The ICC does not try individuals in absentia; thus, the case depends on Banda's appearance in The Hague, whether voluntarily or otherwise.

Alexis Herr

See also: African Union; African Union Mission in Sudan; African Union–United Nations Mission in Darfur; Ibrahim, Khalil; Justice and Equality Movement; Zaghawa

Further Reading

Coalition for the International Criminal Court. n.d. "Abdallah Banda Abakaer Nourain." Available at http://www.coalitionfortheicc .org/cases/abdallah-banda-abakaer -nourain.

Bashir, Omar Hassan Ahmed al-

Since Omar Hassan Ahmed al-Bashir overthrew the civilian government of Prime Minister Sadiq al-Mahdi on June 30, 1989, the condition of human rights in Sudan rapidly deteriorated. In the years that followed, Bashir intensified Islamic rule throughout the country and continued Africa's longest-running civil war against rebels in southern Sudan. Bashir reintroduced multiparty politics in 1999 and won presidential elections in December 2000 and April 2010, although opposition candidates boycotted and disputed the authenticity of both elections. In January 2005, he brokered a historic peace agreement with southern rebels, but a conflict in the nation's western Darfur region continues. In 2019, he was overthrown and was sent to prison, where he remains to date.

Bashir was born in 1944 in the rural village of Hosh Bannaga in the far north of Sudan. At the time of his birth, Hosh Bannaga was still part of the colonial Kingdom of Egypt and Sudan. An Islamic fundamentalist, Bashir enlisted as a young man in the Sudanese army, graduating from the country's military academy in the capital, Khartoum, in 1966. While fighting alongside the Egyptians in 1973 Israeli-Arab War (also known as the Yom Kippur War, Ramadan War, or October War), Bashir distinguished himself in combat. Following the war, he was appointed to a military attaché in the United Arab Emirates in 1975, and

after having returned to Sudan, he became head of an armored parachute brigade in 1981. The National Islamic Front (NIF) recruited Brigadier Bashir and its leader, Islamic ideologue Hassan al-Turabi, to lead a coup against Prime Minister Sadiq al-Mahdi and his government in 1989.

Prime Minister Mahdi had reestablished democracy in Sudan but failed to end the war between the north and south or to enforce Islamic rule to the satisfaction of the fundamentalists. Upon taking power, Bashir, who was believed to be merely the public face of the political aspirations of al-Turabi, suspended the constitution, set up a new ruling Revolutionary Command Council for National Salvation (RCC-NS), and banned all political parties except for the NIF (renamed the National Congress Party) in 1999. He also pledged to end the war with the south, in which non-Muslim black Africans were fighting Arab domination and the imposition of Islamic Sharia law. The enforcement of Islamic law led to the intensification of the ongoing war with the south that led to the deaths of some 2 million people and the displacement of an estimated 4 million Sudanese.

The imposition of Sharia law under Bashir derailed much of the progress that women had made in Sudan since the 1950s. Founded in 1951, the Sudanese Women's Union (SWU) had grown and become a highly effective lobbying force for women's rights in Africa. Fatima Ibrahim, president of the SWU, had become the first woman elected to the Sudanese parliament in 1965, the same year women won the right to vote and hold office. Since her election, women had continued to make strides in holding public positions, and Sudan had even appointed women justices in the Sharia legal system.

However, Bashir's assumption to power and the Islamic coup brought an end to women's political and leadership advancement. Under Bashir, women were forced to obey a strict dress code and could be flogged by the religious police if they did otherwise. As a result, some women resorted to returning to life under the *khimar* (veil used to cover the head, and sometimes also the chest) or the burka (a loose garment covering he whole body from head to foot). A poignant example of the decline of women's rights under Bashir is the following statistic: in the mid-1980s, 25 percent of Sudan's diplomats were women, but by 1993, none held office (Crockett 2010, 139–140).

The intensified enforcement of Sharia law, however, did more than just affect women. It also informed Sudan's relationship to other nations and terrorist groups in the region. For example, from 1990 to 1996, the government provided a safe haven to Al-Qaeda terrorist leader Osama bin Laden (who later planned the September 11, 2001, attack on the twin towers of the World Trade Center in New York). Additionally, Bashir did not make good on his promise to end the war with southern rebels, and in the spring of 1992, he launched a major new offensive. Bashir and the RCC-NS made a gesture toward restoring democracy when they appointed a 300-member provisional National Assembly with legislative powers in February 1992. But in October of the following year, the RCC-NS was dissolved, and Bashir was announced as the president of Sudan. He formed a new government composed mostly of outgoing ministers. Bashir's cabinet continued to support Islamic rule, and it allowed the formation of other political parties in Sudan except for the NIF.

In December 1999, Bashir ousted al-Turabi from his position as speaker of parliament and secretary-general of the National Congress Party after the latter introduced a bill to curb the president's powers. Bashir dissolved the parliament and imposed a state of emergency. Until elections a year later, Bashir ruled Sudan alone. New parties sprang up to oppose his rule, including one led by al-Turabi, but they boycotted the December 2000 elections. After ten days of voting, Bashir won a second term as president, receiving 86.5 percent of the vote. No voting took place in the rebel-controlled areas of the south. Bashir was sworn in for a five-year term in February 2001. Not long after, he placed al-Turabi under house arrest. He was released in October 2003, but he was subsequently jailed again in 2004 and released in 2005.

Under increasing international pressure to end the civil war between the north and south, Bashir signed a peace agreement with the southern rebels in May 2004, followed by a permanent cease-fire settlement on December 31. The agreement, which was two years in the making, called for the central government and the Sudan People's Liberation Movement/Army (SPLM/A) to share political power, divide up Sudan's oil wealth, and merge the armies. It also contained a clause that would allow the southerners to vote to secede from Sudan in 2011 (which southerners voted overwhelming in favor of in January 2011). The final provisions of the accord were worked out, and the document was ratified in a landmark ceremony in January 2005.

As Bashir was reaching a tenuous peace with the south, however, another bloody conflict in the country's western Darfur region erupted in 2003, resulting from long-simmering tensions between "Arab" pastoralists and "black African" farmers over land and water resources. Accusing the government of favoring Arabs and marginalizing black Africans, Darfurian rebel groups began attacking government targets in 2002. The government response included support for local Arab militias called *Janjaweed*, which engaged in raids characterized by rape, mass murder, and wholesale destruction against Fur, Zaghawa, and Massalit groups. Bashir denied involvement with the Janjaweed, but most international investigators and such groups as Human Rights Watch believe that the Janjaweed militias were financed and armed by the government. Janjaweed raids often followed government air raids on villages. In 2004, the violence had intensified to the point that the United Nations (UN) called Darfur one of the world's worst humanitarian crises in the world and the U.S. government labeled the Darfur conflict as a genocide. From 2003 to mid-2008, when an international peacekeeping force was deployed, the conflict had displaced some 2.7 million people and killed more than 300,000, according to UN estimates.

Bashir has voiced his disdain for UN and international intervention in the Darfur crisis. In 2006, for example, Bashir refused to accept UN peacekeepers in Darfur and accused the United Nations of practicing neocolonialism. He has repeatedly accused Western nations and global institutions of seeking to enforce political, social, and religious ideals in opposition to Islamic law in Africa. Likewise, Bashir criticized U.S. president George W. Bush when he formally announced new economic and diplomatic sanctions against Sudan in 2007. The sanctions made it illegal for U.S. citizens or companies to do business with or promote the work of some thirty companies supporting Sudan or supplying arms to its military forces. In response to international condemnation of Bashir and his government's murder of Darfurians, he ordered the expulsion of aid agencies in 2009. At that time, these agencies were providing approximately 50 percent of the total aid capacity in Darfur. While the UN Commission of Inquiry on Darfur stopped short of calling the conflict genocide, saying that the campaign's roots in counterinsurgency made it difficult to prove "genocidal intent," as per the UN definition of genocide, it also noted that this did not mean that the crimes against humanity in Darfur were any less horrific than genocide was.

On July 14, 2008, the prosecutor of the International Criminal Court (ICC) filed for Bashir's arrest on charges of genocide, crimes against humanity, and war crimes in Darfur. On March 4, 2009, the ICC issued an arrest warrant for Bashir on charges of war crimes and crimes against humanity. In July 2010, the ICC officially charged him with three counts of genocide (for actions intended to "bring about the physical destruction," as per the UN definition of genocide, of the Fur, Massalit, and Zaghawa peoples). The 2009 charges were widely cheered by those living in Darfur's displacement camps, although Bashir's supporters took to the streets in protest. Fanning the flames of anger, Bashir himself denounced the 2009 warrant as an attack on Sudan's sovereignty and the Islamic religion of its government.

Attempts at resolving the conflict, including several rounds of peace talks between Bashir's government and different rebel groups in Darfur, and the presence of a joint UN–African Union (AU) peacekeeping force have been met with only partial success. Some international observers criticized both the 2009 and 2010 ICC arrest warrants for potentially destabilizing the country further; however, most rights groups say the warrants were necessary to focus world attention and condemnation on ongoing abuses by the Sudanese government. In any case, the government has ignored the warrants, as have many other AU member-states that have allowed Bashir to visit their nations. For example, Bashir traveled to Kenya, Egypt, Nigeria, and Saudi Arabia without fear of arrest. In 2015, however, a visit to South Africa was cut short when a South African court weighed whether to arrest him.

Bashir remained popular in the north due to infrastructure improvements and a higher standard of living among some Sudanese due to increasing oil production. He was reelected in April 2010 to another five-year term as president. The 2010 balloting was boycotted by leading opposition candidates, though, who cited irregularities in voter registration lists and feared vote-rigging and intimidation—activities that international observers' reports confirmed. Condemnation by the international community has been muted, however, by a sense that the flawed election was nonetheless an important step toward democracy. Many observers doubted that Bashir would let the south—with its oil resources—secede without a fight, but in the run-up to the election, he vowed to accept the results, which he did once it was announced that more than 98 percent of southerners had voted for independence. His cooperation in the matter won him plaudits both internationally and at home.

South Sudan's independence did not forestall conflict in the region and violence has continued to dominate Sudan and South Sudan relations. Under Bashir's direction, government forces have continued to attack towns along the border region between the north and south that are known to have oil reserves. In response, the United Nations passed Resolution 2046, which called for an end to hostilities in Sudan and South Sudan and demanded that Bashir permit humanitarian access to civilians affected by the violence. Despite repeated negotiations over the Abyei region (currently part of South Sudan), attempts at peace have failed. Meanwhile, new fighting erupted in Darfur, which has caused hundreds of more deaths and thousands to flee.

Under the Donald Trump administration, the United States has softened its approach to Sudan and its leader. On October 12, 2017, Washington lifted some sanctions, with the exception of those imposed on April 26, 2006, in relation to the conflict in Darfur. In November 2017, a State Department official said the Trump administration would remove Sudan from its terrorism list if it sees more progress on human rights. In 2018, Bashir took steps to improve his image and that of his government on the international stage by ordering the release of political prisoners and freeing two journalists working for foreign news agencies. These efforts, however, are limited, and it remains to be seen whether the United States will lift all the sanctions.

In April 2018, Sudanese citizens gathered in Khartoum to protest rising food prices, which quickly evolved into chants demanding the removal of Bashir from power. In 2019, Bashir's military dictatorship came to an end on April 11, when the military removed Bashir and placed him in Khartoum's high-security Kobar prison. To date, he has not been seen since his arrest, and it is unclear whether he will be tried for his crimes as dictator of Sudan.

Alexis Herr

See also: African Union–United Nations Mission in Darfur; Denial of the Darfur Genocide; National Islamic Front; Sudanese Civil Wars; Sudan People's Liberation Movement/Army; Turabi, Hassan al-; United Nations Commission of Inquiry on Darfur; United States Involvement in Darfur

Further Reading

Anderson, Scott. 2004. "How Did Darfur Happen?" *The New York Times*. October 17.

Brockman, Norbert C. 1994. *An African Biographical Dictionary*. Santa Barbara, CA: ABC-CLIO.

Crockett, Richard. 2010. *Sudan: Darfur and the Failure of an African State*. New Haven, CT: Yale University Press.

Moore, Jina. 2017. "U.S. Is Open to Removing Sudan from Terrorism List, Diplomat Says." *The New York Times*. November 16.

Bassolé, Djibril

Djibril Yipènè Bassolé is a diplomat and politician from Burkina Faso who headed the joint African Union (AU) and United Nations (UN) peace negotiations in Doha, Qatar, between the government of Sudan and the Liberation and Justice Movement (LJM), a coalition of Darfurian rebel groups. The resulting agreement signed between the two parties in 2011 attempted to conclude the bloodshed in Darfur and provide some semblance of support for Darfurian victims. At this time, Bassolé is awaiting trial for his alleged role in a governmental coup in Burkina Faso.

Born November 30, 1957, Bassolé is an experienced mediator in inter-African affairs. He was a member of international committees monitoring elections in Togo (1993–1994) and mediating a peace agreement during the Tuareg rebellion in Niger (1990–1995). He served as Burkina Faso's minister of security, and then as the minister of foreign affairs and regional cooperation, from 2000 to 2008, during which time he played a key role in implementing a 2007 accord between President Laurent Gbago of Côte d'Ivoire and Guillaume Soro, the leader of the rebel group Forces Nouvelles and, later, prime minister of Côte d'Ivoire from April 2007 to March 2012.

In June 2008, UN secretary-general Ban Ki-moon named Bassolé the joint chief mediator for Darfur, representing both the African Union and the United Nations. Three weeks later, the African Union also authorized the High-Level Implementation Panel on Darfur (AUHIP), led by former South African president Thabo Mbeki. Egypt, Libya, and Qatar offered to organize renewed peace initiatives. The latter was endorsed by the League of Arab States, and new peace talks began in Doha, Qatar's capital.

Bassolé faced multiple challenges in February 2009 as the Doha talks began. He urged the fragmented Darfurian rebel groups to form a united front so they could speak with one voice on the issues under discussion. However, the Abdel Wahid faction of the Sudan Liberation Army (SLA) refused to participate in negotiations until the Janjaweed militias were disarmed and on-the-ground security was established. Khalil Ibrahim's Justice and Equality Movement (JEM), on the other hand, threatened to withdraw from the talks if other insurgents were invited. Bassolé met separately with Wahid in Paris and Ibrahim in Libya, attempting to persuade them to commit themselves to the Doha peace process.

Bassolé came under criticism from Mbeki at one point. Whereas Bassolé had attempted to map a path forward through the conflicts between the government and the various Darfurian rebels, Mbeki thought it important to include representatives of the general public not associated with the government or rebel groups. According to Mbeki, if a negotiated peace was to prove strong and stable, it needed broader civil participation. With that censure in mind, Bassolé, along with Qatari foreign minister Ahmad bin Abdullah al-Mahmoud, hosted an All-Darfur Stakeholders' Conference in Doha in April 2011. The meeting was attended by representatives of the Sudanese government, opposition groups, civil society, and displaced persons and endorsed a framework for further negotiations on issues such as power and wealth sharing, women's rights, human rights and fundamental freedoms, and the return of displaced persons.

On July 14, 2011, the Sudanese government signed a peace accord with LJM, an umbrella organization of minor rebel groups, including the SLA-Juba faction led by Ahmed Abdel Shafi. JEM and the SLA factions of both Abdel Wahid and Minni Minawi declined to sign. Bassolé left his post as mediator on July 19, 2011, to resume his position heading the foreign ministry of Burkina Faso. In August 2012, he was engaged in mediating a crisis in Mali.

In September 2015, at the age of sixty, Bassolé and a former minister of security in Brukina Faso were detained after a failed coup. His accusers claimed that Bassolé had supported the attempted overthrow of the government and charged him with threatening state security, colluding with foreign powers, treason, and murder. UN experts have called on authorities in Burkina Faso for the immediate release of Bassolé, arguing that the claims against him were groundless. In the fall of 2017, he was allowed to leave prison and placed under house arrest and military surveillance. At present, the trial of eighty-three individuals accused of participating in an aborted coup in September 2015 has nearly concluded. Due to his deteriorating health, Bassolé has not yet faced the military court of Ouagadougou.

Karl A. Yambert

See also: Abdel Shafi, Ahmad; African Union; Doha Document for Peace in Darfur; Ibrahim, Khalil; Justice and Equality Movement; Liberation and Justice Movement; South Sudan; Sudan Liberation Army; Sudan People's Liberation Movement/Army; Wahid, Abdel

Further Reading

Flint, Julie, and Alex de Waal. 2006. *Darfur: A Short History of a Long War.* London: Zed Books.

Jolie, Angelina. 2007. "Justice for Darfur." *The Washington Post.* February 28.

Black Book, The

In May 2000, *The Black Book: Imbalance of Power and Wealth in Sudan* mysteriously began circulating in Khartoum, the capital of Sudan. It appeared on the desks of high-ranking government officials, copies were handed out on the streets, and photocopies were passed out as people left mosques following Friday prayers. All told, in just three days, 1,600 copies were released: 800 in Khartoum, 500 in the eastern and western zones of the country, and 300 abroad (Flint and De Waal 2008: 16). The publication criticized the power imbalance between the northern region of Sudan (currently the River Nile and Northern states), where the wealthiest people lived, and the rest of the country. It openly criticized the northern government as using ethnic, racial, and religious prejudice to justify its suppression of Sudan's so-called black African population.

The Black Book broke the silence surrounding the imbalance of power in Sudan and denounced the government's favoritism toward the northern region. It includes statistical information about Sudan's population, natural resources, and a breakdown of regional representation in government. It detailed how those residing in the north unfairly dominated the political and economic landscape, and in so doing marginalized those in Sudan's southern (Upper Nile, Bahr Alghazal, and Equatorial states), eastern (Gadharif, Kasala, and Red Sea states), and western (Kordofan and Darfur states) regions. The authors articulated a well-known fact that until that time was not publicly acknowledged: the vast majority of government, police, judiciary, financial, and military positions were held by members of three northern groups (Shayqiyya, Ja'aliyyin, and Danaqla Arab tribes), which represented just 5.4 percent of Sudan's total population.

The authors of the detailed and meticulous study called themselves "The Seekers of Truth and Justice." The book was the fruit of a twenty-five-member group formed in late 1996 with the goal of collecting information about Sudan's power imbalance and using it to educate ordinary Sudanese. Many of the group members were dissidents of the National Islamic Front (NIF), an Islamist political party founded and led by Dr. Hassan al-Turabi in 1976. When Part Two of *The Black Book* came out in August 2002, it was published on the website of the Justice and Equality Movement (JEM), a Darfurian rebel group. Like the first one, in the second version, JEM called for political, social, and economic change in Sudan. It criticized the marginalization of black Sudanese and proposed forming a more inclusive government to meet the needs of all Sudanese, not just those in the capital. But while the first version of *The Black Book* advocated for change through civil politics, the second expressed that its goal could not be accomplished without the use of an armed movement. After publicly announcing their movement in 2001, JEM began reaching out to other groups, including the Sudan Liberation Army (SLA).

In drawing attention to the disenfranchisement of Sudanese in the south and west, *The Black Book* helped polarize an already mounting division between "Arabs" (those in the north of the country, who claimed to be descendants of Arab invaders) and indigenous Africans. And, perhaps most important, it helped unite multiple elements of Darfur resistance groups.

Alexis Herr

See also: Justice and Equality Movement; Khartoum; National Islamic Front; Sudan Liberation Army; Turabi, Hassan al-

Further Reading

Flint, Julie, and Alex de Waal. 2008. *Darfur: A New History of a Long War*. New York: Zed Books.

Seekers of Truth and Justice. 2004. *The Black Book: Imbalance of Power and Wealth in Sudan*. Trans. Abdullahi Osman El-Tom. Self-published; available at http://www.sudanjem.com/sudan-alt/english/books/blackbook_part1/book_part1.asp.htm.

Totten, Samuel. 2011. *An Oral and Documentary History of the Darfur Genocide*. Santa Barbara, CT: Praeger.

British Involvement in Darfur

The connection between the British and Darfur is complex and long lasting. The colonization of Sudan marks the start of British involvement in Darfur. As a member of the United Nations (UN) Security Council, Great Britain has played a significant role in the international politics that have helped shape the genocide.

Early Colonial Period

When British colonial forces captured Egypt in 1882, Sudan automatically became a British protectorate. Prior to the arrival of the British, Egyptian forces (at that time part of the Ottoman Empire) had settled in Sudan as early as the 1820s and captured Darfur in August 1821. When the British overtook Egypt, they inherited its occupied territories, including Sudan and Darfur. As the British stationed soldiers in Khartoum, the place where Egyptian troops had coalesced their power, they were met with great resistance from the Mahdi (a religious leader of the Samaniyya order of Sudan since 1881), who had rallied the Arab tribes against the Turco-Egyptian rulers. The Mahdi and his supporters were already headed to Khartoum to overthrow the Egyptian forces when the British troops arrived. Once the Mahdi arrived, however, they found the British and directed their outrage at the new occupiers. The Mahdi captured and decapitated General Charles Gordon, an icon of British imperialism, and skewered his head on a stick. In response, Great Britain evacuated all their nationals, only to return in 1898 to retake Sudan.

Anglo-Egyptian Condominium

The British colonial period lasted from 1898 to 1956. In 1899, Great Britain established the Anglo-Egyptian Condominium, a dual colonial government between Great Britain and Egypt. Despite the pretext of shared administration, however, Britain called the shots and Egypt remained second in command. The Anglo-Egyptian Condominium helped polarize the division between the territories of present-day Sudan and South Sudan. Eager to separate the largely Islamic and Arabic-speaking north from the more religiously and ethnically diverse south, the British oversaw the colonization of the south and put the north in the hands of Egyptians. Under the tutelage of Egypt, the northern half of Sudan was homogenized: Islam was the official religion and Arabic the main language spoken. In the British zone, the Sudanese learned English and were encouraged (or, rather, coerced) to adopt Christianity. In the north, the British established a network of government schools that coexisted with Egyptian schools. In the south, Christian missionaries (namely the Anglican Church Missionary Society, the Roman Catholic Verona Fathers, and the American Presbyterian Mission) were given free range.

Given the province of Darfur's remote position in the west of Sudan, seventeen years had passed since the establishment of the Anglo-Egyptian Condominium before British troops conquered Darfur in 1916. From 1898 to 1916, Darfur existed as an independent entity under Sultan Ali Dinar. By the time that British forces arrived in Darfur, the region was emerging from a devastating famine. British troops quickly annexed Darfur and killed Sultan Dinar. After seizing Darfur, the British spent little time and effort in the region.

While British colonizers invested energy in setting up advanced agricultural schemes throughout the Nile zones, Darfur's remote location meant that British forces did not see the economic benefit of extending trade resources so far west. The British simply left a small outpost of colonial officers there and made little to no effort to improve the lives of Darfurians. According to Ahmed Ibrahim Diraige, the former governor of the Sudanese province of Darfur, the British purposefully underdeveloped Darfur to maintain their control over it. For this reason, they did not provide education because they feared that it would create trouble for the colonists (Cocket

2010: 32). When the British left Sudan in 1956, they grafted Darfur, a region as big as France, onto Sudan.

Responding to the Genocide

News of mass atrocities in western Sudan attracted global attention to Darfur in 2003; however, at that time, the United Kingdom (UK) was already involved in the peace negotiations to bring an end to Sudan's decades-long civil war. The Inter-Governmental Authority for Development (IGAD), a coalition attempting to negotiate peace between north and south Sudan, was comprised of representatives from Sudan, Eritrea, Ethiopia, Uganda, Kenya, and Djibouti and was supported by the International Partners Forum, formed in 2001, which included the United States, the United Kingdom, and Norway. UK officials worried that putting pressure on Sudan's president, Omar Hassan al-Bashir, to stop the killing in Darfur would motivate him to withdraw from the precarious peace negotiations that had been ongoing since 2002.

Global attention shifted from the peace negotiations to the genocide when U.S. secretary of state Colin Powell referred to the killings in Darfur as genocide in September 2004. Until that time, the United States had prioritized the peace negotiations, too. For most of 2003, British officials had described the killing in Sudan's western region as a continuation of historical tribal classes between tribal groups in Darfur competing for access to food and water. But when Amnesty International, a London-based nongovernmental organization focused on human rights, challenged the UK government's misleading characterization of the killings in Darfur, it was advised that if it highlighted the crisis in Darfur, the north-south peace process would be threatened.

Despite its failure to respond immediately when the killings broke out, the UK government led the way in responding to Darfur's humanitarian needs. By the time the United Nations made an appeal to its member-states for $534 million in March 2004, the United Kingdom had already given $18.5 million. As of 2005, Britain had contributed $167 million to the UN fund, which accounted for 12 percent of all funds collected at that time.

By 2004, the British involvement in Darfur was based on coalition building, and as such, it was filtered through Britain's membership on the UN Security Council and in the European Union (EU). On September 18, 2004, for example, the United Kingdom voted with Germany, Romania, Angola, Benin, Brazil, Chile, Philippines, Spain, and the United States to adopt Resolution 1564, which threatened to impose sanctions against Sudan if it failed to comply with its obligations on Darfur. In 2004, the United Kingdom also supported the EU measures to prohibit the supply of technical, financial, and other assistance related to military activities for use in Sudan.

Alexis Herr

See also: Amnesty International; Bashir, Omar Hassan Ahmed al-; Denial of the Darfur Genocide; Egyptian Involvement in Darfur; Khartoum; United Nations Commission of Inquiry on Darfur; United States Involvement in Darfur

Further Reading

Crockett, Richard. 2010. *Sudan: Darfur and the Failure of an African State*. New Haven, CT: Yale University Press.

Prunier, Gerard. 2008. *Darfur: A 21st-Century Genocide*. 3rd ed. Ithica, NY: Cornell University Press.

Seri-Hersch, Iris. 2017. "Education in Colonial Sudan, 1900–1957." In *Oxford Research Encyclopedia of African History*. February. Accessed November 12, 2018, from http://africanhistory.oxfordre.com/view/10.1093/acrefore/9780190277734.001.0001/acrefore-9780190277734-e-12?print=pdf.

United Kingdom House of Commons International Development Committee. 2005. "Darfur, Sudan: The Responsibility to Protect." In *Fifth Report of Session 2004–2005, Volume I*. Available at https://publications.parliament.uk/pa/cm200405/cmselect/cmintdev/67/67i.pdf.

C

Cheadle, Don

Don Cheadle is an American actor, producer, author, and humanitarian. Born on November 29, 1964, in Kansas City, Missouri, in 1986 he graduated from the School of Theater at the California Institute of the Arts. For his role in the 2004 film *Hotel Rwanda* (directed by Terry George), Cheadle was nominated for an Academy Award for Best Actor. He has also starred in *Iron Man 2* and *3, Traffic, Ocean's Eleven*, and many more movies, as well as the television series *House of Lies*. In addition to his show-business successes, Cheadle has put significant energy, money, and time into addressing the Darfur Genocide and other atrocities.

At the end of 2005, Cheadle teamed up with writer and activist John Prendergast (founding director of the Enough Project, an initiative to end genocide and crimes against humanity) and embarked on a fact-finding mission in Darfur. Cheadle described the trip as having had a profound impact on him. He found it difficult, he wrote later, to return to "my comfortable life and take stock in all the privileges . . . and do nothing" (Steib 2007). The relationship that he forged at this time with Prendergast would be both lasting and fruitful, leading to their first book together in 2007, a work entitled *Not on Our Watch: The Mission to End Genocide in Darfur and Beyond*. Their book became a *New York Times* bestseller, and the National Association for the Advancement of Colored People (NAACP) named it nonfiction book of the year. It chronicled the Darfur crisis and urged readers to take action to stop

genocide, both there and across the globe. The book also considered tragedies beyond Darfur, such as in northern Uganda and eastern Congo. Holocaust survivor Elie Wiesel wrote the book's foreword, and then-Senator Barack Obama and Senator Sam Brownback coauthored the introduction. Throughout the book, as well as in the press surrounding its release, Prendergast and Cheadle sought to inspire people to find ways to undertake concrete action to help stop genocide.

Inspired by his work on Darfur and the success of the book, in 2006 Cheadle cofounded the organization Not on Our Watch with fellow actors George Clooney, Matt Damon, and Brad Pitt, as well as Jerry Weintraub (an American film producer and former chairman and chief executive officer of United Artists) and David Pressman (an American human rights lawyer and former aide to U.S. secretary of state Madeleine Albright). The mission of Not on Our Watch is to focus global attention and resources towards putting an end to mass atrocities around the world. Drawing upon the powerful voices of artists, activists, and cultural leaders, Not on Our Watch generates lifesaving humanitarian assistance and protection for the vulnerable, marginalized, and displaced. The organization encourages governments to take meaningful and immediate action to protect those in harm's way. Where governments remain complacent, Not on Our Watch is committed to stopping mass atrocities and giving voice to their victims. The organization's charitable activities have raised millions of dollars to help those suffering, with much of the money being channeled through the United Nations (UN) World Food Programme.

Cheadle and his colleagues have made good use of their celebrity status to bring attention to the Darfur Genocide and advocate on behalf of the victims. In late October 2007, Cheadle and Clooney led an unofficial delegation to China and Egypt to meet with government officials, hopeful that they could convince two of Sudan's biggest trading partners to stop doing business with Sudan and thus pressure the Sudanese government to end its genocide in Darfur. This move was strategic, as China, a permanent member of the UN Security Council, a fifteen-member council with five permanent members (France, Russia, Britain, and the United States are the others) that each have the ability to vote and determine when and where a UN peacekeeping operation should be deployed, had a vested interest in supporting President Omar Hassan al-Bashir. As such, Beijing has proved reluctant to take any action that would threaten Bashir's place in power. For example, in 2006, some 7 percent of China's imported oil came from Sudan. With the crisis in the Middle East disrupting the global supply, maintaining a steady stream of oil from outside the Middle East was a priority for the Chinese government. For this reason, it was clear by as early as July 2004 that China would not support sanctions against the government or authorize direct UN intervention.

Cheadle and Clooney followed up their trip to China and Egypt by intensifying their efforts to end the violence in Darfur. For this, the Nobel Peace Prize Laureates presented the actors-humanitarians with the Summit Peace Award in Rome on December 13, 2007. That same year also saw the release of a documentary entitled *Darfur Now* (directed by Ted Braun), filmed between January and May of that year. The film was coproduced by Cheadle and Cathy Schulman, the producer of the award-winning 2005 movie *Crash* (in which Cheadle costarred). *Darfur Now* followed six people from around the world who were trying to help end the civil war and genocide in Darfur, and Cheadle was one of the subjects examined.

For his pains on behalf of Africa's oppressed, Cheadle was honored with the BET Award in 2007. The BET Awards were established in 2001 by the Black Entertainment Television (BET) network to celebrate African Americans and other minorities in music, acting, sports, and other fields of entertainment over the previous year. This award once again helped draw attention to the conflict in Darfur, which at the time was in its fifth year.

In June 2010, Cheadle was named as a United Nations Environment Programme (UNEP) goodwill ambassador. The ceremony, which took place in Rwanda to mark World Environment Day, heralded a new role for Cheadle. In his capacity as UNEP goodwill ambassador, his task is to utilize the influential voice of the entertainment industry to mobilize the public to embrace more sustainable lifestyles, promote the greening of the entertainment industry and other sectors, and take part in UNEP public outreach initiatives.

While this is a new area of responsibility for Cheadle, his primary concern remains the saving of lives—in particular, from genocide, mass murder, and massive human rights violations. In *The Enough Moment: Fighting to End Africa's Worst Human Rights Crimes* (2010), Cheadle and his coauthor Prendergast argue that engaged citizens have the power to force their governments to save people from the most heinous of crimes. Referring to such people as "Upstanders"—as a contrast to the word bystanders—Cheadle and Prendergast provided a number of case studies and showed how even small actions can have a snowball effect that can make every concerned citizen part of a broader movement for good.

Cheadle's main goal is to empower others to take meaningful action to stop genocide. While he has used his celebrity status to encourage change, he makes it clear in his books that an individual does not have to be famous to make a difference. Raising awareness must be for a purpose, and in his view, that purpose is to let the political leadership know that their constituents want action.

Paul R. Bartrop

See also: Bashir, Omar Hassan Ahmed al-; Clooney, George; Damon, Matt; Denial of the Darfur Genocide; Enough Project; Prendergast, John; Save Darfur Coalition; Talisman Energy Corporation; United States Involvement in Darfur

Further Reading

Cheadle, Don, and John Prendergast. 2007. *Not on Our Watch: The Mission to End Genocide in Darfur and Beyond.* New York: Hyperion.

Cheadle, Don, and John Prendergast. 2010. *The Enough Moment: Fighting to End Africa's Worst Human Rights Crimes.* New York: Three Rivers Press.

Steib, Aspen. 2007. "Cheadle Acts to Stop Darfur Genocide." CNN. May 4. Available at https://www.cnn.com/2007/SHOWBIZ /books/05/04/darfur.book/index.html.

Child Soldiers

Political unrest, an unstable economy, civil war, and genocide have made children vulnerable to forced recruitment by militias and government troops in Africa. The sobering data about child soldiers in Sudan speaks to the particular dangers facing children in Darfur.

The Darfur Genocide began when two Darfurian rebel groups, the Justice and Equality Movement (JEM) and the Sudan Liberation Movement (SLM) attacked government installations in Darfur. The government responded with brute force and employed the Janjaweed, a militia group comprised mainly of Arab tribes from northern Darfur, to stop the JEM and SLM rebels. In addition, the government in Khartoum deployed its military in Darfur. As the conflict intensified, Darfurian children were either recruited or abducted by all forces involved.

Refugee camps in Chad and other neighboring nations were frequented by militias to recruit or capture children. The United Nations (UN) estimates that in 2007, between 7,000 and 10,000 children were recruited forcibly in Chad, where a quarter-million Darfurian refugees had escaped. The children range in age from nine to seventeen years old, and they are frequently captured by camp leaders, who then sell them to militias. Some parents have sold some of their children to rebel groups in order to get money to support the rest of their family. According to the United Nations, every armed faction and group in Darfur has exploited children to fight and/or carry weapons.

JEM rebels, in particular, are credited with being the most prolific and aggressive abuser of children during the genocide. After joining an armed group (voluntarily or otherwise), children are coerced to fight through threats, physical and sexual violence, and drugs. In response, the African Union– United Nations in Darfur (UNAMID), in partnership with UNICEF (the UN

International Children's Emergency Fund), launched a Darfur-wide campaign named "No Child Soldiers—Protect Darfur" on December 9, 2014. The campaign aims to raise awareness of the need to end recruitment of child soldiers by armed forces. The campaign managers lead informational workshops in refugee camps. In the workshops, the leaders explain that 126 countries have ratified a UN treaty that prohibits the use of children in hostilities. The mission also hands out vests with messages that call for the protection of children. As part of this campaign, five centers were set up in northern Darfur to help rehabilitate and reintegrate former child soldiers back into the community. Between 2009 and 2014, more than 200 former child soldiers received such support. Most of those who have gone through the rehabilitation centers have enrolled in secondary school or college and/ or received vocational training.

According to a December 2018 investigative report from David Kirkpatrick of *The New York Times*, since 2016 Saudi Arabia has recruited Sudanese fighters—many of them children—to fight Houthi rebels in Yemen. Desperate for money, Darfur families are willing to send their children abroad to fight in exchange for much-needed capital. To some families rendered destitute from the fifteen years of genocide, this opportunity represents a lifeline, despite the sacrifices required.

Alexis Herr

See also: Janjaweed; Justice and Equality Movement; Lost Boys and Girls of Sudan; Sudan People's Liberation Movement/Army

Further Reading

Totten, Samuel. 2010. *An Oral and Documentary History of the Darfur Genocide.* 2 vols. Santa Barbara, CA: Praeger Security International.

World Health Organization. 2009. "Healing Child Soldiers." *Bulletin of the World Health Organization* 87, no. 5, 325–404. Available at http://www.who.int/bulletin/volumes/87/5/09-020509/en/.

Clooney, George

George Clooney is an award-winning American movie actor, film director, producer, and screenwriter. Born in Lexington, Kentucky, on May 6, 1961, he is the son of television personality Nick Clooney and the nephew of singer Rosemary Clooney. His acting has earned him two Golden Globes and an Academy Award, and he is considered one of the premier actors in Hollywood. In addition to his celebrity, Clooney has dedicated himself to a myriad of human rights initiatives, which include pressing the governments of the United States and other countries to stop the genocide in Darfur, Sudan.

Politically, Clooney describes himself as a liberal, and he has long been an activist for many social and humanitarian causes worldwide. On January 18, 2008, the United Nations (UN) announced his appointment as a UN messenger of peace, a position he began thirteen days later and held for three years. Nationally, he has focused his efforts on alleviating poverty. He is a supporter of the poverty-fighting ONE Campaign, spearheaded by Bono, the lead singer of U2; and he also is on the board of trustees for the United Way charity. He has raised funds to assist victims of the 2010 Haiti earthquake, the Pacific tsunami of 2004, and the families of victims of the September 11, 2001 terrorist attacks on the United States.

In addition to his humanitarian work in the United States, he is deeply invested in upending the genocide in Darfur. In April 2006, he spent ten days on the Chad-Sudan border with his father, and while there, he made a documentary called *A Journey to Darfur*, examining the situation of Darfur's refugees. The Clooneys had hoped to enter Darfur from Chad, but were—perhaps not unsurprisingly—prevented from crossing the border by threat of violence. The documentary was initially broadcast on January 15, 2007, on the American Life television network in the United States. Later, it was broadcast on cable stations in the United States, as well as in Britain and France. In 2008, it was released on DVD. The intention of the Clooneys was to try to move Darfur from a footnote to a front-page story. Clooney was to say later that he was pessimistic about any improvement in the plight of the refugees in the short term, although he hoped that an increase in political pressure for international action could make a difference eventually.

The film advocated U.S. intervention in Darfur, and accompanying its release, both George and his father campaigned energetically for widespread international action. Upon his return from Darfur, Clooney spoke at the massive Save Darfur rally in Washington, D.C., on April 30, 2006. He continued to champion his cause on the *Oprah* talk show and across other media outlets. On March 25, 2007, he sent an open letter to German chancellor Angela Merkel, calling on the European Union to take "decisive action" in the Darfur region. Then, in September 2007, he addressed the UN Security Council alongside the famed Holocaust survivor, author, and activist Elie Wiesel to demand that the United Nations work to resolve the Darfur conflict.

In December 2007, he led an unofficial delegation to China and Egypt with fellow actor Don Cheadle, seeking to persuade those countries to use their economic and social power to pressure the government of Sudan to stop the genocide. Upon his return, he briefed UN secretary-general Kofi Annan about the trip. On December 13, 2007, Clooney and Cheadle were presented with the Summit Peace Award by the Nobel Peace Prize Laureates in Rome, although Clooney was forced to acknowledge at this time that when it comes to the atrocities in Darfur, the people of the region were no better off than they had been several years earlier.

Clooney continued to use the emotive power of film to inspire action in Darfur, even after the release of *A Journey to Darfur*. He appeared in *Darfur Now* (directed by Ted Braun), a documentary released on November 2, 2007, that called for worldwide action to stop the Darfur Genocide. Clooney also narrated and was co–executive producer of another documentary, *Sand and Sorrow* (directed by Paul Freedman), an intense examination of the Darfur crisis, that also appeared in 2007 to much critical acclaim. In February 2009, Clooney visited Chad with *New York Times* columnist Nicholas Kristof, again working to raise awareness through the prestige of the *Times* and his own media presence.

Perhaps most tellingly, Clooney has been at the forefront of mobilizing other Hollywood actors to use their celebrity to raise consciousness about Darfur. In pursuit of this, in 2006 he founded Not on Our Watch, alongside actors Cheadle, Matt Damon, and Brad Pitt, as well as David Pressman (an American human rights lawyer and former aide to U.S. secretary of state Madeleine Albright), and Jerry Weintraub (an American film producer and former chairman and chief executive officer of United Artists). Not on Our Watch aims to focus global attention and resources to end mass atrocities worldwide. Drawing upon the voices of cultural leaders, Not on Our Watch generates lifesaving humanitarian assistance and protection for the vulnerable, marginalized, and displaced. The organization encourages governments to take meaningful and immediate action to protect those in harm's way. Where governments remain complacent, Not on Our Watch was committed to stopping mass atrocities and giving voice to their victims. The organization's charity activities raised millions of dollars to help those suffering, with much of the money being channeled through the UN World Food Programme. In February 2019, Not on Our Watch merged with The Sentry, a team of policy analysts, regional experts, and financial forensic investigators that follows the money in order to create consequences for those funding and profiting from genocide or other mass atrocities in Africa. George Clooney remains deeply involved in The Sentry's work.

At the 2010 Emmy Awards Clooney was presented with the Bob Hope Humanitarian Award—its fourth recipient since it was created in 2002. This award is presented to an individual in the telecommunications industry whose humanitarian works have brought credit to the industry and whose deeds and actions have a lasting impact on society.

In 2017, Clooney used his clout to speak out against a U.S. law firm that had agreed to work with the Sudanese government to encourage the United States to lift its economic sanctions on Sudan. The sanctions, which had been in place since 1997, were eventually lifted. In protest, Clooney and his longtime associate, writer and activist John Prendergast, questioned the integrity of the law firm for choosing to work for known genocidaires.

Paul R. Bartrop

See also: Cheadle, Don; Damon, Matt; Enough Project; Kristof, Nicholas; Prendergast, John; Save Darfur Coalition; Wiesel, Elie

Further Reading

Burr, J. Millard, and Robert O. Collins. 2006. *Darfur: The Long Road to Disaster.* Princeton, NJ: Markus Weiner.

Cheadle, Don, and John Prendergast. 2007. *Not on Our Watch: The Mission to End Genocide in Darfur and Beyond.* New York: Hyperion.

Coalition for International Justice

The Coalition for International Justice (CIJ), an international nonprofit organization that operated from 1995 to 2006, endeavored to support the work of courts and international criminal tribunals addressing human rights atrocities in Rwanda, the former Yugoslavia, Cambodia, Sudan, East Timor, and Sierra Leone. From 2004 to 2005, the CIJ sponsored a team of historians and other experts to conduct some 1,200 interviews with refugees in Chad who had sought a safe haven from the violence in Darfur.

The CIJ was headquartered at The Hague in the Netherlands and maintained an office in Washington, D.C. as well. Among other things, the organization provided legal and technical assistance to international tribunals and individual governments, conducted outreach and public-education programs related to war crimes and atrocities, and compiled analyses and critiques of cases being assembled by tribunals in order to maximize the effectiveness of prosecutorial teams.

The CIJ also worked to educate and reach out to world leaders and decision-makers and maintained an archive of all reports from various war crimes trials held between 1995 and 2006, which are available for research purposes at University of Connecticut. It ceased its operations on March 31, 2006. Its board issued a statement at that time to the effect that the organization was not designed to be a permanent group.

Paul G. Pierpaoli Jr.

See also: Darfur Atrocities Documentation Project; Enough Project; United Nations Commission of Inquiry on Darfur; United Nations Convention on the Prevention and Punishment of the Crime of Genocide

Further Reading

"A Guide to the Coalition for International Justice Records." University of Connecticut Archives and Special Collections. Available at https://archives.lib.uconn.edu/islandora/object/20002%3A860116155#accessAnd Use.

Comprehensive Peace Agreement

In the forty-eight years since Sudan achieved independence from colonial occupation in 1956, all but eleven were dominated by a vicious civil war between the north and south. The signing of the Comprehensive Peace Agreement (CPA) on January 9, 2005, signified a step toward ending the decades-long civil wars and achieving peace between north and south Sudan.

Throughout the civil wars, a plethora of foreign and neighboring nations attempted to help broker a peace deal between the north and south to put an end to the bloody conflict. However, the immensely complicated situation undermined all but one attempt at peace. In the course of the fighting, more than 2 million people died, 4 million were displaced, and some 600,000 individuals fled Sudan as refugees. When the National Congress Party (NCP) in the north and the Sudan People's Liberation Movement/Army (SPLM/A) in the south signed the CPA, Sudan came one step closer to creating peace.

The CPA introduced an interim constitution that stipulated power sharing between the NCP and SPLM/A, provided for a semi-autonomous regional government led by the SPLM/A in the south, established a formula for dividing oil revenues, and committed the nation to holding a vote for self-determination in 2011 in the south. Additionally, SPLM/A leader John Garang was appointed the first vice president of Sudan, and the regional government in the south came under the guidance of the SPLM/A leadership. The result of the 2011 referendum was South Sudan's independence.

While the United Nations (UN) supported the CPA, it knew that the government of Sudan was simultaneously attacking civilians in Darfur but chose to avoid direct engagement in the conflict until the CPA was signed. A UN Security Council press release on February 8, 2005, reported that Garang "was confident that the Comprehensive Peace Agreement enhanced the chances for a comprehensive and lasting solution to the Darfur conflict." He also warned that for a lasting solution to the Darfur conflict to exist, "the Janjaweed militia must be reined in and eventually brought to justice . . . otherwise the cart would be placed before the horse, in which case neither would move" (United Nations Security Council 2005).

While the CPA did reduce the fighting between the north and south, an everlasting peace was not achieved. Garang died in late July 2005, just months after the signing of the CPA, when the Ugandan presidential Mi-172 helicopter he was flying in crashed. And even after South Sudan achieved its independence, fighting over oil resources along the north-south border (particularly in Abyei, the Southern Blue Nile, and the Nuba Mountains) continue to cause conflict.

Alexis Herr

See also: British Involvement in Darfur; Garang, John; Nuba; South Sudan; Sudanese Civil Wars; United States Involvement in Darfur

Further Reading

Totten, Samuel, and Eric Markusen, eds. 2006. *Genocide in Darfur: Investigating the Atrocities in the Sudan*. New York: Routledge.

United Nations Security Council. 2005. "Sudan Peace Agreement Signed 9 January Historic Opportunity, Security Council Told." UN Press Release SC/8306. February 8. Available at https://www.un.org /press/en/2005/sc8306.doc.htm.

D

Damon, Matt

Matt Damon is an internationally known, award-winning film star, screenwriter, producer, and philanthropist who has expended much time and effort on ending the genocide in Darfur.

Damon was born Matthew Paige Damon on October 8, 1970, in Cambridge, Massachusetts. He grew up in the Boston area and studied English at Harvard University from 1988 until 1992. After becoming involved in theater there, he left school without receiving his degree. Damon had his first film part in *Mystic Pizza* (1988), which featured just one line of dialogue. He thereafter appeared in a number of plays and had small parts in subsequent movies. His breakout performance came in 1997, when he starred in *Good Will Hunting.* Damon had cowritten the screenplay with childhood friend and fellow actor Ben Affleck. For the film, a box-office hit, Damon and Affleck won the Academy Award for Best Original Screenplay, which cemented both of them as major Hollywood players.

Damon has since starred in a wide range of movies, including *Saving Private Ryan* (1998); *The Talented Mr. Ripley* (1999); *Ocean's Eleven, Twelve,* and *Thirteen* (2001, 2004, and 2007); the *Bourne* spy movie series (2002, 2004, and 2007); *Syriana* (2005); *The Good Shepherd* (2006); *The Departed* (2006); *Invictus* (2009); *We Bought a Zoo* (2011); and *The Martian* (2015). Damon, along with Affleck and two others, also established LivePlanet, a film production company dedicated to helping find and fund newcomers who seek careers as filmmakers. The company also produced *Project Greenlight,* an award-winning documentary series focusing on the efforts of young filmmakers.

Damon has been very active in a number of philanthropic and charitable causes. He founded the H20 Africa Foundation, which is dedicated to providing clean and plentiful water to Africans, and he also supports the ONE Campaign, which is focused on fighting poverty and AIDS in the developing world. Damon has frequently appeared in advertisements for the ONE Campaign and has been a spokesperson for Feeding America, a hunger relief organization dedicated to ending hunger in the United States.

Damon has become closely associated with Darfur Genocide relief efforts and activities designed to bring world attention to the crisis and relieve the suffering of its survivors. He has supported virtually every major protest against the Darfur Genocide since 2005 and has raised millions of dollars in aid with fellow actors George Clooney, Don Cheadle, and others. A poker fan, Damon has taken part in celebrity poker tournaments, the proceeds of which are donated to the victims and survivors of the genocide in Darfur.

In 2007, Damon, along with Cheadle, Clooney, Brad Pitt, and studio executive Jerry Weintraub, founded the nonprofit organization known as Not On Our Watch, which is dedicated to preventing mass killings in Darfur and other areas of the world. The organization was an offshoot of the 2007 book by the same name, coauthored by

Cheadle and the activist John Prendergast, which focused attention on the Darfur Genocide. In 2008, Damon appeared in a series of print ads designed to draw attention to the cataclysm in Darfur. In one ad, he is shown destroying a dollhouse with a baseball bat, signifying how the genocide has destroyed children's lives. The ad was released in conjunction with an international day of protest against the conflict in Darfur.

Paul G. Pierpaoli Jr.

See also: Cheadle, Don; Clooney, George; Enough Project; Prendergast, John; United States Involvement in Darfur

Further Reading

Altman, Sheryl, and Sheryl Berk. 1998. *Matt Damon and Ben Affleck: On and Off Screen.* New York: HarperCollins Publishers.

Cheadle, Don, and John Prendergast. 2007. *Not on Our Watch: The Mission to End Genocide in Darfur and Beyond.* New York: Hyperion.

Darfur

Darfur, located in western Sudan, is an ethnically diverse region approximately the size of France. Starting in 2003, Darfur became home to the first genocide in the twenty-first century, and violence in the region has continued to disrupt life there.

The region of Darfur is subdivided into a collection of smaller states. From 1994 to 2011, it was comprised of three states—North, South, and West Darfur—each of which has a capital (El Fasher, Nyala, and Geneina, respectively). The three-state system, much like the five-state division that currently exists, was determined by the political will of Sudan's government.

Following Omar Hassan al-Bashir's coup in 1989, his party, the National Islamic Front (NIF), sought to undermine support in the Darfur region for his political rival, the Umma Party. To accomplish this goal, the government of Sudan fractured Darfur into three states in order to weaken the voting power of the Fur people. While they had composed the majority ethnic group when Darfur was one state, after the division, the Fur became a minority ethnic group in each state. Some have argued that this division of the region allowed ethnic tensions to mount and played a role in creating an environment that was ripe for genocide. In 2011, the government of Sudan carved out two more states in the region, bringing the total to five. The addition of Central Darfur, with Zalingei as its capital, and Eastern Darfur, with El Daein as its capital, has been criticized as another attempt by the Sudanese government to divide Darfurians and undermine their resistance to oppressive government policies.

Approximately eighty tribes live in the region. The tribes fall within two broad ethnic categories: Arab (nomadic pastoralists) and non-Arab African (sedentary farmers); the majority practice Islam and have a long history of intermarriage. It should be noted, however, that the distinctions of "Arab" and "non-Arab African" are largely inaccurate and there is little to no truth behind the labels. Despite this fact, identity politics plays a role in the genocidal violence that erupted in 2003. Arabic-speaking groups live throughout Darfur but form a substantial majority in the arid north, while the Fur (*dar Fur* means "land of the Fur" in Arabic) dominate the more fertile south. Other major groups include the Zaghawa, Massalit, and Daju.

The earliest-known rulers of Darfur were the agriculturalist Daju, whose chieftains were overpowered in the late fourteenth century by the Tunjur, a nomadic, camel-driving people who emigrated from the deserts of Egypt. Arab pastoralists began migrating into the Darfur region at approximately the same time, bringing Islam with them. The Fur dynasty began in approximately 1640, when Suleiman Solongdungu ("Suleiman the Arab"—so known among the Fur because his mother was an Arab) ousted the Tunjur rulers and then expanded his empire through conquest and marriage, seizing outlying lands populated by Arab nomads and consolidating power through an ethnic Zaghawa wife. The Fur dynasty's greatest rivals were the state of Wadai to the west and the Funj sultans to the east.

Darfur remained independent for several more decades than the rest of the states encompassed by modern Sudan, resisting Ottoman Egyptian forces until 1874, when the Fur dynasty's capital of El Fasher fell and Sultan Ibrim wad Huseyn was killed. Members of the royal family attempted to lead several uprisings against the occupying forces for the next few years, but with little success. During the decline of the Ottoman Empire, Darfur, along with the rest of Sudan, came under joint British-Egyptian rule, and Sudan later gained independence on January 1, 1956.

The recent ethnic conflicts in Darfur began in the 1980s due to competition between various groups over limited resources, although the violence was intermittent until the nature of the conflict shifted dramatically between 2002 and 2003. The critical turning point was the formation of the Sudan Liberation Army (SLA)—composed largely of ethnic Fur, Massalit, and Zaghawa—and a series of attacks that it staged against government installations in 2003. The SLA

demanded that the government allow Darfurians greater representation in the government and help stimulate economic opportunity for them.

Following the SLA attacks, national security interests intersected with nomadic ("Arab") groups' desire to expand their territory and resources, and consequently, the government recruited, sponsored, and armed Arabic-speaking militias—the so-called Janjaweed—to lead an ethnic cleansing campaign against the agriculturalist Fur, Massalit, Zaghawa, and other groups associated with the SLA. The Janjaweed's attacks have not typically targeted SLA positions but have rather been aimed against villages of unarmed civilians. The attacks have been characterized by such atrocities as rape, torture, and the burning of entire settlements to the ground. These events have led to rapid polarization in what was once an ethnically fluid state, although only a few of Darfur's Arab tribes have actually participated in the cleansing campaign. Some Arab groups have, in fact, allied themselves with the SLA, while certain "non-Arab African" groups have fought alongside Janjaweed forces.

The ethnic warfare in Darfur has killed at least 300,000 people since 2003. This has created an enormous displacement crisis, forcing some 2.5 million Darfurians from their homes and into refugee camps, many of them in neighboring Chad and the Central African Republic. This refugee crisis has strained the resources of the entire region, and similar patterns of ethnic violence have recently emerged in these borderlands. A 7,000-member African Union (AU) peacekeeping force began arriving in Darfur in 2004, but it proved incapable of preventing the conflict's continued escalation, partly due to lack of funds. In June 2007, the Sudanese government agreed to allow the United Nations (UN) to form a 26,000-member hybrid UN-AU peacekeeping force. Full deployment was a slow process, hindered by the Sudanese government, as well as a lack of troops and supplies from UN member-states. Despite a stronger international peacekeeping presence, violence in Darfur persisted. When charges by the International Criminal Court were placed against President Omar Hassan Ahmed al-Bashir in May 2009, a number of foreign aid organizations working in refugee camps were expelled from the country. Although further attempts at peace, including the 2011 Doha Documents for Peace in Darfur signed by government officials and the Liberation and Justice Movement (LJM), have been made, violence continues in Darfur.

David Paige

See also: Bashir, Omar Hassan Ahmed al-; British Involvement in Darfur; Egyptian Involvement in Darfur; Famine of 1984–1985; Fur; Massalit; Religion; Sudan People's Liberation Movement/Army

Further Reading

Burr, J. Millard, and Robert O. Collins. 2006. *Darfur: The Long Road to Disaster*. Princeton, NJ: Markus Weiner.

De Waal, Alex. 2005. *Famine That Kills: Darfur, Sudan*. Oxford: Oxford University Press.

Flint, Julie, and Alex de Waal. 2006. *Darfur: A Short History of a Long War*. London: Zed Books.

Prunier, Gerard. 2005. *Darfur: The Ambiguous Genocide*. Ithaca, NY: Cornell University Press.

Rolandsen, Øystein H., and M. W. Daly. 2007. *Darfur's Sorrow: A History of Destruction and Genocide*. Cambridge: Cambridge University Press.

Darfur Atrocities Documentation Project

The Darfur Atrocities Documentation Project was a U.S. State Department enterprise that conducted systematic interviews of Sudanese refugees in Chad. The survey revealed a widespread pattern of atrocities committed against so-called non-Arab villagers in Darfur, a pattern that U.S. secretary of state Colin Powell publicly called a genocide.

In light of the evident humanitarian and human-rights crisis in Sudan that erupted in 2003, the U.S. State Department commissioned an Atrocities Documentation Team (ADT) to conduct interviews in Chad in July and August 2004. Using data from 1,136 interviews, as well as information from various United Nations (UN) offices, the ADT reported that more than 405 villages had been destroyed in Darfur, approximately 200,000 persons had sought refuge in Chad, and another 1.2 million people had been displaced in western Sudan. Furthermore, the displaced populations were acutely threatened by hunger and infectious diseases.

The interviews also exposed a close collaboration between government forces and mounted Arab militias known as the Janjaweed in carrying out systematic attacks against non-Arab villages in Darfur. Attacks on the villages followed a typical pattern of air strikes by government planes or helicopters, followed by coordinated ground assaults by government troops and the Janjaweed. Civilians were variously killed, raped, abducted, or driven away, and their villages were looted and burned.

Numerous respondents reported racial and ethnic epithets aimed at the villagers by the attacking military and militia personnel.

The ADT report was cited by Powell in his testimony before the Senate Foreign Relations Committee on September 9, 2004, when he addressed the specific issue of whether events in Darfur constituted a genocide. In 1948, shortly after the Holocaust (1938–1945), the United Nations had adopted the United Nations Convention on the Prevention and Punishment of the Crime of Genocide (the Genocide Convention), which defined genocide as acts intended to destroy (in whole or in part) a national, ethnic, racial, or religious group. Based on the evidence from the ADT, Powell concluded that genocide had been committed in Darfur, was perhaps still occurring, and that the government of Sudan and the Janjaweed bore responsibility. Powell then called upon the United Nations to investigate violations of international humanitarian and human-rights laws in Darfur, as provided for under the Genocide Convention.

Six weeks earlier, the U.S. Congress had resolved that atrocities in Darfur constituted genocide, but Powell was the first member of the executive branch to use the term publicly. He did so when many were declining to use the term out of concern that the Genocide Convention then would require forceful action from its signatories, perhaps involving them in an African war. However, Powell read the convention differently. He called for further investigation into the Sudan crisis and for greater numbers of African Union monitors, but not necessarily for military intervention. Powell asserted that whether the situation in Darfur was called a civil war, ethnic cleansing, or genocide did not change the reality that the people of Darfur needed the help of the international community.

Karl A. Yambert

See also: African Union; Janjaweed; United Nations Commission of Inquiry on Darfur; United States Involvement in Darfur

Further Reading

Anderson, Scott. 2004. "How Did Darfur Happen?" *The New York Times*. October 17.

Kostas, Stephen A. 2006. "Making the Determination of Genocide in Darfur." In Eric Markusen and Samuel Totten, eds., *Genocide in Darfur: Investigating Atrocities in the Sudan*. New York: Routledge, 111–126.

Darfur Development Front

The Darfur Development Front (DDF) formed in 1963 to bring attention to the unmet needs of Darfurians by the government in Khartoum. Prior to South Sudan's independence in 2011, Sudan had the distinction of being the largest nation in Africa. Darfur, located in the west, was isolated from the seat of government in Khartoum, located in the east. The DDF advocated for Darfur's greater political representation in government and became the forerunner of the organized armed resistance movements to Khartoum's governance in the 1990s and 2000s.

Khartoum's indifference to Darfur echoed the colonial treatment of the entire region. Under Anglo-Egyptian rule (1916—1956), the British and Egyptian militaries paid little attention to Darfur, given its remote location in western Sudan, far from the trade routes and the Nile River in the east. For example, in 1935, after nearly two decades of colonial rule, all of Darfur had only three schools for a school-age population of 500,000. After

Sudan achieved independence (January 1, 1956), the lack of reliable road and train routes between the west and east allowed the government of Sudan to ignore Darfur just as the occupying forces had done.

The DDF was a regionalist movement formed in December 1963 to defend Darfur interests legally, demand greater autonomy, and spur economic development. It was created by Ahmed Ibrahim Diraige, son of a local Fur chief (*shartay*). Many ethnic Fur supported the DDF because of its leader's tribal identity, but membership was open to everybody. The Fur are the largest ethnic group in Darfur, and in addition to following their tribal beliefs, they are Sunni Muslims. Other supporters of the DDF belonged to tribes that identified as Arab, not African like the Fur. In the beginning, all Darfurians, Arabs and non-Arabs alike, shared the frustration of being forsaken by the Sudanese government. However, as time went by, the fight for Darfur had fragmented into two warring camps, driven apart by perceived ethnic lines.

During parliamentary elections held in 1968, Diraige aligned the DDF with a splintered faction of the Umma Party, which had recently split into two. The DDF chose the side of Sadiq al-Mahdi's Umma faction, which was competing for power against Sadiq's uncle, Iman al-Hadi. As the nephew and uncle campaigned for support, they sought constituents along perceived ethnic lines: African and Arab tribes. While in reality, all Darfurians are African, and most practice Islam, the war between Africans and Arabs mirrored the language employed by Khartoum to disenfranchise south Sudan. Sadiq courted the so-called African tribes (Fur, Massalit, and Zaghawa), and because the Fur were considered the largest African tribe in the region, Sadiq struck an alliance with Diraige and the DDF. According to

Sadiq, the Arabs were to blame for Darfur's problems, while al-Hadi blamed Africans. While Darfur's problems were shared by all residing in the region, the splintered Umma parties blamed different ethnic groups. In the end, thanks to the DDF's support, Sadiq's Umma Party came out on top during the election.

When Colonel Gaafar Muhammad an-Nimeiry toppled the government in a military coup in May 1969, he focused on ruthlessly marginalizing the Umma and other sectarian parties. Nimeiry had Sadiq and Diraige jailed, and al-Hadi was murdered while trying to escape to Ethiopia. Although Nimeiry's seizure of power had stampeded the Umma, the legacy of divisionism ushered in by the Umma campaign remained intact and continued to sow resentment along ethnic lines for decades to come.

Alexis Herr

See also: Diraige, Ahmed Ibrahim; Fur; Khartoum; Religion; South Sudan

Further Reading

Prunier, Gerard. 2005. *Darfur: The Ambiguous Genocide*. Ithaca, NY: Cornell University Press.

Denial of the Darfur Genocide

Nations and scholars disagree as to whether the conflict in Darfur, characterized by targeted attacks against non-Arab ethnic groups since 2003, constitutes a genocide, as defined by the United Nations (UN). The disputed classification of the killings has provoked essential questions regarding what is at stake when a nation or individual opts for a different word to describe the violence. Historically, delayed global recognition of genocide has been attributable to a lack of knowledge about the conflict, unfamiliarity with the warning signs of genocide, or both. In the case of Darfur, the denial of genocide is rooted in various motivations, including an unwillingness among UN member-states to get involved in Darfur and prioritizing of different aims within Sudan at large.

In February 2003, members of two rebel groups, the Justice and Equality Movement (JEM) and the Sudan Liberation Army (SLA), took up arms in Darfur and attacked Sudanese military installations in protest of the government's neglect of Darfurian needs. The government responded forcefully to eliminate the rebellion, deploying a two-pronged strategy of aerial bombardment and sustained ground assault. The Janjaweed, an Arab militia recruited and armed by the Sudanese government, carried out the ground assaults, while the government itself attacked from above with aerial bombardments. Between 2003 and 2005, and again in 2007 and 2008, the armed attacks specifically targeted non-Arab tribal ethnicities, including the Fur, Massalit, and Zaghawa. To date, the violence has caused more than 300,000 deaths and has driven 2.5 million people from their homes.

While the evidence of mass murder within Darfur is undisputable, how that killing is codified has been inconsistent. The United Nations adopted the Genocide Convention on December 9, 1948, which defines genocide as acts committed with "intent to destroy, in whole or in part, a national, ethnical, racial, or religious group." The challenge with defining an act as genocide hinges on the ability of a court to prove a perpetrator's intent.

Several international criminal tribunals, including the International Military Tribunals for Nuremberg and Tokyo, the International Criminal Tribunal for the former Yugoslavia, and the International Criminal Tribunal for Rwanda, have produced jurisprudence on the crime of genocide and the resulting obligations under the UN Convention. As elaborated upon by these entities, the convention requires that three elements exist for an atrocity to be considered a genocide. First, the victims must constitute a national, ethnic, racial, or religious group. Second, the members of that group must be the target of either harm, willful neglect, or both. Third, the intent to destroy or partially destroy the group must be the purpose of those harmful acts. The specificity of these elements in practice sets a high standard for officially labeling a conflict as genocide.

While consensus exists that the violence in Darfur amounts to war crimes and crimes against humanity, there is disagreement as to whether it constitutes genocide under the increasingly specific articulated standards of the Genocide Convention. The debate commenced in March 2004, when Nicholas Kristof, a columnist for *The New York Times,* published a series of articles describing the conflict as genocide. Following these articles, several loosely defined American associations and organizations, including the Jewish American, African American, liberal, and conservative constituencies, as well as the United States Holocaust Memorial Museum, called on the U.S. government to label the conflict as genocide and take appropriate action to stop further violence. Despite this growing movement, several notable human rights and humanitarian organizations, including Amnesty International and Human Rights Watch, refrained from labeling the conflict a genocide.

In early September 2004, the U.S. government officially determined that the violence in Darfur constituted a genocide, based on the pattern of widespread atrocities committed by the Janjaweed militia and government forces and their targeting of non-Arab villagers. Shortly thereafter, the International Association of Genocide Scholars (an international nonpartisan organization that seeks to further research and teaching on genocide) likewise determined that genocide was occurring.

The rest of the international community, however, was more reluctant to call the killings a genocide. In late September 2004, the UN Security Council passed Resolution 1564, calling for the establishment of a UN Commission of Inquiry to determine whether acts of genocide had occurred. On February 1, 2005, the commission reported that, despite other serious violations of international humanitarian and human rights law, Sudanese government forces and the allied Janjaweed militia had not pursued an actual policy of genocide in Darfur. The commission explained that although the Darfur violence satisfied the first two requirements for a finding of genocide, there was a lack of the requisite genocidal intent. Shortly after the report was released, the UN Security Council referred the situation to the International Criminal Court (ICC). While initially omitting the crime of genocide from the arrest warrant for Sudanese president Omar Hassan Ahmed al-Bashir, the ICC amended the indictment in July 2010 to include the crime of genocide.

Since the conclusion of the Commission of Inquiry, the joint African Union (AU) and UN Observer Mission in Sudan has continued to dispute the occurrence of genocide in Sudan. Former UN secretary-general Kofi Annan has also resisted calling the conflict a genocide, instead referring to it as consistent with violations of human rights. In addition, former U.S. president Jimmy Carter stated in late 2007 that while the atrocities in Darfur were deplorable, they did not meet the legal standard for genocide. Other notable figures, including Samantha Power, have also hesitated to characterize the conflict as a genocide, pointing to the inability to determine whether all elements of genocide are satisfied in the midst of an ongoing conflict. The African Union and the League of Arab States have also consistently refused to characterize the conflict as genocide. Similarly, the European Union (EU) and British and Canadian officials have also hesitated to call it genocide, instead labeling it as tantamount to genocide or ethnic cleansing.

Throughout the terminology debate, several nations have also either consistently denied that genocide is occurring in Darfur or have refused to take action pursuant to a threat of genocide. China and Russia threatened to veto any UN Security Council resolution to impose sanctions on Sudan, and Pakistan and Algeria also expressed hesitance to such an action. Throughout, members of the Sudanese government, including President Bashir and, most vocally, John Ukec Lueth Ukec, Sudan's ambassador to the United States, have consistently denied that the armed attacks in Darfur constitute acts of genocide, insisting that the exaggerated reporting on the conflict is only hampering efforts at peace.

There are two primary reasons for the denial that the violence in Darfur amounts to genocide. First, many are hesitant to directly invoke the obligations and responsibilities that such a label demands for nations who have signed the UN Genocide Convention. Second, many avoid labeling the conflict at all, for fear of alienating the Sudanese government and upsetting the ongoing peace processes in the region.

In the first category, states may seek to avoid the serious diplomatic, political, and legal obligations that result from labeling a conflict as genocide pursuant to the UN

Convention. In particular, parties to the convention are obligated to undertake necessary measures to prevent and punish genocide and likewise may call upon the United Nations to take actions to prevent and suppress genocide. State parties are also obligated to punish or prosecute acts of genocide and take measures to establish jurisdiction in those circumstances. Related to this, states may fear that overusing the designation "genocide" will detract from the serious response and international criminal responsibility that it is intended to invoke.

The second category of denial relates to the desire of the United Nations and regional organizations, such as the African Union and the League of Arab States, to facilitate the ongoing peace negotiations between the Sudanese government and the Darfur rebels, as well as between the Sudanese government and the government of South Sudan. Indeed, the African Union, in response to the decision of the ICC to include the crime of genocide in the indictment against President Bashir, issued a communiqué expressing deep concern that the decision would negatively affect the peace process in Darfur. Likewise, the United Nations has avoided calling the conflict a genocide, emphasizing that labeling it will not facilitate its resolution.

Other nations' reasons for not calling the killing in Darfur a genocide may be motivated by a desire to maintain a neutral relationship with Sudan for financial or political gain (or both). Nations like China and Russia, for example, have economic partnerships with the Sudanese government centered on oil and weapons trade.

The debate over whether the Darfur conflict constitutes genocide and the resulting inability of the international community to effectively resolve the conflict indicate that the existing framework, as set forth in the UN Convention, is ineffective at galvanizing concerted international efforts to fulfill the framework's purpose of preventing and suppressing genocide. Remembering the consequences of having failed to intervene in a timely way into Rwanda's 1994 genocide, many scholars and international commentators lament that the debate over the violence in Darfur has detracted from genuine efforts to resolve the conflict and have called for the formulation of a different, more effective approach.

Elinor O. Stevenson

See also: African Union; Amnesty International; Annan, Kofi; Bashir, Omar Hassan Ahmed al-; Darfur Atrocities Documentation Project; Enough Project; Save Darfur Coalition; United Nations Commission of Inquiry on Darfur; United States Involvement in Darfur

Further Reading

Fowler, Jerry. 2006. "A New Chapter of Irony: The Legal Definition of Genocide and the Implications of Powell's Determination." In Samuel Totten and Eric Markusen, eds., *Genocide in Darfur: Investigating the Atrocities in the Sudan*. New York: Routledge, 127–138.

Lippman, Matthew. 2007. "Darfur: The Politics of Genocide Denial Syndrome." *Journal of Genocide Research* 9, 193–213.

Slim, Hugo. 2004. "Dithering over Darfur? A Preliminary Review of the International Response." *International Affairs* 80, 811–828.

Dinka

The Dinka are among the most numerous ethnic groups in South Sudan. During the Sudanese Civil Wars, tens of thousands of

Dinka were killed, and even more fled their homes and sought refugee status in neighboring nations.

The Dinka belong to what is commonly referred to as the *Nilotic peoples,* or *Nilotes.* A subgroup of the Nilo-Saharan languages, Nilotic languages are spoken by several ethnic groups, including the Ateker, Dinka, Kalenjin, Luo, Nuer, and Shilluk, who typically reside in South Sudan, northern Tanzania, Uganda, and Kenya. Most Dinka live in present-day South Sudan, but civil war and climate change have driven Dinka beyond their ancestral lands and into northern Sudan, as well as other African nations, Europe, and the United States. According to a 2011 census, the Dinka are the largest ethnic group in South Sudan and account for 35.8 percent of the population, followed by the Nuer, who make up 15.6 percent, and then a myriad of smaller ethnic groups.

Religion, geography, and greed have resulted in the loss of many Dinka lives. Most Dinka practice a combination of Christianity and traditional beliefs, which made them vulnerable to Arab militia raids from the north during Sudan's significant civil wars. Victims of the government of Sudan's Islamization campaigns, many Dinka fled Sudan during the fighting and compose the ethnic identity of many of Sudan's so-called Lost Boys and Lost Girls. During the Second Sudanese Civil War (1983–2005), the discovery of oil on Dinka land elevated government-sponsored attacks on the Dinka beyond the traditional religious scope. The forced relocation of Dinka from oil-rich regions began in 1983 and reached its peak between 1986 and 1988. While Dinka are traditionally agriculturalists, they were sent to live on land with little to no agricultural potential.

The 2005 cease-fire that ended the Second Sudanese Civil War reduced the government's violence against the Dinka, but it did not stop completely, as the oil-rich Abyei region remains contested between Sudan and South Sudan, which became an independent state in 2011. Likewise, many Dinka have been killed, raped, or forcibly recruited into the Lord's Resistance Army of Uganda.

Despite the decades of displacement and violence, the Dinka have upheld their strong tradition of oral literature, which includes folktales, fables, myths, folk songs, fairy tales, and legends. These stories and lyrics passed from generation to generation by word of mouth and recently, with the exodus of Dinka out of Sudan, some of these stories have been translated and published. Animals are often the main characters, and their exploits are used as analogies for human behavior.

Alongside the publication of traditional Dinka stories, Dinka survivors of the Sudanese Civil Wars have published their own personal stories. In so doing, they have brought greater attention to their people and homeland.

Alexis Herr

See also: Child Soldiers; Comprehensive Peace Agreement; Lost Boys and Girls of Sudan; Sudanese Civil Wars; *What Is the What*

Further Reading
Johnson, Hilde F. 2016. *South Sudan: The Untold Story from Independence to Civil War.* New York: I. B. Tauris.

Turse, Nick. 2016. *Next Time They'll Come to Count the Dead: War and Survival in South Sudan.* Chicago: Dispatch Books.

Walzer, Craig, ed. 2008. *Out of Exile: Narratives from the Abducted and Displaced*

People of Sudan. San Francisco: Voice of Witness.

Diraige, Ahmed Ibrahim

Ahmed Ibrahim Diraige served as governor of Darfur between 1961 and 1963, formed a movement called the Darfur Development Front (DDF) in December 1963, and more recently, created the Sudan Federal Democratic Alliance (SFDA) to advocate for the social and political interests of Darfur, an area that had been ignored and marginalized by the government of Sudan. Since then, he has continued to fight for the recognition and rights of Darfurians, and as a result, he has been forced to flee the country.

Diraige is from the Fur tribe in Darfur. He was the son of a chief and assumed the chiefdom himself at the age of eleven, when his father died. He attended Hantoub School (known colloquially as "the Eton of Sudan") in the town of Wad Madani, just south of Khartoum. He excelled there and was captain of athletics for three years and captain of the cadet force. While at Hantoub, he even played sports with Gaafar Muhammad an-Nimeiry, the future president of Sudan from 1969 to 1985. He became the leader of the Fur community, which is the largest ethnic group in Darfur, but he stepped down from that post in 1953 to continue his studies in the United Kingdom.

Despite Darfur being incorporated into Sudan following the nation's independence from colonial forces (1956), the nascent Sudanese government in Khartoum looked down on African tribes in Darfur, like the Fur, even though they are also Muslims. Having returned from law school in the 1960s, Diraige arrived home to a postcolonial Sudan, where the traditional chiefdom administrations had been replaced with local administrations. Under this new system of governance, Darfur was given short shrift once again.

Diraige formed the DDF in 1963 to advocate for his countrymen and countrywomen and request that the government do more to support those residing in the Darfur region. In the local elections in Darfur, Diraige's DDF secured thirteen of the twenty-four seats. When Nimeiry, Diraige's old schoolmate from Hantoub, overthrew the government in Khartoum in May 1969, he had Diraige arrested. Diraige's criticism of the government's neglect of ethnic Africans hit too close to home for Nimeiry. Diraige was later released, and in January 1980, after rioting broke out in Darfur province because the current governor, al-Tayeb al-Mardi, had been appointed rather than elected, Nimeiry replaced al-Mardi with Diraige. Diraige was then elected as governor the following year.

From 1980 to 1983, as the governor of Darfur, Diraige continued to give voice to Darfurian demands. He stressed that representation of Darfurians in the political decision-making process in Khartoum was vital. This lack of representation, he asserted, resulted in a lack of social, political, educational, economic, and agriculture development in Darfur. It was at this time, too, that Darfur was experiencing a significant drought, and Diraige was forced to write to President Nimeiry warning that unless the government sent food to the region, Darfur would experience a debilitating famine. Nimeiry declined to respond, forcing Diraige to fly to Khartoum on December 23, 1983, to present his plea in person. Nimeiry denied that any such famine existed and even issued another arrest warrant for Diraige two days later. Diraige avoided capture by flying to Saudi Arabia, and then he had to watch from the sidelines as famine destroyed Darfurian lives.

From his position of exile, Diraige continued his political organizing and created the SFDA. In this capacity, he has been involved in several peace talks alongside better-known Darfur rebel movements—like the Justice and Equality Movement and the Sudan Liberation Army/Movement—which have been active since 2003.

Alexis Herr

See also: Famine of 1984–1985; Religion

Further Reading

Crockett, Richard. 2010. *Sudan: Darfur and the Failure of an African State.* New Haven, CT: Yale University Press.

Doha Document for Peace in Darfur

Named for the city of Doha, Qatar, where the negotiations took place, the Doha Document for Peace in Darfur (DDPD) was a protocol signed between the government of Sudan and the Liberation and Justice Movement (LJM) on July 14, 2011. The stated purpose of the DDPD was to create a framework for achieving a comprehensive peace process in Darfur; however, the success of this protocol is debatable.

The DDPD was the culmination of two-and-a-half years of negotiations, dialogue, and consultations with the government of Sudan, rebel groups representing Darfurian interests, and international partners and stakeholders. The talks were sponsored by the United Nations and African Union and were led by Djibril Bassolé. Bassolé had been appointed by the United Nations and African Union as the joint chief mediator for Darfur, a position

previously held by mediators Jan Eliasson and Salim Ahmed Salim. Bassolé started his new role in a highly tense political climate owing to the International Criminal Court's 2009 indictment of Sudanese president Omar Hassan Ahmed al-Bashir.

During the initial stages of the Doha talks in February 2009, the Justice and Equality Movement (JEM) and the government of Sudan signed an agreement stating that both parties would participate in subsequent negotiations. A year later, on February 20, 2010, representatives of the two groups met in the Chadian capital of N'Djamena to sign a framework agreement for the Doha talks that would take place later that year.

The key points discussed in December 2010 in Doha were wealth sharing, restitution for Darfurian survivors, a cease-fire agreement, release of JEM prisoners in Khartoum, and recognition of JEM as a political party. As both parties advanced toward signing the DDPD, violence in Darfur continued unabated.

By May 2011, the talks started to crumble when JEM removed itself from the process. According to the movement, the government of Sudan was unwilling to meet its demands, so it saw no reason to continue negotiations. To salvage nearly a year of work, international mediators managed to recruit leaders representing eleven Darfurian rebel factions to continue the talks. The representatives formed LJM; however, many of the participants had been living outside Darfur for decades and thus had little knowledge of what was going on there and had no connection to the Darfurians fighting for survival. The absence of JEM, along with the omission of representatives of the Sudan Liberation Army factions in the meetings, may very well have weakened the final protocol signed in July 2011. Some scholars have criticized the agreement as excessively vague, arguing that it has allowed the Sudanese government to easily violate the spirit of the agreement without directly breaking its commitment. For example, the agreement prohibits LJM and the government of Sudan from engaging in "offensive action," but it lacks provisions that would hold the parties accountable for violating it.

The African Union–United Nations Missions in Darfur (UNAMID) provided technical and logistical support to the process and remain involved in monitoring its implementation. The government of Qatar hosted the thirteenth meeting of the Implementation Follow-up Commission (IFC) of the DDPD at the Sheraton Grand Hotel, Doha, on July 11, 2018. Members of the IFC in attendance included Dr. Amin Hassan Omar and Dr. Magdi Khalafallah as representatives of the government of Sudan, as well as leaders from the National Liberation Justice Party, Liberation Justice Party, JEM-Sudan, and the Sudan Liberation Army/Movement. Non-Sudanese IFC members present included representatives from the League of Arab States, the United Kingdom, European Union, the United States, and Selva Ramachandran, the acting resident representative/county director of the United Nations Development Programme. At this meeting, the parties in attendance called on the government of Sudan, JEM, and the Sudan Liberation Army faction led by Minni Minawi to speed up and finalize a negotiation that would lead to a permanent cessation of hostilities agreement.

Ultimately, DDPD failed to bring immediate and long-lasting peace to Darfur. While a fragile cease-fire has been in effect since 2011, the negotiations in Darfur have not implemented lasting change within the Sudanese government, nor have they held government officials responsible for war crimes. While the situation in Darfur has changed since the DDPD was signed, the problem has not been solved.

Alexis Herr

See also: Bassolé, Djibril; Darfur; Justice and Equality Movement; Khartoum; Sudan People's Liberation Movement/Army; United Nations Mission in the Sudan; United States Involvement in Darfur

Further Reading

Brosché, Johan, and Daniel Rothbart. 2013. *Violent Conflict and Peacebuilding: The Continuing Crisis in Darfur.* New York: Routledge.

E

Egeland, Jan

Jan Egeland has spent more than thirty years in the employ of organizations engaged in international work with human rights, humanitarian crises, and conflict resolution. Throughout his tenure at the United Nations (UN), he vocally criticized governments, institutions, and leaders whose actions stymied humanitarian aid and peace. As a result of his negative comments about the Sudanese government's role in committing mass atrocities in Darfur, he was blocked entry into Sudan.

Egeland was born on September 12, 1957, in the small Norwegian city of Stavanger and educated at the University of Oslo. He has been a Fulbright scholar at the University of California, Berkeley, and a fellow at both the International Peace Research Institute, Oslo, and the Truman Institute for the Advancement of Peace, Jerusalem.

In 1980, Egeland became chairman of Amnesty International in Norway. During his tenure in that office, he was elected as vice chairman of the organization's International Executive Committee. He remained in both positions until 1986. Then, between 1990 and 1997, Egeland was state secretary in the Norwegian Ministry of Foreign Affairs, during which he engaged in humanitarian relief work. He joined the United Nations as Secretary-General Kofi Annan's special adviser on Colombia from 1999 to 2002. From 2001 to 2003, he also served as secretary-general of the Norwegian Red Cross. In August 2003, he was appointed by Annan to serve as undersecretary-general

for humanitarian affairs and emergency relief coordinator, a position that he held until 2006. During that period, he helped reform the global humanitarian response system, which he helped implement in reaction to the crises in Darfur, Democratic Republic of Congo, and Lebanon. For that role, he was named by *Time* magazine as one of the "100 people who shape our world." In September 2008, he became Secretary-General Ban Ki-moon's special adviser for conflict prevention and resolution.

As a young diplomat in 1992, Egeland helped establish the back-channel diplomacy that started negotiations between representatives of Israel and the Palestine Liberation Organization (PLO). These initiatives would lead eventually to the Oslo Accord between Israel and the PLO (the so-called Declaration of Principles) in September 1993. In 1996, he helped facilitate the UN-led peace talks leading up to a cease-fire agreement between the government of Guatemala and the Guatemalan National Revolutionary Unity (Unidad Revolucionaria Nacional Guatemalteca, or URNG) guerrillas, an agreement signed at Oslo City Hall. A further success saw the Ottawa Treaty to ban land mines negotiated and adopted in Oslo in 1997, with Egeland as the Norwegian delegation leader.

In December 2003, soon after becoming UN undersecretary-general for humanitarian affairs, Egeland was forced to address the mounting humanitarian crisis in Darfur. He relentlessly tried to bring the situation in Darfur to the world's attention, just as Mukesh Kapila had been attempting to do from Khartoum in his role as the UN resident and humanitarian coordinator for Sudan (2002–2003). In 2004, Egeland went to Darfur, where there were already 1 million people in need; and by 2006, he was telling reporters that 4 million now needed humanitarian assistance. Egeland warned of a possible collapse of humanitarian assistance programs in Darfur and neighboring areas, due to what he referred to as a "meltdown in security" (CNN 2006). He was desperate for urgent action to be taken, although he was all too aware that the response of the international community was haphazard, uneven, and all too often feeble. By 2006, Egeland's vocal criticisms of the regime in Khartoum and the international community's response had led to an unlikely outcome: the Sudanese government forbid him, the most senior humanitarian officer of the United Nations, entry to Sudan.

As well as addressing the crisis in Darfur, Egeland coordinated relief efforts in what otherwise would have been neglected emergency situations, such as in northern Uganda (where the Lord's Resistance Army, under Joseph Kony, had been murdering tens of thousands for decades), Somalia, and the Democratic Republic of the Congo. He traveled to the frontlines of conflicts, meeting with Kony and his deputy, Vincent Otti, in November 2006, as well as other sites of human catastrophe, such as Colombia, Lebanon, and the Palestinian Territories. And while he sought to draw international attention at all times to the need to alleviate distress, he was often just as critical of local conditions and leaders and their part in the crisis situations that he was attempting to ease.

Apart from human-made disasters such as these, during his period with the UN Office for the Coordination of Humanitarian Affairs (OCHA), Egeland was confronted by natural calamities and the need to provide desperately needed relief in these situations. These included earthquakes, droughts, the 2004 Indian Ocean tsunami, and Hurricane Katrina that devastated large parts of the southern United States and the Caribbean.

In July 2006, Egeland launched a huge U.S. appeal to aid the reconstruction of Lebanon following the destruction of parts of the country by Israeli forces and the displacement of many thousands of refugees. Although critical of Israel, referring to its invasion of Lebanon as a violation of humanitarian law, he drew the intense ire of Hezbollah (a Shi'a Islamist political party and militant group based in Lebanon), lashing out at the movement for its use of women and children as human shields.

During Egeland's tenure at the United Nations, he oversaw the creation of the Central Emergency Response Fund (CERF), a humanitarian funding mechanism established to enable more timely and reliable assistance to victims of natural disasters and armed conflicts. It was approved by the UN General Assembly on December 15, 2005, when the former Central Emergency Revolving Fund (a loan facility of $50 million established by the General Assembly in 1991) was upgraded by adding a grant for the disbursement of further emergency assistance. The CERF, which allocates one-third of its resources to core, lifesaving activities in chronically underfunded crises, was launched in March 2006.

On September 1, 2007, Egeland returned to Norway to take up the position of director of the Norwegian Institute of International Affairs. He also became a professor at the University of Stavanger, while remaining an adviser to the UN secretary-general. In 2008, Egeland published a memoir, *A Billion Lives: An Eyewitness Report from the Frontlines of Humanity*, dealing with his time at the United Nations between 2003 and 2006.

From August 2013, Egeland has served as the secretary-general of the Norwegian Refugee Council (NRC), a role that oversees the work of the humanitarian organization in over thirty-one countries affected by disaster and conflict. In 2015, former UN secretary-general Ban Ki-moon appointed him as special adviser to the UN Special Envoy for Syria. He stepped down from this role on December 1, 2018. He now is the secretary-general of the NRC.

Paul R. Bartrop

See also: Amnesty International; Annan, Kofi; Bashir, Omar Hassan Ahmed al-; Darfur; Kapila, Mukesh

Further Reading

Anderson, Scott. 2004. "How Did Darfur Happen?" *The New York Times*. October 17.

CNN. 2006. "Egeland: 'Meltdown' in Darfur." November 22. Available at http://www.cnn.com/2006/WORLD/africa/11/22/un.darfur/index.html.

Lacey, Marc. 2006. "Sudan Blocks U.N. Official from Darfur." *The New York Times*. April 4.

Scherrer, P. Christian. 2002. *Genocide and Crisis in Central Africa: Conflict Roots, Mass Violence, and Regional War*. Westport, CT: Praeger.

Egyptian Involvement in Darfur

Egypt's role in the history of Sudan predates the Darfur Genocide and provides important context to some of the violent conflicts that haunt Sudanese history. In particular, its dual rule over Sudan with Britain during the colonial period (1899–1956) had a long-lasting impact on identity politics in Sudan, as did its geographical proximity to Sudan.

Egypt stretches along the northern border of Sudan, and as a neighbor, it has long been involved in Sudanese affairs. In the 1820s, the Egyptians, at that time part of the Ottoman Empire (also known as the *Turkish Empire*), settled in Khartoum as the first foreign rulers of Sudan. The occupying forces called the region *Sudan,* a term first coined by north-African Arab traders meaning "land of the blacks."

When the Egyptians first landed in Sudan, it had no political tradition or central political leadership. The two exceptions to this were the sultanates of Darfur in the west and Sennar in the east. Historically, Egypt had been the Darfur Sultanate's largest single trading partner. While Sennar quickly fell to the Ottomans, the sultanate of Darfur, by contrast, tried to resist. Despite Darfur being at the height of its power, its fighters were no match for the Egyptian troops, armed with cannons and trained by former officers of Napoleon Bonaparte's army. By August 1821, Darfur fell to the Egyptians.

The Egyptian occupiers' key interest in Sudan was procuring slaves, particularly those from the south of the country. In addition to raping Sudan of its human resources, it imposed taxes to support the foreign occupiers. Egypt's exploitation of Sudan was challenged by the Mahdi (a religious leader of the Samaniyya order of Sudan since 1881), who rallied the Arab tribes against the Turco-Egyptian rulers. The Mahdi and his troops stormed Khartoum in January 1885 to drive out the Egyptian forces, but in 1882, unbeknown to the Mahdi, the British had conquered Egypt and assumed control of the area. The Mahdi found General Charles Gordon in charge, and in short order decapitated the icon of British imperialism and skewered his head on a stick. The British, overwhelmed by the revolt against their colonial forces, evacuated all their nationals.

Great Britain, however, vowed to take back Sudan in the future in retribution for Gordon. That day came in 1898, when the British soldiers returned and conquered Sudan.

Under Great Britain's control, Egypt reimpressed its influence on Sudan. Great Britain established a dual colonial government known as the Anglo-Egyptian Condominium in 1899, an arrangement that lasted until Sudan achieved independence in 1956. The Anglo-Egyptian Condominium helped polarize the division between the territories of present-day Sudan and South Sudan. Eager to separate the largely Islamic and Arabic-speaking north from the more religiously and ethnically diverse south, the British oversaw the colonization of the south and put the north in the hands of Egyptians. Under the tutelage of Egypt, the northern half of Sudan was homogenized: Islam became the official religion and Arabic the main language spoken.

The British conquered Darfur (*dar Fur* means "land of the Fur" in Arabic) in 1916, some seventeen years after taking over Khartoum and establishing the colonial rule of Sudan. Given Darfur's isolated location, far from Khartoum, the British left a small outpost of colonial officers there. When the British left Sudan in 1956, they grafted Darfur, a region as big as France, on to Sudan.

By the time the British left, the Egyptian influence over the north had led the Sudanese in the north to view themselves as Arab, not African. Despite Islam becoming the main religion under the new leadership, the government in Khartoum looked down on citizens it considered of African, not Arab, descent. Thus, the influence of Egypt on identity politics, particularly in the capital of Sudan, informed the Sudanese government's policies toward those it considered non-Arab Africans residing in the peripheries of the state (namely, those places that the

British had overseen, like Darfur and the southern half of the state).

Egypt's response to the Darfur Genocide is informed by its national politics and geographical position. Its proximity to Sudan means that it has a vested interest in the stability of that country, which translates into maintaining a relationship with the Sudanese government in Khartoum. During the genocide, Egypt intervened through the aegis of the United Nations. It provided humanitarian aid and peacekeeping soldiers to the African Union–United Nations Mission in Darfur (UNAMID). In May 2010, two Egyptian peacekeeping troops were killed and three injured in an ambush attack in south Darfur.

Despite its financial and human contributions to the United Nations, some humanitarians and activists have criticized Egypt for not taking on a greater leadership role in pressuring Sudan's president, Omar Hassan Ahmed al-Bashir, to end the killings. In mid-May 2010, however, Egypt became more involved when President Hosni Mubarak hosted Khalil Ibrahim, leader of the Justice and Equality Movement. Ibrahim had recently backed out of the Doha Peace Talks, claiming that those negotiating an end to the conflict were favoring Khartoum, and in so doing disadvantaging Darfurians.

Egyptian influence on Sudanese affairs extends into the present, too. Although the International Criminal Court (ICC) issued arrest warrants for Bashir for crimes against humanity (in March 2009) and genocide (in July 2010), Egypt has defied the warrants and permitted him to visit. In so doing, Egypt undermined the authority of the ICC by allowing the man responsible for the genocide to go unpunished. Furthermore, Egyptian leadership has actively criticized the arrest warrants for Bashir.

Alexis Herr

See also: British Involvement in Darfur; Darfur; Ibrahim, Khalil; Justice and Equality Movement; Khartoum; Religion

Further Reading

Crockett, Richard. 2010. *Sudan: Darfur and the Failure of an African State*. New Haven, CT: Yale University Press.

Prunier, Gerard. 2008. *Darfur: A 21st-Century Genocide*. 3rd ed. Ithica, NY: Cornell University Press.

Enough Project

The Enough Project is a Washington, D.C.–based advocacy group focused on atrocity crimes in Africa. At its inception, it aimed to end crimes against humanity in Darfur, northern Uganda, and the eastern Democratic Republic of Congo. It has since addressed issues in Somalia and Zimbabwe, as well as conflicts between Sudan and the newly independent South Sudan. When the Darfur Genocide began, the Enough Project quickly became a key leader of U.S. activism efforts.

The Enough Project was cofounded in March 2007 by Africa experts John Prendergast and Gayle Smith as a joint initiative of their respective employers at the time, the International Crisis Group (ICG) and the Center for American Progress (CAP). Six months later, the Enough Project began to operate wholly in association with the CAP.

In "The Answer to Darfur: How to Resolve the World's Hottest War," a strategy paper released at the launch of the Enough Project, Prendergast presented the organization's "3P" strategy of combating mass atrocities and genocide by promoting peace, protecting people, and punishing perpetrators.

With specific regard to Darfur, Prendergast urged that outside actors—including most prominently the United States, the United Nations (UN), the European Union (EU), and the African Union (AU)—aggressively pursue several policy initiatives simultaneously, including (1) promote rebel unity, not least for presenting a common negotiating position in any peace talks; (2) build an effective peace process by imposing multilateral pressure on the Sudanese government to adhere to clearly stated peace objectives; (3) appoint a full-time U.S. special envoy to communicate with both the government and the rebels; (4) deploy credible UN and AU military forces to protect civilians from atrocities; and (5) impose punitive sanctions, such as freezing government assets and providing information to the International Criminal Court (ICC) for the possible prosecution of senior regime officials for their roles in orchestrating mass atrocities. With the success of the antiapartheid movement of the early 1990s as a model, the Enough Project also seeks to promote citizen activism, such as pressuring managers of investment funds to divest their holdings in companies doing business with the Khartoum government.

The Enough Project, through its reports and analysis, has provided a resource for politicians, activists, humanitarians, and students to learn more about Darfur and consider ways to take action. The project has invested considerable resources in researching and writing investigative reports and blog posts on the violence in Darfur. In so doing, it has gathered substantive data on a conflict that has been difficult to study, owing to the government of Sudan's restrictions on foreign access to Darfur. These reports and articles vary in theme and have included in-depth analysis of many topics, including the economics of ethnic cleansing in Darfur (August 8, 2013), flawed peace processes (August 6, 2011), refugees

(August 24, 2010), weapons (October 3, 2009), and gendered violence (June 2, 2009). In addition to providing a historical record of what is happening on the ground in Darfur and Sudan, the Enough Project always includes a plan of action of how international and national actors can resolve the problem at hand.

Bringing public visibility to its efforts, the Enough Project has received support from numerous professional athletes and celebrities, including Mia Farrow, Charles Barkley, Brad Pitt, Ben Affleck, and Matt Damon. In partnership with the Enough Project, professional basketball player Tracy McGrady founded the Darfur Dream Team, an initiative that links American schools with sister schools in Darfurian refugee camps in eastern Chad. Actor George Clooney was instrumental in launching the Satellite Sentinel Project (SSP) in December 2010, by which the Enough Project analyzes satellite imagery to report on possible threats to civilians on both sides of the border between Sudan and South Sudan. Prendergast has also written two books with actor Don Cheadle on promoting citizen activism on Darfur and other regions of Africa.

In July 2012, the reporter Alan Boswell criticized the Enough Project for its role in shaping U.S. policy toward South Sudan, which became a separate nation in 2011. He claimed that the Enough Project's strategy for U.S. support of South Sudan ignored the new government's rampant corruption and poor human rights record. Jonathan Hutson of the Enough Project responded by citing instances in which the organization, using SSP, had reported on possible war crimes by both Sudan and South Sudan.

Since the signing of the Doha Document for Peace in Darfur (DDPD) in 2011—a mediated peace deal between the

government of Sudan and the Liberation and Justice Movement (LJM)—the Enough Project has actively monitored the successes and failures of the peace treaty and thus has put pressure on the government of Darfur to remain accountable for its promises to stop the killing in Darfur, as well as on the United States to uphold target sanctions. In "Ominous Threats Descending on Darfur," Enough Project senior advisor Dr. Suliman Baldo analyzed the tensions and complications surrounding the mandatory weapon collection underway in Darfur. According to Baldo, the government's attempt to confiscate arms from Darfurian militants has only exacerbated the situation, and if the crisis is not managed, he warned that there is a risk of "large-scale fratricidal bloodshed" (Baldo 2017: 4). He suggested that for the disarmament of Darfur to occur, the government of Sudan first must address the rights of the 2.5 million victims of government-led ethnic purges by pursuing justice and reparations.

The Enough Project continues to leverage its celebrity and its cofounder, Prendergast, brings attention to the situation in Darfur and Sudan as a whole by publishing op-eds in well-respected magazines and newspapers. Similar to the group's research projects and lengthy reports, the op-eds are intended to contextualize the conflicts and suggest possible actions to resolve the problems.

Karl A. Yambert and Alexis Herr

See also: Bashir, Omar Hassan Ahmed al-; Cheadle, Don; Clooney, George; Damon, Matt; Doha Document for Peace in Darfur; Farrow, Mia; Prendergast, John

Further Reading

Cheadle, Don, and John Prendergast. 2007. *Not on Our Watch: The Mission to End*

Genocide in Darfur and Beyond. New York: Hyperion.

Cheadle, Don, and John Prendergast. 2010. *The Enough Moment: Fighting to End Africa's Worst Human Rights Crimes.* New York: Three Rivers Press.

Suliman, Baldo. 2017. "Ominous Threats Descending on Darfur." The Enough Project. Available at https://enoughproject.org/wp-content/uploads/2017/11/OminousThreatsDarfur_Nov2017_Enough1.pdf.

F

Famine of 1984–1985

The so-called Great Drought of 1984–1985 sharpened the ongoing violent confrontation over resources in the Darfur region and brought about a devastating famine. The resulting desertification of Darfurian land heightened the already brewing conflict between nomadic/seminomadic Arab groups and the sedentary/farming non-Arabs who called Darfur their home. The instability caused by the drought also helped to unseat then-president Gaafar Muhammad an-Nimeiry.

Darfur has a long history of famines and droughts, which helps put the 1984–1985 famine in greater historical context. During the twentieth century alone, at least twelve famines are known to precede the Great Drought. These famines took place in 1913–1914, 1926–1927, 1930–1931, 1937, 1939, 1941–1942, 1945, 1949–1950, 1955, 1959, 1969, and 1973. Of these famines, the 1913–1914 famine in Darfur known as *Julu* ("Wandering") was the most devastating. Owing to the destructive nature of that famine, its memory was kept alive by Darfur's oral historical tradition. For this reason, when the famine erupted in 1984, people wondered if they were in store for another *Julu*. Other names for the 1913–1914 famine include *Um Sudur* ("Mother of the Chest") and *Dulen Dor* ("Sun Famine"). Famines in the twentieth century were common and frequent, although none were as deadly as the *Julu* (de Wall 67–69: 72). These earlier famines were caused by a host of causes, including drought, war, revolt, and locusts.

Drought in the early 1980s caused by two years of failed rainy seasons precipitated the 1984–1985 famine. While drought was nothing new in the region, it was far more severe than recent dry periods and had dire consequences for the people of Darfur. The drought extended beyond Darfur's borders and into neighboring Chad and Libya. Hoping to find more fertile pasture and land in Darfur, nomads from Chad and Libya entered Darfur in large numbers and put added stress on the region's already-depleted resources. Furthermore, the great global drought of the 1980s caused increasing tensions for water and fertile land as Arab nomads clashed with the established African residents of Darfur. As a result of the drier than normal rainy seasons and extra strain on available resources, the harvest failed in 1983 in northern Darfur, and then in 1984, it failed in northern and southern Sudan.

The drought that came before the famine should have been a warning to the government in Khartoum of the type of devastation that awaited Darfur if preventative measures were not taken. Ahmed Diraige, the governor of Darfur appointed by President Nimeiry, warned Khartoum of the scarcity of resources in the region. At the end of 1983, he begged Nimeiry to declare an emergency, but the president refused to heed Diraige's pleas. Desperate, Diraige made the long trip from Darfur to the capital to address the Council of Ministers and request immediate action. His trip failed to garner support for Darfur; as a result, tens of thousands died.

By the time the famine ended, an estimated 240,000 had died from starvation and disease. Further, 2.3 percent of Darfurians were displaced by the drought in the two years preceding the famine. The famine of 1984–1985 and the failure of the Sudanese government to take decisive action to help Darfurians sent a clear message to those in Darfur: the government does not care about you. This message later became a rallying call for Darfurian resistance groups, like the Sudan Liberation Army (SLA), which in 2002 sought to get the government to pay attention to the needs of its Sudanese citizens in Darfur.

Alexis Herr

See also: Diraige, Ahmed Ibrahim; Sudan Liberation Army

Further Reading

de Wall, Alex. 2005. *Famine That Kills: Darfur, Sudan.* New York: Oxford University Press.

Young, Helen, Abdul Monim Osman, Yacob Aklilu, Rebecca Dale, Babiker Badri, and Abdul Jabbar Abdullah Fuddle. 2005. *Darfur—Livelihood Under Siege.* Medford, MA: Feinstein International Famine Center. Available at http://fic.tufts.edu/assets/Young -Darfur-Livelihoods-Under-Seige.pdf.

Farrow, Mia

Mia Farrow is an award-winning American actress who has undertaken extensive humanitarian work as a United Nations International Children's Emergency Fund (UNICEF) goodwill ambassador. In that capacity, she has been involved in a range of activities in Darfur, Chad, and the Central African Republic, among others. In 2007, she co-founded the Olympic Dream for Darfur to pressure China to do more to end the genocide in Darfur.

She was born in Los Angeles on February 9, 1945, as Maria de Lourdes Villiers Farrow, the daughter of the Australian film director John Farrow and the Irish actress Maureen O'Sullivan. Across a movie career that began when she was still a child, Farrow has appeared in over forty films, for which she has received a number of awards and nominations. She also appeared in leading television and theater roles and was the first American actress to be accepted as a member of London's Royal Shakespeare Company.

Farrow was appointed a UNICEF goodwill ambassador in September 2000 and remains in that role today. Among her many activities on behalf of human rights in Africa, she has worked to raise awareness of the plight of children in conflict-affected regions. One of the areas in which she has worked has been in the battle to eradicate polio, a disease that she herself contracted as a child. Her concern for Darfur has seen her travel to the region on a number of occasions, in 2004, 2006, and 2007.

In 2007, an organization called Olympic Dream for Darfur was founded by Farrow, Darfur Genocide activist Eric Reeves, and Jill Savitt, the director of public programs at Human Rights First. Olympic Dream for Darfur campaigned to pressure the Chinese government to intervene on behalf of the population of Darfur, in view of China's close relationship with the government of Sudan. The campaign intended to force China's hand by focusing world attention on its support for the Sudanese government, embarrassing it in the lead-up to the 2008 Beijing Olympics. It organized so-called alternative torch relays, boycotts of Chinese products and visits, and an intense publicity campaign to draw attention to what it termed the "Genocide Olympics." By April 2007, it seemed as though Farrow's work was beginning to yield results, as the Beijing government reversed its stance on Darfur and urged Sudan to accept UN peacekeepers in the region.

Another of Farrow's signal achievements was persuading Hollywood's premier movie director, Steven Spielberg—who had been appointed as artistic adviser for the Olympic opening ceremonies—to withdraw from his position on February 12, 2008. In doing so, he wrote a letter to the Chinese government in which he also urged its leaders to take action on the Darfur situation.

Despite the victories of Farrow's advocacy, her direct and at times combative approach drew criticism from some. Her detractors argued that she was wrong in singling out China as she had, saying that the Chinese government was neither committing genocide in Darfur nor bankrolling the Sudanese government. All the Chinese were guilty of, in this assessment, was seeking to make money from commercial deals to buy Sudanese oil. Farrow's critics contended that, in condemning China, she was focusing on the wrong target—China was being blamed only for having commercial relations with Sudan, for which many other Western countries, the United States included, were not being demonized.

Farrow has been prepared to put her physical well-being on the line to publicize her causes on more than one occasion. After the International Criminal Court (ICC) issued a warrant for the arrest of Sudanese president Omar Hassan Ahmed al-Bashir on March 4, 2009, Farrow sought to raise international awareness of the crimes alleged against him by starting a water-only fast on April 27. But on May 8, she was persuaded to cease fasting after medical advisers alerted her to the real prospect of lasting physical damage if she were to continue.

Farrow's humanitarian work has extended beyond Darfur. In May 2010, she returned to Africa, where she visited Guinea in an attempt to generate international funding sources for maternal and children's health care in the aftermath of political and economic turmoil in that country. She also met with youth groups and launched a UN Peacebuilding Fund project that encouraged young people to find peaceful ways to resolve conflicts and lessen their risk of being caught up in violence.

In early August 2010, Farrow testified for the prosecution at the UN Special Court for Sierra Leone (SCSL) in the trial of former Liberian president Charles Taylor at The Hague. Taylor was facing eleven counts of war crimes, crimes against humanity, and other serious violations of international humanitarian law, including the trafficking of so-called blood diamonds through Sierra Leone and Liberia. She was asked to testify regarding the blood diamonds that Taylor gave supermodel Naomi Campbell at a charity dinner in 1997. The appearance at The Hague of international celebrities such as Farrow gave significant publicity to the Taylor trial and to the work of tribunals such as the SCSL and the ICC. This also furthered the aims of Farrow and her campaign for humanitarian justice, for which she has set up a dedicated website, www.miafarrow.org.

In 2009, Farrow agreed to be the narrator for what became a multiple award-winning documentary, *As We Forgive,* directed by Laura Waters Hinson. *As We Forgive* provides an intimate, firsthand view of the encounters between genocide perpetrators and their victims' families. The film tells the story of two Rwandan women who come face to face with the neighbors who slaughtered their families during the 1994 genocide, as well as their personal journeys toward forgiveness.

As a powerful advocate for children, Farrow has campaigned tirelessly for their rights around the world, particularly for those whose lives have been affected by armed conflict. She has worked extensively to raise funds and awareness for children in countries such as Angola, Chad, the Central African Republic, the Democratic Republic of the Congo, Haiti, and Nigeria. Farrow has also been honored for her humanitarian work. In February 2007, on a visit to the Central African Republic, President François Bozizé awarded Farrow his country's Presidential Medal of Honor in recognition of her services to his nation. Then, in 2008, she was selected by *Time* magazine as one of the most influential people in the world. On May 11, 2011, Farrow received the Lyndon Baines Johnson Moral Courage Award from the United States Holocaust Memorial Museum in Washington, D.C., in recognition of her efforts to raise international awareness on behalf of the victims of Darfur.

Paul R. Bartrop

See also: African Union–United Nations Mission in Darfur; Child Soldiers; Lost Boys and Girls of Sudan; Save Darfur Coalition

Further Reading

Cheadle, Don, and John Prendergast. 2007. *Not on Our Watch: The Mission to End Genocide in Darfur and Beyond*. New York: Hyperion.

Prunier, Gerard. 2005. *Darfur: The Ambiguous Genocide*. Ithaca, NY: Cornell University Press.

Fur

The Fur are the most numerous of the "non-Arab" peoples inhabiting Darfur, a western region of Sudan over which they once ruled and to which they gave their name. (*Dar Fur* means "land of the Fur" in Arabic.) In 2019, the Fur constituted nearly one-quarter of Darfur's total population, dominating the fertile Jebel Marra massif at the region's heart, as well as areas to its south. Their language, also called Fur, belongs to a small subbranch of the Nilo-Saharan language family and is related, although only distantly, to those spoken by neighboring tribes such as the Zaghawa and the Dinka.

According to Fur oral tradition, the group's ancient homeland lies in the north of the Jebel Marra mountain range, near the town of Turrah. The Fur associate nearby stone ruins with Daali, a traditional figure believed to be the founder of the Fur state and the giver of law, as well as with other prehistoric Fur rulers. These ruins remain unexcavated and may shed light someday on early Fur history. Oral tradition holds that the Fur expanded their homeland to the southwest by force, driving out their neighbors.

The first ruler of the Fur known to written history was Suleiman Solongdungu, who came to power in approximately 1640 and transformed the Fur state into a vast, multiethnic kingdom. His rise coincided with the decline of the empire of the Tunjur—a nomadic, camel-driving people founded in eastern Chand and western Sudan—of which the early Fur state may have been a vassal. At its dynastic peak in the eighteenth century, the Fur state encompassed an area of some 350,000 square miles, with an estimated 4–6 million subjects. Under Suleiman's reign, the Fur and their subjects slowly began converting to Islam and adopting Arabic names and styles of dress, although they largely retained their native languages. After a long period of decline, the Fur dynasty finally fell to Ottoman Egyptian forces in 1874.

The Fur today are a sedentary and predominantly agricultural people with urban population centers in such cities as El Fasher and Zalingei. Fur farmers are noted for their skill at terrace farming in their mountainous homeland, where they have mastered gravity-fed irrigation techniques. Peanuts, numerous vegetables, and fruits such as strawberries and apples are grown by the Fur, in addition to cereal crops. Their societies are stratified, with certain occupations (e.g., leather tanning) being considered low caste. Many Fur live in multiethnic towns with other sedentary groups.

Tensions between the Fur and many of their pastoralist, Arabic-speaking neighbors have escalated for decades, erupting into the Fur-Arab War of 1987–1989, when drought, famine, and desertification created fierce competition for limited resources. In this conflict, the Fur faced a twenty-seven-tribe alliance. More recently, they have been among the primary targets of the Sudanese government's campaign of ethnic cleansing in Darfur. This campaign followed the rise of the Sudan Liberation Army (SLA), led by ethnic Fur rebel Abdel Wahid. The SLA—a multiethnic force dominated by Fur, Massalit, and Zaghawa—has fought a rebellion demanding greater autonomy and economic opportunity for the people of Darfur since 2002. While the government launched its violent campaign in the name of counterinsurgency in 2003, Fur, Massalit, and Zaghawa civilians became the primary targets of attacks by the government and government-sponsored Arabic-speaking militias. The Fur account for a large percentage of the millions displaced by this conflict.

David Paige

See also: British Involvement in Darfur; Dinka; Famine of 1984–1985; Janjaweed; Khartoum; Massalit; Sudan Liberation Army; Zaghawa

Further Reading

Flint, Julie, and Alex de Waal. 2006. *Darfur: A Short History of a Long War*. London: Zed Books.

Holt, P. M., and Martin Daly. 2000. *The History of the Sudan, from the Coming of Islam to the Present Day*. New York: Longman.

Olson, James S. 1996. *The Peoples of Africa: An Ethnohistorical Dictionary*. Westport, CT: Greenwood Press.

Rolandsen, Øystein H., and M. W. Daly. 2007. *Darfur's Sorrow: A History of Destruction and Genocide*. Cambridge: Cambridge University Press.

G

Gambari, Ibrahim

From January 2010 to July 2012, Ibrahim Gambari was head of the joint United Nations (UN)—African Union (AU) peacekeeping mission in Darfur. His experience negotiating with dictators on behalf of the United Nations made him ideal for that role.

Gambari was born on November 24, 1944, in Ilorin, Kwara State, Nigeria, and graduated from the London School of Economics in 1968 with a bachelor of science degree in economics. He then earned a master's degree in political science (1970) and a PhD in international relations (1974) from Columbia University. Gambari began teaching at City University of New York in 1969 and later taught at the University of Albany. From 1986 until 1999, he taught at Johns Hopkins, Georgetown, and Howard universities. Gambari has also been a research fellow at the Brookings Institution in Washington, D.C.

For a brief time in the mid-1980s, Gambari was Nigeria's minister for external affairs (1984–1985) and subsequently served as Nigeria's ambassador to the United Nations (1990–1999). Next, he was appointed as the first UN undersecretary-general and special advisor to the secretary-general on Africa (1999–2005). Concurrent with that position, he was the resident special representative of the secretary-general and head of the UN Mission to Angola (2002–2003). He has been assigned to a number of trouble spots around the world as a roving UN emissary and commissioner. He has also been recognized as one of the few UN leaders who have been able to negotiate with some success with dictators, having been assigned to deal with leaders in places like Myanmar, Zimbabwe, and Sudan. Given his proclivity to negotiate with dictators, Gambari was a natural fit for helping in the Darfur crisis.

On January 1, 2010, UN secretary-general Ban Ki-moon appointed Gambari as the joint UN-AU special representative for Darfur amid the continuing strife and genocide in western Sudan's Darfur region. In July 2011, Gambari was appointed as interim chief mediator of the peace agreement being negotiated in Doha, Qatar, between Darfurian rebel groups and the government of Sudan. He played an active role in creating the Liberation and Justice Movement (LJM), a coalition of ten rebel groups that stepped in when the Justice and Equality Movement (JEM) refused to continue its negotiations with Khartoum.

In early 2012, Gambari traveled to neighboring Chad to seek President Idris Déby's support for a possible splintering of JEM commanders located on the North Darfur–Chad border. He had hoped that a further weakening of JEM would allow the newly formed LJM greater autonomy and influence. Gambari has been engaged in very delicate talks with Sudanese president Omar Hassan Ahmed al-Bashir in an effort to nudge him toward a comprehensive peace settlement, a job that has been greatly complicated by Bashir's indictment for war crimes by the International Criminal Court (ICC).

The efforts to achieve a lasting peace using the Doha Document for Peace in Darfur (DDPD) have proved illusory, but

Gambari remained optimistic when he issued a statement upon the conclusion of his post in Darfur on September 11, 2012. He praised the goals and objectives outlined and agreed upon in the DDPD and urged all parties involved to ensure its full implementation.

Since his work in Darfur, Gambari has gone on to employ his negotiating skills in other conflicts, such as serving as the special adviser on the International Compact with Iraq. He is currently the founder/chair of the Savannah Center in Abuja, Nigeria, a think tank for research, training, and public policy debate on conflict resolution, democracy, and development in Africa.

Paul G. Pierpaoli Jr. and Alexis Herr

See also: African Union; Annan, Kofi; Bashir, Omar Hassan Ahmed al-; Bassolé, Djibril; Doha Document for Peace in Darfur; Justice and Equality Movement; Liberation and Justice Movement

Further Reading

Brockman, Norbert C. 1994. *An African Biographical Dictionary.* Santa Barbara, CA: ABC-CLIO.

Kiernan, Ben. 2007. *Blood and Soil: A World History of Genocide and Extermination from Sparta to Darfur.* New Haven, CT: Yale University Press.

Sørbø, Grunnar M., and Abdel Ghaffar M. Ahmed, eds. 2013. *Sudan Divided: Continuing Conflict in a Contested State.* New York: Palgrave Macmillan.

Garang, John

John Garang was an important rebel leader who fought for more than twenty years to secure South Sudan's independence. The charismatic commander of the Sudan People's Liberation Movement/Army (SPLM/A), Garang led the fight against the government of Sudan during the Second Sudanese Civil War (1983–2005). Prior to his death, he earned a reputation as a fearless leader, brave fighter, and adept politician; however, his influential legacy is not without controversy.

An ethnic Dinka, he was born on June 23, 1945, as the sixth child of seven in a poor Christian family in Wanglei village, in the upper Nile region of Sudan. Owing to the destruction and dislocation caused during the First Sudanese Civil War (1955–1972), Garang attended school in Tanzania. In 1962, at the age of seventeen, Garang attempted to drop out of school to join the Anyanya (a southern Sudanese separatist rebel army), but instead he was urged by its leader to finish his schooling. A bright and hard-working student, he won a scholarship to attend college in the United States, and by 1969, he had earned a bachelor's degree in economics from Grinnell College in Iowa. After he graduated, the University of California, Berkeley, offered him a graduate fellowship, which Garang declined. Instead, he returned to Tanzania, where he obtained a research fellowship at Dar es Salaam University.

After the Addis Abba Peace Accords brought the First Sudanese Civil War to an end in 1972, Garang returned to Sudan and joined the Sudanese armed forces. In short order, he was promoted to the post of colonel and then sent to attend the U.S. Army Infantry Officer's Advanced Course at Fort Benning, Georgia, in 1974. While serving in the Sudanese armed forces, he took a four-year leave to earn a master's degree in agricultural economics, followed by a PhD at Iowa State University in economics.

In May 1983, the Sudanese armed forces sent Garang to Bor, the capital of Jonglei in southern Sudan, to quell a mutiny of 500 southern troops resisting orders to be shipped north. Instead of putting down their mutiny, he joined his brother officers Samuel Gai Tut, William Nyuon, and Keribino Kuanyin Bol, and from this nucleus formed the Sudan People's Liberation Movement (SPLM)—the "political wing"—and the Sudan People's Liberation Army (SPLA)—the "military wing." Garang became the chairman of the SPLM and commander in chief of the SPLA. By the end of July, he had persuaded over 3,000 soldiers to defect to the SPLA, as other army garrisons at that time were engaging in acts of mutiny against the imposition of Islamic Sharia law by the Muslim-dominated government in Khartoum.

The resistance efforts of the SPLM sparked the Second Sudanese Civil War (1983–2005). From 1983 onward, the government in the north were seeking to rein in the southern rebels as armed conflict, famine, disease, massive destruction, and genocide ravaged Sudan. The civil war had a religious dimension as well, with the Christian and animist peoples of the south suffering at the hands of the Muslim north. The war led to the death of upward of 2.5 million people, placing Sudan near the top of the list of post-1945 death statistics for single-country conflicts.

While the roots of this civil war reach back to the times of colonization, the antagonism of the north toward the south was reinforced in 1983, when President Gaafar Muhammad an-Nimeiry rescinded the autonomy that had been granted to the south in the 1972 Addis Ababa Peace Agreement that had concluded (or paused, depending on who you ask) the First Sudanese Civil War. Henceforth, the north would rule by direct control, with the south's legislative chamber stripped of even its most basic powers. Resource management became a wholly

northern concern, and Islamic Sharia law was introduced throughout the Christian south.

In 1985, two months after the overthrow of President Nimeiry, the transitional president, General Abdel Rahman Suwar al Dahab, looked to Arab tribes in Darfur to intensify the fight against Garang's SPLA. Garang and the SPLA had already infiltrated Kordofan in Darfur. Dahab thus dispatched the minister of defense, General Fadlalla Burma Nasir, to Kordofan to mobilize Darfurian Arab tribes (namely, the Baggara) to attack the SPLA. In return for supporting the government attacks on the SPLA, they were permitted to seize cattle and goods from Dinka and Nuba suspected of supporting the SPLA. The government backed militias in Darfur, known as *Murahaliin* (nomads) or *Fursan* (horsemen), quickly gained a reputation as violent and merciless attackers. News of their actions caught public attention in April 1987, when they shot and burned to death more than 1,000 Dinka in Da'ien (in southeastern Darfur) in response to a series of battles in which the SPLA had killed 150 Baggara Rizeigat (Flint and de Wall 2008: 23–24).

By 1986, the SPLA was estimated to have 12,500 armed men, organized into twelve battalions and equipped with small arms and mortars—much of it from Garang's backers in Libya, Uganda, and Ethiopia. Support grew even more by 1989, when the SPLA's numbers had reached anywhere from 20,000 to 30,000. By 1991, it was estimated that this had risen even further, to between 50,000 and 60,000.

In 1989, following a coup d'état, a new government was installed in Khartoum under a northern radical Islamizer, Omar Hassan Ahmed al-Bashir. He shared power with the civilian leader of the National Islamic Front, Dr. Hasan al-Turabi. Together, they transformed Sudan into an even more fundamentalist Islamic society and intensified the war against the south. Garang refused to enter into negotiations so long as this forced attempt to Islamize southern Sudan remained Khartoum's goal.

While some explanations for the massive number of deaths focus on the destructive nature of the civil war—and it was, certainly, a conflict in which little quarter was given—there is nonetheless enough circumstantial evidence to be able to lay a charge of genocide at the feet of the Bashir government. Throughout the entire period, Bashir's government went out of its way to destroy unarmed southern civilian populations through killing, displacement, expulsion, starvation, and other means.

Initially, the SPLA relied on support from the regime of President Mengistu Haile Mariam in Ethiopia, but his fall in 1991 led to the loss of this base. Fortune was to favor Garang, however. The fact that the United States regarded Bashir's government as a leading sponsor of international terrorism, in which the master terrorist Osama bin Laden was alleged to have been given refuge in Sudan, only served to throw U.S. support behind anyone willing to oppose Khartoum. Accordingly, it has been reported that in 1996, the United States sent nearly $20 million worth of military equipment through Ethiopia, Eritrea, and Uganda to help the Sudanese opposition overthrow Bashir.

The Sudanese government was also known to have made half-hearted attempts to lure Garang into a peace settlement, but he always declined, on the basis that doing so would leave the people of the south vulnerable to northern economic exploitation and religious and ethnic persecution. A painfully slow negotiating process did take place, however, as both sides accepted that they were deadlocked in a war that neither could win.

In July 2002, Garang and Bashir met for the first time in Uganda, and a breakthrough occurred when the south was granted the right to hold a referendum on its future after a six-year transition period. The SPLA agreed to put its demand for secession on hold, and in return, the Sudanese government agreed to a limited separation between religion and the state and to withdraw most of its troops from the south.

The peace process dragged on for another eighteen months, during which haggling took place over how the south's oil revenues would be split in the future. In May 2004, a provisional agreement was signed, and, as a reward, the Arab League pledged $2 billion to help rebuild the south. The Comprehensive Peace Agreement (CPA) that followed, also known as the Naivasha Agreement, was signed on January 9, 2005, between the SPLA and the Sudanese government, providing for Garang's appointment as vice president of Sudan in a power-sharing arrangement that allowed limited autonomy for southern Sudan and a scheduled referendum of possible secession within six years. On July 9, 2005, after twenty-one years of struggle, Garang reentered Khartoum to a rapturous welcome and was sworn in as vice president (as Bashir continued to cling to the presidency).

Less than three weeks later, in late July 2005, Garang was returning by helicopter from a visit to Rwakitura, the country home of his longtime ally, Ugandan president Yoweri Museveni. In circumstances the full details of which are yet to be fully determined, the helicopter crashed, and Garang and all on board were killed. At first, there was uncertainty as to what the effect of Garang's death might be on the Naivasha Agreement, but the peace held sufficiently to enable a referendum to take place from January 9 to 15, 2011, to determine whether the region should remain part of Sudan or become independent. On February 7, 2011, the referendum commission published the final results, with 98.83 percent voting in favor of independence. Accordingly, on July 9, 2011, the Republic of South Sudan became Africa's newest independent country, and the 193rd member-state of the United Nations.

Garang's leadership helped bring about an independent South Sudan; however, his methods have received criticism by some, and his character has been the subject of debate. His enemies portrayed him as a dictator and accused him of executing his rivals. His friends described him as a jokester with a great sense of humor. Some have claimed that his intelligence and military training made him a ruthless and skilled manipulator. Perhaps the most poignant criticism of Garang centers on the SPLA's use of child soldiers. The SPLA was not the only militia group capturing and forcibly recruiting children, but Garang's use of young boys has earned him criticism from human rights groups.

Paul R. Bartrop and Alexis Herr

See also: Child Soldiers; Comprehensive Peace Agreement; Fur; Khartoum; Lost Boys and Girls of Sudan; Religion; South Sudan

Further Reading

Deng, Francis Mading. 1995. *War of Visions: Conflict of Identities in the Sudan*. Washington, DC: Brookings Institution Press.

Flint, Julie, and Alex de Waal. 2008. *Darfur: A New History of a Long War*. New York: Zed Books.

Lacey, Marc. 2005. "Sudan and Southern Rebels Sign Pact to End Civil War." *The New York Times*. January 1.

Rolandsen, Øystein H., and M. W. Daly. 2016. *A History of South Sudan: From Slavery to Independence*. Cambridge: Cambridge University Press.

Gosh, Salah Abdallah

Salah Abdallah Gosh was an important general in the Sudanese army, and until 2009, he was the head of Sudan's national security and intelligence apparatus. He was also a supporter of President Omar Hassan Ahmed al-Bashir's regime, established in Sudan in 1989, and has been charged with instigating the Darfur Genocide.

Gosh was born in Nuri, in northern Sudan, and brought up in the city of Port Sudan. He belongs to the Shaigiya tribe. Because of his involvement in espionage and counterintelligence, the details of Gosh's life remain fragmentary. He apparently studied engineering at the University of Khartoum, graduating in 1981. There, he became involved in Sudan's Muslim Brotherhood, and he soon created an intelligence bureau to keep the movement's leaders informed of political happenings within the university. After graduation, he became involved in intelligence work for the National Islamic Front, while simultaneously working as a civil engineer.

After Bashir took power in Sudan via a coup in 1989, Gosh became a full-time intelligence officer and operative. As such, he made important contacts with militant Islamists throughout the Middle East. In fact, he played a key role in helping to establish Osama bin Laden's Al-Qaeda headquarters in Sudan between 1990 and 1996. In 1995, however, Gosh was removed from his intelligence position when Sudan was accused of having plotted to kill Egypt's president, Hosni Mubarak. Gosh took a position as director of a military arsenal in Yarmouk, Syria, but by the late 1990s, he had been made chief of internal security for Sudan. In the early 2000s, he was named director of the Sudanese National Intelligence and Security Services.

In 1999, when the Islamic movement split, Gosh remained loyal to al-Bashir and the National Congress Party. However, he also came to be seen as a loose cannon and clashed with some of the party's leadership. When the Darfur rebellion began in 2003, Gosh played a central role in creating and equipping government militias, which in turn perpetrated many atrocities against unarmed civilians. In 2006, the United Nations listed Gosh as one of at least seventeen Sudanese officials who were involved in perpetrating the Darfur Genocide.

About the same time, Gosh appeared to be playing both ends against the middle, allegedly having significant contacts with American and British intelligence agencies, providing information on radical Islamists in the region. Although American officials have not commented on these developments, it is believed that the Central Intelligence Agency (CIA) flew Gosh to Washington in 2005 on a counterterrorism mission. Gosh himself claimed to have helped U.S. intelligence efforts in Somalia and Iraq, although that cannot be proven.

Beginning as early as 2008, after the International Criminal Court (ICC) handed down an indictment for war crimes against al-Bashir, Gosh is thought to have begun plotting a change in regime that would bring Ali Osman Muhammad Taha to power. In 2009, Bashir, now suspicious of Gosh's loyalty, fired him as intelligence chief, but he made him a presidential adviser for national security in an attempt to keep him in line. Gosh apparently continued to plot behind the scenes, however, and in November 2012, amid growing unrest, Bashir ordered that Gosh be arrested and jailed. He was eventually released and started a business importing petroleum and chemical products between Sudan and the Gulf. In his early sixties, Gosh was appointed by President Bashir on February 11, 2018, as head of the National Intelligence and Security Service.

Two days after President Bashir was ousted from power in April 2019, Gosh stepped down as intelligence chief. At this time, it is unclear if he was forced out by rival security chiefs and military generals or if he did so voluntarily.

Paul G. Pierpaoli Jr.

See also: Bashir, Omar Hassan Ahmed al-; British Involvement in Darfur; United States Involvement in Darfur

Further Reading
Crockett, Richard. 2010. *Sudan: Darfur and the Failure of an African State.* New Haven, CT: Yale University Press.

Natsiosis, Andrew S. 2012. *Sudan, South Sudan, and Darfur: What Everyone Needs to Know.* Oxford: Oxford University Press.

H

Harun, Ahmad

Ahmad Mohammed Harun (known as Ahmad Harun), Sudan's minister of humanitarian affairs, was charged by the International Criminal Court (ICC) on March 31, 2005, for crimes committed between August 2003 and March 2004. The ICC prosecutor accused Harun of having conducted war crimes and crimes against humanity in Darfur while serving as Sudan's minister of the interior.

Harun was born in 1964 in Sudan's North Kordofan state, which borders North Darfur to the west and Khartoum state to the east. He belongs to a Sudanese tribe of West African descent known as the Bargou. Before beginning his political career, Harun attended Cairo University in Egypt, where he trained to become a judge. However, Harun eschewed his legal career in 1990 to join the National Intelligence and Security Service of Sudan, where he served until 2005.

While Harun earned a reputation during the 1990s as a rising political star within the ruling National Congress Party—an offshoot of the Muslim Brotherhood that came to power in June 1989 during a military coup—in the public eye, he earned a less-flattering moniker: "the butcher of Nuba." Before Harun entered Sudanese politics in 1995, he orchestrated a massacre in Kordofan's Nuba Mountains. This campaign of violence bears a striking resemblance to the later campaign in Darfur, characterized by the targeting of Nuba civilians, forced displacement, rape, and the weaponizing of famine. Harun was involved in the recruitment of local people into militias that staged such attacks against the Nuba, experience that he would use again as Sudan's minister of the interior.

President Omar Hassan Ahmed al-Bashir appointed Harun to his cabinet as minister of the State for the Interior of the Government of Sudan in May 2003. In this position, he was allegedly in charge of the management of the so-called Darfur Security Desk, and thereby coordinated the police, armed forces, National Security and Intelligence Service, and the Janjaweed militia attacks in Darfur. When the Sudan Liberation Army (SLA) attacked military instillations in Darfur, Harun helped direct the government's genocidal response. For the next two years, Harun recruited, funded, and armed the notorious Janjaweed militias of Darfur and encouraged them to commit widespread atrocities against SLA combatants and civilians.

While Harun has not denied that atrocities have taken place in Darfur, he refuses to accept responsibility for them. In February 2007, the ICC issued an international warrant for his arrest, which has been ignored by the Sudanese government. The ICC presented convincing evidence pointing to Harun's extensive knowledge of and involvement in the atrocities, including eyewitness accounts of Harun delivering arms and funds to Janjaweed fighters in his personal helicopter. According to the ICC, Harun traveled extensively in Darfur with large, well-guarded boxes of cash drawn from a limitless budget that was not publicly audited.

Other incriminating evidence against Harun includes his own public comments and speeches. According to the ICC inducement, he gave a speech in August 2003 in the town of Mukjar before a large gathering of Janjaweed, calling for indiscriminate attacks against all civilians—even children. This speech was followed almost immediately by a massive attack on the town. Earlier public speeches referred to his "power and authority to kill or forgive whoever in Darfur," to "cleaning" operations, and to being prepared "to kill 3/4 of Darfur." In 2004, Harun told the United Nations (UN) Commission of Inquiry on Darfur that "the villages are like water to fish" and explained that his objective was to remove the water in order to kill the fish.

In a 2006 cabinet shuffle, President Bashir appointed Harun to the position of minister of humanitarian affairs, making him responsible for the well-being of the more than 2 million refugees that his campaign of violence had created. His controversial appointment has been generally viewed as an intentional snub of the government's international critics. In a similar maneuver in September 2007, Bashir named Harun—already a wanted war criminal—to lead the investigation into human rights abuses committed in Darfur.

The ICC alleges that Harun, by virtue of his high-ranking position, had full knowledge of the crimes committed against civilians by the different bodies of the government and the Janjaweed militia. The prosecutors contend that his public speeches demonstrate that he commissioned and encouraged the attacks on civilians and the pillaging of villages and towns. Further, due to his position at the Darfur Security Desk, he is charged with having recruited, armed, and funded the Janjaweed militia attacks in Darfur. The charges consist of twenty-two counts of crimes against humanity (which include

murder and persecution) and twenty-eight counts of war crimes (which include planned attacks on civilians, rape, and destruction of property).

On April 27, 2007, the ICC issued an arrest warrant for Harun. In May 2010, the Pre-Trial Council for the Harun case informed the UN Security Council that Sudan has failed to cooperate with their arrest requests. Amid mounting protests, President Bashir resigned as leader of his political party, the National Congress Party, in March 2019 and appointed Harun as his successor. Following the overthrow of Bashir a month later, both Bashir and Harun were arrested.

David Paige and Alexis Herr

See also: African Union–United Nations Mission in Darfur; Bashir, Omar Hassan Ahmed al-; Fur; Janjaweed; Massalit; National Islamic Front; Nuba; Rape; Sudan People's Liberation Movement/Army

Further Reading

Flint, Julie, and Alex de Waal. 2006. *Darfur: A Short History of a Long War*. London: Zed Books.

Hagan, John, and Wenona Rymond-Richmond. 2009. *Darfur and the Crime of Genocide*. New York: Cambridge University Press.

Schabas, William. 2016. *The International Criminal Court: A Commentary on the Rome Statute*. Oxford: Oxford University Press.

Totten, Samuel. 2010. *An Oral and Documentary History of the Darfur Genocide*. 2 vols. Santa Barbara, CA: Praeger Security International.

Hilal, Musa

Musa Hilal, an Arab tribal leader from northern Darfur, is a former Janjaweed leader and chairman of the Revolutionary

Awakening Council. He is a key perpetrator of crimes against humanity, ethnic cleansing, and genocide in Darfur.

Hilal was born in 1961, and his family is a major member of the Arab Mahameed clan. Allegations have been made that Hilal's father relocated the clan to the Amu region of Darfur in 1976 after he acquired land originally owned by so-called black Africans through forgery and bribing a local official.

In 1997, Hilal was arrested, allegedly for killing seventeen black Africans, but the charge did not stick, and no conviction was recorded. However, he was convicted in 1998 for leading an armed robbery against the Central Bank of Nyala, during which a policeman was killed. Hilal served his sentence in a number of prisons around Sudan, always under tight security.

Hilal was again detained during 2002–2003 on the orders of Abdullah Safi al-Nour, the then-governor of North Darfur, who was concerned over increased ethnic tension in the region. In early 2003, Hilal was imprisoned in Port Sudan, but in April 2003, with the outbreak of the Darfur conflict, the government of Sudan released him to help recruit and command militia forces and thereby crush the armed rebellion of the Sudan Liberation Movement (SLM). It is believed that Sudan's first vice president, Ali Osman Mohamed Taha, and the chief of the air force, Major General Abdullah Safi al-Nur, helped to secure his release. Shortly thereafter, he convened a meeting with the top leaders of Arab tribesmen in Darfur, during which he ordered them to attack and burn black African villages (as opposed to those claiming to be ethnically Arab) and to loot the residents' livestock.

Starting in 2003, the Sudanese government troops and Janjaweed carried out widespread ethnic cleansing and genocide against black Africans in Darfur. Initially, the Sudanese government and Janjaweed retaliated against rebel groups of Sudanese blacks who had attacked government installations and the provincial capital of El Fasher as a result of their frustration over the discrimination and marginalization that they were experiencing at the hands of the government. Instead of merely attacking the rebel groups, however, government forces and the Janjaweed carried out wholesale attacks on the villages and farms of Sudanese blacks in Darfur, indiscriminately killing men, women, and children; raping young girls and women; and, prior to burning down hundreds of entire villages, plundering what they could. By 2011, estimates of the dead ranged from 250,000 to over 400,000, with over 2 million internally displaced and another 250,000 subsisting in refugee camps in Chad.

From an early date in the conflict, Hilal's name has been closely associated with the killing. In 2004, the U.S. State Department identified him as one of the top Janjaweed leaders running a terror campaign in Darfur against the black African population, and in a purported meeting that took place in Khartoum with a U.S. diplomat, Hilal allegedly provided detailed information on the Sudanese government's support of the Janjaweed militias in Darfur. In a videotaped interview with Human Rights Watch in 2004, Hilal claimed that the Sudanese armed forces were responsible for the attacks in Darfur, but he did admit he played a key role in recruiting Janjaweed militiamen. At this time, he denied having performed any acts that could be considered crimes against humanity or war crimes.

In April 2006, the United Nations Security Council imposed financial and travel bans against Hilal, having identified him as one who was obstructing peace in Darfur, and pursuant to this action, U.S. president George W. Bush issued an executive order enforcing U.S. sanctions against him. In response, Hilal threatened that should he be indicted, he would fight anyone who tried to hand him over to an international court.

Such international action was not long in coming. In February 2007, the prosecutor of the International Criminal Court (ICC) in The Hague named Hilal for having made a racist and inflammatory speech in July 2003, although he was not yet identified as a war crimes suspect. It was shown that Hilal was enthusiastic about the Arabs of Darfur and Sudan unifying to fight the common enemy, and that he characterized the conflict as a jihad, or holy war. From 2006 onward, international pressure has been urging the Sudanese government to give Hilal to the ICC.

On January 18, 2008 (in a decision announced publicly two days later), Sudanese president Omar Hassan Ahmed al-Bashir appointed Hilal as the new chief adviser to the Ministry of Federal Affairs in Sudan. This position would allow him to coordinate with regional leaders surrounding Darfur, as well as with Arab tribal groups, on relations with the government in Khartoum. It also gave him some measure of authority over decisions made in Khartoum relating to the recruitment of Janjaweed for Sudanese government purposes.

It has been reported that over the years, he met on numerous occasions with militia leaders to coordinate attacks on Fur and Zaghawa villages and has been accused of kidnapping women. On February 27, 2008, Eric Reeves, an American chronicler of the Darfur Genocide, reported the destruction of thirty villages, the assassination of 200 people, the rape of over 200 girls and women, and the kidnapping of 150 women and 200 children. These actions, Reeves argued, were executed by Janjaweed militias acting on Hilal's orders.

There is much about Hilal that is internally contradictory. In an interview with Human Rights Watch on September 27, 2004, he stated clearly that he was "not a criminal." Hilal refuses to accept that he is a military leader or part of the Sudanese armed forces, but he has repeatedly said his fighters are engaged in a jihad. At the same time, he has upheld claims that Janjaweed actions are not spontaneous or directed by him, but rather are organized and directed from Khartoum under President Bashir. A former Janjaweed recruit, called up to join the Janjaweed in 2003 with the lure of earning 60 pounds a month and getting a gun, stated in a press interview that Hilal commanded the Janjaweed in Island Mustariha, in northern Sudan. Witnesses have related accounts of militia members who committed atrocities in Hilal's name, and Hilal was seen at the site of attacks in North Darfur in February and March 2004. It was common knowledge that he was often transported around the country by Sudanese government helicopters, and eyewitnesses have confirmed that he was both uniformed and armed by the Sudanese military.

In a report published in *The New York Times* on June 12, 2006, Hilal was quoted as having said in 2004 that his militias should aim to "change the demography of Darfur and empty it of African tribes." More recently, Hilal has been known to blame the ruling regime in Khartoum for the atrocities that took place in Darfur, and to have expressed regret for the acts committed since 2003.

On November 27, 2017, Hilal was detained by the Sudanese government militia Rapid Support Forces (RSF) after he killed its director of general supplies, Brigadier Abdel-Rahim Gumma, in Mistiriyha,

Darfur. Despite efforts to disarm militia groups in Darfur, Hilal has refused to comply with all the terms of the 2011 peace agreement. He was arrested along with his sons, brothers, and members of his entourage and transferred to Khartoum to await trial.

In May 2018, his trial began, and the charges laid against him may be punishable by death if he is convicted. The Sudanese president and National Congress Party leader Bashir was deposed in April 2019, and to date, Hilal is said to still be in a Sudanese prison, waiting for the conclusion of his trial.

Paul R. Bartrop

See also: Bashir, Omar Hassan Ahmed al; Janjaweed; Jihad; United States Involvement in Darfur

Further Reading

Deng, Francis Mading.1995. *War of Visions: Conflict of Identities in the Sudan.* Washington, DC: Brookings Institution Press.

Holt, P. M., and Martin Daly. 2000. *The History of the Sudan, from the Coming of Islam to the Present Day.* New York: Longman.

Human Rights Watch. 2005. *Entrenching Impunity: Government Responsibility for International Crimes in Darfur.* New York: Human Rights Watch. Available at https://www.hrw.org/sites/default/files/reports/darfur1205webwcover.pdf.

Hussein, Abdel Raheem Muhammad

Abdel Raheem Muhammad Hussein is Sudan's defense minister, and he has been charged by the International Criminal Court (ICC) with war crimes and crimes against humanity in Darfur. Hussein was born in northern Sudan, near Dongola; the exact date of his birth is undetermined. The ICC arrest warrant for Hussein estimated that in 2012, he was over sixty years old.

It was in secondary school in 1964 that Hussein first met the future president of Sudan, Omar Hassan Ahmed al-Bashir. Hussein went on to a career in the Sudanese air force, during which time he was involved with the Islamist Muslim Brotherhood. He played an important role in the 1989 Islamist coup that elevated Bashir to power, and he subsequently served as secretary-general of the Revolutionary Command Council, which ruled Sudan until its powers devolved to President Bashir in 1993. Hussein served as minister of the interior (1993–2005) and simultaneously was Bashir's special representative in Darfur (2003–2004). He is alleged to have worked directly with Osama bin Laden and Al-Qaeda during bin Laden's tenure in Sudan (1992–1996).

Atrocities committed during Hussein's term as presidential representative in Darfur drew international attention and condemnation, especially after the ICC issued arrest warrants for President Bashir himself, charging him with war crimes, crimes against humanity, and genocide in Darfur. On March 1, 2012, the ICC issued a warrant for Hussein's arrest on twenty-one counts of war crimes (including murder, attacks on civilians, and rape) and twenty counts of crimes against humanity (including murder, forcible transfers of civilians, rape, imprisonment or severe deprivation of liberty, and torture).

The ICC warrant charged Hussein with formulating and implementing a counterinsurgency plan with a core component of unlawful, coordinated attacks by Sudanese armed forces and Janjaweed militias against civilian populations presumed to be associated with rebel groups. The charges against

Hussein elucidate an unbroken chain of command, from Janjaweed leader Ali Kushayb, who led the attacks on the ground, to former interior minister Ahmad Mohammed Harun, who coordinated militia attacks and reported to Hussein, who in turn reported to President Bashir. For its part, the Sudanese government dismissed the charges, declaring that it had not been a party to the statutes establishing the ICC and therefore did not recognize the court's authority.

In April 2019, as President Bashir was overthrown from power and put in prison, the Sudanese media reported that Hussein had also been arrested in a sweep by the military against Bashir's inner circle. At this time, it is unclear how the transitional government plans to address Hussein's crimes.

Karl A. Yambert

See also: Bashir, Omar Hassan Ahmed al-; Clooney, George; Kushayb, Ali; Satellite Sentinel Project

Further Reading

Cheadle, Don, and John Prendergast. 2007. *Not on Our Watch: The Mission to End Genocide in Darfur and Beyond.* New York: Hyperion.

Flint, Julie, and Alex de Waal. 2006. *Darfur: A Short History of a Long War.* London: Zed Books.

Ibrahim, Khalil

Khalil Ibrahim (1957–2011) was the founder and the leader of the Justice and Equality Movement (JEM) until his death. He was born in Darfur as a member of the Zaghawa tribe in 1957. Trained as a physician, Ibrahim supported the National Islamic Front (NIF) party that seized power in Sudan in 1989.

Ibrahim worked for the NIF in a number of regional posts, including the ministries of health, finance, and education in North Darfur. As early as the mid-1990s, however, he became disaffected with the Islamist regime due to its withdrawal of economic and educational support from Darfur and for its arming of Arab militias.

Ibrahim turned to other varieties of activism. He was an anonymous coauthor of *The Black Book: Imbalance of Power and Wealth in Sudan,* an exposé on the imbalance of power in Sudan that favored the residents of the northern region at the expense of all other Sudanese. In August 2001, Ibrahim announced the formation of JEM, whose program favored a unified Sudan but called for radical constitutional reform and equitable redistributions of power and wealth. Its embrace of Islamic law for Muslims distinguished JEM from the secular Sudan Liberation Army (SLA), with which JEM cooperated in loosely allied military operations. Chad and Libya provided JEM with political and financial support.

In May 2006, the Sudanese government and the SLA faction led by Minni Minawi signed the Darfur Peace Agreement (DPA) in Abuja, Nigeria. Ibrahim rejected the DPA as merely a partial and divisive solution to the Darfur conflict. The next month, he helped found the National Redemption Front, an alliance of groups in Darfur that were fighting for a federal system of regional self-rule and a just system for sharing wealth and power among Sudan's regions.

JEM forces attacked Omdurman in May 2008. Omdurman is the second-largest city in Sudan and is located on the western banks of the Nile River, opposite the capital city of Khartoum. They were eventually forced to retreat, but the assault showed the rebel group's ability to strike at the heart of the regime. JEM and the government signed a preliminary agreement in February 2010, by which JEM would attain seats in the Khartoum government and become a recognized political party. However, within two months, the agreement disintegrated amid mutual accusations of violating the ceasefire and stalling the peace process.

The neighboring nation of Chad had been a backer of the JEM insurgency, but it withdrew its support after it normalized relations with Sudan in 2010. That February, Chad expelled JEM forces, including Ibrahim. He moved to Libya, where he was suspected of lending mercenary support to the embattled Libyan leader Muammar Gaddafi. After the murder of Gaddafi in October, Ibrahim returned to Sudan. In November, JEM joined the newly formed Sudan Revolutionary Front (SRF), whose stated objective was no longer constitutional reform, but instead the overthrow of the Bashir regime. JEM joined SRF belatedly, only after negotiating with the front's secular members about the contentious issue of the proper role of Islam in a postrevolutionary Sudan. Ibrahim died on December 24, 2011, from wounds suffered while fighting government forces.

Karl A. Yambert

See also: Itno, Idriss Déby; Justice and Equality Movement; Minawi, Minni; Sudan Liberation Army

Further Reading

Flint, Julie, and Alex de Waal. 2006. *Darfur: A Short History of a Long War.* London: Zed Books.

Totten, Samuel. 2010. *An Oral and Documentary History of the Darfur Genocide.* 2 vols. Santa Barbara, CA: Praeger Security International.

Itno, Idriss Déby

Idriss Déby Itno (prior to 2006, he used the surname Déby) is a Chadian politician who has ruled his country as its president since December 2, 1990. The politics of Chad are closely linked to Sudan, in part because of Itno's relationship with the government of Sudan and the fact that the two countries share a border that runs along the Darfur region.

Itno was born on June 18, 1952, in Fada, Chad, then part of French Equatorial Africa (1913–1960). His family belongs to the Zaghawa ethnic group located in the Ennedi region of northeastern Chad. He joined the army in the early 1970s to participate in Chad's civil war, and in 1976, he traveled to France, where he received additional training at a flight school. When Itno returned to Africa two years later, Chad was still embroiled in war, and he lent his support to Hissène Habré, then prime minister; over time, he became the leader of Habré's military forces. In 1982, thanks in part to Itno's military successes, Habré seized power and became president. Habré then promoted Itno to commander in chief of the armed forces, and three years later, Itno returned to France to attend senior officer training at the École Supérieure de Guerre.

In April 1989, Itno fled from Chad to Sudan when Habré accused him of trying to overthrow his government. From his base in Darfur, Itno started launching attacks into Chad. As Habré's forces launched counterattacks into Darfur, Libya rearmed Itno, and the Sudanese government helped him remobilize 1,200 Chadian Arab militiamen. By 1990, Habré fled the country, and Itno's forces, the Patriotic Salvation Movement, seized the Chadian capital of N'Djamena. In short order, Itno formed a new government, appointed himself its head, and suspended the constitution. He has been in power ever since.

When the Darfur Genocide began in 2004, thousands of Sudanese refugees fled to Chad to escape the violence. In late March 2004, Itno offered to host a mediation in N'Djamena between the government of Sudan and the rebel groups representing the interests of the Darfurian victims. Under Itno's guidance, the involvement of Western nations as observers was minimized. In fact, Itno allowed Western observers to attend only the first sessions dealing with humanitarian concerns, and they were excluded from the political talks that followed. A political agreement was signed on April 25, 2004, but it was broken before the ink even dried. Some have asserted that the failure of this agreement was due in large part to the less-than-neutral mediation of President Itno. In January 2012, Itno married the daughter of Musa Hilal, the leader of the feared Sudanese Janjaweed militia.

While Chad and Sudan have not always been on the best terms, a week before Omar Hassan Ahmed al-Bashir was deposed as president of Sudan in April 2019, Itno and Bashir met to discuss continued cooperation between their nations. Since Bashir's overthrow, President Itno met with the UN secretary-general, António Guterres, the following September, wherein he confirmed the continued support of the United Nations (UN). This statement was welcome, given that to date, the United Nations has established twelve camps in Chad that support more than 500,000 persons, including refugees, asylum seekers, and internally displaced persons (IDPs).

Alexis Herr

See also: Janjaweed; United Nations Commission of Inquiry on Darfur; Zaghawa

Further Reading

Totten, Samuel, and Eric Markusen, eds. 2006. *Genocide in Darfur: Investigating the Atrocities in the Sudan*. New York: Routledge.

J

Janjaweed

Janjaweed is an informal name for the armed militias that since 2003 have been the principal perpetrators of the Darfur Genocide. Known by a colloquial Arabic expression that roughly means "mounted horseman," the Janjaweed has become infamous for riding into African farming settlements after bombing raids by the Sudanese air force, massacring the men, raping the women, and stealing anything they can get their hands on. This mass slaughter, characterized by some international observers as genocide and by others more broadly as war crimes, has forced millions of Darfurians to flee to refugee camps.

The militia's members hail primarily from a few traditionally nomadic, Arabic-speaking Abbala and Baggara tribes—camel and cattle herders, respectively—and are often lighter-skinned than most of Darfur's sedentary population. Despite the Janjaweed's Arab-supremacist ideology, *Arab* is a misleading term in Darfur, where nearly the entire population is black as well as Muslim, including those defining themselves as Arab. While Western media has dramatized the conflict in Darfur as a showdown between Arabs and Africans, many Darfurians defining themselves as Arab do so primarily on the basis of their communities' use of Arabic and on their pastoralist way of life. Many of the tribes in Darfur defining themselves as ethnically Arab are not associated with the Janjaweed.

A modern incarnation of the age-old nomadic Arab militia known as *murahaliin* (nomads), the origins of today's Janjaweed reach back to 1988, after former Chadian president Hissène Habré, aided by French- and U.S.-backed forces, drove Libyan president Muammar Gaddafi's invading militia out of Chad into Darfur. There they stayed through the 1990s, continuing to espouse their Arab-supremacist ideology and gathering weapons. Their small-scale territorial incursions at the expense of Darfurian farmers were largely ignored by the Sudanese government in Khartoum.

The conflict between Arab and non-Arab Darfurian groups escalated during 1999–2000, when rebels in Darfur—namely, the Sudan Liberation Army (SLA) and Justice and Equality Movement (JEM)—began to demand more support from the Sudanese government in Khartoum. In February 2003, rebels stepped up their attacks against government installations, and Khartoum responded with a counterinsurgency campaign that involved recruiting, organizing, and providing weapons to the Janjaweed militia. While the campaign aimed to destroy the SLA and JEM, as part of its strategy, the government also orchestrated the Janjaweed's scorched-earth campaign against unarmed, non-Arab civilian populations, particularly those of the Fur, Zaghawa, and Massalit ethnic groups, which are those most associated with the Darfur rebel movements. The Sudanese government has largely denied its role in this campaign; however, the evidence contradicting these denials, beginning with thousands of eyewitness accounts, is overwhelming.

According to a report commissioned by the United Nations (UN) and published in

2005 (see "Excerpts from the United Nations Commission of Inquiry on Darfur (January 25, 2005)," in the "Primary Documents" section of this book), the Janjaweed militia is comprised of three main categories, determined by their affiliation with the Sudanese government. The first category includes militia groups that are loosely affiliated with the government and have received supplies and weapons from Khartoum. They have led attacks at the request of the government and have acted on their own initiative for personal gain. The second category is organized in paramilitary structures, some of which are headed by Sudanese army officers and controlled by senior tribal leaders. The third category includes members of the Popular Defense Force (PDF), a paramilitary group supported by the government, and Border Intelligence, a paramilitary unit of Janjaweed forces created by President Omar Hassan al-Bashir, who fight alongside regular armed forces. The UN commission established that all three categories of Janjaweed fighters have a strong link with the government of Sudan.

In 2005, the International Criminal Court (ICC) started investigating key leaders of the Janjaweed, and in 2007, it issued arrest warrants for Ali Kushayb and Musa Hilal. The ICC also examined Abdel Raheem Muhammad Hussein and scrutinized his role in coordinating the crimes of the Janjaweed in his capacity as a leader of the Sudanese government's forces. Subsequently, the court issued an arrest warrant for him in 2012. As evidenced by the ICC's investigations into Hussein, the Sudanese government's military forces have partnered with the Janjaweed on attacks in Darfur by providing air and ground support.

The union of Janjaweed and governmental forces produced the Rapid Support Forces (RSF). In 2013, President Bashir established the RSF, in what some have called nothing more than a rebranding of the Janjaweed. It has been suggested that Bashir created the RSF to maintain his control of violence in Darfur as his relationship with Hilal became unstable.

In a dramatic reversal of power dynamics, the RSF has played an essential role in the toppling of Bashir in April 2019. Prior to the coup, Bashir referred to the RSF commander, General Mohamed Hamdan "Hemeti" ("Little Mohamed") Dagolo, as "Himayti" (my protector) because the RSF answered directly to Bashir. Dagolo had joined the Janjaweed militia in 2003 and quickly gained a reputation for leading violent attacks against "non-Arab" Darfurians and instigating systematic rape campaigns in the name of jihad. After being tasked to lead the RSF in 2013, he continued to spearhead violent incursions in South Kordofan, the Blue Nile states, Darfur, and central Sudan.

In September 2013, the RPF allegedly killed at least 200 protesters in Khartoum. But according to a recent appearance on television, Dagolo claims that when Bashir instructed him in April 2019 to open fire on the protesters, he refused. Since Bashir's arrest, Dagolo has continued to use his considerable influence to guide the structure and goals of the transitional government (Tubiana 2019). Some fear that he will try to take power for himself, at the expense of peace in Sudan.

Melissa Stallings and Alexis Herr

See also: Hilal, Musa; Kushayb, Ali; Rape

Further Reading

Anderson, Scott. 2004. "How Did Darfur Happen?" *The New York Times*. October 17.

Deng, Francis Mading. 1995. *War of Visions: Conflict of Identities in the Sudan*. Washington, DC: Brookings Institution Press.

De Waal, Alex. 2019. "Sudan Crisis: The Ruthless Mercenaries Who Run the Country for Gold." BBC. July 20.

Tubiana, Jérôme. 2019. "The Man Who Terrorized Darfur Is Leading Sudan's Supposed Transition." *Foreign Policy.* May 14. Available at https://foreignpolicy.com/2019/05/14/man-who-terrorized-darfur-is-leading-sudans-supposed-transition-hemeti-rsf-janjaweed-bashir-khartoum/.

Jihad

Sharia law is the political system and body of laws that shape the Islamic religion. *Jihad,* the name of a component of Sharia (Islamic canonical law based on the Koran), literally means "to struggle" or "to strive" in Arabic. The government of Sudan has proclaimed a jihad to help galvanize militants to attack civilians and opposition groups, and in so doing justify state-sponsored murder in Darfur and south Sudan.

Despite popular discourse in Western media, particularly in the wake of the September 11, 2001, terrorist attacks in the United States, jihad is not synonymous with terrorism and violence. Instead, it may be associated with any activity that a Muslim performs that is in conformity with the will of Allah (the Arabic word for God). According to the Muslim faith, the Koran is God's word as dictated to and recorded by the Prophet Muhammad. According to the Koran, *jihad* has many meanings and can refer to both internal and external efforts to glorify God.

All Muslims are called to engage in different types of jihad, which include jihad of the heart, jihad of the mouth, jihad of the pen, jihad of the hand, and jihad of the sword. Each jihad is considered a fight against evil. Jihad of the heart is the struggle for moral reformation and faith and calls on Muslims to struggle against their sinful tendencies. Jihad of the mouth is the struggle to proclaim God's word through righteous speech. Jihad of the pen is the struggle to do good through the study of Islam, legal reasoning, and science. Jihad of the hand is the struggle to promote the cause of Allah against evil by accomplishing praiseworthy deeds.

Finally, jihad of the sword, perhaps the most contested of all, refers to armed combat on behalf of Islam; it is often linked with the word *qital* (Arabic for "fighting with a weapon to kill or subdue") in the context of dealing with nonbelievers. Not all Muslims agree on how to interpret jihad of the sword, with some believing that a jihad of the heart is the greater type of jihad and jihad of the sword a lesser type.

According to the Koran, a military jihad can be permitted only if it is intended to protect believers, strengthen Islam, protect the freedom of Muslims to practice their faith, protect Muslims against oppression, punish enemies who break an oath, and right a wrong. And the Koran has strict rules regarding attitudes of war, such as "Fight in the way of Allah against those who fight against you, but begin not hostilities. Lo! Allah loveth not aggressors" (Koran 2:190), and "But if the enemy incline towards peace, do thou (also) incline towards peace, and trust in Allah: for He is One that heareth and knoweth (all things)" (Koran 8:61). Not all those who practice the Muslim religion agree on how to interpret jihad and best honor its meaning.

In the hands of President Omar Hassan al-Bashir, the issuance of the jihad was wielded as a weapon to fuel hatred and spur violence. For example, in 1992, a jihad was issued against the southern rebels. Officially, the governor of South Kordofan state in Sudan declared the jihad, but its issuance was supported and conceived by Bashir and his ally, Hassan al-Turabi. The jihad helped the Sudanese government recruit young men to join the Popular Defense Forces (PDF), a paramilitary army established in 1989, which was waging war against the rebels in the south. Those who had been trained to fight against the south in training camps in the 1990s were later tasked by the Sudanese government to train Janjaweed soldiers to kill civilians and rebels in Darfur during the genocide there (Cockett 2010, 108, 190).

Alexis Herr

See also: Janjaweed; Nuba; Turabi, Hassan al-; South Sudan

Further Reading

Cockett, Richard. 2010. *Sudan: Darfur and the Failure of an African State*. New Haven, CT: Yale University Press.

Elass, Mateen. 2004. *Understanding the Koran: A Quick Christian Guide to the Muslim Holy Book*. Grand Rapids, MI: Zondervan.

Kelsay, John. 2015. "Jihad." In Gerhard Bowering, ed., *Islamic Political Thought: An Introduction*. Princeton, NJ: Princeton University Press, 86–104.

Jolie, Angelina

Angelina Jolie is an award-winning actress and humanitarian. In addition to her well-received film career, she is widely known for her work as a United Nations High Commissioner for Refugees (UNHCR) goodwill ambassador and a vocal advocate of humanitarian causes worldwide. Since the Darfur Genocide began, Jolie has called upon the United Nations and the United States to save Darfurians and stop the killing.

Born in Los Angeles on June 4, 1975, she is the daughter of the actors Jon Voight and Marcheline Bertrand. As a child, she attended the Lee Strasberg Theatre and Film Institute, followed by Beverly Hills High School. She went on to study drama at New York University, model, act, and appear in music videos.

During the filming of *Lara Croft: Tomb Raider* (directed by Simon West in 2001), much of which was shot on location in Cambodia, Jolie not only fell in love with the environment and culture of the country, she also became aware of the dire economic situation caused in large part to the Khmer Rouge regime's genocide there from 1975–1979. Wanting to learn more about the genocide and the plight of refugees, she reached out to UNHCR. The organization supported her inquiry and facilitated a series of field trips for the actress to various refugee camps around the world. In February 2001, she visited Sierra Leone and Tanzania, and soon she became actively involved in humanitarian causes. On August 27, 2001, she was appointed a UNHCR goodwill ambassador at the group's headquarters in Geneva, Switzerland.

The UNHCR appoints high-profile celebrities, often from the media or entertainment industry, as goodwill ambassadors that serve as its representatives and use their talent and fame to advocate on behalf of refugees. During her tenure as a goodwill ambassador from 2001 to 2012, Jolie worked hard to attract more attention to the plight of refugees. Among the many overseas trips that she made as an advocate for humanitarian causes, Jolie traveled through countries such as Pakistan, Sudan, and Chad to talk personally with internally displaced persons (IDPs) and refugees. She also visited refugee camps in Thailand and Kenya, and, in 2003, she undertook a six-day mission to Tanzania, where she investigated camps hosting

Congolese refugees on the western border. She inspected the situation of vulnerable people in Sri Lanka and the North Caucasus, as well as Iraqi refugees in Jordan and Sudanese refugees in Egypt. In June 2004, she flew to Chad to inspect refugee camps for those fleeing the genocidal policies of the government of Sudan against the people of Darfur, and a few months later, she went directly into Darfur itself. The same year, she also visited Afghan refugees in Thailand, and a year after that, she went to Pakistan to meet with Afghans closer to the scene who had fled the fighting in their country. All told, during her eleven-year tenure as a goodwill ambassador, she carried out nearly sixty filed missions and became an influential and leading advocate on refugee and displacement matters. And she has continued to do so since then, as the UNHCR appointed her a special envoy in April 2012, a role that she has filled to this day.

Jolie's energy and enthusiasm for visiting crisis areas around the world have been boundless. In the cause of raising the world's conscience through her own exposure to these situations, the list of places she has entered is so extensive that they would seem to defy categorization. She on more than one occasion has been to Haiti (where, after the earthquake in early 2010 that devastated that country, she and her former husband, Brad Pitt, donated $1 million to relief efforts); India (where she has met with Afghan and Burmese refugees in New Delhi); San José, Costa Rica (where she has talked with Colombian refugees); Syria; Iraq (again, to investigate the refugee situation); and, while filming the movie *Beyond Borders* (directed by Martin Campbell in 2003) in Namibia, she also took the opportunity to meet with Angolan refugees.

Beyond Borders focused on humanitarian aid workers during the 1980s and 1990s, and in many respects it is Jolie's personal manifesto on film. Set in Ethiopia, Cambodia, and Chechnya, it provides a dramatic perspective of the dangers and difficulties faced by aid workers in situations of war, genocide, and natural disasters. Besides Jolie, the movie stars British actor Clive Owen. In the United States, it received an R rating for language and war-related violence, the latter of which was re-created for the screen with impressive effectiveness. While critics responded negatively to what they perceived as a moralizing "issues movie," the passion for the cause that it attempts to portray shines through. In fact, on one level, *Beyond Borders* can be viewed as Jolie's call to arms for a world in danger. At the same time as the film's release, she published a book, *Notes from My Travels*, a collection of journal entries that chronicled her early field missions from 2001 to 2002 as a UNHCR goodwill ambassador. Despite its many merits, however, *Beyond Borders* was unsuccessful in the box office.

In the United States, Jolie has investigated the conditions of detained asylum seekers at the southern border in Arizona and has been closely involved in World Refugee Day events in Washington, D.C. She has worked hard on a range of lobbying activities and has conducted numerous meetings with members of Congress seeking the introduction of bills assisting refugees (especially relating to children at risk) in the Third World. In 2007, Jolie became a member of the U.S. Council on Foreign Relations.

The various initiatives introduced by Jolie include the National Center for Refugee and Immigrant Children, which she founded in 2005 with a personal grant of $500,000 to oversee its operations for its first two years. The center provides free legal aid to asylum-seeking children with no legal representation. Then, in 2006, Jolie and Pitt established the Jolie-Pitt Foundation (later renamed the Maddox Jolie-Pitt Foundation in honor of the couple's son, Maddox, whom they adopted from Cambodia), to alleviate extreme rural poverty, protect the environment, and conserve wildlife in rural northwestern Cambodia. At its launch, Jolie and Pitt also donated $1 million to Doctors Without Borders, $1 million to Global Action for Children, and an additional $1 million to aid groups working in Darfur. The foundation works with impoverished rural villagers and governments to alleviate food insecurity and provide access to basic primary health care and education.

In 2003, Jolie was the first recipient of the newly created Citizen of the World Award by the United Nations Correspondents Association, and in 2005, she was awarded the Global Humanitarian Award by the United Nations Association of the United States for her work with UNHCR and refugees. On August 12, 2005, Cambodia's King Norodom Sihamoni awarded Jolie Cambodian citizenship for her conservation work in that country. The International Rescue Committee has also bestowed upon Jolie a Freedom Award.

Jolie made her directorial debut in 2011 with *In the Land of Blood and Honey*, a film set during the 1992–1995 Bosnian war. In part, the movie was made to communicate the plight of survivors of that vicious conflict. Her next directorial effort, the 2014 movie *Unbroken*, received much attention and acclaim. In 2017, Jolie again wedded her film career to her humanitarian interests in *First They Killed My Father*, a movie she directed about the Cambodian Genocide.

Paul R. Bartrop

See also: Save Darfur Coalition

Further Reading

Jolie, Angelina. 2003. *Notes from My Travels*. New York: Pocket Books.

Jolie, Angelina. 2007. "Justice for Darfur." *Washington Post*. February 28.

Justice and Equality Movement

The Justice and Equality Movement (JEM), founded in 2000, is a largely Islamist Sudanese armed group operating out of Darfur and demanding regime change within Sudan. While sharing many of the same basic founding principles as the Sudan Liberation Army (SLA), particularly in its demands for greater regional autonomy and economic opportunity, JEM is distinct from the SLA in that it has firm roots in Islamist political ideologies. The organization is also notable for having a strong tribal affiliation with the Zaghawa people, whereas the SLA is not dominated by any one tribe and instead draws its ranks from a broad tribal base that includes the Fur, Massalit, and Zaghawa, among others.

JEM emerged as a distinct political entity in 2001 under the leadership of the Dutch-trained doctor and former Darfur government minister Khalil Ibrahim. Its formation was intricately tied to a 1999–2000 power struggle between Sudanese president Omar Hassan Ahmed al-Bashir and his former mentor, Hassan al-Turabi, then speaker of the National Assembly. During the peak of this dispute, a mysterious diatribe outlining the imbalance of power in Sudan known as *The Black Book* appeared in print in Khartoum, and soon thereafter, al-Turabi broke from the ruling National Congress Party to form the opposition Popular Congress Party (PCP). Ibrahim and other non-Arab Darfurian politicians joined al-Turabi in founding the PCP during this period and then went on to create JEM, adopting *The Black Book* as their political manifesto. While al-Turabi denies government claims that he is the puppet master behind JEM's rebellion, the organization's leadership is intricately linked with him and his PCP.

During early fighting in 2003, when the crisis in Darfur was beginning to escalate, Ibrahim told reporters that the goal of his movement was not secession, but rather to secure a role in government. The group had strongholds in several large towns in West Darfur, including Tina and Karnoi. In April, the group launched a major joint operation with the SLA against government installations in Darfur's principal cities of Nyala and El Fasher. In a major symbolic victory during the attacks, JEM forces captured Major General Ibrahim Bashra, head of Sudan's air force.

In October, some 1,000 JEM fighters launched another major assault, this time in the Kulbus district of West Darfur, killing dozens. They followed this in December with a second operation against the town in coordination with the SLA. The government of Sudan responded to the rapid expansion of rebel-held territory in January 2004, when it launched aerial bombardments against JEM's urban strongholds, including Tina and Karnoi, and followed these strikes with ground campaigns. As the government captured these towns, JEM was driven back into rural areas of West Darfur.

In April, JEM and SLA both agreed to a cease-fire, which was violated by the government within days. During this period of tense negotiations, JEM showed its first signs of fracturing, and by May, the first major rift in JEM ranks had occurred, leading to the creation of the rival National Movement for Reform and Development, led

by Colonel Gibril Abdel-Karim Bari. The Ibrahim-led faction of JEM, meanwhile, signed an alliance with the Free Lions, a rebel movement by the Rashaida (a tribe of nomadic ethnic Bedouin Arabs) in eastern Sudan, vowing to continue fighting until the current government was toppled. Soon thereafter, JEM was implicated in an alleged coup attempt led by al-Turabi.

JEM refused to sign a May 2006 peace deal brokered by the African Union (AU) between the government and one of the two major factions of the SLA. JEM has refused to back down from its conditions for peace: a Darfurian regional government, a vice presidential post, greater representation at the national level, a share of national oil revenue, and compensation for victims of government abuse. JEM's unwillingness to compromise on these points has earned it a reputation as one of the chief barriers to reconciliation, and the United States placed sanctions against Ibrahim in an effort to curb the group's ongoing violent activities.

Another splinter group, the JEM–Eastern Command, formed around Abdallah Banda Abbaker Nourain (commonly known as Abdallah Banda) in July 2007, after he was dismissed by Ibrahim from his position as JEM commander general on the grounds that he discriminated against non-Zaghawa JEM members. The continued disintegration of JEM into rival factions has earned its leaders a reputation of being unable to control their own forces—an unsurprising situation considering that the vast majority of JEM's leadership operates from exile in Europe. (Ibrahim himself commanded JEM from France until 2007.) Renegade JEM factions have been among the prime culprits in attacks against aid workers and AU peacekeepers in Darfur. Presently, Banda is wanted by the International Criminal Court (ICC) for his role in a 2007 attack against the African Union Mission in Sudan (AMIS), during which twelve AMIS soldiers were killed and eight were severely wounded.

In July 2011, JEM leaders refused to sign the Doha Document for Peace in Darfur (DDFP). Later that year, Ibrahim was killed by a government airstrike. Al-Tahir el-Feki, a local surgeon, filled in for Ibrahim until JEM leadership finally gathered and elected Khalil's brother, Jibril Ibrahim, its new chairman on January 26, 2012.

David Paige

See also: Banda, Abdallah; *Black Book, The;* Ibrahim, Khalil; Sudan Liberation Army; Turabi, Hassan al-; Zaghawa

Further Reading

Burr, J. Millard, and Robert O. Collins. 2003. *Revolutionary Sudan: Hasan al-Turabi and the Islamist State, 1989–2000.* Boston: Brill Academic Publishers.

Burr, J. Millard, and Robert O. Collins. 2006. *Darfur: The Long Road to Disaster.* Princeton, NJ: Markus Weiner.Flint, Julie, and Alex de Waal. 2006. *Darfur: A Short History of a Long War.* London: Zed Books.

K

Kapila, Mukesh

Mukesh Kapila served as the United Nations (UN) Resident and Humanitarian Coordinator for Sudan from 2003 to 2004. His vocal reproach of the Sudanese government's genocidal attacks in Darfur resulted in his transfer from Sudan just twelve months into his twenty-four-month assignment.

Born in India on April 4, 1955, he holds degrees in medicine, surgery, and public health from Oxford and London universities. His earlier career focus was in public health, although he is best known for his later work in international development and humanitarian affairs. Between 1987 and 1990, he served as deputy director of the first UK National AIDS Programme (which he helped create), and from 1990 to 2002, he worked at Britain's Department for International Development, where he became the first head of a new Department of Conflict and Humanitarian Affairs, which expanded greatly under his direction.

In 1994, within hours of the liberation of the Rwandan capital of Kigali by the Rwandan Patriotic Front, Kapila arrived as part of the first British team into the freed city. He then went to Goma in Zaire (now known as the Democratic Republic of Congo) to provide aid to Rwandan refugees. Other humanitarian assignments saw him at Srebrenica, Bosnia. In 2002, Kapila was appointed a special adviser to the UN special representative of the secretary-general in Afghanistan, and then special adviser to UN High Commissioner for Human Rights Sergio Vieira de Mello.

When Kapila took up his post as the UN Resident Humanitarian Coordinator, he became the top UN official in Sudan. He took on this role just a few months after Darfurian rebels had attacked military outposts in Darfur; the government's retaliation was so brutal that early UN human rights monitors feared that genocide was on the horizon.

Kapila's UN apparatus did not possess any international observers in Darfur, so it took some time to fully appreciate that what was happening was not an anomaly, but instead something that was systematic and catastrophic. From the middle of 2003, firsthand stories began to trickle out with the first displaced people arriving in Khartoum. Local UN personnel were also passing on reports to Kapila's office. As reports of atrocities mounted from late 2003 onward, Kapila began to see a pattern. Reports from UN workers and independent foreign aid organizations showed that Sudanese government forces and government-armed Arab militia members known as Janjaweed were using scorched-earth tactics against so-called black African civilians. Villages were being burned, wells poisoned, and women and girls were being raped. He was forced to conclude that what was taking place in Darfur was ethnic cleansing. As more information about the violence filtered in, he arrived at the view that he witnessing the first genocide of the twenty-first century.

Kapila's immediate reaction was that he should attempt to develop a deeper understanding of the violence in Darfur, having promised himself in his earlier assignments that if ever he were in a position of responsibility, he would do all he could to avoid genocide or massive human rights violations. He soon developed a more determined approach and began to work actively to stop the carnage.

In early 2004, Kapila informed his superiors at the UN headquarters in New York that genocide was occurring in Darfur. The response he received was that the United Nations had a humanitarian role to play in Sudan, and he should not get involved in politics. A second response was that the peace process was in the hands of powers other than the United Nations (although with that body's approval), and that little would be achieved by the Department of Political Affairs in New York getting involved.

Kapila was disgusted but not discouraged. He attempted to make the international community aware of the situation, beginning with the government of Sudan itself. He also spoke with members of the international community, starting with the foreign diplomatic corps stationed in Khartoum. From there, he began to make personal visits to governments. He first went to his own government in London, then to Washington, D.C., where he met with the National Security Council (NSC) in the White House, and then to Paris, Oslo, Brussels, Rome, and many other cities. In some countries, his discussions were at the ministerial level; in others, with senior bureaucrats. Wherever he went, he was told that the governments in question knew what was happening but that, because of the delicate negotiations then taking place to try to end the civil war between northern and southern Sudan, now was not the time to rock the boat by making a fuss over Darfur. Only in Washington did he obtain anything like a full hearing, although no concrete action was taken. The general attitude seemed to be that a greater provision of humanitarian aid was needed rather than resolving what were, in reality, political problems requiring immediate resolution.

In frustration, Kapila abandoned the route of normal international diplomacy. He went public, divulging to the media what he knew about Darfur and the treatment that his overtures in the capitals of the world had received. From Nairobi, Kenya, he conducted an interview with BBC Radio in March 2004, comparing the situation in Darfur to the 1994 genocide in Rwanda. His comments succeeded in bringing Darfur to the attention of the world's media for the first time. Newspapers around the world picked up the story, which was immediately challenged by the government of Sudan.

His outspokenness landed Kapila in trouble with the United Nations, and in April 2004, he was transferred out of Sudan, just thirteen months into a twenty-four-month assignment. His ongoing regret is that he left with his job only half done and failed to prevent the worst of what happened in Darfur.

After this, Kapila was taken on by the World Health Organization (WHO) as director in the Department of Health Action in Crises and adviser to the director general, and he remained in this capacity between 2004 and 2006. Since September 2006, he has been at the International Federation of Red Cross and Red Crescent Societies in Geneva, Switzerland, serving in different positions as a director and as special representative of the secretary-general. Among his many other activities in international development and humanitarian affairs, Kapila has been part of the World Bank Global Facility for Disaster Risk Reduction and Recovery and the UN International Strategy for Disaster Reduction, as well as serving on many other boards and executive committees. In 2006, he founded the Alliance for

Direct Action Against Rape in Conflicts and Crises.

Currently, he is professor of global health and humanitarian affairs at the University of Manchester, England. He is also chair of Nonviolent Peaceforce (a global nonprofit organization working to protect civilians in violent conflicts through unarmed strategies), founder and chair of Manchester Global Foundation (which works in fostering global health), adjunct professor at the International Centre for Humanitarian Affairs Nairobi, associate fellow of the Geneva Centre for Security Policy, special representative of the Aegis Trust for the prevention of crimes against humanity, special adviser to Syria Relief, and more.

In 2003, he was honored by his own government for his work in international humanitarian relief with the award of Commander of the Order of the British Empire (CBE) by Queen Elizabeth II, and in 2007, he received the Dr. Jean Mayer Global Citizenship Award from the Institute for Global Leadership.

Paul R. Bartrop

See also: African Union-United Nations Mission in Darfur; Khartoum; Sudanese Civil Wars; United Nations Commission of Inquiry on Darfur

Further Reading

Anderson, Scott. 2004. "How Did Darfur Happen?" *The New York Times.* October 17.

Burr, J. Millard, and Robert O. Collins. 2006. *Darfur: The Long Road to Disaster.* Princeton, NJ: Markus Weiner.

Khartoum

Khartoum is the capital city of Sudan and seat of the central government. Located in the northern region of Sudan, the city's name is derived from the Arabic word *al-Khurtum,* meaning "elephant's trunk." Although it comprises just over 5 percent of the entire country's population, the seat of government in Khartoum controls nearly all of Sudan. During the Darfur Genocide, as well as in the years leading up to it, the government in Khartoum issued decrees that brought about the destruction of the so-called non-Arab Darfurians. The geographical position and historical legacy of Khartoum offer important context to the genocide and what motivated it.

Located just south of the point where the Blue and White Nile rivers meet, Khartoum is located 666 miles from Darfur in the west. In the United States, this is almost equivalent to the distance between the cities of San Francisco and Portland, Oregon; however, the time spent traveling between the two points in the United States and Sudan is widely different. While someone in Portland can drive to San Francisco in ten to twelve hours depending on traffic, no all-weather road or railroad connects Khartoum to Darfur. As a result, the vast majority of Darfurians have never visited Khartoum, as the journey can take a week to months, depending on the time of year. Because of this, Darfur has remained isolated.

Khartoum's dramatic history lends context to the Darfur Genocide. The perceived differences between the wealthier residents of Khartoum and those in Darfur are rooted in the theory that people residing in the capital (this is excluding refugees and slaves from the hinterlands who have relocated to the city's slums) are descendants of the *awlad al-bahar* ("people of the river" in Arabic), Arab migrants who came to Khartoum in the sixteenth and seventeenth centuries. As a result, the political leadership of Khartoum identified itself as ethnically Arab, and the tribes in Darfur as predominantly African. This ambiguous distinction made between the so-called racial identity of capital residents as Arab and Sudanese living in the west, east, and south of Sudan as African has helped fuel conflict and genocide for decades.

After the Islamist coup d'etat of June 30, 1989, Sudan's new leader, Omar Hassan Ahmed al-Bashir, and his party, the National Islamic Front (which became the National Congress Party in 1998) sought to undo what centuries of intermarriage (forced or otherwise) between Arab descendants and Africans had accomplished. Through the efforts of Bashir and his party, the racial distinctions between those considered Arab and those considered African sparked new conflict between those in the Arab capital and those residing in peripheral regions like Darfur, whom the government called *zuruq* ("black") or the more pejorative *abid* ("slave"). This discrimination was used to justify the racially motivated killing, rape, and persecution of Darfurians by government-sponsored soldiers, troops, and militias like the Janjaweed. Although the vast majority of Sudanese are Muslim, the conflict between those in Khartoum and those outside it is couched in perceptions of race.

The genocide in Darfur occurred in part because the region's obscurity allowed perpetrators to commit crimes without fear of being discovered. Additionally, the lack of roads and infrastructure made it difficult for victims to escape their attackers who arrived on camel and horseback. The historical legacy of Arab settlers coming to Khartoum also set up a false pretext for Bashir to persecute black Africans, whom he viewed as inferior to Arabs.

Alexis Herr

See also: Bashir, Omar Hassan Ahmed al-; Darfur; Janjaweed; South Sudan; Sudan

Further Reading

Totten, Samuel, and Eric Markusen, eds. 2006. *Genocide in Darfur: Investigating the Atrocities in the Sudan.* New York: Routledge.

Kiir, Salva

Always seen in public with his trademark cowboy hat, Salva Kiir Mayardit (commonly referred to as Salva Kiir) is the current president of South Sudan, a position he has held since the nation seceded from Sudan in 2011. Within two years of taking office, however, Kiir was presiding over yet another civil war, which has the distinction of having created both a famine and the largest refugee crisis in Africa today.

Kiir was born in 1951 to a Dinka family in the Gogrial district of the small Bahr el-Ghazal province, located in northwestern South Sudan (then part of Sudan). He received an elementary school education at a Christian mission; there his formal education was concluded, but his Christian faith was not. At age nineteen, he joined the Anya Nya (a southern rebel movement that sought independence for the southern part of Sudan from the north) and fought in the First Sudanese Civil War (1955–1972). By the time President Gaafar Muhammad an-Nimeiry of Sudan signed the Addis Ababa Peace Agreement with the south Sudanese rebels in 1972, Kiir had risen to the rank of a low-level officer. With a cease-fire in place and a semblance of peace returning to the nation, Kiir joined the Sudanese army, and by the time the next civil war erupted in 1983, he had attained the rank of lieutenant colonel.

The Addis Ababa Peace Agreement ceased to exist after just a decade, and once again, the south and north found themselves locked in violent conflict. In 1983, President

Nimeiry nullified the peace agreement and imposed traditional Islamic law (Sharia) throughout Sudan, including in the mainly Christian and animist south, sparking a new rebellion. When Kiir and his friend John Garang were sent by Nimeiry to put down a mutiny among government troops in the south, they joined the rebels instead of fighting them, bringing together a number of resistance organizations to form the socialist-leaning resistance faction known as the Sudan People's Liberation Movement (SPLM).

Kiir and Garang were friends and close allies against the Sudanese government throughout the bloody Sudanese Civil Wars (1955–1972 and 1983–2005), which claimed some 2.5 million lives. A highly respected negotiator and military strategist, Kiir had a pragmatism and willingness to compromise in the interest of peace that were instrumental in negotiating the long-sought-after Comprehensive Peace Agreement (CPA) with Sudanese president Omar Hassan Ahmed al-Bashir, passed on January 9, 2005.

Known as a firm, direct, intelligent man who dislikes long speeches and ceremonial pomp, after assuming the vice presidency of Sudan in 2005 following the untimely death of Garang in a helicopter crash on July 10, just three weeks after being sworn in, Kiir pledged to maintain his friend's commitment to achieving peace and security in the south and working toward a united Sudan. Despite speculation that Kiir would not be able to maintain the support of southerners without Garang, he was initially received warmly, especially due to rumors that he would vote to secede from the Muslim north in the 2011 referendum that was stipulated in the 2005 CPA—a popular stance in the south. Initially, however, Kiir insisted that he wanted to keep the country united and pledged to focus on improving security and enacting

development initiatives in the south. Kiir also discussed with Khartoum a plan to end the massive conflict that has plagued the western Darfur region since 2003.

Although initial fears that the country would descend into sectarian violence following Garang's death were well founded, the transfer of power to Kiir was remarkably smooth. Despite his charisma and the support of the SPLM, Garang had not been popular with the southern public, and the SPLA's repeated violence toward civilians, intraorganizational feuds, notorious corruption, and suffocating control of local governments left traditional and community leaders with little or no power to effect change in their regions. Additionally, Garang had been known for making nearly all decisions independently, and in so doing, he provoked repeated criticism from members of his own party for his irresponsible management style. In fact, Kiir was often his most forceful critic, arguing endlessly for accountability.

Kiir was not only a harsh judge of Garang's leadership style, but also of the party itself, which is known for its strong-arm politics and resistance to peace initiatives. In 1999, he oversaw the signing of a covenant between the Nuer and Dinka tribes, despite strong opposition within the SPLA and indifference from Garang. To show his seriousness about creating peace between the groups, Kiir used a display of military force at the meeting and vowed to strike down anyone who challenged the proceedings. The alliance proved invaluable when government forces from the north attacked the oil-rich eastern banks of the Nile River just one year later, displacing tens of thousands of Nuer, who then were taken in by the Dinka people of Bahr al-Ghazal province.

One of Kiir's main priorities as the leader of South Sudan was overseeing the implementation of the referendum for independence. Although many southerners initially doubted whether he favored independence, he eventually made his support clear by refusing to run for the national presidency in the April 2010 elections. Instead, he sought election to the presidency of the south, which he won with an overwhelming majority. After the formal announcement of the referendum's success on February 7, 2011—98 percent of southerners voted for independence—Kiir said that a priority as president of the independent nation would be a war against corruption in his own government in order to help attract foreign investment. He also pledged cooperation with the north and said there would be freedom of movement between the two countries.

Despite his optimistic words, the South Sudan of today is far from the peaceful nation that South Sudanese had hoped and fought for. The possibility of uniting South Sudan after independence was never going to be easy owing to its size (it is larger than Kenya, Rwanda, and Burundi combined), immensely undeveloped economy, lack of infrastructure, and its diversity of some sixty-four ethnic groups who speak more than eighty languages. Kiir also faced mounting pressure between the SPLA and other southern rebel groups that quickly took on an ethnic character.

The escalating ethnic tensions that were playing out in Sudan came to a head in 2013, when Kiir accused Riek Machar, vice president and leader of the Sudan People's Liberation Movement (SPLM), of trying to overthrow the government. Kiir fired Machar and cleansed his cabinet of Machar's supporters, which ultimately took on the appearance of a Dinka (Kiir) removing ethnic Nuer (Machar) from the government. In short order, a civil war erupted between the Nuer and Dinka ethnic groups, and it has continued to claim innocent lives and destroy South Sudan's economy and society.

Alexis Herr

See also: Comprehensive Peace Agreement; Garang, John; Sudanese Civil Wars; Sudan People's Liberation Movement/Army

Further Reading

Deng, Francis Mading. 1995. *War of Visions: Conflict of Identities in the Sudan*. Washington, DC: Brookings Institution Press.

Flint, Julie. 2005. "Meet Salva Kiir, an SPLA Democrat." *The Daily Star*, August 9.

Terse, Nick. 2016. *Next Time They'll Come to Count the Dead: War and Survival in South Sudan*. Chicago: Haymarket Books.

Kristof, Nicholas

Nicholas D. Kristof is a dual Pulitzer Prize–winning journalist, author, and columnist for *The New York Times*, renowned for his in-depth reports focusing attention on the genocide in Darfur and other underreported human rights issues.

Born on April 27, 1959, in Chicago, he was raised in Oregon and educated at Harvard University and Magdalen College, Oxford. In 1984, Kristof joined *The New York Times* as an economics reporter, serving as a correspondent in Los Angeles, Hong Kong, Beijing, and Tokyo, until he was promoted to the position of associate managing editor. In November 2001, he began writing op-ed columns, often tackling issues relating to human rights abuses and genocide. As a journalist, Kristof has lived on four continents, reported on six, and traveled to over 140 countries.

Kristof won his first Pulitzer Prize for international reporting in 1990, after he and his wife, Sheryl WuDunn, reported on China's prodemocracy student movement and the related Tiananmen Square protests of 1989. WuDunn was the first Asian American to win a Pulitzer Prize for journalism, and they were the first married couple to do so. Kristof considers this period to have been the most formative period in his journalistic development. He realized that at this time, the idea of journalistic neutrality in the face of oppression was wrong and that he would have to take sides. In his view, he could not stand by as the students facing down government troops were being murdered simply for expressing their opinions. Since then, Kristof has become especially well known for his advocacy of human rights issues around the world, particularly in Asia and Africa. His concerns have embraced such matters as human trafficking, global health, poverty, gender issues, and genocide.

He has become a leading voice on the Darfur Genocide and a vocal critic on the lack of an effective response from the global community to this crisis. He first learned about Darfur in early 2004 from reports by Doctors Without Borders and the International Rescue Committee. Initially, his awareness was of a terrible situation brewing along the Sudan-Chad border. As it happened, there was another story he had wanted to do in Chad, so he decided to look into Darfur as well. When he arrived, he was told repeatedly that Darfurian villages were being destroyed by Janjaweed militias and the Sudanese army, and that men and boys were being killed and women and girls were being raped by these same forces. From this point on, Kristof has written dozens of columns exposing the atrocities taking place in Darfur. After publishing his first articles on Darfur, Kristof was upset that inaction remained the world's response. Determined to continue exposing what was happening,

he decided to return to Darfur two months after his first trip to see how the crisis had escalated. It was the start of what became a one-man campaign to raise awareness of the Darfur situation through the pages of *The New York Times*.

After covering the genocide for several years, Kristof has detected some measure of change, at least with regard to global awareness. On the ground in Darfur, however, he views the situation as just as hopeless for the victims now as it was when the killing began. On a personal level, Kristof has experienced considerable frustration at seeing how slowly things change, and especially how difficult it is to translate concern into positive action. Over many years of observing and reporting on international affairs, he has come to the conclusion that intervention can occur more easily in the early stages of a conflict than later.

Indeed, Kristof is most concerned about the reluctance of governments to get involved in stopping genocide. Genocide, he has concluded, rarely rises to the top of governments' priorities, whether it concerns the Armenian Genocide, the Holocaust, the Rwandan Genocide, or the Bosnian Genocide. In this regard, he has been critical of the mass media for not focusing sufficiently on genocidal governments.

Throughout the 2000s and right up to the present, Kristof has shown himself to be a distinctive voice in the mainstream media, a journalist-as-activist who employs his column as a vehicle for social justice. For his powerful series of articles on Darfur, Kristof won his second Pulitzer Prize in 2006. (Earlier, he had been a finalist for the Pulitzer in 2004.) Then, in 2009, the Brooklyn-based filmmaker Eric Daniel Metzgar produced and directed *Reporter*, a documentary focusing on Kristof that showed him and two young colleagues working in the Democratic Republic of Congo. Kristof's reporting style was revealed as a model of where international broadcast journalism might be heading in the future. Kristof shows in this film how witnessing and reporting on the world's atrocities can lead people to act, as was the case for actor George Clooney. *Reporter* was nominated for the Grand Jury Prize at the Sundance Film Festival in 2009. The same year, Kristof and WuDunn were awarded the Dayton Literary Peace Prize's Lifetime Achievement Award, and in 2010, Kristof was notable in his calls for immediate action to stave off the prospect of a new genocide taking place in southern Sudan.

Kristof continues to be a voice for the voiceless in Sudan and has been actively reporting on the overthrow of Bashir in April 2019. In an article published in October 2019, he reflected on some of the stories that during his nearly thirty-five years of reporting at *The New York Times* he described as being "particularly meaningful to me." The Darfur Genocide is one of the ten stories that he profiles. Reflecting on his experience meeting with victims, he writes, "Darfur showed me the evil that humans are capable of—and the indifference of most of the international community. Yet the ordinary citizens of Darfur showed extraordinary strength . . ." (Kristof 2019).

Paul R. Bartrop

See also: Clooney, George; Prendergast, John; Rape; Save Darfur Coalition

Further Reading

Anderson, Scott. 2004. "How Did Darfur Happen?" *The New York Times*. October 17.

Kristof, Nicholas. 2019. "In a Career of Reporting, These Are the Stories That Still Touch Me." *The New York Times*. October 1.

Available at https://www.nytimes.com /2019/10/01/opinion/kristof-new-york -times.html.

Totten, Samuel. 2010. *An Oral and Documentary History of the Darfur Genocide*. 2 vols. Santa Barbara, CA: Praeger Security International.

Kushayb, Ali

Ali Muhammad Ali Abd-al-Rahman (commonly known as Ali Kushayb) was a top commander of the Janjaweed militias in the Darfur region of western Sudan. In April 2007, the International Criminal Court (ICC) in The Hague, Netherlands, issued a warrant for his arrest, pursuant to charges of war crimes and crimes against humanity stemming from his involvement with and leadership in attacks against civilians during village raids throughout Darfur from August 2003 to March 2004.

While details of his early life remain unclear, Kushayb is thought to have been born in the mid-1950s. He is of mixed tribal origin; his father was a member of the cattle-herding Taisha (Taicha) tribe of southwestern Darfur, while his mother was part of the Dangaoui tribe of South Sudan. Kushayb's first known work was as a soldier in the Sudanese army. Although it is unclear how Kushayb was able to gain local power, it is known that he became an important tribal leader in the Wadi Salih area of the Sudanese state of West Darfur. He is also known to have been involved with the Popular Defense Force or PDF (a paramilitary force that reports to the government of Sudan) in Darfur. From August 2003 to March 2004, he was considered the *aqid al-ogada* (colonel of colonels) for the PDF in the Wadi Salih region and a top commander of the Janjaweed forces. He was also called an "emir of the mujahideen"—a leader of Muslim religious militants—and is thought to have personally recruited and commanded thousands of militia members.

Kushayb became an important intermediary between Janjaweed forces in Darfur and the government of Sudan and is thought to have been in direct contact with the government regarding operations targeting civilian populations in the region. According to local sources, he coordinated efforts with local police and government officials, including the Garsila town commissioner Ja'afar Abdul el Hakh (the current governor of West Darfur since 2005), and he was given a satellite phone and a vehicle to make himself more available. He allegedly orchestrated attacks on numerous villages between August 2003 and March 2004, targeting local populations of ethnic Fur, Massalit, and Zaghawa. Troops under his command raped, killed, tortured, imprisoned, and forcibly expelled civilians from many villages and destroyed large amounts of property and livestock during the attacks. Eyewitnesses said Kushayb was personally present at many of the attacks and played an active role in the atrocities. From February to March 2004, forces under his command carried out a series of executions and mass burials that were intended to be a form of ethnic cleansing.

In response to early charges against Kushayb stemming from these attacks and executions, the Sudanese government issued a warrant for his arrest in April 2005, which most see as merely a move by Khartoum to improve its international image. In November 2006, the government arrested Kushayb and kept him in custody until October 2007. At that time, government officials issued a statement claiming that he had been released, although no other details were offered. The ICC Pre-Trial Chamber I issued an arrest warrant for Kashyab on April 27, 2007. The arrest warrant from the ICC is still outstanding, and Sudanese officials have refused to comply with it because Sudan is not a signatory of the ICC.

Evan Brown

See also: Harun, Ahmad; Janjaweed

Further Reading

Burr, J. Millard, and Robert O. Collins. 2006. *Darfur: The Long Road to Disaster.* Princeton, NJ: Markus Weiner.

Flint, Julie, and Alex de Waal. 2006. *Darfur: A Short History of a Long War.* London: Zed Books.

L

Liberation and Justice Movement

International mediators scrambled to bring together a coalition of ten Darfurian rebel factions in February 2010, when the Justice and Equality Movement (JEM) walked away from peace negotiations with the government of Sudan being held in Doha, Qatar. The coalition, known as the Liberation and Justice Movement (LJM), helped bring about a peace treaty that slowed, but did not stop, the genocide in Darfur. The role of LJM in the peace process and the coalition's formation by the international community have been the focus of much criticism and praise (and, thus, debate). Since the signing of the Doha Document for Peace in Darfur (DDPD) in July 2011, the LJM has unwound, and some of its former groups have been absorbed by JEM.

LJM was an umbrella group of ten movements. Unlike JEM, a key player in advocating and fighting for Darfurian lives, LJM was a small coalition of splintered rebel factions, and some of its leaders had not resided in Darfur for decades. Dr. Tijani Sisi, who had served as governor of Darfur in the 1980s, was selected by the international community to lead LJM. While Sisi was a prominent intellectual among the Darfur diaspora, he had spent the last few decades living in exile, and thus was not as engaged in the conflict in Darfur or as influential as a JEM leader would have been. Prior to leading LJM, Sisi had been living in Addis Ababa, Ethiopia, and working for the United Nations Economic Commission for Africa.

After years of working toward a peace treaty with JEM, when JEM walked away from negotiations, LJM stepped in as a Band-Aid measure put in place by international representatives (namely, the Qatari government and a mediation team from the African Union–United Nation mission to Darfur). The international players involved thought that LJM would be more flexible and open to negotiations with the government of Darfur. While this may have been true, not all members of LJM were willing to bend to the priorities of the government of Sudan or the international community involved. For example, in March 2011, some of the military strongholds of LJM left the coalition, including the Sudan Liberation Army–Justice (SLA-Justice) and the Sudan Liberation Army–Field Leadership (SLA-Field Leadership). After the departure of the SLA-Justice and SLA–Field Leadership, as well as defections from some Massalit leaders and troops, the LJM's main military force was the United Resistance Front.

The eventual Doha peace treaty signed by LJM and the government of Sudan had serious flaws, the most significant of which was that it contained no clear language as to how to deal with violations of the treaty. Implementation of the DDPD has been and continues to be limited. Positive steps included the appointments of some LJM leaders to different governmental positions. Haydar Galukoma, for example, a Massalit leader and member of LJM, was appointed as governor of West Darfur. While appointments such as that of Galukoma do demonstrate a step in the right direction, the financial commitments of the international community and government of Sudan noted in the DDPD have not been fulfilled.

What has become clear in the years since LJM signed the DDPD is that the agreement was focused on peacekeeping, not peacemaking. According to Al-Tahir al-Feki, a senior JEM official, the DDPD was nothing more than a meaningless cease-fire agreement without any authority. However, the Sudanese vice president, Ali Osman Muhammad Taha, viewed the Doha treaty as an important step that would give moment to peace efforts in Darfur.

Alexis Herr

See also: Doha Document for Peace in Darfur; Justice and Equality Movement; Massalit; Sudan Liberation Army; Sudan People's Liberation Movement/Army; United Nations Mission in the Sudan

Further Reading

"Darfur Rebel Alliance Makes Peace with Sudan." BBC. March 18, 2010.

Sørbø, Grunnar M., and Abdel Ghaffar M. Ahmed, eds. 2013. *Sudan Divided: Continuing Conflict in a Contested State.* New York: Palgrave Macmillan.

Lost Boys and Girls of Sudan

In the context of conflict in Sudan, the phrase *Lost Boys* refers to a group of young boys displaced during the Second Sudanese Civil War. The media images of these unaccompanied boys walking barefoot across rough African terrain, desperate to survive and hopeful for a peaceful existence, have become an indelible manifestation of the human spirit and a raw image of how children suffer in areas of immense conflict. While boys have been the focus of the young refugee group, girls were also among the masses of children fleeing the conflict; for this reason, the phrase *Lost Girls* is just as relevant.

The combination of war, famine, and disease has killed more than 2 million and displaced more than 4 million Sudanese since the second civil war between the north and south erupted in 1983. Some fled to southern cities like Juba; others trekked as far north as Khartoum and even into Ethiopia, Kenya, Uganda, Egypt, and other neighboring countries. Those refugees were unable to grow food or earn money to feed themselves, and malnutrition and starvation were widespread. The government's de facto scorched-earth policies, which aimed to divide and conquer the already internally divided militia groups, extended the fighting throughout the south, with devastating results. Male children were subjected to the horror of witnessing their families being slaughtered before their eyes as militia or rebel groups forced them into military conscription. Females of all ages were put into slavery, raped, and/or killed, and entire villages, including cattle and crops, were burned to the ground.

Beginning in the late 1980s, roughly 26,000 Sudanese boys, mostly from the Dinka and Nuer tribes and predominately Christian, were compelled to flee their villages to escape the bloodshed and forced recruitment as child soldiers. Snaking their way through Sudan, hordes of boys aged five through approximately thirteen gathered in a massive confluence in the hope of finding safety. The Lost Boys (so dubbed by aid workers after Peter Pan's cadre of orphans) fled their homeland on foot across 1,000 miles of rugged and dangerous terrain to a refugee camp in Ethiopia. The trek through the sub-Saharan heat and wilderness took two months.

Many of the boys perished along the way, having succumbed to heat exhaustion, dehydration, starvation, and attacks from lions, crocodiles, and other wild animals. The boys ate whatever they could, and when there was no water, they would suck liquid from mud. As a result, some of the boys died from eating poisonous leaves or drinking dirty water. Occasionally, aid from the International Committee of the Red Cross and other humanitarian groups would be flown in for the boys, but the civil war would most always interfere.

Once in Ethiopia, the boys spent three years in camps until civil strife in that region forced them to flee once again. Chased by the Ethiopian military in tanks and by other militia groups, the boys frantically tried to cross the River Gilo. Thousands of the Lost Boys drowned, were eaten by crocodiles, or were shot. Those who survived the river crossing began the arduous journey back through Sudan to Kenya, which was a common destination for thousands of African refugees forced from their homes by war or natural disaster.

Walking for more than a year, only 10,000 of the original 26,000 boys arrived at the Kakuma Refugee Camp in 1992. The majority of the survivors were now between the ages of eight and eighteen (most did not know their age and were given approximate ages). Many still live at the camp in Kenya, while others have been placed around the world in programs to help them acclimate to new surroundings and survive on their own.

As the civil war continued to ravage south Sudan, international aid agencies like the International Rescue Committee (IRC) and the United Nations High Commissioner for Refugees (UNHCR) worked to resettle thousands of the Lost Boys. UNHCR determined that repatriation and family reunification were no longer viable or realistic options and thus recommended that 3,600 be resettled in the United States. The United States welcomed nearly 4,000 Lost Boys in 2001, and the IRC helped resettle them in Atlanta, Boston, Dallas, Phoenix, Salt Lake City, San Diego, Seattle, and Tucson. Many have gone on to attain U.S. citizenship, graduate high school and then college, and start new families.

In 2003, the feature-length documentary *Lost Boys of Sudan* made its debut. The movie featured the stories of two Sudanese refugees, Peter Nyarol Dut and Santino Majok Chuor. It has won numerous awards and helped turn the name *Lost Boys* into a phrase widely associated with the violence in Sudan.

While films, memoirs from Lost Boys, and popular media have helped disseminate stories of male adolescent refugees, it is important to tell the less discussed story of the girls that were among the youths fleeing violence in Sudan. It is estimated that of the nearly 4,000 refugees resettled in the United States, just 89 of them were female. This statistic, however, misrepresents the much larger number of girls who also walked thousands of miles and faced countless challenges before reaching relative safety in Kenya.

Unlike boys, girls were discouraged from telling their stories of flight and abuse to rescue workers, in part because of the stigma around sexual violence and rape. When girls reached the age of twelve or thirteen in the camp, they were typically prevented from attending school and forced into marriage against their will. For this reason, they fell through the cracks of humanitarian assistance and became the "property" of their spouses.

The film *The Good Lie* (2014), starring Academy Award–winning actress Reese Witherspoon, has helped bring much needed attention to the plight of these girls and young women. Sasha Chanoff, the executive director and founder of Refuge-Point, served as an adviser on the film. Chanoff created RefugePoint (previously known as Mapendo) to help refugees like the Lost Girls whom the international aid community has overlooked.

Alexis Herr and Regina Rainwater

See also: Child Soldiers; South Sudan; *What Is the What*

Further Reading

Burr, J. Millard, and Robert O. Collins. 2003. *Revolutionary Sudan: Hasan al-Turabi and the Islamist State, 1989–2000.* Boston: Brill Academic Publishers.

Holt, P. M., and Martin Daly. 2000. *The History of the Sudan, from the Coming of Islam to the Present Day.* New York: Longman.

Park, Linda Sue. 2010. *A Long Walk to Remember.* New York: Houghton Mifflin.

M

Massalit

The Massalit (also spelled *Masalit*) constitute an ethnic group of approximately
330,000 people who are concentrated in the
Dar Massalit district of Northern Darfur
province in Sudan, as well as across the border in the Adré district of Chad. Another
25,000 Massalit live farther west, in the Oum
Hadjer-Am Dam region of Chad. Tens of
thousands of other Massalit have migrated in
recent years to points in eastern Sudan, such
as in Khartoum and the Gedaref and Kassala
states. During the Darfur Genocide, Janjaweed forces and the Sudanese military targeted the Massalit for annhiliation.

Most Massalit live as nuclear families in
villages composed of conical wood and
thatch houses. They speak a language that is
part of the Maba division of the Nilo-Saharan
linguistic family. Most Massalit are bilin-
gual, speaking both Massalit and Arabic.
Tribal tradition places their origins in Tuni-
sia in North Africa, from where they
migrated through Chad to Sudan. Most Massalit are small farmers, raising millet and
peanuts. In the southern reaches of Massalit
territory, the farmers also raise sorghum,
okra, sesame, mangoes, and coriander. In
recent years, increasingly large numbers of
Massalit young men have taken to seasonal
migration to towns and cities in eastern
Sudan, where they labor for cash. Although
there are still elements of pre-Islamic religious rituals in Massalit culture, the people
are becoming increasingly orthodox in their
religious devotion. Their conversion to Islam
began in the seventeenth century, when
traveling holy men reached the Massalit
communities.

In the early 1990s, the Massalit were in a
state of warfare with the neighboring Fur
peoples of Sudan. During the Darfur Genocide in the early years of the twenty-first
century, they were one of the three main
groups of so-called black Africans, along
with the Fur and Zaghawa, that were targeted by the Sudanese government and Janjaweed militias.

James S. Olson

See also: Fur; Janjaweed; Zaghawa

Further Reading

Flint, Julie, and Alex de Waal. 2006. *Darfur:
A Short History of a Long War*. London:
Zed Books.

Holt, P. M., and Martin Daly. 2000. *The History of the Sudan, from the Coming of Islam
to the Present Day*. New York: Longman.

Olson, James S. 1996. *The Peoples of Africa:
An Ethnohistorical Dictionary*. Westport,
CT: Greenwood Press.

McGrady, Tracy

Tracy Lamar McGrady is a former professional basketball player for the National
Basketball Association (NBA). He has also
been actively involved in humanitarian
efforts dealing with the Darfur crisis and
genocide. McGrady has played for the Toronto
Raptors, the Orlando Magic, the Houston Rockets, the New York Knicks, the
Detroit Pistons, and the Atlanta Hawks. In

October 2012, he signed a one-year agreement to play for the Chinese Basketball Association's Qingdao Eagles and then officially retired in 2013. Since retiring, he has worked as a basketball analyst for ESPN.

McGrady was born on May 24, 1979, in Bartow, Florida. He attended Auburndale High School, in Auburndale, Florida, averaging 23.1 points and 12.2 rebounds in basketball as a junior in 1995. In May 1996, Alvin Jones, basketball coach at neighboring Kathleen High School, told Joel Hopkins, basketball coach at Mount Zion Christian Academy in Durham, North Carolina, about McGrady. Hopkins gave McGrady a basketball scholarship and much stricter discipline. McGrady averaged 28 points, 9 rebounds, and 8 assists in 1996.

McGrady skipped college to play professional basketball. The Toronto Raptors selected the 6-foot-8-inch, 210-pound shooting guard in the first round as the ninth pick overall of the 1997 NBA draft. During his thirteen-year career playing professional basketball in the United States and China, McGrady played shooting guard and small forward. He also signed a lucrative contract with Nike and donated $300,000 to his alma mater, Mount Zion Christian Academy.

In the midst of his professional successes in the mid-2000s, McGrady became active in relief efforts for the victims and survivors of the Darfur Genocide in western Sudan. He joined a growing number of high-profile celebrities and entertainers, including the actors George Clooney and Matt Damon, who sought to bring the bloodshed to the world's attention and to support genocide survivors. McGrady visited various refugee camps for displaced Darfurians in Chad, working with the Enough Project. In 2009, McGrady also made a documentary that followed his movements in Chad during a 2007 visit, entitled *3 Points*. He has also recruited several NBA players to help support an adopt-a-school project named the Darfur Dream Team, which links U.S. schools and universities with schools in the Darfurian refugee camps. Between 2008 and 2014, the program raised over $1 million for primary school education for Darfurian refugees in eastern Chad. In the process, the Darfur Dream Team project engaged over 350 high schools and universities throughout the United States. While the program concluded in 2014, its impact has endured.

David L. Porter

See also: Clooney, George; Damon, Matt; Enough Project

Further Reading

Crothers, Tim. "Onward Christian Soldier." *Sports Illustrated* 86 (February 10, 1997): 40–44.

Crothers, Tim. "A Tough Question." *Sports Illustrated* 87 (December 29, 1997–January 5, 1998): 55–59.

Minawi, Minni

Suliman Acrua Minawi, known as Minni Minawi, is a Sudanese politician and the leader of a principal faction of the Sudan Liberation Army (SLA) known as SLA-MM, one of the rebel groups in Darfur fighting for greater autonomy for the region.

Minawi was born on December 12, 1968, in Shamal Darfur, Sudan, to a Zaghawa family. Prior to joining the SLA, Minawi had been living with his uncle, Bahr el Arabi, in Nigeria, had a secondary school education, and had no prior experience in either civil politics or combat.

In 2001, leaders of the Fur and Zaghawa tribes agreed to work together to oppose Arab supremacist policies in Darfur. Abdel

Wahid of the Fur was chosen as the chair of what would become the SLA, while Abadallah Abakir of the Zaghawa became deputy chair. Minni Minawi was named Abakir's secretary, chiefly because he could read and write. SLA rebels soon scored successes against government garrisons, at which time Minawi issued a declaration opposing the Khartoum government's policies of Arabization, political and economic marginalization of non-Arabs, and genocide in Darfur.

When Abakir was killed in January 2004, Minawi began to act as secretary-general of the SLA, even though he did not have that formal title. He promoted other Zaghawa, and especially members of his own clan, to key offices within the SLA. His ambition alienated not only the Fur and other tribes, but even members of the Zaghawa, including civilians, who wished for greater cooperation and less ethnic divisiveness within the resistance movement. Furthermore, forces loyal to Minawi soon committed atrocities against members of the Arab Zayadiya tribe farmers, establishing a reputation for brutality that distressed Arabs and non-Arabs alike.

With Abdel Wahid in self-exile in Paris, Minawi pressed his advantage against his rivals within the SLA. In June 2004, Minawi troops attacked a number of Fur civilians. Other, smaller tribes of Darfur were also subject to Zaghawa extortion and duress.

In October 2005, Minawi convened an SLA conference in southern Darfur that his rivals in the organization (notably Abdel Wahid) declined to attend. He was elected chair, formalizing the rift between the SLA factions loyal to Abdel Wahid and to himself (SLA-AW and SLA-MM, respectively). The Justice and Equality Movement (JEM), led by Khalil Ibrahim, constituted yet a third major rebel group.

On May 5, 2006, the SLA-MM became the only rebel faction to sign the Darfur Peace Agreement (DPA) with the government of Sudan. The DPA was brokered with the assistance of the United States, and Minawi was flown to the White House for a meeting and photograph with President George W. Bush to publicize the agreement. As a result of the DPA, Minawi was sworn in on August 5, 2006, as senior assistant to President Omar Hassan Ahmed al-Bashir, becoming Sudan's fourth-ranking official after the country's president and two vice presidents. He also became head of the Transitional Darfur Regional Authority, charged with administering the DPA in Darfur.

Minawi's position as senior assistant was not renewed after the April 2010 Sudanese general election. In December, he moved from Khartoum to Juba in the south, denouncing the government for its slow implementation of the DPA and its lack of progress on issues of sharing power and wealth. Then, in November of the following year, the SLA-AW, SLA-MM, JEM, and the Sudan People's Liberation Movement–North (a political party and military organization formed in 2011 that sought to create a more ethnically and religiously inclusive government in Khartoum) announced a new rebel alliance, the Sudan Revolutionary Front, and pledged to topple the Khartoum regime through political action and armed struggle. SLA-MM and other Darfurian rebel factions have repeatedly tried and failed to broker lasting cease-fires and peace between Darfur and the government of Sudan.

Since the overthrow of President Bashir in April 2019, Minawi has participated in the ongoing negotiations for a peaceful governmental transition. In late October of that year, Minawi traveled to Khartoum to participate in discussions about what will come next for Sudan.

Karl A. Yambert

See also: Fur; Gambari, Ibrahim; Justice and Equality Movement; Wahid, Abdel; Zaghawa

Further Reading

Flint, Julie, and Alex de Waal. 2006. *Darfur: A Short History of a Long War*. London: Zed Books.

Prunier, Gerard. 2005. *Darfur: The Ambiguous Genocide*. Ithaca, NY: Cornell University Press.

N

National Islamic Front

The National Islamic Front (NIF) was the architect of the 1989 presidential coup that helped propel Omar Hassan Ahmed al-Bashir into power. Gaafar Muhammad an-Nimeiry and the Sudanese Muslim Brotherhood founded the NIF in 1985. It played a pivotal role in forcibly spreading Islamic law in Sudan, and it has labored to enforce Sharia law throughout the country.

The NIF is a coalition of fundamentalist Islamic groups, of which the Muslim Brotherhood is its strongest supporter (and, according to some, its originator). For decades, the NIF has existed under various guises, including the Islamic Charter Front (ICF) in the 1960s, NIF in the 1980s, and presently the National Congress Party. The Sudanese branch of the Muslim Brotherhood (an Islamic revivalist organization that originated in Egypt) was founded by Sudanese students in Cairo in the 1940s. It broke away from the Egyptian Muslim Brotherhood because unlike its associates in Cairo, the Sudanese Muslim Brotherhood wanted independence from Egyptian and British colonialists (which was finally obtained in 1957).

The Muslim Brotherhood in Sudan founded the ICF in 1964 to advocate for a new Sudanese constitution steeped in Islamic law. Following the 1969 political coup by Nimeiry, the party's push for Islam was derailed. From that point forward, the Muslim Brotherhood sought out high-ranking positions in the government, the military, and secondary schools. However, it was outperformed in general elections by the National Umma Party (a moderate Islamic centrist political party in Sudan previously led by Sadiq al-Mahdi, who served as prime minister from 1966–1967 and 1986–1989).

In 1985, the Muslim Brotherhood created the NIF and participated in the 1986 elections. The elections, however, failed to secure the NIF and its leader, Hassan al-Turabi, a clear majority. While the Umma Party won ninety-nine seats in parliament (38.2 percent), the Democratic Unionist Party got sixty-three (29.5 percent), and NIF won just fifty-three (18.5 percent), of which twenty-three were reserved for university students. While the NIF did not gain a majority of the seats in parliament, it did demonstrate that it was not to be ignored (Collins 2008: 162). Indeed, when Bashir removed Nimeiry from power in a military coup in 1989, he did so with the support of the NIF, which had deployed several hundred militants who had been trained in the 1970s in a Libyan terrorist training camp.

In July 1991, Bashir sent NIF activist al-Tayib Ibrahim Mohamed Khair, commonly known as Sikha, to take charge of Darfur and regain control of the province, which had come under the influence of Libya. Libya had begun arming Arab tribal militias in Darfur, with the intent of launching an onslaught on President Idriss Déby Itno of Chad. The proxy war waged between Libya and Chad in Darfur resulted in thousands of casualties, and Arab Darfurians commonly raided what they viewed as African (as opposed to Arab) villages. For their part, Sudanese government officials in Darfur supported the Libyan incursion by arresting many Fur (the largest ethnic group in Darfur and codified as "African") and sending them to prison. The Sudanese Popular Liberation Army (SPLA) from south Sudan, who had been locked in civil war with Khartoum and northern Sudan, sent representatives to Darfur to try and engage Chadian support for the Fur rebels. When the NIF leader Sikha arrived in Darfur in 1991, he was charged with upending SPLA influence using brute force. He quickly gained a reputation for the utter ruthlessness with which he targeted and attacked the Zaghawa and the Fur, both considered "African" tribes within Sudan.

President Bashir continued to rely on the NIF to bolster his military efforts. The Popular Defense Force (PDF), the military wing of the coalition, was created in 1989 and has been deployed alongside government army units against various rebel groups. According to a 2004 country report by the U.S. Library of Congress, the PDF consisted of 10,000 active members and 85,000 members in the reserve. When Bashir launched his genocidal attack on Darfur in 2004, once again he turned to the PDF to support his efforts. It has participated in attacks on African Darfurians and has played a major role in the distributions of weapons to and military training for Arab militias.

In the wake of Bashir's removal from power in April 2019, it remains to be seen whether the NIF will weather the storm or if its members will be weeded out of government and replaced by more moderate leaders.

Alexis Herr

See also: Bashir, Omar Hassan Ahmed al; Turabi, Hassan al-

Further Reading

Collins, Robert O. 2008. *A History of Modern Sudan*. Cambridge: Cambridge University Press.

Crockett, Richard. 2010. *Sudan: Darfur and the Failure of an African State*. New Haven, CT: Yale University Press.

Prunier, Gérard. 2008. *Darfur: A 21st-Century Genocide*. 3rd ed. New York: Cornell University Press.

Nuba

The Nuba people inhabit chiefly the South Kordofan region of Sudan in the Nuba Mountains. They are not one ethnic or cultural group, but rather are composed of multiple distinct groups, many of whom speak their own language or dialect. What binds them together are their geographic location and their socioeconomic status. Most of the Nuba are small farmers, cattle ranchers, and herders. According to the purview of the government of Sudan, the Nuba are "Black Africans," a term usually used to describe the non-Arab population of Darfur. Some Nuba practice Islam and some practice Christianity. Still others believe in traditional shamanism. The Nuba tend to be religiously tolerant, which rankles the Sudanese government because it wants to homogenize Sudanese society by forcing all citizens to observe Islam. The current Nuba population is 2.5 million, of which some 1 million reside in the Sudanese state of South Kordofan; the rest are mostly internally displaced people (IDP) living near the capital city of Khartoum.

Historically, the Nuba have been relegated to third-class citizenship within Sudan and have been repeatedly marginalized and disenfranchised. In 1986, the Popular Defense

Force (PDF), a militia group with direct ties to the Sudanese government, began a campaign of terror and intimidation against the Nuba people. This escalated into a broader, more destructive war against the Nuba and became part of the larger Second Sudanese Civil War (1983–2005). Atrocities against the Nuba increased dramatically as villages were destroyed and civilians killed in large numbers. Some human-rights groups classified these actions as de facto genocide. The war also badly fractured the Nuba economy and led to widespread starvation because many could no longer engage in agricultural pursuits.

The Sudanese government justified its actions against the Nuba by asserting that they were not Arab and that many were not Muslim or practicing Muslims. Also at work in this incipient genocide was the fact that many Nuba inhabited areas that held high economic value. By exterminating the Nuba or driving them out of the country, Sudanese leaders hoped to profit from the former Nuba farmland. Most of the atrocities against the Nuba subsided with the end of the civil war in 2005, although the remaining Nuba continue to fight for basic rights while at the same time holding on to their unique culture and social institutions. Although the precise number of Nuba who died in the conflict is difficult to determine with any accuracy, estimates range from 500,000 to as many as 1 million.

In 2011, as South Sudan gained its independence, violence was renewed in the Nuba Mountains, and once again the Nuba were targeted for removal and elimination by the government of Sudan. Because United Nations (UN) agencies, journalists, and aid workers were denied access to the region, gathering information on the situation poses many challenges. The stories that have escaped the government-enforced silence indicate that the Nuba have yet again become victims of war crimes and crimes against humanity. The Sudan People's Liberation Army–North (SPLA-N), commanded by Abdel Aziz Adam al-Hillu, is waging war against the government of Sudan and demanding self-determination and power sharing for the Nuba. For its part, the government of Sudan's intermittent bombing of Nuba towns and villages has killed countless civilians.

In 2012, Valerie Amos, the UN undersecretary-general for humanitarian affairs and emergency relief coordinator, issued an urgent statement highlighting the growing concerns for the safety and well-being of citizens in the Nuba region. Her statement was issued alongside reports that women and girls in the Nuba Mountains were being raped and subjected to repeated sexual assault. Journalist Nicholas Kristof of *The New York Times* has continued to urge the international community to pay greater attention to the plight of the Nuba and to do more to help. He has categorized the government attacks as ethnic cleansing and urged the U.S. government to do more to support the takedown of Sudanese president Omar Hassan al-Bashir. In April 2019, after Bashir was forcibly removed from power, the United Nations announced that the governments of South Sudan and Sudan, with the support of SPLA-N, had welcomed the first UN humanitarian mission to the Nuba Mountains in South Kordofan in more than eight years.

Paul G. Pierpaoli Jr. and Alexis Herr

See also: Bashir, Omar Hassan Ahmed al-; Khartoum; Kristof, Nicholas; Rape; Sudanese Civil War

Further Reading

Deng, Francis Mading. 1995. *War of Visions: Conflict of Identities in the Sudan*. Washington, DC: Brookings Institution Press.

DeRouen, Karl R., and Uk Heo. 2007. *Civil Wars of the World: Major Conflicts Since World War II*. Santa Barbara, CA: ABC-CLIO.

Kristof, Nicholas. 2019. "Marching Toward a Massacre." *The New York Times*. January 16.

P

Power, Samantha

Samantha Power was a special assistant to U.S. president Barack Obama, administering the Office of Multilateral Affairs and Human Rights as senior director of multilateral affairs on the staff of the National Security Council (NSC). From April 5, 2013, until January 20, 2017, she served as the U.S. ambassador to the United Nations (UN). She was also the Anna Lindh Professor of Global Leadership and Public Policy at Harvard University and was the founding director of Harvard's Carr Center for Human Rights Policy.

An award-winning journalist and writer, Power was born on September 21, 1970, in Dungarvan, Waterford, Ireland. She migrated to the United States in 1979 and grew up in Pittsburgh and Atlanta. Although she originally aspired to become a sports reporter, upon graduation from Yale University, her journalistic career took her down a different path. She began covering genocidal conflicts and gross human rights violations, including those in Bosnia, Burundi, Sudan, East Timor, Kosovo, Rwanda, and Zimbabwe. Seeing firsthand the all-too-frequent impotence of international efforts to combat genocide, particularly those of the United States, led her to write the Pulitzer Prize–winning book *"A Problem from Hell": America and the Age of Genocide* (2002), for which she also received the National Book Critics Circle Award for general nonfiction and the Council on Foreign Relations Arthur Ross Prize for the best book on U.S. foreign policy, both in 2003. She followed this up with an article in the *New Yorker* in August 2004 titled "Dying in Darfur: Can the Ethnic Cleansing in Sudan be Stopped?" which won the 2005 National Magazine Award for best reporting.

As a working journalist, scholar, and government official, Power continued to write on foreign policy issues for a number of major periodicals syndicated throughout the world. With Graham Wilson, she coedited *Realizing Human Rights: Moving from Inspiration to Impact* (2000). In *Chasing the Flame: Sergio Vieira de Mello and the Fight to Save the World* (2008), Power tells the story of Sergio Vieira de Mello, the UN envoy killed by a suicide bomber in Iraq along with fourteen others in 2003.

Prior to the release of *A Problem from Hell*, Power published the article "Bystanders to Genocide" in *Atlantic Monthly*, which in many ways summarized the arguments that would follow in the larger work. In this lengthy piece—the result of a three-year investigation—she criticized the administration of President Bill Clinton for its ongoing failure to do anything substantive to halt the genocide in Rwanda in 1994. Power asked a range of questions that would frame her investigation regarding the lack of past U.S. involvement in previous cases of genocide. These included: Why did the United States not do more for the Rwandans at the time of the killings? Did President Clinton really not know about the genocide, as marginal comments in his memoranda suggested? Who in his administration made the life-and-death decisions that dictated U.S. policy? How did they arrive at their decisions? Were any voices inside or outside the U.S. government demanding that the United States do more? If so, why were they not heeded? And, most crucially, what could the United States have done to save lives?

Power argued that her research conclusively showed that the absence of U.S. involvement was not a case of inactive "bystanderism," but instead the result of what she called "active noninvolvement." The scenario of active noninvolvement, in fact, was consistent with what Power regarded as the "major findings" of *A Problem from Hell* relating to U.S. policy responses to genocide.

Power wrote this book, she said later, for "the screamers," those persons in positions of responsibility who choose to speak out against government policies, often at great personal and professional sacrifice (a number of whose stories are told throughout the book), as well as in the hope that the learning curve concerning what is and what is not genocide—and what can and what cannot be done in the future—will prove far less difficult to surmount than it has been in the past.

Given her desire to foster greater U.S. support for upending genocide, she soon became colleagues with then-senator Barack Obama. From 2005 to 2006, she worked in his office as a foreign policy fellow and later became an early and outspoken supporter of Obama's presidential campaign. Her support for him was prompted in part by his advocacy of U.S. and UN action over the ongoing genocide in Darfur while he was senator. Power was a senior adviser on Senator Obama's campaign until she resigned in March 2008 after she was reported to refer to Obama's main political rival (and later his secretary of state), Hillary Clinton as "a monster." After the 2008 presidential election, Power returned to work for Obama,

where she became a member of the transition team and worked for the State Department. In January 2009, President Obama appointed Power to the NSC staff. In April 2013, she succeeded Susan Rice as ambassador to the United Nations, which at the time made her the youngest person to be appointed to that position.

For several years, Power was held by many to be the most important figure within the Obama administration, pushing for military intervention in Libya on moral and humanitarian grounds. As UN ambassador, she took the Syrian government to task for gross human rights abuses during the ongoing Syrian civil war and pointedly criticized the United Nations for its failure to react to the Syrian carnage. Power also slammed Russia's 2015 intervention in the Syrian civil war, saying that it was not a counterterrorism effort aimed at the Islamic State of Iraq and Syria (ISIS), but rather was barbarism aimed at aiding Syrian president Bashar al-Assad's warmaking capabilities. Before vacating her position at the end of Obama's second term, Power gave a speech in which she was highly critical of Russia's attempts to upend the global world order by tampering with the 2016 presidential election and its military forays in Ukraine and Syria.

After her time at the United Nations, Power went to Harvard University, where she was given a joint faculty appointment (April 2017) at Harvard Law School and the John F. Kennedy School of Government. She also serves as a senior member, board member, and director of the International Peace and Security Project, as well as an affiliated faculty member at Harvard's Carr Center and Belfer Center for Science and International Affairs.

Overall, Power has been an important critical voice on policies regarding genocide. She continues to bring to the table the intellect and insights of a scholar, the eye and talents of a journalist, and the moral passion of a human being truly concerned about others caught in the grip of a crime that shows few signs of abating. She has not been without her detractors, some of whom have argued that her reliance on an idealized vision of political will as a way to stop genocide does not take into account the actuality of a world system that is still founded on political realism. She discusses this point in her newest work, *The Education of an Idealist: A Memoir.* In it, she defends the same idealism that drove her to write *A Problem from Hell,* while discussing the complicated nature of diplomacy, international relations, and the United Nations while trying to combat genocide, crimes against humanity, and war crimes while serving as U.S. ambassador.

Paul R. Bartrop

See also: United Nations Mission in the Sudan; United States Involvement in Darfur

Further Readings

Power, Samantha. 2007. *"A Problem from Hell": America and the Age of Genocide.* New York: Harper Perennial.

Power, Samantha. 2008. *Chasing the Flame: Sergio Vieira de Mello and the Fight to Save the World.* New York: Penguin.

Power, Samantha. 2019. *The Education of an Idealist: A Memoir.* New York: HarperCollins.

Prendergast, John

John Prendergast is an American author and human rights activist who has made a major contribution to raising awareness about genocide in Africa, particularly (though not exclusively) in relation to Darfur.

He was born on March 21, 1963, in Indianapolis. After drifting through his education and early adult years—during which time he attended five different universities before finishing his degree at Temple University, Philadelphia—he saw a breaking news story about the famine in Ethiopia (1983–1985) that changed his life forever. In 1984, he decided to travel to Africa to investigate what he was hearing about only secondhand. Unable to fly directly to Ethiopia, he landed instead in the west African nation of Mali. Working his way across the Sahara, he developed a love for Africa and a deep desire to do something to alleviate the distress he was witnessing. In subsequent years, and after further trips to Africa, Prendergast decided that he would dedicate himself to raising awareness in the United States of what could be done to help Africans at the grassroots level—not through government policies alone, but via concerted action from citizens on behalf of a shared humanity.

In the mid-1990s, under President Bill Clinton, Prendergast served as director of African affairs at the National Security Council (NSC) and special adviser to Susan Rice, assistant secretary of state for African affairs at the Department of State. In this capacity, he was involved in a number of U.S. peace initiatives in Africa. In 2003, when news of the genocide in the Darfur region of Sudan began to break, Prendergast had already established himself as an advocate of some note for African rights and a voice that deserved to be heard. By that stage, he had already worked for two members of Congress, the United Nations International Children's Emergency Fund (UNICEF), Human Rights Watch, the International Crisis Group, and the U.S. Institute of Peace. Part of his work involved a trip to the Democratic Republic of Congo in the fall of 2003 with activist-actress Angelina Jolie, the results of which were publicized by the United States Holocaust Memorial Museum.

In mid-2004, Prendergast went to Darfur on a fact-finding trip with *New Yorker* columnist Samantha Power. This was his first direct exposure to the genocide that was in full swing by then. Eighteen months later, he returned, this time with Academy Award–nominated actor Don Cheadle. The relationship forged between the two men was to be both lasting and fruitful, leading to the appearance in 2007 of their first book together, a work entitled *Not on Our Watch: The Mission to End Genocide in Darfur and Beyond*. This became a *New York Times* bestseller and was named nonfiction book of the year by the National Association for the Advancement of Colored People (NAACP).

While outlining the Darfur tragedy, the book's major focus was on finding strategies both to raise consciousness and to develop practical approaches in which ordinary citizens could take action to improve the situation and assist the victims. It also considered tragedies beyond Darfur itself, such as in northern Uganda and eastern Congo. Holocaust survivor Elie Wiesel wrote the book's foreword, and then Senators Barack Obama and Sam Brownback cowrote the introduction. *Not on Our Watch* offered six strategies that readers could employ to shape change: raise awareness, raise funds, write letters, call for divestment, start an organization, and lobby the government. Each of these actions, the authors argued, can make a huge difference in the fate of a nation and a people.

Much of Prendergast's work went to support the Enough Project, an organization he cofounded with another Africa expert, Gayle Smith. A project of the Center for American Progress, an organization committed to stopping and preventing genocide and crimes against humanity, Enough was launched in early 2007. Dedicated to creating "noise and

action both to stop ongoing atrocities and to prevent their recurrence," the project conceived its mission as being to help people from every walk of life understand the practical actions that they can take to make a difference. In framing its policy prescriptions, Enough utilizes what it refers to as a "3P" approach: promoting peace, protecting civilians, and punishing perpetrators. A fourth and all-encompassing "P," prevention, is also important, and Enough works to develop the policies, tools, and investments that can prevent crimes against humanity and genocide.

Due to the nature of his activism, Prendergast is often a featured expert on television and in print media. He has authored ten books on Africa and has written op-eds in a variety of national publications. In the visual media, he has appeared on or contributed to a number of television shows to raise awareness about human rights issues in Africa. In addition, he was a consultant on two episodes of *Law and Order: Special Victims Unit*, one focusing on the recruitment of child soldiers and the other on rape as a war strategy.

His movie and documentary credits include *Sand and Sorrow* (directed by Paul Freedman, 2007), *Darfur Now* (directed by Ted Braun, 2007), *3 Points* (directed by Josh Rothstein, 2009), *War Child* (directed by Christian Karim Chrobog, 2008), and *After Kony: Staging Hope* (directed by Bil Yoelin, 2011). He also coproduced *Journey into Sunset* (directed by Rick Wilkinson, 2006), a documentary examining the children known as the "Night Commuters" of northern Uganda. These children migrate into the towns each night so as not to be kidnapped by the soldiers of Joseph Kony's Lord's Resistance Army to be conscripted as child soldiers. In the music industry, he partnered with Downtown Records and Mercer Street Records to create a compilation album, *Raise*

Hope for Congo, which shines a spotlight on sexual violence against women and girls there.

With Tracy McGrady and other National Basketball Association (NBA) stars, Prendergast cofounded the Darfur Dream Team Sister Schools Program to fund schools in Darfurian refugee camps and create partnerships with schools in the United States. He also helped create the Raise Hope for Congo Campaign, highlighting the issue of so-called conflict minerals (mainly tin, tungsten, coltan, and gold ore) that fuel the war in Congo.

Prendergast was an early board member of Not on Our Watch, a human rights and antigenocide body founded by George Clooney, Matt Damon, Cheadle, and Brad Pitt, among others. The mission of Not on Our Watch was to focus global attention and resources on ending mass atrocities. Drawing on the powerful voices of artists, activists, and cultural leaders, Not on Our Watch generated lifesaving humanitarian aid and encouraged governments to take meaningful and immediate action to protect those in harm's way.

In 2010, Prendergast wrote another book with Cheadle, *The Enough Moment: Fighting to End Africa's Worst Human Rights Crimes*, which focuses on building a popular movement against genocide and other human rights crimes. The book was intended to help empower engaged citizens from all societies and walks of life to combat genocide, rape, and the enforced servitude of child soldiers in Africa and showed how all individuals can become part of the movement to stop these crimes. It was an important follow-up to *Not on Our Watch* for those seeking to understand the region, in particular Sudan, Congo, and northern Uganda. In 2019, Not on Our Watch merged with The Sentry, an investigative initiative seeking to dismantle the networks of perpetrators and facilitators that benefit from Africa's deadliest conflicts. The Sentry was cofounded by Clooney and Prendergast. One of its main focuses is tracking and analyzing how armed conflict and atrocities are financed, sustained, and monetized. In so doing, the organization hopes to upend the economic support for atrocities. Former president of Sudan Omar Hassan Ahmed al-Bashir has been the subject of many such reports.

Prendergast remains a highly visible activist in human rights and antigenocide initiatives and a much-sought-after speaker in the United States and worldwide. As the Darfur Genocide continues, he draws attention to the enduring conflict through his public talks and many op-eds.

Paul R. Bartrop

See also: Cheadle, Don; Child Soldiers; Clooney, George; Damon, Matt; Jolie, Angelina

Further Reading

Cheadle, Don, and John Prendergast. 2007. *Not on Our Watch: The Mission to End Genocide in Darfur and Beyond*. New York: Hyperion.

Cheadle, Don, and John Prendergast. 2010. *The Enough Moment: Fighting to End Africa's Worst Human Rights Crimes*. New York: Three Rivers Press.

Prosper, Pierre-Richard

Pierre-Richard Prosper is a U.S.-based attorney and former ambassador-at-large within the Office of War Crimes Issues, which advises the U.S. secretary of state and formulates policy responses to atrocities committed in areas of conflict and elsewhere throughout the world. He attracted worldwide attention when he successfully prosecuted the first case at the International

Criminal Tribunal for Rwanda (ICTR) to bring in a guilty verdict for the crime of genocide.

Born in Denver in 1963, Prosper is the son of two medical doctors who were refugees from Haiti. Raised in New York State, he graduated with a bachelor of arts at Boston College in 1985 and earned his law degree from Pepperdine University in 1989. Upon graduation Prosper became a deputy district attorney for Los Angeles County, California, where he remained until 1994. He then entered service with the federal government as an assistant U.S. attorney for the Central District of California in Los Angeles, where he investigated and prosecuted major international drug cartels while assigned to the Narcotics Section of the Drug Enforcement Task Force.

Prosper first went to Rwanda in April 1995 as part of a fact-finding mission to examine the national justice system. He was then appointed as a special legal consultant of the U.S. government mission in Kigali, where he assessed the postgenocide Rwandan justice system and assisted in developing an action plan to reinstate some kind of judicial operation in a country that had been stripped of its legal infrastructure. To do so, he consulted with Rwandan, UN, and donor country representatives, and coordinated activities to maximize international efforts. He remained in this position until May 1995.

He was then offered a position by the United Nations to be one of two American prosecutors at the ICTR, sitting in Arusha, Tanzania. The more he learned, the more he came to regard the horrors committed in Rwanda as a crime not just against Rwandans, but against all humanity. It was in this position that he successfully prosecuted the ICTR case against the former mayor of the town of Taba, Jean-Paul Akayesu.

For Prosper, serving as lead prosecutor became a life-transforming experience. He and the judges on the tribunal were confronted with the task of having to determine, for the very first time, what constitutes genocide in a legal sense. Reviewing the language of the 1948 Convention on the Prevention and Punishment of the Crime of Genocide and a half-century of legal scholarship, they had to establish how the concept of genocide applies in the contemporary context. They studied legal precedent, investigated the astonishing circumstances not only of the specific case being tried, but also of the overall situation in Rwanda, met with victims and survivors, and stood before mass graves—all prior to even starting the trial.

The result was a powerful prosecution that resulted in the first conviction by an international tribunal for the specific crime of genocide, with Akayesu sentenced to life imprisonment. The trial was also the first case of genocide ever argued before an international tribunal under the 1948 Convention. An important part of the judgment saw the further development of genocide case law, as the three trial judges—Laity Kama, from Senegal, presiding; Navanethem Pillay, from South Africa; and Lennart Aspegren, from Sweden—ruled that rape could henceforth be considered within the general legal definition of genocide and crimes against humanity. In the fourteen-month trial, Prosper won additional life-sentence convictions against Akayesu for crimes against humanity. In developing his case, Prosper traveled widely, supervising investigations throughout Africa, Europe, and North America.

Reflecting on his Rwanda experience later, Prosper said that it both altered his professional life and challenged his fundamental assumptions about human nature. It changed his views concerning the nature of human evil and how important it is that all people contribute to making the world a better place.

Prosper remained a trial attorney with the ICTR until October 1998. In January and February 1999, he served as a special assistant to the assistant U.S. attorney general (where he helped with the development of international justice initiatives), prior to a secondment to the State Department as special counsel and policy adviser to the Office of War Crimes Issues within the Office of the Secretary of State in the administration of President Bill Clinton. Here, he worked directly with the first U.S. ambassador-at-large for war crimes issues, David Scheffer, developing policy and assisting in formulating U.S. responses to serious violations of international humanitarian law around the world. He traveled to affected areas in Europe, Africa, and Asia to promote initiatives and build coalitions, as well as engaging in negotiations in support of U.S. government positions.

On May 16, 2001, President George W. Bush nominated Prosper to succeed Scheffer as ambassador-at-large for war crimes issues. After being confirmed by the U.S. Senate, he was sworn in on July 13, 2001, thereby becoming an official who served in high office in the administrations of both a Democrat (Clinton) and a Republican (Bush). He served in this capacity until October 2005, and, as such, was responsible to two secretaries of state—Colin Powell and Condoleezza Rice—on all matters relating to violations of international humanitarian law around the world. His role was important, in that he advised not only the secretary of state, but also the president of the United States, secretary of defense, attorney general, national security adviser, chairman of the Joint Chiefs of Staff, director of the Central Intelligence Agency, White House counsel, and other senior U.S. government officials.

The human rights violations that formed the centerpiece of Prosper's brief included genocide, crimes against humanity, and war crimes. He was often required to speak publicly on behalf of the United States as the face of U.S. policy against war crimes, genocide, and crimes against humanity around the world. As with his earlier appointments, Prosper traveled extensively, conducting diplomatic negotiations and consultations with heads of state, foreign ministers, and senior government officials from over sixty different countries. He regularly visited conflict zones in efforts to secure peace, stability, and the rule of law. After the terrorist attacks in the United States on September 11, 2001, Prosper played a key role in helping to develop antiterrorism policies within a legal human rights framework.

In October 2005, Prosper resigned his position to run for the Republican nomination for attorney general of California in the 2006 primaries. He withdrew his candidacy in February 2006 and did not proceed with his campaign.

In November 2006 and April 2007, he headed an International Republican Institute election observation mission to observe and monitor the 2007 Nigerian presidential and National Assembly elections. He led a team of fifty-nine international observers, meeting and consulting with candidates, political leaders, voters, and international observers. In February 2007, the UN General Assembly elected him to serve as an independent expert to the UN Committee on the Elimination of Racial Discrimination, a human rights treaty body located in Geneva, Switzerland. This monitors compliance by state parties to the Convention on the Elimination of All Forms of Racial Discrimination. Then, in April 2008, he was appointed by

President Bush to serve as a member of the United States Holocaust Memorial Council.

Currently, Prosper is an attorney in the Los Angeles office of the California law firm Arent Fox LLP, having joined on January 1, 2007. That same year, he told reporters that he thought the International Criminal Court (ICC) was a bad instrument for promoting healing in war-torn societies. This rationale underlined the Bush administration's proposal that the United Nations and African Union create a regional court to investigate atrocities in Darfur.

Paul R. Bartrop

See also: United States Involvement in Darfur

Further Reading

Jokic, Aleksandar, ed. 2001. *War Crimes and Collective Wrongdoing: A Reader.* Malden, MA: Blackwell Publishers.

Neier, Aryeh. 1998. *War Crimes: Brutality, Genocide, Terror, and the Struggle for Justice.* New York: Times Books.

Taylor, Stuart. 2005. "Genocide in Darfur: Crime Without Punishment?" *The Atlantic.* Available at https://www.theatlantic.com/magazine/archive/2005/02/genocide-in-darfur-crime-without-punishment/303813/.

R

Rape

Since the Darfur Genocide began in 2003, tens of thousands of Sudanese, primarily women and girls, have been sexually assaulted and/or raped by the Sudanese army and the Janjaweed militia group. From testimony given by the survivors and witnesses of rape in Darfur, it is now known that sexual violence is a central component of the dehumanization, humiliation, and destruction of Darfurian communities.

United Nations (UN) fact-finding missions, journalists, humanitarian groups, and human rights researchers have all described a pattern of systematic attacks on civilians in Darfur by government troops and government-sponsored militias. When a village (mainly those belonging to the Fur, Massalit, and Zaghawa ethnic groups) is attacked, the men are typically killed and the women are brutally and often repeatedly raped. This violence has led to the displacement of at least 1.2 million Darfurians, and more than 170,000 have fled to neighboring Chad, seeking safety in refugee camps.

Amnesty International sent delegates to Chad in 2004 to interview Darfurian refugee women at three of the UN refugee camps there: Goz Amer, Koungoungo, and Mile. In so doing, they collected more than 100 personal testimonies from refugees, documented the names of 250 women who were raped, and recorded stories of an estimated 500 rapes. They also learned of other human rights abuses targeting women and girls, including sexual slavery and torture. In addition, it was learned that gang rapes are not uncommon. Survivors told Amnesty International researchers the names of more than 50 women and girls who were abducted by Janjaweed and government troops at night who were never seen again.

According to a 2014 report by Human Rights Watch (HRW), researchers confirmed that the systematic rape that began in 2004 has continued unabated for more than a decade. HRW has documented, for example, Sudanese army attacks against civilians in Tabit, Darfur, during which at least 221 women and girls were raped over a period of thirty-six hours in October 2014. More than 450,000 people have been displaced by the fighting in 2014 alone.

According to reports, the more than 2 million Darfurians living in internally displaced persons (IDP) settlements in Darfur are incredibly vulnerable to sexual violence and exploitation. Women are forced to leave the settlements, located on the periphery of towns and large villages in the region, to collect firewood and gather what food they can. Janjaweed groups often patrol outside the settlements, but the women have few other options because men who leave the sites are typically killed. Additionally, women and girls are vulnerable to sexual exploitation and rape within IDP sites.

As a consequence of rape, women often experience social stigmatization and ostracism. The perpetrators frequently rape women in public in front of their husbands, relatives, or the wider community. Amnesty International reported that some women raped in Darfur, fearing rejection from their relatives in Chad, refuse to go to refugee camps across the border. Women and girls who became pregnant as a result of rape are likely to suffer further abuses of their rights, as well as additional trauma.

The situation for IDP civilians in Darfur is desperate and requires greater attention from international aid groups; however, the government of Sudan has restricted and denied foreign aid to the region, making it all the more challenging to help IDPs. International peacekeepers have been present in Darfur since 2004, and on July 31, 2007, the UN Security Council authorized the African Union–United Nations Hybrid Mission in Darfur (UNAMID). Although the mission is mandated specifically to report on sexual and gender-based violence, it is ill prepared to prevent sexual violence. In 2018, UNAMID documented 122 incidents of sexual violence involving 199 victims, of whom 85 were women, 105 girls, and 9 boys. According to the United Nations, 80 percent of the perpetrators were described as armed, and 31 percent were members of the security forces. Witnesses described the perpetrators as members of specific armed groups, including the Sudan Liberation Army–Abdel Wahid faction, government security forces including the Sudanese armed forces, Rapid Support Forces (RSF), and police. In a 2019 report on sexual violence, UN secretary-general António Guterres encouraged Sudanese authorities to cooperate with the United Nations to facilitate greater access throughout Darfur for service provisions, humanitarian aid, and monitoring.

Alexis Herr

See also: Amnesty International; Darfur Atrocities Documentation Project; Lost Boys and Girls of Sudan; United Nations Mission in the Sudan; Wahid, Abdel

Further Reading

Amnesty International. 2004. *Sudan, Darfur: Rape as a Weapon of War: Sexual Violence and Its Consequences.* Available at https://www.refworld.org/docid/4152885b4.html.

Human Rights Watch. 2015. *Mass Rape in North Darfur: Sudanese Army Attacks Against Civilians in Tabit.* Available at https://www.hrw.org/report/2015/02/11/mass-rape-north-darfur/sudanese-army-attacks-against-civilians-tabit.

United Nations. 2019. *Conflict-Related Sexual Violence: Report of the United Nations Secretary-General.* March 29 (S/2019/280). Available at https://www.un.org/sexualviolenceinconflict/wp-content/uploads/2019/04/report/s-2019-280/Annual-report-2018.pdf.

Reeves, Eric

Eric Reeves is a professor of English at Smith College, Massachusetts. He was born in Los Angeles in 1950 and educated at Williams College, Massachusetts, and the University of Pennsylvania, from where he obtained his PhD in 1981.

Reeves's work to alleviate suffering in Darfur has served as a key source of information since the catastrophe emerged in 2003, although in this, he built on his earlier research and activist work relating to the long civil war between north and south Sudan. Since 2003, he has effectively worked full time as an independent Sudan researcher and analyst. He has testified several times before the U.S. Congress, lectured widely, and served as a consultant to a number of human rights and humanitarian organizations operating in Sudan. He has written extensively on Sudan's recent history and published the results of his research both in the United States and internationally.

Since 2003, Sudanese government troops and Janjaweed militias have been carrying out widespread ethnic cleansing and genocide against the so-called black Africans in the Darfur region of Sudan. Initially, the Sudanese military and Janjaweed retaliated against rebel groups who attacked government installations. These groups, in particular the Sudan Liberation Army (SLA), were frustrated over the fact that Sudanese blacks had been and were being discriminated against and marginalized and the victims of injustice at the hands of the Sudanese government. In response, the Sudanese military and Janjaweed carried out wholesale attacks on the villagers and farmers of Darfur, indiscriminately killing men, women, and children; raping young girls and women; and, prior to burning down hundreds of entire villages, plundering settlements for all they could carry.

By collecting information from numerous sources via telephone, email correspondence, Internet searches, and interviews with relief workers, diplomats, reporters, and others who have returned from Darfur and the refugee camps in Chad, Reeves has managed to keep the world knowledgeable about the genocide in Darfur as it has been taking place. In this capacity, he is effectively a one-man nongovernmental organization, although he has been fortunate in receiving support for his research and travel from the Humanity First Initiative of the Omidyar Network, a philanthropic investment firm established in 2004 by eBay founder Pierre Omidyar.

International observers have considered that it has been the work of Reeves that has kept the Darfur crisis on the agenda of political leaders and the general public since 2003. His reports on southern Sudan and Darfur have generated hundreds of lengthy essays. On Darfur alone, he produces a 5,000-word analysis each week (published at www.sudanreeves.org) and disseminates his analysis on a weekly blog that reportedly is read by hundreds of scholars and policymakers involved with Sudan. As early as December 2003, he began declaring on his blog, as well in opinion pieces in various newspapers, that what was taking place in Darfur was (and is) genocide.

In May 2007, a collection of the most important of Reeves's writings on Darfur between 2003 and 2006 was published as *A Long Day's Dying: Critical Moments in the Darfur Genocide*. The book's main theme was that the Sudanese government is committing genocide in Darfur while the international community looks on passively. The book provides an in-depth critical assessment of the situation and a stinging indictment of the international community's diplomatic efforts in responding to the crisis. It also provides a record of Reeves's relentless advocacy for Darfur, making it an indispensable archival reference for any serious student of the Darfur conflict.

Reeves has studied the genocide more thoroughly and knowledgeably than most other commentators or scholars and has stimulated responses from politicians, journalists, and academics for at least the last decade. In recognition of his work on Sudan, he received an honorary degree from Smith College on March 6, 2008, the first time a current member of the faculty at Smith has ever been accorded such an honor. In addition to his own work, he is a consultant to several human rights and humanitarian organizations within Sudan itself.

Paul R. Bartrop

See also: Janjaweed; Rape; South Sudan

Further Reading

Anderson, Scott. 2004. "How Did Darfur Happen?" *The New York Times*. October 17.

Reeves, Eric. 2007. *A Long Day's Dying: Critical Moments in the Darfur Genocide.* Toronto: Key Publishing House.

Religion

While perceptions of race (or what some call "tribe") have motivated the Darfur Genocide, Sudan has a long history of religious and ethnic diversity. Of the estimated 6 million people residing in Darfur, divided into a host of ethnic groups or tribes (ranging from 40 to 90, depending on one's definition), 70 percent of the population practice Islam, 5 percent identify as Christian, and the remainder adhere to indigenous religions, including animism, the religious belief that nonhuman entities like animals and plants possess souls or spirits (Cheadle and Prendergast 2007: 52). And according to a U.S. Department of State report released in 2011, approximately 25 percent of the population infuse their practice of Islam or Christianity with indigenous beliefs.

Traditional African religions existed before the arrival of Christianity and Islam. Of the more than 570 ethnic groups that call Sudan home, each had its own religious practice and customs. With the arrival of Arab tribes in Darfur, indigenous beliefs were replaced by Islam. Of the main ethnic groups residing in the Darfur region—Fur, Zaghawa, Massalit, Daju, Berti, and Baqqara—nearly all are Muslims, some of whom infuse indigenous beliefs with Islam. In the early nineteenth century, Egyptians launched a military expedition into Sudan and set up the Turkiya, or Turkish regime. The Egyptian forces endeavored to restructure Sudan to foster the wider adherence and adoption of Islamic law and practice. They divided Sudan into provinces (Bahar al Ghazal, Equatoria, and Upper Nile) and sent garrisons into each one to spread Islam and capture thousands of Sudanese and force them into slavery. The Turkiya conquered and annexed Darfur in 1874, which by that time had already adopted Islam.

Christianity has a long history in Africa, and Sudan in particular. The Roman Empire ushered in Christian teachings in the area now known as Sudan in the first century CE. In the mid-sixth century, the Byzantine emperor Justinian turned Nubia (a region stretching along the Nile River between Aswan in southern Egypt and Khartoum in central Sudan) into a Christian stronghold. Until the sixteenth century, Christianity continued to spread throughout the region. Islam arrived along with slave traders in the 1500s and over time, it replaced Christianity as the dominant religion. Today, the vast majority of Darfurian Muslims belong to the Sunni sect of Islam.

Mahdism entered into Sudan from West Africa in the 1880s. It is named for Mohamed Ahmed ibn Abdallah who declared himself "al Mahdi" (literally, "the guided one"). The Mahdi was the leader of a messianic revolution who endeavored to create a new caliphate (Islamic state). The Madhi set his sights on western Sudan, despite not originating from that country. His declared aim, to overthrow the Turco-Egyptian administration that oversaw Sudan at the time, earned him a popular following from the nomadic tribes in west and north Sudan.

British colonialism (1898–1956) reintroduced Christianity in a predominantly Arab society, most acutely in south Sudan. The arrival of the British in the late nineteenth century resulted in the decision to have Egypt administer northern Sudan and the British to oversee the south. Under the British, Christianity spread. Meanwhile, Egypt led an Islamization of the north. It is important to note, too, that the south was also home to indigenous religions as well as Christianity, with some Sudanese practicing elements of both. As for the western region of Darfur, the British and Egyptian leadership had little to contribute. Lacking a reliable road or railway to connect Darfur with British-Egyptian outposts in Khartoum or in the south, during the colonial period Darfur was loosely administered by a few British officers, local African chiefs, and Arab *shaykhs* (chiefs).

The end of colonial Sudan exacerbated long-held tensions between the Muslim north and what was viewed as a largely Christian south. Even before Sudan's independence on January 1, 1956, the mounting tensions between the north and south had erupted. The seat of the new government in the north sought to suppress Christian and animist beliefs in the south so that the whole country would become a united Islamic state. In response, the south sought independence from the north. As a result, from 1955 to 1972, and again from 1983 to 2005, the southern and northern parts of Sudan collided in bloody civil wars.

While many centuries of Arab influence in Sudan led to the widespread acceptance and practice of Islam in Darfur and throughout the rest of the country, the historical influx of Arabs in the region eventually became a point of contention in the Darfur Genocide. Although Arabs had been in Darfur for centuries, intermarried with the indigenous African population, and practiced Islam alongside tribes indigenous to Darfur, the government in Khartoum in the 1980s attempted to politicize and problematize one's ethnic identity. As such, the fact that those in Khartoum and Darfur practiced Islam was not enough to prevent genocide.

Alexis Herr

See also: Darfur; Fur; Massalit

Further Reading

Cheadle, Don, and John Prendergast. 2007. *Not on Our Watch: The Mission to End Genocide in Darfur and Beyond.* New York: Hyperion.

Crockett, Richard. 2010. *Sudan: The Failure and Division of an African State.* 2nd ed. New Haven, CT: Yale University Press.

Flint, Julie, and Alex de Waal. 2008. *Darfur: A New History of a Long War.* New York: Zed Books.

U.S. Department of State. 2011. "Sudan." September 13. Available at https://www.state.gov/j/drl/rls/irf/2010_5/168432.htm.

S

Satellite Sentinel Project

Through analysis of digital globe imagery captured by satellites, the Satellite Sentinel Project (SSP) has discovered evidence of mass graves, razed villages, forced displacement, bombardments and attacks, and more in Sudan. The SSP hopes that in documenting such atrocities, the perpetrators will be held accountable.

The actor George Clooney and Enough Project cofounder John Prendergast had the idea to start SSP following a trip to southern Sudan in October 2010. It is the first sustained public effort to monitor and report systematically on potential hot spots and threats to human security in near real time. The satellite images of destruction captured by the SSP prove, despite the Sudanese government's denial of wrongdoing in Darfur and elsewhere, that violence has continued to destroy Sudanese communities and lives.

Reports released as recently as 2014 by the SSP used satellite imagery to document Janjaweed attacks in Darfur. In a report entitled *Darfur in Flames with Janjaweed's Return,* published on March 25, 2014, the SSP used satellite images to show that over a two-week period, approximately 150 homes on the western side of the Darfurian town of Saraf Omra were destroyed by Janjaweed forces. In *The Economics of Ethnic Cleansing in Darfur,* the SSP reports on renewed ethnic cleansing in Darfur. The evidence that SSP has collected using satellite images and the reports documenting such evidence demonstrate that the Sudanese government has continued to instigate, deny, and/or allow violence against Darfurians to continue, thus invalidating peace treaties created to end the bloodshed.

As of 2015, the SSP stopped collecting and analyzing satellite imagery. Its founding organizations, the Enough Project and Not on Our Watch, are now working with The Sentry, an investigative initiative seeking to dismantle the networks of perpetrators and facilitators that benefit from Africa's deadliest conflicts. Like the SSP, The Sentry was cofounded by George Clooney and John Prendergast. One of its main focuses is tracking and analyzing how armed conflict and atrocities are financed, sustained, and monetized. In so doing, the organization hopes to upend the economic support for atrocities. Former president of Sudan Omar Hassan Ahmed al-Bashir has been the subject of many such reports.

The Sentry's team is composed of financial forensic investigators, international human rights lawyers, regional experts, and former law enforcement agents, intelligence officers, policymakers, investigative journalists, and banking professionals. It currently focuses its work on South Sudan, Sudan, the Democratic Republic of Congo, and the Central African Republic.

Alexis Herr

See also: Clooney, George; Enough Project; Janjaweed; Prendergast, John

Further Resources

Satellite Sentinel Project. Home page. Available at http://www.satsentinel.org.

The Sentry. Reports. Available at https://
thesentry.org/reports/.

Save Darfur Coalition

Largely through grassroots efforts, the Save
Darfur Coalition has raised awareness of
atrocities committed in Sudan's western
region of Darfur and mobilized a unified
response to end the conflict. The nonprofit
advocacy coalition includes 190 faith-based,
advocacy, and human rights organizations,
with more than 1 million activists and hundreds of community groups committed to
ending the genocide in Darfur.

On July 14, 2004, the Save Darfur Coalition was created at the Darfur Emergency
Summit, which was held in New York City
and sponsored by the United States Holocaust Memorial Museum and the American
Jewish World Service. Keynote speaker Elie
Wiesel, a Holocaust survivor and author,
encouraged participants to join together and
act on behalf of civilians in Darfur, who have
been targeted by the Sudanese government
since 2003. Dozens of organizations have
signed the coalition's Unity Statement, which
describes the killing, displacement, rape, and
ongoing attacks against civilians by the
government-sponsored militia known as
the Janjaweed as genocide.

Save Darfur has held various campaigns
to draw attention to the humanitarian crisis
and to motivate people to work for peace and
security in the region. In January 2006, the
organization called on individuals to send 1
million postcards to the White House urging
U.S. president George W. Bush to support
plans for a multinational force to protect the
people of Darfur. In April 2006, Save Darfur organized a rally in Washington, D.C.,
with 50,000 people in attendance. Later that
year, it coordinated the first Global Days for
Darfur campaign, in which events across the
United States and in more than fifty countries drew unprecedented crowds. Coalition
leaders have met with and petitioned President Bush and officials at the Sudanese
embassy to intercede.

In January 2007, the Save Darfur Coalition dispatched New Mexico governor and
former United Nations (UN) ambassador
Bill Richardson to meet with President
Omar Hassan Ahmed al-Bashir of Sudan.
Negotiations led to a peace agreement that
included a sixty-day cease-fire between the
Sudanese government and a rebel group. As
part of the Voices from Darfur tour, Sudanese refugees traveled across the United
States and shared their experiences in the
fall of 2007. Anticipating the 2008 Olympics in Beijing, China, the coalition started
its own Olympic torch relay to protest China's strong business relationship with the
Sudanese government.

Along with its international and national
events, the Save Darfur Coalition encourages local efforts. To generate publicity, the
group has paid for newspaper, television, and
billboard ads, and lawn signs and green
wristbands with the motto "Not on Our
Watch" have been made available for individuals to use to show their support for the
cause. Other campaigns have encouraged
community gatherings, student fundraisers,
prayer weekends for people of faith, and
requests to investment firms to avoid contributing to companies that are involved in
the crisis.

In April 2009, Save Darfur launched the
first annual Genocide Prevention Month. In
its first rendition, the coalition and its activists coordinated 220 events in forty-two
states, 118 religious organizations incorporated Darfur into faith services and events,
and forty bookstores across twenty states
featured books on genocide.

In spite of the wide publicity that the Save Darfur Coalition has brought to the conflict in Darfur, the organization also has drawn criticism for its aggressive campaigns, including ads in the United States and the United Kingdom that reported a death toll at 400,000 people since 2003. (Although the complexity of such crises complicates accurate casualty counts, conservative estimates at that time had placed the number of deaths closer to 200,000.) The aims of the coalition have also been characterized as out of touch with the nature of the conflict. Initially, campaigns called on the international community to establish a no-fly zone and to send a multilateral force to the region. However, relief organizations opposed such initiatives, claiming that such actions would impede their work and potentially cause further conflict if imposed without the consent of the Sudanese government. Additionally, some aid groups operating in Darfur contend that Save Darfur's budget is not directly applied to humanitarian services for refugees.

The organization was overseen by a board of directors who are selected from its member-organizations. An executive director coordinates the coalition's strategy and budget, advises the board on policies, and promotes cooperation among international, national, and local efforts. The Save Darfur operates on an annual budget of about $14 million, which it receives mostly through foundation grants and donations. Its 180 current member-organizations include Amnesty International, the Anti-Defamation League, the Council on American-Islamic Relations, the National Association for the Advancement of Colored People, and the National Association of Evangelicals.

In July 2011, the Save Darfur Coalition merged with the Genocide Intervention Network and the Sudan Divestment Task Force to become United to End Genocide, under the leadership of current president Tom Andrews.

Jane Messah

See also: Coalition for International Justice; Enough Project; United States Involvement in Darfur

Further Reading

Burr, J. Millard, and Robert O. Collins. 2006. *Darfur: The Long Road to Disaster.* Princeton, NJ: Markus Weiner.

Flint, Julie, and Alex de Waal. 2006. *Darfur: A Short History of a Long War.* London: Zed Books.

South Sudan

South Sudan seceded from Sudan and became an independent country on July 9, 2011. While many hoped that statehood could bring peace to the conflict-ridden nation, South Sudan has not yet escaped its violent past.

Colonial Period

The area now known as South Sudan became part of the colony of Equatoria in 1870, when it was discovered by British explorer Samuel Baker. During the Mahdist War (1885–1898) Equatoria became a state under the Anglo-Egyptian Condominium in 1899. In this dual colonial government between Great Britain and Egypt, the British oversaw the south, while the Egyptian forces administered the northern half of the country.

Under colonial command, division between the Sudanese in the north and south intensified, due in large part to the identity of the colonizers. Under the influence of Egypt, the northern half of Sudan was taught Arabic and Islam became the official religion, while in the British south, Sudanese learned English and attended Christian churches. The southern and northern zones continued to be ruled differently until the British colonial administrators combined the two colonies at the 1947 Juba Conference in the aftermath of World War II (1939–1945). Between 1945 and 1953, life for those in the south changed little. The British neglected to foster self-government in the south as an Arab and Islamic Sudanese nationalism mounted in the north.

Although no document proves this, many Southerners insist that they were promised self-determination by the departing colonialists, a commitment that those in the north broke (Johnson 2016: 2). When colonial rule came to an end, the northern and southern zones of Sudan still spoke different languages, practiced different religions, and had even taken on codified ethnic identities, with those in the north identifying as Arabs and those in the south as black Africans.

Civil Wars

From 1953 to 1963, Sudan transitioned from colonial rule to independence. The departure of colonial forces in the mid-twentieth century sparked conflict almost immediately. When the British left, they had intended the north and south to participate together in the new nation's political system. However, when the Arab government in Khartoum acted to exclude those in the south, the first civil war erupted.

The First Sudanese Civil War started in 1955 and concluded in 1972. It was fought between the Arab government in the north and the largely Christian and animist (a spiritual belief system that views all objects as possessing a distinct spiritual essence) south. The rebel groups in the south demanded greater representation in government affairs and the freedom to practice their own traditions and beliefs.

In 1969, a group of socialist and communist officers under the command of Colonel Gaafar Muhammad an-Nimeiry took control of Sudan in a government coup in the north. Under Nimeiry, a peace agreement was brokered and signed in 1972, thus ending the civil war by awarding partial autonomy to the south. From 1972 to 1983, the fighting that had dominated the first seventeen years of independence halted.

The Second Sudanese Civil War (1983–2005) was sparked by Nimeiry's decision to abolish the south's semiautonomous government in order to consolidate his power in the north. To do so, he instituted decrees and reforms intended to Islamize the country, which was an affront to the Christian-animist south. He declared Arabic the official language and instituted Sharia law countrywide. The declaration of Sharia law reignited conflict between the north and south. To fight the mounting forces in the south, Nimeiry plunged Sudan into debt and the Sudanese economy plummeted. Inflation, famine, and joblessness plagued the country.

In response to Nimeiry's about-face on the south's involvement in the government, Dr. John Garang formed a rebel movement in the south known as the Sudan People's Liberation Army (SPLA). The SPLA starting fighting the north in the summer of 1983, with an initial force of about 2,500 guerrilla fighters. Garang believed in a united Sudan, and along with his followers, he fought the forced institutionalization of Islamic law and called for a more open government.

In 1985, while Nimeiry was out of the country to meet with President Ronald Reagan in Washington, D.C., the Sudanese dictator was overthrown. Despite his removal from power, the war continued. In 1989, Colonel Omar Hassan Ahmed al-Bashir mounted a military coup and seized control of the government. Like Nimeiry, Bashir sought to expand the influence of Islam throughout Sudan and within its government. In 1993, he appointed himself president of Sudan, and three years later, he founded the National Congress Party (NCP).

Over the course of the two civil wars (1955–1972 and 1983–2005), an estimated 2.5 million people—mostly civilians—died due to starvation, drought, and violence. Some 26,000 boys and girls became the Lost Boys and Girls of Sudan, children who were orphaned and/or displaced during the Second Civil War. It has been suggested by some that the civil wars should be classified as a government-sponsored genocide given the perceived religious and ethnic divisions between north and south Sudan during the warfare.

Comprehensive Peace Agreement

Thanks to continued pressure from African nations, the United Nations (UN), and key Western governments, Bashir finally agreed to meet with leaders from the south to negotiate a peace treaty. After a lengthy mediation, on January 9, 2005, the warring parties signed the Comprehensive Peace Agreement (CPA) and brought the second civil war to an end. Many have argued that the focus of foreign countries and the United Nations on achieving the CPA came at the expense of lives in Darfur, as those involved in mediations feared that confronting Bashir about the killings occurring there would prompt him to walk away from the peace negotiations.

The CPA created a Government of Unity between Bashir's NCP and Garang's SPLA and appointed Garang as Sudan's first vice president. When Garang died in a helicopter crash on July 30, 2005, he was replaced by his deputy, Salva Kiir Mayardit.

Importantly, the CPA also called for a referendum vote for southern Sudan's independence to occur in 2011. After fifty-six years of strife, on July 9, 2011, south Sudanese citizens went to the polls and voted overwhelmingly for independence. Despite South Sudan's independence from Sudan, however, the two countries continue to fight over the contested oil-rich area of Abyei, which is located on the border between the two countries.

Present-Day Conflicts

At this time, South Sudan is again burdened by geographical and political violence and poor governance. Since achieving independence, conflict has erupted. Civil war broke out again in South Sudan in 2013, this time between those loyal to President Kiir and those backing his former vice president, Riek Machar. Along with Machar, President Kiir fired his entire cabinet in July 2013 owing to political disagreements. The conflict between Kiir and Machar has taken on an ethnic dimension because members of the Dinka tribe (the largest tribe in the country) are typically loyal to Kiir, a Dinka, and members of the Nuer tribe (the second largest) are loyal to Machar, who is a Nuer.

Months after Machar was fired, tensions between the two groups they represented reached a breaking point. On December 15, 2013, fighting erupted in the headquarters of the army, in South Sudan's capital city of Juba, between Dinka and Nuer members of Kiir's presidential guard, also known as the Tiger Division. Fighting that had begun in the army barracks quickly spread into the streets of the capital. Dinka members of the Sudan People's Liberation Army (SPLA) set up impromptu checkpoints through Juba and started stopping and attacking Nuer civilians. Thousands of Nuer managed to skirt the checkpoints and make their way to relative safety on two bases managed by the United Nations Mission in South Sudan.

Despite claiming to have launched investigations into the violence that occurred in Juba, the government has failed to release reports of its findings or hold people accountable for crimes against civilians. Since December 2013, an estimated 383,000 people have been killed, and nearly 4 million have been internally displaced or have fled to neighboring countries. The United States has instituted targeted sanctions against the leaders of the conflict, and the United Nations has passed an arms embargo. Although a series of peace treaties was signed between Kiir and Machar in June, July, and August 2018, the fighting continues.

Of the country's estimated population of 12.8 million, some 7 million require humanitarian assistance and protection, and 1.96 million have been forced to flee their homes to escape the fighting. In addition, sexual violence continues to destroy lives and communities throughout the nation. Attempts at forming a unity government in South Sudan continue to flounder, however, despite U.S., UN, and international pressure.

Alexis Herr

See also: Egyptian Involvement in Darfur; Garang, John; Kiir, Salva; Lost Boys and Girls of Sudan; Nuba; Rape

Further Reading

Johnson, Hilde F. 2016. *South Sudan the Untold Story: From Independence to Civil War*. New York: I. B. Tauris.

Turse, Nick. 2016. *Next Time They'll Come to Count the Dead: War and Survival in South Sudan*. Chicago: Dispatch Books.

Walzer, Craig, ed. 2008. *Out of Exile: Narratives from the Abducted and Displaced People of Sudan*. San Francisco: Voice of Witness.

Steidle, Brian

Brian Steidle is a former U.S. Marine Corps officer best known for his work documenting the humanitarian disaster and genocide that have been taking place in the Darfur region of Sudan since 2003. Born in 1976, as the son of a naval officer, he spent his childhood moving from location to location. He received his university education at Virginia Tech (at which he earned a science degree), and then joined the Marine Corps. By the time he left the service at the end of 2003, he had reached the rank of captain.

In January 2004, after having served in Kosovo and elsewhere, Steidle saw a job opening for a U.S. monitor working in the Nuba Mountains of Sudan with a group called the Joint Military Commission, assisting with the creation and implementation of a north-south cease-fire between the government of Sudan in the north and the largely Christian south. Within seven months, he had become a senior operations officer. In September 2004, he moved into a different role as an unarmed military observer and U.S. representative to the African Union (AU) in the region of Darfur. He was one of only three Americans serving with a coalition of African countries monitoring the cease-fire between the government of Sudan and black African rebel groups such as the Sudan Liberation Army (SLA).

Steidle served for six months in Darfur as an unarmed military observer. While there, he documented every day of his experience with his pen, his computer, and his camera. He emailed reports home almost every day, documenting systematic attacks against civilians as he watched the situation worsen. In a classic instance of deliberate destruction, he witnessed the following set-pattern formula: a fighter plane would arrive and circle a village to conduct reconnaissance, followed by helicopter gunships that would hover above the village and shoot at anything that moved. Then, on the ground, the Janjaweed militia, together with Sudanese forces, would close in on trucks or a combination of horses, camels, and motor vehicles. The village would then be burned and looted, but not before the Janjaweed plundered all its valuable goods. All too often, Steidle would see the remains of people who were locked inside their home as it was burned to the ground. Some of these so-called villages were in reality small towns of up to 20,000 inhabitants. Steidle saw them burned to ashes, resulting in hundreds of thousands of displaced civilians. He also saw the results of violent atrocities, including rape, torture, and murder.

The impotence that Steidle felt by being unable to physically help the people he was observing played on his conscience to such an extent that after six months—and having taken nearly 1,000 photographs and a large number of witness statements—he resigned his position. In February 2005, he returned to the United States. He concluded that he had become a silent witness to genocide, a situation he could not abide. Convinced that he could be more effective by bringing the story of what he witnessed in Darfur to the world, and feeling that he could not stay quiet about the horrors he had witnessed, he decided to publicize his observations.

Steidle began talking to people and groups about what he had seen and sought appointments with influential leaders and policymakers. Within a short period, he had addressed more than 500 public-awareness functions across the United States, including university events at Harvard, Princeton, Stanford, the University of California at Los Angeles, West Point, and the U.S. Naval Academy. He met with members of Congress and such eminent leaders as former U.S. secretary of state Condoleezza Rice. He testified in the Congress and the British Parliament as well. He took his material to *The New York Times* and any other media outlet that would have him and worked hard to raise awareness of the human rights violations and atrocities that were taking place in Darfur. Overall, his outrage and frustration brought Darfur to the attention of the United States and helped pave the way for renewed efforts on the part of the United Nations.

With his sister, Gretchen Steidle Wallace, he coauthored the 2007 book *The Devil Came on Horseback: Bearing Witness to the Genocide in Darfur*. It addressed the atrocities that Steidle had seen in Darfur and showed how international inaction had cost the lives of hundreds of thousands of people. Steidle and Wallace drew heavily on the many emails that had passed between them during the crisis, as well as extensive notes taken in the field and the large number of photographs taken by Steidle, many of which have since become iconic images of the Darfur Genocide. An impassioned memoir, *The Devil Came on Horseback* took its name from the feared nickname given to the the Janjaweed, the Arab militias that did so much to terrorize the black African population of Darfur; the "devils on horseback."

At the same time as the book's appearance came a documentary of the same name, featuring Steidle's photographs and narration. Directed by Ricki Stern and Anne Sundberg, and produced by Wallace and Jane Wells, it premiered at film festivals in early and mid-2007 and won numerous awards. The film alternates between contemporary footage shot by the filmmakers and Steidle's own images from his time in Darfur. The viewer sees civilians who have been murdered and whole villages that have been burned and devastated. A confrontational movie, it charges its viewers to become educated about the ongoing genocide in Darfur and find ways to direct political leaders to take action to stop the killing. On this note, it also laments the failure of the United States and other countries to end the crisis. An up-close and uncompromising look at the Darfur catastrophe, the film does not hold back in its attempt to raise public awareness about the atrocities in Sudan.

Today, Steidle remains an activist against genocide. His campaigning originally ignited American public awareness of the Darfur Genocide and continues to do so today. He is an adviser to a variety of nongovernmental organizations on their current operations in Sudan and Chad on such subjects as intelligence gathering, Sudanese military operations, and war crimes. He has also assisted the International Criminal Court in its investigation of war crimes in Sudan, in particular with regard to Bashir, who was indicted in July 2008 by prosecutor Luis Moreno Ocampo for genocide, crimes against humanity, and war crimes in Darfur.

Paul R. Bartrop

See also: African Union Mission in Sudan; Bashir, Omar Hassan Ahmed al-; Janjaweed; Nuba; Wallace, Gretchen Steidle

Further Reading

Steidle, Brian, and Gretchen Steidle Wallace. 2008. *The Devil Came on Horseback:*

Bearing Witness to the Genocide in Darfur. New York: Public Affairs Books.

Sudan

Sudan is the third-largest country in Africa, with a land area more than three times larger than France. Located in North Africa, its northern half is a desert through which the Nile River flows on its way to Egypt. The southern half contains vast regions in which there are great swamps caused from the meanderings of the White Nile. The population in the south is African and Christian or animist, and the residents of the northern desert area are generally Arab and Muslim. In 2011, South Sudan seceded from Sudan to form its own nation.

Throughout most of its history, Sudan, especially the northern half, has been dominated by Egypt. In the late nineteenth century, the British colonized both Egypt and Sudan. The decision to have the northern area administered by the Egyptians and the southern area administered by the British eventually led to the Christianization of the south and the Islamization of the north. Following independence (January 1, 1956), the First Sudanese Civil War, which had begun in 1955, flared into a full revolt. The cause of the war was rooted in the goal of the Islamic leaders in the north to destroy Christian and animist control of the south so that the whole country could be transformed into an Islamic state.

The fighting mainly took place in the south. Occasionally, there was fighting among groups of rebels, as well as against the Sudanese army. In 1958, a military coup brought General Ibrahim Abboud to power in Khartoum. A resistance movement in the south intensified when Khartoum tried to force abandonment of the use of English and native languages, the imposition of Arabic, and conversion to Islam.

The rebels, operating with captured weapons, conducted a guerrilla-style war. The exile community, meanwhile, organized around the Sudan African Nationalist Movement. The Anyanya movement of southern blacks, led by Joseph Lagu, conducted the war against the Islamic government. The war ended with the Addis Ababa Peace Agreement in 1972. It has been estimated that 500,000 people were killed during the first civil war, and thousands more were driven from their homes. Crimes against humanity during the first civil war included the sacking and burning of villages, rape, the execution of prisoners or civilians deemed not useful as slaves, and cultural extermination through the prohibition of the use of English and native languages. The enslavement of young women and children was often accompanied by their forced conversion to Islam.

The Second Sudanese Civil War began in 1983, when Gaafar Muhammad an-Nimeiry, the Sudanese leader of the Free Officers Movement, sought to take control of the south by abrogating the Addis Ababa Peace Agreement. The conflict raged until 2005. The south formed the Sudan People's Liberation Army (SPLA) to resist Nimeiry. In 1989, Omar Hassan Ahmed al-Bashir led a coup that took control of the north. As the leader of the Muslim Brotherhood, he called for a jihad against the south. The country was opened to Islamic radicals and international terrorists such as Osama bin Laden. Driving the Second Sudanese Civil War was the battle for control of oil-producing areas located mainly in the Abyei area. By 1999, oil began to flow, providing revenue for the government to use to buy arms. The burning

of villages and expulsion or killing of civilians have been less than systematic, but they lasted long enough to have killed or displaced thousands, including some who came to be known as the Lost Boys and Girls (children who were orphaned and/or displaced during the Second Sudanese Civil War). Amnesty International and other nongovernmental organizations have alleged that war crimes and crimes against humanity were committed by all sides in southern Sudan.

Starting in 2003, global attention started to focus on Darfur, whose name is Arabic for "the home of the Fur." It is an arid area in western Sudan about 1,000 miles south of the Mediterranean Sea. It borders the Sahara Desert in the north and the Sahel in the south and is about the size of mainland Spain. The mass killing of the so-called black African residents of Darfur by the troops of the Sudanese government beginning in 2003 constituted what the United States identified as a genocide. Although the methods (bombings from airplanes, automatic weapons fire, stabbings, burning people alive, poisoning of wells, and chasing victims into forbidding deserts without water or food) have remained constant over the years, the number of killings has ebbed and flowed as the government of Sudan has turned the spigot of violence on and off according to its wiles in its game of brinkmanship with the international community.

To date, it is estimated that at least 400,000 people have been murdered. Some 3 million persons have been forced from their villages, and more than 225,000 have fled to Chad, a neighboring state. The killings, rapes, ethnic cleansing, and expulsions have been inflicted largely by the Janjaweed, seminomadic and nomadic Arab Muslim herders from northern Sudan. They have been accused of genocide by killing, raping, and expelling great numbers with the connivance of the Sudanese government.

The causes of any genocide are extremely complex, and the Darfur Genocide is no exception. The issues and events that combined to make it possible include extreme drought that resulted in a dramatic decline in the yield of produce, loss of pastureland, and loss of livestock. Along with the resulting famine, the impact of the drought increased tensions over land use and access to water and ultimately resulted in ever-increasing conflict and violence between the nomadic/seminomadic "Arab" groups and the sedentary/farming group of "non-Arabs." Arab supremacism, an ideology that promotes the notion that Arab beliefs and way of life are superior to all others, is also a contributing factor, and authoritarianism has taken its toll as well: for nearly thirty years, Sudan was led by the authoritarian ruler Bashir, whose regime controlled virtually every aspect of Sudanese life. The "non-Arab" population was perceived and treated as second-class citizens, and the government ruthlessly suppressed any signs of opposition and dissent. Further more, "black Africans" are largely disenfranchised, with just a single region of Sudan, the north (where Khartoum, the capital, is located and accounts for just over 5 percent of the country's population), controlling virtually all the country. This naturally feeds long-standing hostilities among Sudan's various regions.

In April 2007, the United Nations (UN) sent materials to the International Criminal Court (ICC) accusing fifty-one individuals of war crimes in Darfur. On May 3, 2007, the ICC, meeting in The Hague, issued warrants for Ahmad Mohammed Harun, the humanitarian affairs minister of Sudan, and Ali Muhammad Ali Abd al-Rahman (aka Ali Kushayb), a top commander of the Janjaweed, for crimes against humanity. Harun

was interior minister at the height of the Darfur Genocide. In August 2007, the UN Human Rights Office charged the Sudanese army and its allied militias with war crimes. Specifically, it alleged that the Sudanese army had made sex slaves of women and young girls abducted from Darfur villages. The enslavements came after raids on the east Jabel Marra region in southern Darfur in December 2006.

In March 2009, after months of bureaucratic wrangling, the ICC issued an arrest warrant for President Bashir. In July 2010, the court specifically charged him with three counts of having helped orchestrate the genocide in Darfur. However, Bashir remained at large in Sudan and was not brought to justice. The ICC and other international officials warned him that he faced apprehension and detention should he leave Sudan and travel to a nation that supports the court's authority. However, Bashir received support from numerous nations, including Egypt and Qatar, who refused to arrest him even when he visited there. The African Union likewise refused to abide by the ICC's arrest warrant.

Meanwhile, in May 2006, the Darfur Peace Agreement (DPA) was finalized between the SPLA and the Sudanese government. This accord lasted until December 2010, when the SPLA abrogated it. That same month, more peace talks commenced in Doha, Qatar. The Doha Document for Peace in Darfur (DDPD) talks, however, broke down; since then, some parties have agreed to a comprehensive peace accord, but several key groups have yet to endorse it. In the meantime, the region has seen a general reduction of fighting, but tensions remain high and the possibility of renewed bloodshed seems ever present.

In January 2012, President Bashir formally announced the creation of two new states in Darfur: Central Darfur and East Darfur, each to be administered by a government-appointed governor. Oil revenues have rejuvenated the Sudanese army in recent years, particularly since oil prices spiked beginning in 2011. The army in turn has supplied the Janjaweed with weapons. The Sudanese army has also conducted ethnic cleansing in the disputed border region between Sudan and South Sudan to pave the way for oil companies to explore the area and exploit its resources.

In December 2018, amid years of U.S. sanctions and loss of oil revenue owing to emergency austerity measures and a sharp currency devaluation, government cuts to bread and fuel subsidies gave rise to popular protests in Khartoum. Although most sanctions had been lifted in 2017 to help the failing country after it had lost many of its oil fields to South Sudan upon its independence in 2011, the Sudanese economy plummeted. The protesters first gathered to rally against the rising costs of food, but their calls quickly demanded the removal of Bashir and his government. The demonstrations have been led by the Sudanese Professional Association, a collaboration of health workers, lawyers, and doctors. Women have also played a prominent role in the protests despite reports of sexual assaults by military police.

On April 11, 2019, the military removed Bashir from power and stepped in to oversee the government. Currently, Bashir is being held in a jail in Sudan, and the provisional government has suggested that it will send him to The Hague to face the charges levied by the ICC. The protesters have not dispersed from the capital and are demanding that the military set up a civilian government.

Andrew J. L. Waskey

See also: British Involvement in Darfur; Lost Boys and Girls of Sudan; South Sudan; Sudanese Civil Wars; United States Involvement in Darfur

Further Reading

Burr, J. Millard, and Robert O. Collins. 2003. *Revolutionary Sudan: Hasan al-Turabi and the Islamist State, 1989–2000*. Boston: Brill Academic Publishers.

Holt, P. M., and Martin Daly. 2000. *The History of the Sudan, from the Coming of Islam to the Present Day*. New York: Longman.

Sudanese Civil Wars

Prior to South Sudan's independence from Sudan in 2011, the two nations had been embroiled in nearly forty years of fighting. The First Sudanese Civil War (1955–1972) and the Second Sudanese Civil War (1983–2005) elucidate the underlying religious, ethnic, political, and economic conflicts that came to a head as colonial forces planned their withdraw from Sudan. While often defined as two separate civil wars, some argue that the brief period of reprieve (1972–1983) belies the fact that a war of identity was being waged between the north and south even after the outright fighting abated. For this reason, some scholars and journalists refer to the civil wars collectively instead of as two separate periods. And although independence has been won by the south, fighting between Sudan and South Sudan over oil reserves located along their border has continued.

First Sudanese Civil War (1955–1972)

The roots of the ethnic and religious tensions that gave rise to the First Sudanese Civil War are connected to Sudan's colonial past. From 1899 to 1955, the country was jointly ruled by British and Egyptian forces in the so-called Anglo-Egyptian Condominium. In the northern region administered by Egyptian forces, the national language was Arabic and the religion Islam. In the southern zone, the British taught the residents English and brought with them Christian missionaries who succeeded in converting them. Furthermore, in the north, the population came to view itself as Arab, not African, and those in the south as "black Africans." As a result, by the time the British-led Anglo-Egyptian Condominium was set to return Sudan to the Sudanese, the north and south spoke different languages, practiced different religions, and viewed themselves as belonging to different ethnic groups and tribes.

Even before the colonizers departed, fighting had erupted between those in the north and south. In February 1953, the Anglo-Egyptian government announced its intent to withdraw its forces in three years. The British viewed those in the south as less capable of leading themselves and thus tied their fate to that of the north. Despite a three-year transitional period, those in the south were essentially left out. The north, the British reasoned, had the necessary infrastructure and economic resources to lead the country, and so it focused its efforts on preparing national elites in the north for self-government. As the residents of the south became angry that they were being denied a voice in the future of Sudan, fighting soon broke out between the two regions.

It took almost two decades for the hostilities to abate. In 1972, the Addis Ababa Peace Agreement was signed between the southern rebels, known as the Anyanya, and the government of Sudan in Khartoum. The deal included power-sharing agreements, security guarantees, and greater economic stimulation for the south. Furthermore, the militaries of the north and south were to be slowly intermixed.

Interwar Period (1972–1989)

During the relatively brief period between the civil wars, oil was discovered by the U.S.-based Chevron Corporation in 1976 in Bentiu in southern Sudan. This motivated lingering discord between the Sudanese government and southern rebel leaders over the economic development of the south. By the time fighting broke out again in 1983, the Sudan People's Liberation Movement (SPLM), a new organization created that year and headed by John Garang, called for the overthrow of all Islamic leaders from national power.

Influenced by communist theories of social and economic reform, the movement's leaders emphasized a Sudan based on equality rather than factors of race, ethnicity, religious persuasion, gender, or cultural beliefs. Those in the south, in the purview of the SPLM, were as deserving of the same rights, benefits, and protection as those in the north. Wary that such a theory could come into practice under the current government, an Islamic fundamentalist movement grew in northern Sudan. Islamic clerics seized control of the government on June 30, 1989, and began to rule the country through the military and Sharia (Islamic law).

Second Sudanese Civil War (1989–2005)

The Second Sudanese Civil War was fought between the Sudanese government forces and the Sudan People's Liberation Movement/Army (SPLM/A), representing the south. Hostilities ebbed considerably in the early 1990s as international leaders and the United Nations (UN) attempted to broker a peace settlement. Fighting had severely affected the entire nation and had even led to starvation and bloodshed in neighboring nations, a development that threatened to widen the war beyond Sudan.

In 1992 and 1993, a peace agreement was reached through the auspices of the Inter-Governmental Authority on Drought and Desertification. The organization offered a secularization plan to separate religion from the state to reduce the ethnic and religious tensions fueling the conflict.

Although the Islamic government rejected the plan for religious reasons in late 1993, they reached a peace agreement with rebel groups four years later. The government, however, still adamantly refused to remove Islamic values from the functions of the state, which has prompted rebel factions to reject the government's recent call for peace and unity. A cease-fire agreement was never established and fighting resumed.

On January 19, 2002, a cease-fire agreement was mediated by the United States and Switzerland. The agreement called for a cessation of fighting in the Nuba Mountain region, a key stronghold for southern forces; a halt to the aerial bombardment of civilians; and the establishment of so-called tranquility zones to allow humanitarian aid to resume unfettered. Further negotiations on power- and revenue-sharing between the north and south eventually led to the signing of the CPA in January 2005, formally ending the two-decade-plus second phase of the war, which is estimated to have killed more than 2 million people and internally displaced more than 4 million others from their homes due to fighting or war-related famine.

The CPA established a semiautonomous region for ten states in the south of Sudan and called for a referendum in which southerners could elect to secede and form an independent country. In that referendum, held in January 2011, more than 98 percent of southern voters opted to secede. The Republic of South Sudan was formally declared on July 9, 2011; however, hostilities along border areas and in the disputed region of Abyei have continued.

Alexis Herr and Dennis Moran

See also: Comprehensive Peace Agreement; Garang, John; Lost Boys and Girls of Sudan; South Sudan; Sudan People's Liberation Movement

Further Reading

Deng, Francis Mading. 1995. *War of Visions: Conflict of Identities in the Sudan*. Washington, DC: Brookings Institution Press.

Holt, P. M., and Martin Daly. 2000. *The History of the Sudan, from the Coming of Islam to the Present Day*. New York: Longman.

Rolandsen, Øystein H., and M. W. Daly. 2007. *Darfur's Sorrow: A History of Destruction and Genocide*. Cambridge: Cambridge University Press.

Sudan Liberation Army

The Sudan Liberation Army (SLA) first formed to demand justice for Darfurians who had been driven from their homes, seen their cattle and crops stolen, and even been murdered for trying to protect their land from plunder and unjust theft. Their reason for leading a rebellion against the Sudanese government in 2003 was about more than economic marginalization, however; they were rising up against the political isolation of Darfurians because of their perceived African ethnicity, as opposed to the assumed Arab identity of the perpetrators.

The SLA's origins reach back to the 1980s, when young Fur people first banded together to protest the Arab domination of the central government in Sudan's capital, Khartoum, and the harassment of their people by Arab nomads. This group of Fur would evolve into what became known as the Darfur

Liberation Front (DLF). In February 2003, the DLF took control of Gulu, the main town in Darfur's central province of Jebel Marrah. Led by Abdel Wahid, the DLF set up camps in Gulu and began staging attacks against the Sudanese military.

In March 2003, the DLF announced that it had changed its name to the SLA. The same day, it released a political declaration that the SLA's goal was to create a united democratic Sudan, and they were willing to use force to do so. A few days after the declaration was released, the SLA entered into a short-lived cease-fire with Khartoum.

The SLA draws the core of its membership from three Darfurian ethnic groups: the Fur, Zaghawa, and Massalit. The original members of the SLA ranged in age from teenagers to men in their fifties, most of whom had far more experience tilling the land than fighting. Some had worked as police or in the army and for a time had turned a blind eye to the ethnic violence spreading throughout Darfur, but once the government started attacking their villages and killing their families, they could no longer ignore the situation. A smaller number of SLA fighters were teachers, lawyers, and other professionals who also were drawn into the conflict as their families came under fire.

The SLA took control of the village of Tine, on the border with Chad, on March 26, 2003. The conflict between the SLA and government forces intensified, and by the beginning of August, the government had recruited Darfurian Arab militias to help with the fighting. These fighters, known as the *Janjaweed*, entered into very few direct battles with the SLA during the next three years; instead, they carried out a scorched-earth campaign against the mostly unarmed people of Darfur, raping, pillaging, and murdering in village after village. The guerrilla

SLA, though it had far fewer troops than the Janjaweed, enjoyed strong popular support. Headquartered in the mountains of central Darfur, the SLA was supported by villagers who provided its fighters with food, shelter, and intelligence on its adversaries. As of 2006, the SLA was estimated to have 16,000 fighters.

Unsuccessful peace talks were held in Chad in December 2003, and so the conflict continued. In January 2004, Sudan's government filed a complaint with neighboring Eritrea, which it claimed had been helping the SLA. Neither the SLA nor Eritrea confirmed these claims.

Along with Darfur's other major rebel group, the Justice and Equality Movement (JEM), the SLA signed a cease-fire in Chad in April 2004. The agreement included safe passage for humanitarian aid teams and the disarmament of the Janjaweed, and Sudan's government made plans to return many refugees to the country. In July, SLA, JEM, and the government began peace talks. They fell apart in December, however, because of alleged cease-fire violations. The African Union, which sent 7,000 peacekeeping troops to Darfur, said that the cease-fire was frequently violated by all the groups involved.

November 2005 marked the beginning of the splintering of the SLA into numerous factions that have competed for territory and fought one another, a phenomenon that has had drastic consequences for the peace process and increased the complexity of the conflict. The first split within the SLA occurred following the election of Minni Minawi as SLA leader during a conference boycotted by Abdel Wahid, who had led the DLF during the siege of Gulu. Wahid loyalists, who primarily shared his Fur ethnicity, did not recognize the election of Minawi, an ethnic Zaghawa, and the two emerging factions soon engaged in bloody fighting in North Darfur.

While the predominantly Fur SLA-Wahid and the predominantly Zaghawa SLA-Minawi remain the two largest factions, as of September 2007, the extent of these internal power struggles was reflected in the existence of an estimated dozen rival factions. On May 5, 2006, the SLA-Minawi faction signed a peace agreement with the government. For his cooperation, Minawi was made senior assistant to the president. Both SLA-Wahid and JEM continued to hold out for the government to agree to such demands as greater compensation for Darfur war victims, an SLA role in disarming the Janjaweed, and providing aid for refugees to return to their homes.

Shifting alliances and splintering within the SLA has complicated peace efforts in Darfur. In 2010, Ahmad Abdel Shafi allied the Juba faction of the SLA with other rebel groups to create the Liberation and Justice Movement (LJM). The LJM signed, in July 2011, the Doha Document for Peace, though Abdel Shafi has since distanced himself from his organization, believing that the government is not truly invested in peace. Later in 2011, two major factions of the SLA joined with JEM and the Sudan People's Liberation Movement-North to continue resistance.

Alexis Herr

See also: Abdel Shafi, Ahmad; African Union Mission in Sudan; Minawi, Minni; Wahid, Abdel

Further Reading

Anderson, Scott. 2004. "How Did Darfur Happen?" *The New York Times*. October 17.

Deng, Francis Mading. 1995. *War of Visions: Conflict of Identities in the Sudan*. Washington, DC: Brookings Institution Press.

Sudan People's Liberation Movement/Army

The Sudan People's Liberation Movement (SPLM) was a rebel organization that opposed the imposition of Islamic law (Sharia) in the southern, non-Muslim part of Sudan, and through its military wing, the Sudan People's Liberation Army (SPLA), fought for south Sudanese rights during the Second Sudanese Civil War (1983–2005). Both groups have gone on to play key roles in the running of South Sudan since its statehood was realized in 2011.

The SPLM emerged in response to the radicalized policy of President Gaafar Muhammad an-Nimeiry. In 1983, the president introduced Sharia law and reneged on the provision in the Addis Ababa Peace Agreement for a referendum on the future of the oil-rich Abyei region. The enactment of Sharia law and the breaking of the Addis Ababa Peace Agreement went against the mediated peace that had concluded the First Sudanese Civil War (1955–1972) between the predominantly Muslim north and the Christian south. In short, Sharia law criminalized the south's ability to practice Christianity and local traditions that conflicted with radicalized Islamic law. And the infringement on the Abyei region demonstrated that the government of Sudan had no intention of allowing the south to operate with any autonomy.

At the time that President Nimeiry was instituting his aggressive policies, John Garang was an officer in the Sudanese army. He had been sent by Nimeiry in February 1983 to negotiate with a group of mutineers at the Bor garrison, a group of 500 southern troops who refused to be sent to the north of the country. Instead of suppressing the mutiny in Bor, Garang joined in and encouraged other such mutinies throughout Sudan. In fact, it has been convincingly argued that Garang instigated the Bor mutiny in the first place. Garang, like those who joined his movement, was from the south, and with support of his fellow Sudanese southern combatants, he formed the SPLM, the political wing of his movement, on April 6, 1983, and the SPLA, the military wing, in the summer of 1983, with an initial force of about 2,500 guerilla fighters. The SPLA soon became the dominant rebel force in the south of the country, although its growth was undermined by infighting. The establishment of a new regime under Omar Hassan Ahmed al-Bashir in 1989 did not help the SPLM's cause, but with a force of about 25,000 troops, Garang and his SPLA had gained control of most of the south's nonurban areas.

Early in its existence, the SPLM sought to establish a people's democratic and socialist government, but in 1987, it began to downplay its emphasis on Marxism-Leninism and press for the south to be given a greater role in national affairs and an increased share in economic development projects. In 1992, the group began to call for the creation of a confederation that would enable the south to be an autonomous, secular state. Among its major complaints was that the government had uprooted thousands of southern Sudanese to open land for oil drilling.

In April 1993, after several years of severe internal dissension, several factions opposed to Garang split from the SPLM and formed a new group called SPLA-United. Again, however, internal fighting disintegrated the rival group. The main branch continued to hold sporadic peace talks with representatives of the northern government. After several cease-fire attempts in the late 1990s and early 2001, the SPLM and the Sudanese government agreed on January 19, 2002, to a cease-fire brokered by the United States and Switzerland. Additional negotiations began in May 2002 and talks, held over the next two years, resulted in the Machakos Protocol in July 2002, an additional cease-fire in 2003, the Security Protocol in September 2003, and the Wealth-Sharing Protocol in January 2004.

In May 2004, Garang and the government signed an additional three protocols as part of the Comprehensive Peace Agreement (CPA). The deal gave the southern Sudanese increased religious freedom, a greater share of national oil revenues and governmental power, and the right to decide on secession from the north after a six-year interim period, among other points. Additionally, Garang was named president of the south and first vice president in the federal government of President Bashir under the umbrella of "National Unity." Soon after the May 2004 signing, Garang sent out a return-to-base call to SPLM members worldwide, urging them to return to their units.

In December 2004, under a United Nations (UN) Security Council mandate, a permanent cease-fire was signed, followed by the signing of the final landmark CPA in January 2005. Under the accord, which cemented the May 2004 provisions, southerners were no longer subject to Sharia law.

With the CPA finalized in 2005, the SPLM became a Sudanese political party, as well as the dominant party in what the CPA established as the Southern Sudan semiautonomous region. Garang remained vice president of the federal government and president of the south until his untimely death in a helicopter crash on July 30, 2005. Salva Kiir assumed Garang's governmental capacities, as well as his role as head of the SPLM. In Sudanese legislative elections held in April 2010, the SPLM dominated in the south, winning all but 10 of the 170 seats for the semiautonomous region's legislature. Kiir was elected president of the south (a position he had held since Garang's death) with 93 percent of the vote. Election monitors said that the conduct of the election did not measure up to international standards, but the results were widely accepted internationally.

In January 2011, the residents of South Sudan, including many thousands of exiles voting from abroad, overwhelmingly approved the referendum promised by the terms of the CPA on becoming an independent country. The Republic of South Sudan was formally declared on July 9, 2011.

Since the declaration of the independent South Sudan, the SPLM has remained the dominant political party and the SPLA the national army. The two are often referred to together as the SPLM/A.

The SPLM's leadership overwhelmingly comprises members of the Dinka, the largest of South Sudan's ethnic groups, comprising about a quarter of the population. Critics within South Sudan believe that the party favors Dinka interests in a region that has long suffered from tribal rivalries for resources. In recent years, rebel militias have formed, sometimes including ex-SPLA members; and during the preparations for statehood in 2011, clashes between the SPLA and rebel militias within South Sudan increased, causing an estimated death toll of more than 2,000 in the first six months of the year. SPLM/A officials believe that the rebel militias are being funded by the Sudanese government in Khartoum in an effort to destabilize the new country, an assertion denied by both the rebel militias and Sudanese government officials.

Alexis Herr

See also: Garang, John; Kiir, Salva; South Sudan; Sudanese Civil War

Further Reading

Deng, Francis Mading. 1995. *War of Visions: Conflict of Identities in the Sudan.* Washington, DC: Brookings Institution Press.

Holt, P. M., and Martin Daly. 2000. *The History of the Sudan, from the Coming of Islam to the Present Day.* New York: Longman.

T

Talisman Energy Corporation

The Talisman Energy Corporation is a Canadian oil company that withdrew its operations in Sudan in the wake of criticism that revenue from those operations was enabling the government to commit human rights abuses.

In October 1998, the Talisman Energy Corporation acquired a 25 percent share in the Greater Nile Petroleum Operating Company (GNPOC), a consortium in which Chinese, Malaysian, and Sudanese companies held 40, 30, and 5 percent, respectively. Within months, advocacy groups such as Amnesty International and the American Anti-Slavery Group (AASG) launched campaigns protesting Talisman's alleged complicity in human rights violations occurring during the war in Sudan.

The United States had already placed Sudan on its list of states sponsoring terrorism in 1993, and President Bill Clinton had signed the Anti-Terrorism Act in 1997, prohibiting Americans from engaging in business with governments on the list. In a letter to Canadian foreign affairs minister Lloyd Axworthy in 1999, U.S. secretary of state Madeleine Albright urged Canada to press Talisman to withdraw from Sudan. Axworthy commissioned the diplomat John Harker to investigate Talisman's affairs in Sudan. Harker's January 2000 report confirmed some complaints of critics by concluding that oil was exacerbating the conflict in Sudan, although it did not charge Talisman with actively aiding in atrocities. The government of Sudan had used oil company airstrips and roads for military actions against rebels, while oil revenues financed its war effort and lessened the incentive for it to seek a negotiated peace. Furthermore, the government's imperative to secure access to oil led it to commit forced mass displacements of civilians.

The advocacy groups lobbied Canadian and American politicians to act against both Sudan and Talisman. They appealed to Talisman shareholders to compel the company to withdraw from the GNPOC. The AASG led a campaign to induce major institutional investors to divest themselves of Talisman stock—U.S. pension funds sold millions of Talisman shares in 1999 and 2000 as a result of activist pressure. In 2001, an attorney on the board of the AASG filed a $1 billion class-action suit against Talisman, charging it with collaborating with the Sudanese government in committing genocide, war crimes, and crimes against humanity to clear access to oil fields. However, the case was eventually dismissed in a district court in 2006.

Facing continued negative publicity and shareholder discontent, Talisman sold its share of GNPOC in March 2003, despite the fact that its Sudan oil production was exceeding expectations. Talisman's chief executive officer, Jim Buckee, attributed the sale to the depressing effect that the political fallout was having on the company's stock prices, as well as U.S. threats to exclude Talisman from American financial markets.

Defenders of the company have pointed to its dedication to building health and educational infrastructure in Sudan and its potentially moderating influence on government policies. Furthermore, with Talisman's departure, Sudan's oil industry was now being managed by those who, like the Chinese, were relatively impervious to human-rights pressure.

Karl A. Yambert

See also: Nuba

Further Reading

Burr, J. Millard, and Robert O. Collins. 2006. *Darfur: The Long Road to Disaster*. Princeton, NJ: Markus Weiner.

Kobrin, Stephen J. 2004. "Oil and Politics: Talisman Energy and Sudan." *NYU Journal of Law and Politics*. 36, nos. 2–3: 425–456.

Turabi, Hassan al-

Hassan al-Turabi (1932–2016) was one of the most influential figures in Sudanese politics as a leader of the National Islamic Front (NIF), which later became the National Congress Party (NCP). In the 1990s, he played a key role in radicalizing and politicizing Islam in Sudan. He also played an important role in the 1989 coup that propelled President Omar Hassan Ahmed al-Bashir to power.

Commonly referred to as the grandfather of modern political Islam in Sudan, al-Turabi had deep religious roots. Born on February 1, 1932, in Kassala, the capital of eastern Sudan, he was the son of a *qadi,* or religious judge. His family was noted for its long lineage of Islamic scholarship and practice of Qadiri Sufism, a religious order steeped in Islamic mysticism. His father spent a substantial amount of time teaching al-Turabi religious law and science, an education that was furthered by his time at Khartoum University. For his postgraduate studies, al-Turabi attended the University of London, where he earned a master's degree in law, followed by a doctorate in law at the Sorbonne in Paris.

Two months after finishing his studies abroad, al-Turabi delivered a speech in September 1964 at Khartoum University calling for deposing the military regime of Ibrahim Abboud. Abboud was a career soldier who had become deputy commander in chief of the Sudanese military in 1949, and then, after Sudan's independence from colonial rule, he served as the head of state in Sudan (1958–1964) and president of Sudan in 1964. Just a month after his speech criticizing the president, al-Turabi played an important role in overthrowing Abboud in the October Revolution. Capitalizing on his popularity and the successful takedown of Abboud, al-Turabi founded the Islamic Charter Front (ICF), a precursor of the NIF (founded in 1985), and headed the Islamic Movement. Mobilizing his influence and power, al-Turabi joined with other religious right-wing parties like the Umma Party and the Democratic Unionist Party to advocate for an Islamic constitution in Sudan.

In 1969, al-Turabi's demand for an Islamic constitution was derailed when President Ismail al-Azhari was overthrown by Gaafar Muhammad an-Nimeiry. For the next seven years, al-Turabi and the ICF opposed the Nimeiry regime, but following a failed coup attempt in 1976, he changed tactics and aligned himself and his party with the president. This opened many doors for him and helped him implement his religious ideology and zeal in Sudan.

In 1979, President Nimeiry appointed al-Turabi as attorney-general and then tasked him with leading a commission to revise the legal system to comply with Sharia, or Islamic canonical law based on the teaching of the Koran and the traditions of the Prophet Muhammad. This ultimately led to the passage and enactment of the September Laws in 1983. During this same period, al-Turabi expanded ICF membership to include supporters in western Sudan. However, growing distrust between Nimeiry and al-Turabi resulted in the latter's arrest and imprisonment. Fortunately for him, Nimeiry was overthrown a month later while meeting President Ronald Reagan in Washington, D.C.

Al-Turabi hitched himself to yet another dictator when he formed an alliance with Bashir, who overthrew the Sudanese government in 1989. That year, he became Sudan's foreign minister and encouraged Osama bin Laden, the leader of al Qaeda, to transplant his organization to Sudan. In 1996, he became a speaker for the Sudanese parliament and continued to promote his radical Islamic agenda. Two years later, Bashir dissolved the parliament, and in so doing, he stripped al-Turabi of his position. At this point, the dominant Islamic movements in Sudan broke into two camps: the supporters of Bashir formed the NCP, and the followers of Turabi formed the Popular Congress Party.

Then al-Turabi went on to criticize Bashir and called for him to surrender himself to the International Criminal Court (ICC) for his role in the Darfur Genocide. As a result, al-Turabi was arrested and imprisoned on numerous occasions. At the age of eighty-four, he passed away at Khartoum's Royal Care International Hospital on March 5, 2016, from an unspecified illness.

Alexis Herr

See also: Bashir, Omar Hassan Ahmed al-; National Islamic Front

Further Reading

Crockett, Richard. 2010. *Sudan: Darfur and the Failure of an African State*. New Haven, CT: Yale University Press.

Prunier, Gérard. 2008. *Darfur: A 21st-Century Genocide*. 3rd ed. New York: Cornell University Press.

U

United Nations Commission of Inquiry on Darfur

The United Nations (UN) Commission of Inquiry on Darfur was created to examine the growing human rights abuses taking place in the Darfur region of Sudan. It operated between October 2004 and January 2005. By 2004, it had become clear to much of the international community that a potential genocide was unfolding—or was about to unfold—in Darfur. The situation had resulted from brutal attacks on the black Africans of Darfur by Sudanese government forces and the Arab militia force known as the Janjaweed. On September 9, 2004, the U.S. government alleged that these forces were in the process of committing genocide against the Darfurian people. The allegation was referred to the UN Security Council, which agreed to assess the situation. On September 18, the Security Council passed UN Resolution 1564, which formally empowered the secretary-general to form a commission of inquiry to investigate the situation then unfolding in Darfur.

On October 25, 2004, the commission was formally organized in Geneva, Switzerland, and commenced its work. The commission had five commissioners, from five different nations: Antonio Cassese, the chairperson (Italy); Mohamed Fayek (Egypt); Hina Jilani (Pakistan); Dumisa Ntsebeza (South Africa); and Therese Striggner-Scott (Ghana). They were aided in their work by a secretariat headed by an executive director, Mona Rishmawi, in addition to a legal research team

and an investigative team composed of criminal investigators, forensic experts, military analysts, and investigators specializing in gender violence. They were all appointed by the Office of the UN High Commissioner for Human Rights.

The commission concluded its work and submitted its final report on January 25, 2005. It detailed the many human rights violations that had occurred in Darfur prior to 2005. These included attacks on villages, murders of civilians, mass rapes, the pillaging and destruction of property, and other atrocities. Although the commission deplored these acts, it said that they did not rise to the level of genocide because the parties responsible for the human rights abuses had not, as a whole, intended to undertake them specifically to annihilate or exterminate a group of people on racial, ethnic, religious, or national grounds. In the end, the commission concluded that while serious and deadly human rights abuses were occurring in Darfur, it was not equipped to determine with any certainty that they rose to the level of genocide. But it also stated in its report that the crimes against humanity and war crimes that were unfolding in Darfur were, in fact, as serious as genocide itself, and that the differences among them were more semantic than practical. Finally, the commission identified specific perpetrators of the crimes in Darfur and suggested that they should be pursued by an international tribunal. But the report's conclusion was greeted with skepticism among some in the international community, who considered it something of a whitewash (so to speak).

Ultimately, the allegations of genocide were sent to the International Criminal Court (ICC) at The Hague, Netherlands, which opened an investigation on June 6, 2005. That investigation continues, and as of 2012, the ICC has indicted seven suspects involved in war crimes or crimes against humanity in Darfur. They include Sudanese president Omar Hassan Ahmed al-Bashir, Ahmad Harun, Ali Kushayb, Bahar Abu Garda (whose charges were dropped based on insufficient evidence in 2010), Abdallah Banda, Saleh Jerbo (whose charges were dropped in 2013 following his death), and Abdel Rahim Mohammed Hussein. Trials have not yet occurred, however, as Sudan is not a party to the Rome Statute that established the ICC in 2002 and thus is not obligated to turn anyone over to the court. In mid-April 2019, Bashir, Harun, and Hussein were imprisoned by the military during the government coup that is still occurring. It remains unclear whether they will be handed over to the ICC or if Sudan will hold independent trials.

Paul G. Pierpaoli Jr.

See also: Banda, Abdallah; Bashir, Omar Hassan Ahmed al-; Harun, Ahmad; Hussein, Abdel Raheem Muhammad; Kushayb, Ali

Further Reading

Deng, Francis Mading. 1995. *War of Visions: Conflict of Identities in the Sudan*. Washington, DC: Brookings Institution Press.

Hamilton, Rebecca. 2011. *Fighting for Darfur: Public Action and the Struggle to Stop Genocide*. London: Palgrave Macmillan.

Prunier, Gerard. 2005. *Darfur: The Ambiguous Genocide*. Ithaca, NY: Cornell University Press.

United Nations Convention on the Prevention and Punishment of the Crime of Genocide

The United Nations Convention on the Prevention and Punishment of the Crime of Genocide (UNCG), known as the Genocide Convention for short, is a comprehensive, international legal document that details the definition and meaning of genocide and that provides very general guidelines for the punishment of genocide perpetrators. The UN General Assembly officially enacted the UNCG on December 11, 1948, when twenty-two member-states signed the declaration to proceed to ratification by their own home governments. The convention, which remains in force, recognizes that genocide is a crime under international law.

The UNCG's definition of genocide has not been without its critics. Some have argued that it is unnecessarily expansive, as it enumerates behaviors that are not necessarily lethal and thus seems to fly in the face of the term *genocide,* which literally means "the killing of people." Others have asserted that it does not go far enough because its definition does not include the killing of people on the basis of political or social affiliation. This was the result of several nations' efforts, including those of the United States and Soviet Union, to exclude politics and social affiliations from the definition for specific internal reasons. Despite these concerns, however, the UNCG has remained an important component of international law and has been invoked many times since 1948.

The UNCG would probably not have been approved when it was had it not been for the herculean effort of one man: Raphael Lemkin (1900–1959). Lemkin, a Polish Jew, was a lawyer and historian who had fled Poland in 1939 and settled in the United States in

1941. By then, he had already spent much time contemplating mass murder and its implications for the international community. He published and lectured widely on the subject, and in 1944, he was credited with coining the term *genocide* in his *Axis Rule in Occupied Europe: Laws of Occupation, Analysis of Government, Proposals for Redress*. That book made Lemkin famous, but more important, it placed his quest to enact an international convention against genocide in the public spotlight. In 1945, he published an article, "Genocide—A Modern Crime," in *Free World*, a monthly magazine in New York, which was read widely and lent even more credence to his efforts.

After the Holocaust (1939–1945), Lemkin served as a legal adviser to the Nuremberg war-crime trials in Germany from 1945 to 1946, during which he redoubled his efforts to enact a global convention against genocide. In 1946, he was told that his idea of a genocide convention would be formally considered by a UN committee. Although the proposal encountered some turbulence early on, the General Assembly unanimously approved the UNCG on December 11, 1948. By then, however, Lemkin had seriously undermined his own health in his quest to establish a genocide convention. It went into effect on January 21, 1951, and for about eight years, until the end of his life, Lemkin worked tirelessly to secure U.S. ratification of the measure. That ultimately would not occur until November 4, 1988, however, when President Ronald Reagan signed the ratification agreement.

As of 2019, 151 UN member-states have ratified or acceded to the UNCG; Sudan is among the members that have yet to do so. the UNCG is regarded as the bedrock of international law dealing with war crimes, crimes against humanity, and genocide. A number of courts that have since been established to indict and prosecute such crimes—including the International Criminal Court, the International Criminal Tribunal for the Former Yugoslavia, and the International Criminal Tribunal for Rwanda—owe at least part of their jurisdiction to the UNCG.

Paul G. Pierpaoli Jr.

See also: African Union; Bashir, Omar Hassan Ahmed al-; Coalition for International Justice; Denial of the Darfur Genocide; Sudan; United Nations Commission of Inquiry on Darfur

Further Reading

LeBor, Adam. 2008. *"Complicity with Evil": The United Nations in the Age of Modern Genocide*. New Haven, CT: Yale University Press.

United Nations. 2008. *Atrocities and International Accountability: Beyond Transitional Justice*. New York: United Nations.

United Nations Mission in the Sudan

The United Nations (UN) Security Council established the United Nations Mission in the Sudan (UNMIS) on March 24, 2005, by passing Resolution 1590. UNMIS was launched while the Darfur Genocide was already in progress in the west of the country, to support the implementation of the Comprehensive Peace Agreement (CPA) that had been signed by the government of Sudan and the Sudan People's Liberation Movement/Army (SPLM/A) on January 9 of that year.

UNMIS was established to support Sudan as it transitioned from nearly four decades of civil war (1955–1972 and 1983–2005) to relative peace between the north and south. The two civil wars were the result of ethnic and religious tensions between the government in the north, which self-identified as ethnically Arab and religiously Muslim, and the so-called black African and Christian-animist south. Since colonial independence, those in the south had fought for greater representation in government, and the CPA contained a plan to do so.

The Security Council installed UNMIS to help ensure the success of the CPA. Its mission was to support its implementation, which included: to monitor and verify the implementation of a cease-fire agreement and to investigate violations; to liaise with bilateral donors on the formation of Joint Integrated Units; to observe and monitor the movement of armed groups and redeployment of forces in the areas of UNMIS deployment; to assist in the disarmament and reintegration of rebel members; to promote greater understanding of the CPA; to help restructure the police service in Sudan; to promote the rule of law and jurisprudence; to help prepare for elections and referenda, as provided for by the CPA; to help coordinate refugee and internally displaced persons return to their homes; to cooperate with other international partners in the mine action sector (which includes safely removing land mines) by providing humanitarian and technical assistance; and to promote human rights in Sudan. The UNMIS headquarters were located in Khartoum and the Joint Monitoring Coordinating Office was in Juba.

With the expanding crisis in Darfur, the Security Council decided on August 31, 2006, in Resolution 1706 to expand the UNMIS mandate to include its deployment to the Darfur region in the west. The Security Council called for UNMIS to increase its forces from 8,727 troops, 695 military

observers, 186 staff officers, and 666 police officers (as of September 2006) to 17,300 military personnel, up to 3,300 civilian police units, and up to 16 Formed Police Units (specialized, cohesive, and armed mobile police units that provide security support to UN operations by protecting personnel and assets). In the following months, however, the government of Sudan's opposition to a solely UN peacekeeping mission in Darfur blocked UNMIS's deployment there. In response, the United Nations created a joint African Union and UN peacekeeping force.

The mandate of UNMIS concluded on July 9, 2011, when South Sudan became the newest country in the world. That same year, the United Nations established the United Nations Mission in South Sudan, which continues to operate in South Sudan.

Alexis Herr

See also: African Union Mission in Sudan; Comprehensive Peace Agreement; Lost Boys and Girls of Sudan; South Sudan

Further Reading
Straus, Scott. 2016. *Fundamentals of Genocide and Mass Atrocity Prevention.* United States Holocaust Memorial Museum.

United States Involvement in Darfur

The United States has the distinction of being the first (and to date, the only) country to label the violence in Darfur as genocide. On September 9, 2004, U.S. secretary of state Colin Powell accused the Sudanese government and Arab militia groups loyal to Omar Hassan Ahmed al-Bashir, president of Sudan, of waging a campaign of genocide. He described the violence as "consistent and widespread" and as a "coordinated effort, not just random violence" (Powell 2004). He advocated that the United States and the international community not just stand by as Darfurians die at the hands of their government and its allies. Despite his public outcry, the U.S. actions in Darfur and dealings with Bashir were tempered by the Sudanese government's collaboration with the U.S. worldwide counterterrorism campaign. As a result, the U.S. relationship to and involvement in the conflict is multifaceted and complicated.

U.S. involvement in Sudan began in the 1970s as a result of the Cold War (a political war waged between the U.S.-led Western powers and the Soviet-bloc countries from 1945 to 1990). Sudan received hundreds of millions of dollars in U.S. aid in the 1970s and bought weapons from the United States in the 1980s. By supporting Gaafar Muhammad an-Nimeiry (president of Sudan from 1969 to 1985), the United States intended to block Soviet infiltration into Sudan; in so doing, it became Nimeiry's main foreign backer. Furthermore, Sudan gained U.S. praise for its support in evacuating the Jews from Ethiopia in the early 1980s. When the Ethiopian Jews fled to Sudan after facing undue persecution at home, Sudan welcomed them and allowed the United States to relocate the refugees to Israel.

Nimeiry's close relationship with the United States caused Islamic fundamentalists to criticize the president. Fearful of losing office, Nimeiry reasserted his Islamic identity and fused Islamism with Sudanese nationalism. In 1983, he issued the so-called September Laws, which called for Sharia law—Islamic canonical law drawn from the Koran, which in this case called for retributive penalties for disobeying religious law—throughout Sudan. He also suspended the Addis Ababa Peace Agreement with the largely Christian south. This in turn led to the resumption of civil war in Sudan between the predominately Arab north and African south.

These actions ultimately tarnished Nimeiry's image in the United States. Members of the U.S. Congress, outraged by images of African Christians in the south being killed and forced into slavery by Arabs in the north, ultimately forced the United States to play a role in negotiating a peace treaty between the north and south.

The U.S. relationship with Bashir, the man who overthrew Nimeiry in 1989 and held the office of the president until he was forcibly ousted in 2019, was equally (if not more) turbulent than the one with Nimeiry. U.S. diplomatic relations with Sudan were tense for decades owing to Osama bin Laden's residency in the Sudanese capital of Khartoum from 1991 to 1996. Bin Laden (1957–2011) founded al-Qaeda, the pan-Islamic militant organization responsible for the terrorist attacks in New York on September 11, 2001. U.S. president Bill Clinton had imposed sanctions against the Sudanese government in November 1997 and accused it of supporting terrorism, citing bin Laden's former residency in Khartoum as evidence. That same year, President Clinton responded to terrorist bombings of U.S. embassies in Tanzania and Kenya on August 7 by ordering the U.S. air force to attack a factory in Khartoum that was allegedly linked to bin Laden. However, investigations later showed that this was untrue. The government of Sudan used the rubble of the factory to provoke anti-Western sentiment and preserved debris from the factory as proof of Western criminality.

After the terrorist attacks in 2001, the relationship between Sudan and the United States changed owing to the Sudanese government's immediate offer to support the

U.S. counterterrorism campaign. The United States accepted Khartoum's offer, which caused some Sudanese to criticize President Bashir, who had assumed power on June 30, 1989. Bashir's critics viewed his partnership with the United States as eroding Sudan's Islamist agenda, while others supported Bashir's offer to help fight terrorism and regarded it as a strong and strategic move for power. The United States for its part, benefited from the vital intelligence that Sudan provided about al-Qaeda. Sudanese agents managed to infiltrate the terrorist group and thus provide information that prevented attacks on American military in Iraq.

During his second term as president of the United States, George W. Bush responded to the calls for greater action in Darfur. The United States commissioned a study of the patterns of violence in that region, and upon viewing its results, Secretary of State Colin Powell declared that the brutality was consistent with the United Nations (UN) definition of genocide. President Bush went on to reiterate this interpretation before the UN General Assembly. Congress reinforced the genocide assessment and encouraged the United States to take unilateral action if necessary. Ultimately, Washington did not send troops or take direct military actions in Darfur; it later chose to abstain from a UN Security Council vote to refer Darfur to the International Criminal Court.

The U.S. involvement in negotiating a peace treaty to end the north-south civil war, in addition to its partnership with Sudan in the so-called war on terror, ultimately tempered its response to the genocide in Darfur. When the Sudanese government began killing Darfurians in 2003, the United States (along with a coalition of international partners) was committed to brokering the Comprehensive Peace Agreement (CPA), a treaty that ultimately concluded the decades-long north-south civil war when it was signed on January 9, 2005. As a result of its commitment to brokering peace between north and south, the United States feared that pressuring President Bashir to stop the violence in Darfur would disrupt the delicate negotiations already underway.

With the CPA signed, the United States issued sanctions on thirty-one Sudanese companies in May 2007, which barred them from conducting business with the United States. The United States also imposed sanctions on Ahmed Mohammed Haroun, state minister for humanitarian affairs in Sudan; Khalil Ibrahim, head of the Justice and Equality Movement; and Awad Ibn Aug, director of military intelligence and security. Many scholars and humanitarians have criticized the U.S. sanctions as too ineffective and blunted to stop the human rights abuses in Darfur. For example, on the tenth anniversary of the genocide, actor Don Cheadle and activist John Prendergast lamented the mild international response to Sudan and called on U.S. president Barack Obama to send a team of diplomats to Sudan to better support Sudanese efforts toward peace. For its part, the Obama administration offered to relieve Sudan from a two-decade-old trade embargo instituted by the Clinton administration in the 1990s, an offer that was ultimately achieved by U.S. president Donald Trump in 2018. Despite the United States lifting the trade embargo and acknowledging that Sudan is no longer a terrorist stronghold, it is one of six Muslim countries whose citizens were prevented from entering the United States under Trump's executive order on immigration.

In conclusion, the U.S. role in the Darfur Genocide is complicated and influenced by its turbulent relationship with Sudan during the Cold War and the war on terror.

While U.S. nongovernmental organizations have encouraged mass civilian protests of the genocide and sparked an international network of activists fighting for Darfurians, the U.S. government response has not been as robust.

Alexis Herr

See also: British Involvement in Darfur; Doha Document for Peace in Darfur; Enough Project; Garang, John; Ibrahim, Khalil; Khartoum; Save Darfur Coalition

Further Reading

Brosché, Johan, and Daniel Rothbart. 2013. *Violent Conflict and Peacebuilding: The Continuing Crisis in Darfur.* New York: Routledge.

Cheadle, Don, and John Prendergast. 2010. *The Enough Moment: Fighting to End Africa's Worst Human Rights Crimes.* New York: Three Rivers Press.

Cheadle, Don, and John Prendergast. 2013. "Cheadle/Prendergast: Lessons from Darfur, 10 Years Later." *USA Today.* March 19.

Crockett, Richard. 2010. *Sudan: Darfur and the Failure of an African State.* New Haven, CT: Yale University Press.

Powell, Colin. 2004. "The Crisis in Darfur." U.S. Department of State Archives. September 9. Available at https://2001-2009 .state.gov/secretary/former/powell/remarks /36042.htm.

Wahid, Abdel

Abdel Wahid Mohammad Ahmad al-Nur, commonly referred to as Abdel Wahid, was a founder of the Sudan Liberation Army/Movement (SLA/M) and is the current leader of a principal faction of the SLA/M known as SLA–Abdul Wahid (SLA-AW). He has been a prominent advocate for equality and secular democracy in Sudan for decades.

Wahid was born in 1968 in Zalingei, West Darfur, Sudan. He graduated with a degree in law from the University of Khartoum in 1995. While in school, he founded the Sudan Liberation Movement (SLM) in June 1992. In 1996, he and other Fur activists, including Ahmed Abdel Shafi, began organizing against the government. In 2001, Fur and Zaghawa leaders joined forces to fight Arab supremacist policies in Darfur by forming the Sudan Liberation Army (SLA).

The following year, Wahid was named chairman of the SLA. That same year, the Sudanese government arrested him. A letter of his, smuggled from prison and published, brought international attention to the Darfur conflict. In it, he pleaded for the protection of the people of Darfur from the aggression of the national government. Upon his release, the SLA issued a manifesto that called for a secular state and self-determination for Darfur, but also promoted concerns beyond Darfur by denouncing the oppression of all of Sudan's marginalized peoples and urging Arabs to join the movement to redefine Sudan.

Wahid's leadership style created organizational difficulties for the SLA. He failed to delegate authority or to create administrative structures; meanwhile, he tended to be indecisive. Dissatisfaction with his exercise of authority was exacerbated by the ethnic tensions within the SLA. In November 2005, Minni Minawi formed a Zaghawa faction of the SLA (SLA-MM) that broke from the SLA-AW.

The international community, including notably the United States and the United Kingdom, pressed the SLA-AW, SLA-MM, and Khalil Ibrahim's Justice and Equality Movement (JEM) to sign the Darfur Peace Agreement (DPA) with the government of Sudan in 2006. The SLA-MM was the only group that heeded the call; they signed the agreement on May 5. Wahid, however, refused to commit to the agreement without first having a strong North Atlantic Treaty Organization (NATO) presence on the ground to provide security and bring about the disarming of Janjaweed militias. Other nonsignatories to the DPA then formed the National Redemption Front (NRF), which Wahid also refused to join. The SLA's uncertain political direction following Wahid's rejection of both the DPA and the NRF induced a number of commanders to switch their loyalty from Wahid to Shafi in July 2006, further fracturing the SLA.

After fleeing for a time to Eritrea soon after the Darfur Genocide began, Wahid moved to Paris in 2007 and has not returned to Sudan. His refusal to participate in the peace talks in Doha, Qatar, exasperated

French officials, and he decided to leave Paris at the end of 2010 to shuttle between Nairobi, Kenya, and Kampala, Uganda. His absence from Sudan has drawn criticism from many rebel commanders.

Nonetheless, the SLA-AW joined the SLA-MM, JEM, and the Sudan People's Liberation Movement–North to form the Sudan Revolutionary Front (SRF) in 2011. The SRF, which calls for toppling the Sudanese government by all political and military means, elected Wahid as vice-chair of its leadership council and the head of its political wing. After Sudanese president Omar Hassan Ahmed al-Bashir was forced out of power on April 11, 2019, Wahid has expressed optimism for his country and his people. On November 12, the governor of North Darfur, Major General Malik al-Tayeb Khojali, announced his intention to do everything in his power to accelerate humanitarian access to Darfur, including those areas currently controlled by the SLA-AW.

Karl A. Yambert

See also: Darfur Peace Agreement; Justice and Equality Movement; Minawi, Minni; Sudan People's Liberation Army/Movement

Further Reading

Burr, J. Millard, and Robert O. Collins. 2006. *Darfur: The Long Road to Disaster.* Princeton, NJ: Markus Weiner.

Flint, Julie, and Alex de Waal. 2006. *Darfur: A Short History of a Long War.* London: Zed Books.

Wallace, Gretchen Steidle

Gretchen Steidle Wallace is an American humanitarian dedicated to advancing women's rights and well-being in Rwanda and other countries affected by genocide. She has worked with survivors of the Darfur Genocide, coauthored a book about the killings, and produced a documentary on the atrocities.

Born in 1974 as the daughter of a U.S. navy admiral, she grew up in a variety of settings around the world. Living in the Philippines for a time as a child, she saw the effect that desperate poverty can have on a community, and she has worked since to address the injustices of wealth disparities. She attended the University of Virginia (from which she graduated with a bachelor of arts degree in foreign affairs in 1996) and the Tuck School of Business at Dartmouth College, where she obtained a master of business administration in 2001. Between 1996 and 1999, she worked in international project finance for PMD International, Inc., a boutique investment banking firm specializing in infrastructure development in poor countries.

In 2004, Wallace went to South Africa to help with the HIV/AIDS epidemic. Studying the AIDS initiatives of major multinational corporations, she learned of the financial consequences of AIDS with regard to healthcare costs and lost production. She also began to study the extent to which various companies developed and applied efficient solutions to these problems. She learned that many solutions were in fact flawed, due largely to a poor understanding of health care and the stigma attached to HIV/AIDS. It became apparent that many employees were reluctant to undergo AIDS testing or to seek assistance if they knew they were infected. Culturally, women faced the problem of not being empowered to insist that their partners use condoms.

Wallace came to the realization that some form of social initiative was needed to promote the rights of women regarding sexual freedom and HIV/AIDS prevention. She knew that some women in South Africa were already employing enterprising techniques at the grassroots level and realized that they were determined to address critical issues facing women and girls, but they were struggling without the training and resources necessary to ensure their success. Wallace dedicated herself to supporting these emerging agents of change and their ideas.

As a result, later the same year, Wallace established Global Grassroots, a nonprofit organization supporting conscious social change for women in postconflict and developing countries, particularly in Africa. Through personal transformation work and social entrepreneurship training, the organization helps marginalized women and genocide survivors reclaim their lives and discover their value to society through the development of their own ideas for social change. Global Grassroots offers seed funding grants and twelve months of advisory support for launching projects that advance the well-being and rights of women. It also engages in creative campaigns to raise awareness of critical women's issues globally.

With Global Grassroots established, Wallace saw an enormous amount of work awaiting her. Her first initiative, in 2005, connected her interests with those of her brother, Brian Steidle, who had already been doing significant work in raising awareness around the world about the ongoing genocide in Darfur. Steidle and Wallace took their respective campaigns to the refugee camps of eastern Chad, where they worked on issues that were being overlooked by aid organizations, such as establishing a human rights library and providing education about refugee rights, domestic and sexual violence, and female genital mutilation. Wallace also provided on-site training to try to ensure that her projects would be sustained in the long term.

Returning to the United States, Wallace began to develop her new social entrepreneurship program, but she saw a great need to return to Africa to work with genocide survivors in Rwanda, where mass rape during the 1994 genocide had led to a huge spread of HIV/AIDS. In 2006, she trained 180 Rwandan women, many of them widows raising several children and many of them rape victims, in the development of social projects in Kigali.

Dealing with the aftermath of rape is one of the issues for which Global Grassroots soon became best known. In Africa, as elsewhere, mass rape is a common problem, especially in situations of war and civil strife. The promotion of dialogue about rape is an important, although difficult, first step in raising awareness and addressing the issue. Again, her knowledge of mass rape was brought home through the observations of her brother, Brian, in Darfur, where the Janjaweed militias engaged in the practice of raping female genocide survivors, often en masse.

Since 2006, Global Grassroots has trained 250 so-called change leaders, managing to fund several important locally designed projects serving thousands of vulnerable women and girls. These initiatives deal with issues relating to domestic violence, water access, child rape, prostitution, property rights, HIV/AIDS, discrimination, and illiteracy. Most of these are in postgenocide Rwanda, which has become the main field of operations for Global Grassroots, but projects among Darfur refugees in eastern Chad are also now underway. This organization is one of the major providers of assistance to female genocide survivors and focuses almost exclusively on the promotion of what Wallace calls "conscious social change" driven by and on behalf of marginalized women in postconflict Africa.

In early 2007, Global Grassroots and Wallace were also heavily involved in producing an Emmy-nominated documentary about the Darfur Genocide, *The Devil Came on Horseback* (directed by Ricki Stern and Anne Sundberg). Based on her brother's memoir of the same title (which Wallace coauthored), *The Devil Came on Horseback* tells the story of Steidle's direct encounter with genocide in Darfur.

As a social entrepreneur, Wallace has always believed in inner-driven change, holding that decisions made with the greatest level of awareness will ensure the wisest response and most potent, effective results. This was one of her key motivators behind the establishment of Global Grassroots in 2004. Wallace's interests lay in looking for gaps in existing systems and fostering ideas of what to do about them, but the greatest measure of success at Global Grassroots is the impact that locally chosen projects can have on transforming communities for the better. There is a focus on training and project design. Monitoring of progress and the provision of high-engagement advisory support take place for a minimum of twelve months after a project begins.

In recognition of her contribution to the betterment of the human condition through management and entrepreneurship strategies, Wallace was honored in 2007 by *World Business* magazine and Shell as one of the top International Thirty-five Women Under Thirty-five. By the end of the twenty-first century's first decade, the antigenocide enterprise created by one woman's vision had become an inspiration to communities throughout many parts of Africa, not to mention a model for others to follow.

Paul R. Bartrop

See also: Rape; Steidle, Brian

Further Reading

Cheadle, Don, and John Prendergast. 2007. *Not on Our Watch: The Mission to End Genocide in Darfur and Beyond.* New York: Hyperion.

Steidle, Brian, and Gretchen Steidle Wallace. 2008. *The Devil Came on Horseback: Bearing Witness to the Genocide in Darfur.* New York: Public Affairs Books.

Weintraub, Jerry

Jerry Weintraub is a highly successful talent agent and manager, Hollywood film producer, and studio executive who has become a fixture for charitable causes aimed at mitigating the Darfur Genocide. He was born on September 26, 1937, in Brooklyn. He was raised in the Bronx and eventually found employment with MCA Records (now Universal Music Group). In the early 1960s, he founded an entertainment management company, through which he eventually handled such groups and individuals as the Four Seasons, Joey Bishop, and John Denver. He also promoted or managed a wide variety of concerts and musical events that featured Elvis Presley, Led Zeppelin, the Carpenters, Neil Diamond, Frank Sinatra, and the Moody Blues, among others.

In the mid-1970s, Weintraub became a movie producer; his first film, *Nashville* (1975; directed by Robert Altman), was critically acclaimed. His next movie was *Oh God!* (1977), starring George Burns and Denver. The film proved to be a popular box-office draw. Other films that Weintraub has produced include *Diner* (1982), *The Karate Kid* (1984), and the *Ocean's* trilogy (2001, 2004, and 2007). Weintraub also served as chair and chief executive officer of United Artists, a top-flight movie and entertainment company.

Weintraub has become widely known for his philanthropic endeavors. He has been a major patron of the Los Angeles County Museum of Art, the Children's Museum of Los Angeles, and the Museum of Contemporary Art. Weintraub became involved in charitable work involving Darfur in 2007, when he joined with Matt Damon, George Clooney, Don Cheadle, and Brad Pitt to cofound the nonprofit organization known as Not on Our Watch, which is dedicated to preventing mass killings in Darfur and other areas of the world. The organization was an off-shoot of a 2007 book by the same name, coauthored by Cheadle and John Prendergast, which focused attention on the Darfur Genocide. That same year, Weintraub, Clooney, Pitt, Damon, and Cheadle launched a major initiative to raise $9.3 million for various relief efforts in Darfur. That sum was quickly raised, and since then, Weintraub has remained committed to helping the victims and survivors in Darfur, as well as preventing mass killings in other regions of the world.

Paul G. Pierpaoli Jr.

See also: Cheadle, Don; Clooney, George; Damon, Matt; Enough Project; Kristof, Nicholas; Prendergast, John

Further Reading

Cheadle, Don, and John Prendergast. 2007. *Not on Our Watch: The Mission to End Genocide in Darfur and Beyond.* New York: Hyperion.

What Is the What

In *What Is the What: The Autobiography of Valentino Achak Deng,* the best-selling author David Eggers tells the story of Valentino Achak Deng, one of the refugees known as the Lost Boys of Sudan. A work of fiction inspired by fact, the novel is based on a series of interviews that Eggers had with Deng over the course of many years. *What Is the What* follows Deng from Marial Bai, his village in southern Sudan, to Ethiopia, Kenya, and finally Atlanta.

Egger's novel is responsible for helping to bring to public attention the Lost Boys and Girls, the name ascribed to tens of thousands of children that were driven from their homes and, for the lucky ones, amassed in refugee camps boarding Sudan. Many of the 17,000 Sudanese children who ended up with Deng in Ethiopia were recruited or abducted into the ranks of the Sudan People's Liberation Army as child soldiers. As Eggers traces Deng's flight, which began during the Second Sudanese Civil War (1989–2005), the reader gains a greater appreciation for the mass exodus of Sudanese children out of Sudan, through a war zone, and into refugee camps. It took the real Deng four months to cross Sudan, barefoot, and it was another five years before he settled in the Kakuma Refugee Camp in northern Kenya, where he remained for nine years before finally arriving in the United States.

The novel begins in Atlanta, wherein a couple and a young boy break into Deng's apartment and hold him captive. This youth, Deng observes, was the same age as he himself had been when the violence in Sudan had unearthed his village life. As he reminisces about his upbringing in the Dinka tribe of Marial Bai, he recalls a local legend that his father used to tell. According to the story, God first created Dinka men and women, and then he offered them the gift of cattle. After showing them that cattle could bring milk, meat, and prosperity, God said, "You can either have these cattle, as my gift to you, or you can have the What." The man asked God, "What is the What?" to which

God refused to explain; rather, He asked the man to make his choice. He picked the cow, and the question "What is the What?" remained unanswered (Eggers 2006: 63). God offered the same deal to the Arabs in the north, but they chose the "What." This allegory serves as an explanation for the northerners attacking the south—while those in the south were satisfied with what God had given them, the north wanted more.

What Is the What meditates on the challenges that refugees face both when fleeing their countries and seeking safety abroad. Home becomes a common thread throughout, as the novel oscillates between the present, where Valentino is a hostage in his Atlanta apartment, and the past, where war forces Valentino from his village in Sudan. Violence occurs worldwide, not just in Africa or places of known conflict.

Eggers and the real-life Deng decided to use the royalties from the best-selling novel to build a school in the latter's hometown. Eggers donates all his royalties from *What Is the What* directly to the Valentino Achak Deng (VAD) Foundation, and that will continue indefinitely. In 2009, VAD opened the Marial Bai Secondary School, the first fully functional high school in the entire region. Because of the school's success, the government of South Sudan granted the VAD Foundation an entire campus in 2017, which VAD hopes to transform into a boarding school for Sudanese women.

Alexis Herr

See also: Child Soldiers; Dinka; Lost Boys and Girls of Sudan; South Sudan; Sudan People's Liberation Movement/Army

Further Reading

Eggers, David. 2006. *What Is the What: The Autobiography of Valentino Achak Deng.* New York: Random House.

VAD Foundation. "Foundation History." Available at http://www.vadfoundation.org/foundation-history/.

Wiesel, Elie

Elie Wiesel was a Romanian-born American writer, thinker, and teacher, world renowned for his work in raising awareness of the Holocaust and its meaning for contemporary society. For many, he was the conscience and expression of all Holocaust survivors. A prolific author, his work has been extremely influential in dealing with the moral responsibility of any person to fight hatred, racism, and genocide. He spent much of his life speaking out about international indifference to genocide, including the Darfur Genocide.

Wiesel was born on September 30, 1928, in the town of Sighet, in Transylvania (when it was still part of Romania, prior to its occupation by Hungary in 1940). With the Nazi invasion of Hungary in the spring of 1944, all the Jews in his village were forced into two ghettos. He was then deported to the Auschwitz concentration camp, where he was tattooed with the number A-7713. He and his father were at that time separated from his mother and sisters. The two remained together for a year, surviving a death march to Buchenwald in the winter of 1944–1945, but then Wiesel's father died just a short time before the camp was liberated by the Americans in April 1945. Both of Wiesel's parents and one of his sisters perished during the Holocaust.

After the liberation, Wiesel was taken to Paris, where he lived in an orphanage. Between 1947 and 1950, he studied the Talmud, philosophy, and literature at the Sorbonne, attending lectures by Jean-Paul Sartre and Martin Buber. Working as a teacher of Hebrew and a choirmaster to supplement his income, he then became a journalist. He steadfastly refused, however, to write about or discuss his Holocaust experiences. However, a meeting with François Mauriac, who won the Nobel Prize for Literature in 1952, convinced him of the need to begin writing about his experiences, and his best-known work, *Night* (1960), was the result. *Night* came to be a symbolic record of the experience of all Jews during the Holocaust, and as a result, Wiesel dedicated his life to ensuring that no one can forget what happened at that tragic time. For Wiesel, "never again" is more than a phrase; it was his life's mission. He was recognized as one of the most powerful voices in Holocaust consciousness in the world

In 1955, Wiesel moved to the United States and made his home in New York. In 1963, he became an American citizen. His work received recognition from the U.S. government in 1978, when he was appointed chair of the Presidential Commission on the Holocaust, established by President Jimmy Carter. In 1980, the commission was renamed the U.S. Holocaust Memorial Council, and Wiesel retained his position as chair until 1986. In further acknowledgment of his contribution to the betterment of society, Wiesel was awarded the Congressional Gold Medal of Freedom in 1985, the Nobel Peace Prize in 1986 (for advocating worldwide against violence, repression, and racism), and an honorary knighthood in recognition of his advocacy work for Holocaust education in the United Kingdom. He was elected to the American Academy of Arts and Letters in 1996.

Wiesel's many writings show his highly diverse range of skills. He made compelling and profound contributions to literature and theology, and it might be said that his input to Holocaust writing has been among the most important ever composed. His opposition to indifference, as well as his quest to ensure that "never again" becomes the guiding principle directing the actions of everyone, led Wiesel to condemn, over and over again, what he called the sin of indifference. Putting his own words into practice, one of the first things Wiesel and his wife, Marion, did after he won the Nobel Peace Prize in 1986 was to establish the Elie Wiesel Foundation for Humanity, a foundation to promote peace and human rights throughout the world. Its mission, rooted in the memory of the Holocaust, is to combat indifference, intolerance, and injustice through international dialogue and youth-focused programs that promote acceptance, understanding, and equality, and in fulfilment of this mission, it runs multiple programs, both domestic and international.

In November 1992, during the Bosnian War, Wiesel went to Belgrade, Sarajevo, Banja Luka, and the Manjača concentration camp. Upon his return, he publicly urged U.S. secretary of state Lawrence Eagleburger to speak out against the genocide that was occurring. He was unsuccessful, but eighteen months later, at the opening of the United States Holocaust Memorial Museum in Washington, D.C., he made a further public plea to President Bill Clinton about the necessity of addressing the Bosnian Genocide. Again, however, he did not succeed.

Such initiatives were not isolated; for decades, Wiesel's was an imposing voice in speaking out against injustice and genocide around the world, notably with regard to apartheid in South Africa, the so-called disappearances of political dissidents in Argentina, the treatment of dissidents in the Soviet Union, Serb actions in Bosnia and Herzegovina, Saddam Hussein's actions against the Kurds in northern Iraq, and the Darfur

Genocide. In September 2006, Wiesel addressed the United Nations (UN) Security Council, in the company of George Clooney, about the humanitarian crisis in Darfur, urging immediate international action for the purpose of saving lives.

In 2007, the Wiesel Foundation issued a letter, signed by fifty-three Nobel laureates, condemning Armenian genocide denial by the Turkish government and its supporters. Alongside such activities, he was a major advocate for Jewish rights around the world, and in earlier times, he was an outspoken critic regarding the respective difficulties faced by Soviet and Ethiopian Jewry.

Wiesel's major concern was that in the decades since the end of World War II, nothing substantial had been learned from that terrible conflict. All the cries of "never again," so frequently uttered at the time of the liberation of the camps, amounted to little of substance in his view. According to him, after a cataclysm such as the Holocaust, people should be looking out for the welfare and safety of each other, but that had not yet happened. Having survived the Holocaust, Wiesel devoted his life to fostering the kind of understanding that would enable people to see the necessity of developing compassion and defeating indifference, and thus prevent more atrocities and other genocides.

Wiesel died at his home in New York City on July 2, 2016, after a lengthy illness. His passing sparked an international outpouring of grief and remembrance.

Paul R. Bartrop

See also: Clooney, George; United States Involvement in Darfur

Further Reading

Downing, Frederick L. 2008. *Elie Wiesel: A Religious Biography*. Macon, GA: Mercer University Press.

Wiesel, Elie. 1960. *Night*. New York: Hill and Wang.

Z

Zaghawa

The Zaghawa are an African people whose homeland extends from eastern Chad into the northwest of Sudan's Darfur region. In this harsh desert and savanna environment, they have traditionally lived a seminomadic lifestyle, thriving through the herding of camels, sheep, and goats; trading; and some agriculture, particularly the cultivation of millet. Their language, also called *Zaghawa,* belongs to the Nilo-Saharan language family and is closely related to Kanuri, the language spoken by the descendants of the people of the great medieval empire of Kanem-Bornu in Chad, Niger, and Nigeria. It is more distantly related to the languages spoken by the Fur of Sudan and the Luo of Kenya.

The Zaghawa are the earliest people of the Sahara Desert whose existence is documented in writing, with Arabic records mentioning them as early as 700 CE. Today, they are almost exclusively Muslim, but the date of their conversion to Islam is a subject of debate. According to Zaghawa oral history, Abdullah Boru—founder of a Kobé clan dynasty—introduced Islam in the early 1600s. The thirteenth-century Arab geographer Ibn Said, however, places their conversion several centuries earlier, in the 1200s, following the Zaghawa's submission to the rulers of Kanem-Bornu, who embraced Islam in 1085.

Regardless of the exact date of conversion, earlier rituals have survived in local Islamic practice into the present. Of particular importance is the ritual sacrifice of animals directed at *ha manda* (sacred mountains) and other holy sites. Certain Zaghawa clans venerate animals associated with their founder, including the Imogu clan, who are traditionally forbidden to eat the meat and eggs of the ostrich. While adherence to such practices declined significantly beginning in the twentieth century, many Zaghawa still follow these traditions, seeing them as integral to—rather than exclusive of—their practice of Islam.

In modern politics, the Zaghawa have often found their allegiance split between their neighbors, Arabic-speaking pastoralists, and such sedentary agriculturalist groups as the Fur, who, like them, are dark-skinned and speak an indigenous African language. In Chad, they have enjoyed a privileged status since the rise to power there of President Idriss Déby Itno, a Zaghawa, in 1991. In Darfur, Zaghawa allegiances have shifted rapidly with the balance of power.

As recently as the 1980s, Darfur's Zaghawa largely aligned themselves with Arabic-speaking tribes against aggressive regional governments dominated by the Fur. Today, they are mostly allied with other groups persecuted in the government-sponsored ethnic cleansing campaign carried out by the Janjaweed, Arabic-speaking militias. Ethnic Zaghawa form the backbone of one of Darfur's two major rebel groups, the Justice and Equality Movement, and are also well represented in the Sudan Liberation Army, particularly in a faction led by the Zaghawa leader Minni Minawi which broke ranks in signing a peace deal with the government of Sudan in May 2006. Sudan's government accuses Chad's Itno of supporting the Zaghawa rebellion in Sudan.

David Paige

See also: Darfur; Fur; Itno, Idriss Déby; Justice and Equality Movement; Massalit; Minawi, Minni; Sudan Liberation Army

Further Reading

Flint, Julie, and Alex de Waal. 2006. *Darfur: A Short History of a Long War*. London: Zed Books.

Olson, James S. 1996. *The Peoples of Africa: An Ethnohistorical Dictionary*. Westport, CT: Greenwood Press.

Primary Documents

I. U.S. Department of State Describes the Janjaweed Militia (March 6, 2004)

The document cited here provides valuable insight into the determination by the United States that the killing in Darfur, Sudan, constituted genocide. Unlike other human rights crimes defined by international law, the crime of genocide relies on proving the "intent to kill in whole, or in part" a national, ethnical, racial, or religious group. While the United Nations did not consider the killings of Darfurians by the Janjaweed militia and its backers (mainly the government of Sudan) to be genocide, the United States viewed the organized slaughter of so-called non-Arab Darfuris by Arab militias and the government to be indicative of organized and intentional slaughter. The following declassified cable was penned by Gerard M. Gallucci, the U.S. ambassador in Khartoum (August 2003–September 2004) and sent to numerous other embassies on March 6, 2004.

P 060701Z MAR 04

FM AMEMBASSY KHARTOUM
TO SECSTATE WASHDC PRIORITY
  0281
INFO AMEMBASSY ADDIS ABABA
  PRIORITY

AMEMBASSY ASMARA PRIORITY
AMEMBASSY BANGUI PRIORITY
USEU BRUSSELS BE PRIORITY
AMEMBASSY CAIRO PRIORITY
CJTF HOA
AMEMBASSY KAMPALA PRIORITY
AMEMBASSY KHARTOUM PRIORITY
AMEMBASSY LONDON PRIORITY
AMEMBASSY NAIROBI PRIORITY
AMEMBASSY NDJAMENA PRIORITY
NSC WASHDC
AMEMBASSY OSLO PRIORITY
AMEMBASSY PARIS PRIORITY
AMEMBASSY ROME PRIORITY
AMEMBASSY THE HAGUE PRIORITY
USMISSION US UN NEW YORK NY
  PRIORITY

CONFIDENTIAL KHARTOUM 000228

DEPT FOR AF/SWG
E.O. 12958: DECL: 3/6/2014
TAGS: PGOV, PHUM, PINR, PREF,
  PREL, ASEC, SU
SUBJECT: THE JINJAVVEED
  (C ORRECTE D)
REF: A) KHARTOUM 0220

CLASSIFIED BY: GALLUCCI, COM,
  US EMBASSY, DOS.
REASON: 1.5 (B), (D)
CORRECTED COPY

1. (c) Summary: The Arab militia known as "Jinjaweed" [Janjaweed] continues to terrorize Darfur civilians and presents a dilemma for the government. With a strength of 11,000 to 15,000 and mounted on horses or camels, the Jinjaweed [Janjaweed] are burning and looting villages and attacking civilians. UN and NGO's report that some displaced people in Darfur will not accept badly-needed food or other assistance, fearing that the Jinjaweed [Janjaweed] will injure or kill them for the loot. Following is information on the Jinjaweed [Janjaweed] we have obtained from multiple sources. End Summary.

2. (C) when the Sudanese armed forces was unable to defeat the SLA following the April 2003 attack on el Fasher, the GOS engaged a proxy force of Arab militia which, because they ride horses and camels, are known as the Jinjaweed [Janjaweed]. While the air force has bombed towns, the Jinjaweed [Janjaweed], working in concert with the army, have continued on the rampage. The UN told us on March 4 that the Jinjaweed [Janjaweed] had killed over 100 civilians in a recent attack on Tawila west of el Fasher. There are numerous accounts by IDP's, Darfur tribal leaders, and NGO's of Jinjaweed [Janjaweed] abuses of non-Arabs in Darfur. Apparently as part of a strategy to defeat the SLA by removing its support base, the GOS has provided support to the Jinjaweed. At the same time, the Jinjaweed [Janjaweed] are able to loot whatever they can and have been promised prime land at the expense of non-Arab farmers.

3. (C) the Jinjaweed [Janjaweed] are mostly camel herders from the four main tribes of north Darfur—the "Rezagat from the north". (note: the northern Rezagat should not be confused with the southern Rezagat who are cattle herders and who have tried to stay out of the conflict.) Non-Arab tribal leaders have told us that some of the Jinjaweed [Janjaweed] are not Sudanese, but imported—or emigrated—from Chad, the CAR [Central African Republic], Niger, Burkina Faso, and Mali. According to multiple sources, there are three main leaders, but the most important is Sheikh Moussa Hilal. Originally from Kutum, Moussa most likely is based in Misteriha, between Kebkabyia and Birka Sayira in north Darfur. (note: UN security official was told by Jinjaweed manning checkpoints at the entrance of villages west of Kekabyia that they took their orders from Misteriha.) Sheikh Moussa was banned from Darfur by the previous Walt (governor) of north Darfur because of his role in tribal conflicts. Moussa remained in Khartoum until after the SLA attack on el Fasher and the subsequent removal of the [governor]. Moussa returned to Darfur to lead the Jinjaweed [Janjaweed]. He reportedly once belonged to the NIF [National Islamic Front].

4. (C) Although an irregular militia, the Jinjaweed [Janjaweed] is most likely better organized than previously believed. Prior to the operation in Tawila, UN security witnessed a large number of Jinjaweed [Janjaweed] coming from different directions to meet at a makeshift camp. This indicates an internal structure and communications. In addition to attacks, the Jinjaweed [Janjaweed]—according to IDP's—also extort money from towns, abduct people for ransom, target males during operations, destroy irrigation systems, require payment of up to SD [Sudanese dollars] 4000 per month for people to return to their homes an[d] land, and prohibit freedom of movement. The government, according to IDP's, NGO's, and Darfur political leaders in

Khartoum, makes no attempt to curb the Jin-jaweed [Janjaweed] abuses nor to maintain order.

5. (C) Comment: the Jinjaweed [Janjaweed] are not a government creation but a tradi-tional element of the tribal conflicts of Dar-fur (and beyond). However, the government has been arming and encouraging them since mid-2003, and this has shifted the bal-ance of tribal power in Darfur in a way that may be difficult to undo in the future. Non-Arabs have been pushed from their land by the Jinjaweed [Janjaweed], and the "rebels" fighting to protect their communities and to convince the government to accept a politi-cal negotiation are under intense pressure from the military. It also appears that the Jinjaweed [Janjaweed] have been expanding their attacks since president Bashir launched his Darfur "initiative" on February 9 and are using more brutal tactics reminiscent of the LRA [Lord's Resistance Army] in Uganda—including mass rapes and killings of defenseless civilians (especially dis-placed people). Given reports from the field increasingly pointing to army complicity in the coordination and implementation of attacks, there seems little way to avoid the conclusion that the government of Sudan is pursuing a full-fledged war on the non-Arab peoples of Darfur While the international community is focused on the IGAD [Inter-national Authority on Development] peace process.

End Comment.

Gallucci

Source: U.S. Department of State Virtual Reading Room. "The Jinjaweed (Corrected)." March 6, 2004, Case No. F-2013-09087. Available at the National Security Archive, https://nsarchive.files .wordpress.com/2016/03/document-4-20040306 -the-janjaweed.pdf.

2. U.S. Department of State Memo on Genocide in Darfur (June 25, 2004)

The following is a secret Department of State memo written by William Taft IV, the legal advisor to U.S. secretary of state Colin Powell, to Deputy Secretary of State Richard Armitage entitled "Genocide and Darfur." The June 25, 2004 memo dis-cusses the determinations that go into deciding whether the conflict in Darfur should be considered genocide. Taft explains that while defining the killing in Darfur as a genocide could have moral, policy, and political consequences, it would not have legal ones. Furthermore, he determines that it is difficult to deter-mine whether the acts committed in Darfur are in accordance with the 1948 Conven-tion on the Prevention and Punishment of the Crime of Genocide, which specifies that acts of genocide are committed "with the intent to destroy, in whole or in part, [the group] as such."

UNCLASSIFIED
RELEASED IN FULL

200415443
United States Department of State

Washington, D.C. 20520
JUN 25 2004

2004 JUN 25 PM 6 26
INFORMATION MEMORANDUM
S/ES

SECRET
Decl: 6/25/14

TO: The Deputy Secretary

FROM: L—William H. Taft, IV
DRL—Lorne W. Craner
S/WCI—Pierre R. Prosper
AF—Donald Y. Yamamoto, Acting

SUBJECT: Genocide and Darfur

In the context of our review of whether the atrocities in Darfur constitute genocide, we are providing the following overview of genocide and the legal and practical consequences of any such U.S. determination.

What is genocide?

- Although Sudan is not a Contracting Party to the 1948 Convention on the Prevention and Punishment of the Crime of Genocide (hereinafter, the "Genocide Convention"), the prohibition on genocide reflected in the Genocide Convention applies to Sudan both as a matter of customary international law and as a preemptory norm of international law (i.e., "jus cogens").
- In determining the meaning of "genocide" under customary international law, the Genocide Convention provides the internationally accepted definition. Article II of the Genocide Convention requires that three conditions be met:

o specified acts are committed:

a) killing;
b) causing serious bodily or mental harm;
c) deliberately inflicting conditions of life calculated to bring about physical destruction of a group in whole or in part;
d) imposing measures to prevent births; or
e) forcibly transferring children to another group;

o these acts are committed against members of a national, ethnic, racial or religious group; and
o they are committed "with the intent to destroy, in whole or in part, [the group] as such".

- As is often the case in contemporaneously assessing whether genocide is occurring, the third required element (intent) is the most difficult to determine.

o When ratifying the Convention, the United States included the following understanding: "(1) That the term 'intent to destroy, in whole or in part, a national, ethnical, racial, or religious group such appearing in article II means the **specific intent** to destroy, in whole or in **substantial** part, a national ethnical, racial or religious group as such by the acts specified in article II." (Emphasis added.)
o The difficult question with respect to the application of article II to the situation in Darfur is whether the Arab perpetrators or Sudanese Government supporters have the specific intent to destroy the non-Arab members of certain ethnic groups, as such, in whole or substantial part.
o In the case of Bosnia (Tab 1), the Secretary imputed genocidal intent based on the nature and scale of the atrocities associated with ongoing ethnic cleansing.

Who decides whether genocide has occurred?

- Our records reflect that the Secretary of State typically makes a determination whether genocide has occurred in a particular country.
- In recent years, after a careful evaluation of the facts in question, the Department has concluded that genocide

occurred in Cambodia, Bosnia, Rwanda, and Burundi. In all cases but Cambodia, policy bureaus analyzed the acts of violence in the respective countries and, with L, recommended that the Secretary find that genocide was taking place.

What are the consequences of such a finding?

- Contracting Parties to the Genocide Convention have an obligation to prevent and punish acts of genocide in their territory. Article VI provides that persons charged with genocide "shall be tried by a competent tribunal of the State in the territory of which the act was committed, or by such international penal tribunals may have jurisdiction with respect to those Contacting Parties which shall have accepted its jurisdiction."
- As Sudan is not a Contracting Party to the Genocide Convention, its obligations apart from not directly engaging or participating in genocide are not dearly established under customary international law.
- Based on the available facts, a determination that genocide has occurred in Darfur would have no immediate legal—as opposed to moral, political or policy—consequences for the United States.

o In prior years, the Department rejected arguments by some human rights advocates for an expansive reading of article I ("The Contracting Parties confirm that genocide . . . is a crime . . . which they undertake to prevent and punish") that would impose a legal obligation on all Contracting Parties to take particular measures to "prevent" genocide in areas outside of their territory.

- From a policy perspective, however, a finding of genocide can act as a spur to the international community to take more forceful and immediate actions to respond to ongoing atrocities.

o Article VIII of the Genocide Convention provides that any Contracting Party "may call upon the competent organs of the United Nations to take such action under the Charter of the United Nations as they consider appropriate for the prevention and suppression" of genocide and related genocidal acts. Attachments: Tab I; October 1 and February 10, 1993 Action Memoranda on Genocide in Bosnia

SECRET
UNCLASSIFIED

Drafted: L/HRR:RKHarris ext. 7–4035
6/25/04 Doc. No. 117957

Cleared: L/AF:GTaft ok
L/HRR: GBrancato ok
L:SWitten ok
DRL/MLA:Mbutler ok
IO:JSWigert ok
AF/SPG:TSmith ok
INR:WWood ok
S/WCI:EHRichard ok

Source: National Security Archives, U.S. State Department Memo. "Genocide and Darfur." June 25, 2004. Available at https://nsarchive2.gwu.edu//dc.html?doc=3983552-Document-01-Genocide-and-Darfur-William-H-Taft.

3. U.S. Government Calls for International Resolve to Combat Darfur Genocide (July 2, 2004)

This cable from Secretary of State Colin Powell elucidates Washington's view on the

Darfur crisis and urges greater collaboration among the African Union (AU), United Nations (UN), European Union (EU), and other international groups to support the more than 1 million internally displaced persons (IDPs) in Sudan and 200,000 refugees in Chad dying of starvation, dehydration, and violence sponsored by the government of Sudan. Secretary Powell had visited Sudan on June 29 and 30, 2004, when he met with government officials and relief workers. Having met with Sudanese president Omar Hassan Ahmed al-Bashir and received his verbal commitment to allow humanitarian support for those in need, Powell asks in the cable that partner organizations help hold Bashir accountable and, if necessary, enforce sanctions. Above all, this cable demonstrates that intervention and aid are a team effort.

P 020118Z Jul 04
FM Secstate WashDC
To EU Member States Priority
Amembassy [ibid.] Bucharest Priority
Amembassy [ibid.] Bern Priority
Amembassy [ibid.] Oslo Priority
INFO Amembassy Khartoum Priority
USMission USUN New York Priority

Confidential State 145183 . . .
Subject: Sudan Demarche: Crisis in Darfur Requires EU Pressure and Resources
Ref: State 141587

Classified by: AF PDAS Charles R Syner
Reasons 1.4 B/D

1. (U) This is an action message. See para. 11.
2. (U) The secretary [Colin Powell] traveled to Sudan on June 29 and June 30 where he met with President Bashir and traveled to El Fasher, Darfur. The purpose of his trip was to press the GOS [Government of Sudan] on better performance and to call international attention to the dire humanitarian situation in Darfur. He visited a camp for internally displaced persons and met with the African Union ceasefire monitoring team.
3. (U) Since February 2003 the Darfur region of Sudan has been ravaged by conflict, which has resulted in over 1,000,000 internally displaced persons and some 200,000 refugees having fled into neighboring Chad. In Darfur, the government of Sudan and the conflict have severely constrained relief efforts, as have the normal logistical challenges. In Chad, however, it is principally logistics and lack of water that have constrained relief efforts. Nevertheless, lack of financial and human resources have also been a significant constraint to saving lives and relieving suffering. We anticipate that hundreds of thousands of people may die in Darfur due to the high levels of malnutrition and disease resulting from the conflict and inability to reach the victims. Global malnutrition rates on both sides of the border are running at levels of 25% and higher.
4. (U) In the midst of a severe humanitarian crisis, the GOS [government of Sudan] continues to hold up customs clearances for humanitarian assistance, and is insisting on testing medicines needed urgently to stop the spread of disease among [internally displaced persons or] IDPs. Most importantly, the GOS has not taken concrete steps to stop the Jingaweit [ibid., likely a misspelling on Janjaweed] militias, which continue to perpetrate violence and atrocities. This impedes delivery of humanitarian

relief and terrorizes internally displaced persons.

5. (U) During the course of his visit, the secretary obtained three commitments from the government of Sudan (GOS) (I) to protect civilians against attacks by Jingaweit [ibid.], (II) lift all restrictions on the free flow of humanitarian aid, (III) engage in political negotiations in close cooperation with the African Union. These three commitments are to be enacted within a time frame of specific days and weeks.

6. (U) We believe that this new round of commitments, delivered publicly by foreign minister [Mustafa Osman] Ismail in the presence of the secretary, offer a window of opportunity to pressure the GOS while making clear that we will respond to constructive GOS actions.

7. (U) Sudanese president Bashir and vice president [Ali Osman Mohammed] Taha know that we intend to intensify pressure—particularly by seeking a [United Nations Security Council or] UNSC resolution calling for targeted sanction if the necessary actions are not taken immediately. Such an approach has worked in the past. Pressure caused the GOS to sign the ceasefire agreement with the rebel groups (the Sudan Liberation Movement, SLM, and the Justice and Equality Movement, JEM) in earlv [ibid.] April. We helped broker this and then followed up to get agreement to international monitoring led by the African Union. The GOS has reluctantly cooperated in the monitoring.

8. (U) Funding contributed to date has not been sufficient to allow the UN and other international organizations and NGOs to adequately respond to the emergency needs of refugees and IDPs. To date the [United States government or] USF has contributed over $130 million to address the refugee situation in Chad and the crisis in Darfur. It is imperative that other donors also do all that they can to address what the UN has described as its most pressing humanitarian crisis. Immediate and generous donor contributions are critical at this time before the rains further shut down operations and to arrest the decline in nutritional/health status that could lead to hundreds of thousands of deaths.

9. (U) In additions, with the agreement of both the GOS and the Darfur rebels, the African Union had deployed a ceasefire monitoring mission to Darfur. The initial costs to establish the mission are substantial.

10. (C) USUN has circulated a draft UNSC resolution (reftel) [*reftel* stands for "reference telegram"] in NY. As of June 30 all council members have the text, as well as a number of non-council members including Norway and former and present EU presidents [of] Ireland and the Netherlands. Initial reactions have been generally positive, although most delegations have not yet received formal guidance. We have not yet formally tabled the resolution and do not expect to do so before the Security Council is briefed next week on the SYG's [*SYG* stands for "Secretary General of the United Nations"] trip to Sudan.

Action Requests:
—————

11. (U) Posts are requested to meet with appropriate officials in donor countries to explain the urgency of the situation in Darfur and Chad and to press for energetic EU engagement in efforts to forestall an even greater humanitarian tragedy. To aid your discussion of the

situation in Darfur, we have created a web site that contains unclassified aerial imagery.

Please visit the website at www.extranet.state.gov/m/ediplomacy/ and view the first unclassified item under "what's hot". [United States Agency for International Development or] USAID also posts a weekly fact sheet on their website at www.usaid.gov. Go to Sudan. Embassies should draw upon the following points:

- The situation in Darfur and eastern chad remain-grave.

 We anticipate that hundreds of thousands of people will die in Darfur due to the high levels of malnutrition and disease resulting from the conflict and inability to reach the victims. About 1 million people are at imminent risk now and that number is expected to increase to 2 million before the end of the year.
- Secretary Powell visited Khartoum and Darfur on June 29 and 30. He met with President Bashir and witnessed the horrible suffering that the GOS has inflicted on the people of Darfur. During the course of his visit, he obtained three commitments from the government of Sudan (GOS) (i) to protect civilians against attacks by Jingaweit [Janjaweed], and to deploy additional police forces to the region to combat additional militias if the attacks on civilians continue, (ii) lift all restrictions on the free flow of humanitarian aid, (iii) engage in political negotiations mediated by the African Union.
- We asked that you join us in pressing the GOS to abide by the commitment it made to Secretary Powell to take

the steps necessary to end the violence, provide unfettered access to humanitarian relief, and actively support the deployment of the au ceasefire monitors and human rights monitors. in other words, implement the spirit and letter of the N'Djamena humanitarian ceasefire agreement signed on April 8, 2004.
- We asked that you join us pressing the GOS to abide by the commitment it made to Secretary Powell to take the steps necessary to end the violence, provide unfettered access to humanitarian relief, and actively support the deployment of the AU-ceasefire monitors and human rights monitors.
- We are circulating in NY a draft UNSC resolution on Darfur. We havw [ibid.] put Sudan on notice that it must act immediately on the commitments made during the secretary's visit.
- The resolution calls on the GOS to honor the commitments it has already made, including ceasing attacks, disarming the Jinjaweit [Janjaweed], and allowing unfettered humanitarian access, urges support for the AU monitoring mission, and imposes sanctions on the Jinjaweit.
- The resolution demands action but we are prepared to respond positively to dramatic, verifiable actions on Darfur by the GOS.
- Your public support for a resolution is important. Your support will help build pressure on Sudan to act on its commitments.
- Secure access in the Darfur region continues to hamper humanitarian assistance, but so does money. We

must match our efforts those efforts with sufficient financial and human resources for the relief effort and the African Union ceasefire monitoring mission.

- Appeals from the UN, Red Cross, and NGOs are under funded [ibid.] resulting in major gaps in assistance.
- At the Geneva donor conference, we pledged $188 million in new funding for Darfur over this year and next. We have just contributed an additional $8 million in funding to [UN High Commission for Refugees or] UNHCR for the refugees in Chad and $5 million to ICRC for Chad and Darfur.
- At the June 26 U.S.—EU summit, we issued a joint statement calling on the GOS to stop the violence and support all efforts to address the humanitarian crisis. We need to follow up this statement with concrete action. thus, we ask the commission and all EU member states to support the UNSC resolution and provide further assistance.
- Also, it is important to encourage the African union to continue to press forward with the Darfur ceasefire monitoring mission and monitor the violence occurring in Darfur.

12. (u). Please advise on responses, with as much detail as possible on specific pledges/contributions and timing thereof.

Powell

Source: U.S. Department of State. "Sudan Demarche: Crisis in Darfur Requires EU Pressure and Resources." July 2, 2004. Available at the National Security Archive, https://nsarchive2.gwu.edu//NSAEBB/NSAEBB335/Document3.PDF.

4. John Garang: Speech at Signing of Comprehensive Peace Agreement (January 10, 2005)

On January 9, 2005, Sudan People's Liberation Movement (SPLM) leader John Garang and Sudan's first vice president, Ali Osman Taha, signed the Comprehensive Peace Agreement (CPA), and in so doing, they concluded more than two decades of civil war between north and south Sudan. In his remarks, Garang addresses the twisted road to peace and what is required from all of Sudan for the CPA to be fulfilled. He also addressed the ongoing government-sponsored violence in Darfur, Sudan, saying that he was confident that the peace agreement between the north and south enhanced the chances for a lasting peace. The following is the text of Garang's speech at the signing ceremony, held in Nairobi, Kenya.

Your Excellency President Mwai Kibaki [president of Kenya from 2002 to 2013], Your Excellency former president Daniel arap Moi [president of Kenya from 1978 to 2002], Your Excellencies heads of state and government, Your excellencies ambassadors and representatives of the international organizations, distinguished invited guests, ladies and gentlemen, compatriots, fellow countrymen and women, allow me at the outset to convey to you my best wishes for the new year. The year 2005 will mark the year of peace not only for the whole of Sudan but equally throughout our sub-region and Africa as a whole.

On this joyous day and occasion, I greet and salute the people of Sudan from Nimule in the far south to Halfa in the far north, and from Geneinah in the far west to

Hamashkoreb and Port Sudan in the east. I greet and salute all the marginalized rural people in Sudan who have suffered in dignified silence for so long. I greet and salute all the farmers, workers, and professionals who are the creators of wealth but who have no wealth. And who have seen their living conditions deteriorate over the years.

I greet you on the occasion of this peace, which we have just signed, all the Sudanese women everywhere. Women in Sudan, as everywhere in the world, are the marginalized of the marginalized, whose suffering goes beyond description. The Sudanese rural woman, for example, gets up at five o'clock in the morning to walk five kilometers just to get five gallons of water after five hours' walk, spends another five hours working on the family farm and five more hours making the family meal, and then she goes to sleep.

I greet and salute all our students on this occasion of the peace agreement, all our youths who have borne the brunt of the 21 years of this war, and to whom the future belongs, and urge them to invest in their future and that of the nation in the post-conflict period.

Compatriots, fellow countrymen and women, congratulations—*Mabruk all mabruk alaykum.* Your movement, the SPLM [Sudan's People Liberation Movement]-SPLA [Sudan People's Liberation Army], and the National Congress party government have delivered to you a comprehensive peace agreement. A just and honorable peace which we have signed today and which you have all witnessed. This is the best Christmas and New Year's gift for the Sudanese people, to our region, and to Africa for 2005.

With this peace agreement, we have ended the longest war in Africa - 39 years of two wars since August 1955 out of 50 years of our independence. And if we add the 11 years

of Anyanya II [southern Sudanese separatist forces formed in the late 1970s], then Sudan had been at war within itself for 49 years, which is the whole of its independence period. [Anyanya is the word for a poison made in southern Sudan; Anyanya I was the name of the southern Sudanese rebel army of the first civil war, during 1955–1972.]

With this peace agreement, the SPLM and the National Congress party government have brought half a century of war to a dignified end—congratulations.

With this peace agreement, there will be no more bombs falling from the sky on innocent children and women. Instead of the cries of children and the wailing of women and the pain of the last 21 years of war, peace will bless us once more with hearing the happy giggling of children and the enchanting ululation of women who are excited in happiness for one reason or another.

At the political level, this agreement affirms the right of self determination for the people of southern Sudan and the right of popular consultation for the people of the Nuba Mountains and Blue Nile so that the unity of the Sudan becomes based on the free will of the people instead of on wars and the forced and false unity of the last 49 years.

This peace agreement will change the Sudan for ever [ibid]. Sudan cannot and will never be the same again, as this peace agreement will engulf the country in democratic and fundamental transformations, instead of being engulfed in wars as it has always been for the last 184 years since 1821, when our country was first invaded by outside powers and exposed to the ravages of the slave trade and predatory commerce of all sorts, and since before independence from 1955 in civil wars.

This peace agreement coincides with Sudan's 49th independence celebrations.

And I agree with what President Bashir [Omar Hassan Ahmed al-Bashir] said on 31 December [2004] in Naivasha [in Kenya], when we signed the last two documents of the comprehensive peace agreement that Sudan's independence on 1 January 1956 was not complete because [word indistinct] south. The war we are ending today first broke out in Torit on 18 August 1955. Four months before independence. And so the south, like other marginalized parts of the Sudan were really not part of that independence. With this peace agreement, we begin the process of achieving real independence by all Sudanese people and for all the Sudanese people.

The signing of this comprehensive peace agreement thus marks the end of what I will correctly call the first republic of the whole Sudan that has lasted 49 years from 1 January 1956 to 31 December 2004, when we signed the last two agreements on comprehensive cease-fire and implementation modalities. And at a personal note, exactly 42 years to the date when I first left Sudan for the bush on 31 December 1962 to join the first war. I hope I will not go to the bush again.

This peace agreement therefore signals the beginning of Sudan's second republic of the new Sudan. From here on, Sudan for the first time will be a country voluntarily united in justice, honor, and dignity for all its citizens regardless of their race, regardless of their religion, regardless of their gender; or else if the country fails to rise to this challenge of moving away from the old Sudan to the new Sudan of free and equal citizens, then the union shall be dissolved amicably and peacefully through the right of self-determination at the end of the six years of the interim period.

I call on the Sudanese people to join this peace agreement, to join the SPLM and the National Congress party in the peace process, because this peace agreement belongs to them. It does not belong to John Garang or the SPLM leadership, it does not belong to [Vice-President] Ali Uthman Taha or President Al-Bashir or to the National Congress party. This agreement belongs to all of the Sudan, to its neighbors, to Africa, to the Arab world, and indeed to the rest of the world. That is why you see this big attendance today, because this peace belongs to all of them.

Although the comprehensive peace agreement was negotiated by two parties as a matter of necessity and practicality in order to end the war in the first place, and now that the war is ended, I call on all the Sudanese people and their political forces to build consensus around this comprehensive peace agreement, and use it to end war in other parts of Sudan and to relaunch the Sudan to the promised land of the new Sudan of progress and equality, of opportunity for all Sudanese citizens without distinction.

Finally, and last but not least, I salute all our martyrs and all wounded heroes on both sides. I salute and congratulate all officers, NCOs [noncommissioned officers], and soldiers on both sides of the conflict for their heroic sacrifices. I pay tribute and thank our civil population who provided the logistics for the war, especially those in the SPLM-administered areas, for without their contribution this comprehensive peace agreement would not have been possible. It is because of the role played by our civil population in the long war that we have invited some 50 chiefs and traditional leaders representing our civil society at the grassroots. We have also invited the SPLM military band to represent the SPLA rank and file.

On this joyous occasion of the signing of the comprehensive peace agreement, as you will recall that the SPLA has always released prisoners of war, we have released so far more than 3,000 prisoners of war at various times over the last 21 years. I here as of today order the immediate release of all prisoners of war that are still under the custody and care of the SPLA.

It is fitting, as we celebrate this momentous historical landmark, to pause to remember the thousands of fellow human beings who recently perished in both Asia and Africa in one of the planet's worst natural disasters of the modern era.

Our hearts go out in grief and solidarity to the peoples of Southeast Asia in this their hour of tragedy in the hands of a merciless earthquake and tsunamis. As we share the pain and suffering of our fellow human beings in all the countries that have been devastated by the earthquake and the accompanying tsunamis or tidal waves, we also urge the international community, after it has pledged so generously to help alleviate the suffering and rebuild shattered lives in the affected region, to spare some resources to help post-conflict Sudan recover and develop. We therefore look forward to a massive turnout of donors with their pledges at the prospective Oslo donors conference for Sudan which is scheduled soon.

Excellencies, compatriots, fellow citizens. In order to understand and appreciate the present historical moment of the signing of the Sudan comprehensive peace agreement, I beg your indulgence to allow me to talk briefly about the problem that we are solving now and to which [Ugandan] president Museveni [Yoweri Museveni] referred to before as the problem of people with the turbines and people with ostrich feathers.

As I said before, Sudan has been at war within itself for the whole of 49 years of its independence. And as we end this war today, another serious one is intensifying in the western Darfur region while another threatens in eastern Sudan.

Why? What is the problem? Why should a community subject itself to generations of war and suffering in so many parts of the country?

In our view, the attempts by various Khartoum-based regimes since 1956 to build a monolithic Arab Islamic state with the exclusion of other parameters of the Sudanese diversity constitutes the fundamental problem of the Sudan and defines the Sudanese conflict. The Sudanese state hitherto has excluded the vast majority of the Sudanese people from governance and therefore their marginalization in the political, economic, and social fields.

This provoked resistance by the excluded. There have been wars and there continues to be wars in the Sudan simply because the majority of the Sudanese are not stakeholders in the governance.

The solution to the fundamental problem of Sudan is to involve an all-inclusive Sudanese state which will uphold the new Sudan. A new political Sudanese dispensation in which all Sudanese are equally stakeholders irrespective of their religion, irrespective of their race, tribe, or gender and if this does not work, then to look for other solutions, such as splitting the country. But we believe that a new Sudan is possible, for there are many people in northern Sudan who share with us in SPLM/A, including the National Congress party, who believe in the universal ideals of humanity, the ideals of liberty, of freedom, justice, and equality, of opportunity for all Sudanese citizens.

As is the case in the south, the events in Darfur, eastern Sudan and elsewhere have made it clear that we must have an all-inclusive state at the national level and full devolution of power to the various regions of the Sudan, for otherwise it is unlikely that the country would stand a chance of remaining united. But this all-inclusive Sudanese state which we have called the new Sudan must have some basis, for example in history, that makes us one country or one nation. The question is whether there is the basis for the Sudan as a country, and my answer has also been yes, there is. That is, this affirmative answer to this question has guided us and sustained the SPLM for the last 21 years until today. For this purpose I have always wanted to go down the corridors of history and I want to do this very briefly. Again, begging your indulgence, and taking it for that matter—I am guerrilla, I take my time, you see.

My presentation, our presentation in the SPLM, is that we, the Sudanese, are indeed a historical people and that the new Sudan has an anchor in history. If we cannot find an anchor in history, then we either create one or dissolve the union peacefully. Sometimes it is necessary to go back in order to gain momentum in order to go forward. President Museveni called it something in his language. That is why you see sheep, you see rams moving backward first when they fight. They gain momentum before they lock horns. Recently, in southeast Asia, it was noticed [in] the tragedy of the earthquake and the tsunamis. First, the sea receded back, and then came forward with devastating force.

We very much need to do this exercise in the Sudan. To go back thousands of years so as to rediscover ourselves. Gain momentum and then move forward with the momentum of 5,000 years to propel ourselves and snatch ourselves into history once again. And we have a very long history indeed. Peoples and kingdoms have lived, thrived, and disappeared in the geographical area that constitutes the present modern Sudan.

Many people will be surprised that in the Bible, in the Old Testament, the Sudan was part of the Garden of Eden, where it is stated in Genesis, Chapter 2, Verse 8 to 14, that the Garden of Eden was watered by four rivers. One of them is the White Nile, it is Pessian in the Bible. The one is the Gihon and there is a Gihon Hotel in Addis Ababa. It is the Blue Nile. And to the east by the Tigris and Euphrates. So the Garden of Eden was not a small vegetable garden. It was a vast piece of territory. My own village happens to be just east of the Nile. So I fall in the Garden of Eden. It will surprise many of you that the Prophet Moses was probably married to a Sudanese named Siphorah, as narrated in the book of Numbers.

From the Biblical days, we move to the ancient Sudanese kingdoms of Awach, of Ritat, of Anu, of Maida, that are believed to be connected with the present-day Dinka, Shiluk, Nuer, other Nilotic tribes, and the peoples of central and western Sudan. And at the corridors of history we move to the Kingdom of Merowe [Arabic Marawi] that bequeathed an iron civilization to the rest of Africa. Merhawi got transformed into the Christian kingdoms of Nubia. Then followed the spread of Islam and Arab migrations into the Sudan and subsequent collapse of the last Nubian Christian kingdoms of Makuria, Alawa, and Soba in 1504, followed by the rise on the etches of the Islamic Kingdom Sinnar, which was founded by the Fuinsh and Shiluk people.

The rest of Sudanese history is familiar to all of us from the Islamic kingdoms of Sinar to the Teko Egyptian occupation, to the first Islamic Mahadisi state, to Anglo-Egyptian condominium [joint authority, in 1899] to independence in 1956 and the Anyanya movement [during] 1955 to 1972, to the SPLM/SPLA in 1983, to the second Islamic state in the Sudan of Ingas, with which we negotiated from 1989, and to the comprehensive [agreement] which we signed today. This is the history of the Sudan and this is how we got here. It has been a long journey of more than 5,000 years to reach Naivasha and Nyayo Stadium today. It is important to know and appreciate where we came from in order to better be able to chart the way forward with the momentum of historical force. That was Sudan in history.

As for the contemporary Sudan, we have more than 500 different ethnic groups speaking more than 130 different languages. We have two major religions in the country—Islam and Christianity, and traditional African religious. Our contention in the SPLM/SPLA is that the Sudan belongs equally to all the peoples that now inhabit the country, and its history, its diversity and richness, is the common heritage of all Sudanese. The comprehensive peace agreement that we have signed today is based on [these] historical and contemporary objective realities of Sudan. And by implementing the provisions of the comprehensive peace agreement that we signed today, we [evolve] an all-inclusive form of governance that ensures that all Sudanese are equally stakeholders irrespective of where they come from and this is what will keep our country together.

Furthermore, by adapting and applying the form of governance and wealth-sharing arrangements stipulated in the comprehensive peace agreement to other parts of the country with similar afflictions as the south such as Darfur, eastern Sudan and other parts of the country, we can once again become a great nation that is voluntarily united in diversity rather than divided by diversity and forcibly kept under a coerced and fake unity.

This is the context and the value of the comprehensive peace agreement we have signed today. It provides the Sudan with a real and perhaps the last opportunity to make a real paradigm shift from the old Sudan of exclusivity to the new Sudan of inclusivity, achieved not through force but through the exercise of the right of self-determination.

Viewed this way, the right of self-determination, which is one of the cornerstones of the comprehensive peace agreement, is a blessing rather than curse as many northern Sudanese fear. I want to assure you that we will all work together with the National Congress party and other political forces in the Sudan so that we develop a new paradigm so that we keep our country together.

Excellencies, distinguished guests, compatriots, ladies and gentlemen, bear with me. I am almost finished. The transformation which shall be engendered by this agreement, which I have alluded to, shall be reflected first and foremost in democratic [mutation?] and to which the SPLM is fully committed. Surely by democratic we do not mean return to the sham procedural democracy of the past, which was a camouflage for the perpetuation of vested interest. In that sham democracy, civil rights were subject to the whims of rulers. The majority of Sudanese regions remained peripheral to the central power and was treated as an expendable quantum only to be manipulated through political trickery and double-dealing.

The transformation envisaged in the comprehensive peace agreement puts an end to all that since it represents a political and socioeconomic paradigm shift which entails the recognition of political diversity by guaranteeing full freedom for political pluralism. The entrenchment of human rights and peoples' rights in the constitution, the upholding of the independence of the judiciary, including the creation of an inviolable constitutional court and commitment to the rule of law by the government and the governed, and the establishment of a truly independent and competent civil service at all levels of government. It also conceptualizes and seeks to realize a re-creation of the legislature in a manner that shall ensure rigorous checks and balances and guarantees powers to the government of southern Sudan and to the states powers which can neither be withdrawn nor impaired by other centers of power.

Eventually, the comprehensive peace agreement ordains that within a maximum of three to four years, governance at all levels shall be mandated by the supreme will of the people through internationally monitored free and fair elections.

Excellencies, distinguished guests, compatriots, ladies and gentlemen, the long war to which we have put an end to today impoverished our citizens and reduced our country with tremendous resources to destitution. Without claiming that the new economic paradigm shift, which I have alluded to, is the ultimate panacea for curing the nation's ills, it provides at least a vision and modalities to address the problems besetting the nation in the here and now—while I leave the world hereafter to those who claim to have divine qualifications.

In southern Sudan and other war-affected areas, as well as in the slums of our major cities, the baseline from which we shall start development is shocking and I will not bore here with the statistics of the status of these parameters, such as prevalence of child malnutrition, primary education, mortality rates among children, rate of maternal mortality, rate of births attended [by] skilled health staff, access to improved water sources. These statistics in southern Sudan in particular and other war-affected areas are among the worst in the world. To combat this pervasive and humiliating poverty and political disenfranchisement, a general

policy framework has [been] chartered out and published in a booklet entitled "SPLM Strategic Framework for War to Peace Transition."

In summary, the SPLM shall articulate and implement a social, political, and economic development strategy and programs that include the following highlights:

First, the SPLM shall adopt an economic development paradigm that emphasizes growth through rural development and transformation of traditional agriculture that is integrated with agro-industries. We must transform the present subsistence traditional agriculture in southern Sudan and other areas through technological innovations, making agriculture the engine of growth. And agriculture as the engine of growth will literally be fueled [ibid.] by oil—the building of dikes for flood control and canals and underground water development for irrigation will be priorities to guaranteeing crop production.

Secondly, the SPLM will change the urban-based center of focus development paradigm in favor of rural and decentralized development. The SPLM vision, policy, and slogan shall be to take the towns to people in the countryside rather than people to towns, where they end up in slums as [has] happened in many countries, with the consequent deterioration in their quality of life. Rural small town planning and rural electrification will therefore be priorities.

Thirdly, the SPLM shall emphasize and develop new ways of delivery of social services. As we move to the new era of peace, the people of Sudan, particularly the war-affected communities, face formidable social and economic problems and also tremendous opportunities. The major problems there require immediate attention fall in the areas of health, education, and water. We must find new ways to rapidly and efficiently deliver these services. For example, constructing windmills all over rural Sudan to provide clean drinking water and build micro-dams for generating small scale hydroelectric power for rural towns, as well as the use of solar, wind, and bio-gas energy sources.

Fourthly, the SPLM shall exert all efforts to build physical infrastructure—roads, rail and river transport, and telecommunications. There has never been any tarmac road in the new Sudan since creation, since the days of Adam and Eve, and this is an area the size of Kenya, Uganda, Rwanda, and Burundi put together. The SPLM's vision for transport infrastructure is at three levels—to develop regional linkages within southern Sudan and with the neighbors and with northern Sudan and to involve the state and local communities in this infrastructure building.

Fifthly, and finally, in terms of social and cultural parameters, the SPLM shall adopt the strategies and programs that shall restore and achieve dignity of people of the Sudan through social and cultural empowerment. Programs will include information and media, radio, TV, print, promotion of new Sudan art, songs, dances, theater of new Sudan, sports, development of local languages and cultures by the various communities of the Sudan, archives of the struggle and modern history of Sudan, archaeology, [and] antiquities and ancient history of Sudan, Africa, and the Middle East so that we can find our rightful place in the world.

Excellencies, distinguished guests, ladies and gentlemen, to conclude, the comprehensive peace agreement and safeguards, full compliance with the requirements of the agreement, the SPLM will work in partnership with the National Congress party. The objectives of this partnership is to ensure a sincere implementation of the comprehensive peace agreement in both letter and spirit and to provide, within the parameters of this agreement, permanent solutions to the problems inherent in Sudan's cultural, social, and political diversity.

Failure to appreciate the wealth in diversity was another cause of national crisis. For diversity, viewed positively, is a mutually [word indistinct] phenomenon and ultimately a source of national cohesion and strength. Viewed otherwise, that is as a source of dissimilarity or distinction, it shall lead inevitably to the ultimate disintegration of the country as threatens today and which at all costs we must avoid.

Furthermore, the partnership does not mean abandonment of political allies by any of the two parties. However, this partnership, once safeguarded in the new political dispensation, shall in effect nurture the democratic transformation and political multiplicity, which by their very nature may lead to diverse alliances. But so long as those alliances are based on commitment to the letter and spirit of the peace agreements that will put an end to the longest war in Africa, alliances become assets not liabilities. It is our submission that political struggle in the Sudan shall henceforth translate into competing visions of peace, progress, and development and never into the use of force or the threat of the use of force.

The SPLM, ladies and gentlemen, will ensure that the new political dispensation is wide enough to accommodate all legitimate political and social forces in the country. It is therefore our hope to achieve popular consensus on those agreements. As the movement that has been fighting against the marginalization of others, we shall not tolerate the exclusion of anybody from this process. The parties to the comprehensive peace agreement share this conviction and we have included in the agreement inclusiveness. In this regard, the SPLM will play its role at the national level to work with the National Congress party and other political forces to ensure full inclusiveness.

While the SPLM and the National Congress party shall be major partners in the initial interim government unity, our understanding of partnership is well rooted in inclusiveness, which means to bring on board all political forces in the Sudan, chief among them the political parties within the National Congress party umbrella and the political parties within the National Democratic Alliance, which we call upon to complete negotiations with the government of Sudan based on the Jeddah agreement that are holding negotiations in Cairo, and so that they get their share in the government of national unity and participate and participate fully in all the national commissions stipulated in the comprehensive peace agreement, especially the national constitution review commission.

Finally, on issues that concern southern Sudanese, I want to say a little on south-south dialogue. On building national consensus, the SPLM will also spearhead the south-south dialogue. This dialogue, above all, is to heal wounds and restore fraternity and mutual respect so as to create a healthier political environment that is accommodative all southern Sudanese political forces, both at the level of southern Sudan and at the national level. But south-south dialogue is not only about power. It is about all and [enviable?] democratic exercise based on mature and selfless political discourse among southern Sudanese with a view of galvanizing all our human material resources for the service of our people.

Democracy, whether in the north or south, should no longer and solely be a struggle for power but rather as a competition on providing good governance, development, and delivering social services for our people and restoring the dignity and wealth of every man and woman. Yet in terms of power-sharing in southern Sudan, I want to assure all that there will be enough room for everybody, including those who have not been associated with the SPLM/SPLA. Even those who for one reason or another were opposed or against the SPLM. There will room for everybody.

I want in conclusion to quote, in terms of this inclusiveness, the gospel according to St. John, that says in St. John, Chapter 14, Verse 1 and 2: Do not be worried and upset, Jesus told them, believe in God and believe also in me. There are many rooms in my father's house and I'm going to prepare a place for you. I would not say if it were not true.

So I say to all southern Sudanese on the occasion of this signing of this comprehensive peace agreement, that there will be many rooms in an SPLM-based government in southern Sudan and all are welcome.

I also want to assure southern Sudanese in general that the comprehensive peace agreement will not be dishonored like other agreements that [former Sudanese vice president] Abel Alier has written a book about, entitled *Too Many Agreements Dishonoured*. The biggest challenge will be implementation of the peace agreement but we, both the SPLM and the National Congress party, are committed, fully committed, to the implementation of this agreement. There are both external and internal guarantees, organic and external guarantees, that will ensure the implementation of this agreement.

I want also to assure the SPLA that the experience of Anyanya I will not repeat itself, because there are many SPLA soldiers that are worried they will be left by peace.

This regards the issue of funding of the armed forces. We solved the issue of funding of the armed [forces] adequately. The joint integrated units, component of the SPLA, shall be funded by the government of national unity, not as a separate army from the mother SPLM but as part and parcel of it with the same wage and living conditions.

The mother SPLA, on the other hand, will be funded by the government of southern Sudan, and the government of southern Sudan has been empowered by the comprehensive peace agreement to raise financial resources from both local and foreign sources and to seek international assistance for that purpose. So there is no reason for concern or alarm.

As for those who [are] in the Diaspora, I would like to address them and assure them that the government of southern Sudan as well as the government of national unity will [need] their skills, and I take the opportunity of this forum to appeal to all our Diaspora to return home and build our country. As I said before, our house has many rooms and Diaspora are welcome to return home and fully participate in the development of southern Sudan, the two areas—Abyei and the whole of Sudan.

Last but not least, I would like to pay tribute to our fallen heroes and martyrs who sacrificed in order for us to celebrate this day on both sides of the conflict. Those, ladies and gentlemen, are the objectives for whose achievements I have exerted all my faculties and energies and efforts, and for which we will cooperate and work together with the National Congress party. We move in a new direction and achieve the cohesion and the unity of our people and the unity of our country.

Finally, let me pay tribute and salute the courage of the party to reach this agreement and in particular President Omar Hassan al-Bashir and [Vice President] Ustadh Ali Uthman Taha, with whom I sat for 16 months and negotiated this agreement. I salute and congratulate them. I also congratulate the two delegations of the SPLM and the government of Sudan, and of course [Sudanese chief mediator] General [Lazarus] Sumbeiywo and before him Ambassador Daniel Mboya, who was the special envoy, [and] also before them, Zachary Onyango, Bethwel Kiplagat, and foreign minister then Stephen Kalonzo Musyoka and now Minister [for Regional Cooperation John] Koech and other ministers in the Kenya government, who have contributed so much; and to the IGAD [Intergovernmental Authority on Development] envoys of the five countries of IGAD, the facilitators of IGAD, the secretariat. I thank them and congratulate them for guiding the peace process to this successful conclusion.

I would also like to thank and commend the IGAD heads of state, ministers, peace envoys. and indeed the populace who have been with us through thick and thin, guiding, advising, cajoling, and sometimes threatening to abandon the process. They deserve praise. Our thanks go to them and also to the bravery of the people of east Africa, the Horn, the Arab world, and the wider international community, who on numerous occasions either volunteered to bring peace to Sudan or did encourage in meaningful manners the ongoing peace process. In this connection, the Nigerian efforts of [the] Abuja I and Abuja II [agreements], the joint Egyptian-Libyan initiative, the African Union, and the Arab League efforts, who exerted efforts for post-conflict reconstruction.

I must also mention a few of the very many names to thank for their contribution to the Sudan peace process, among them are eminent people like [Nigeria] President Obasanjo [Olusegun Obasanjo], President Babangida [Ibrahim Babangida] of Nigeria, President Kaunda [Kenneth Kaunda of Zambia], Masire [Ketumile Masire of Botswana], Machel [Samora Machel of Mozambique], Nujoma [Sam Nujoma of Namibia], Chissano [Joaqium Chissano of Mozambique], Rawlings [Jerry Rawlings of Ghana], who is here with us today, Mandela [Nelson Mandela] of South Africa, Mubarak [Hosni Mubarak] of Egypt, Qaddafi [Muammar Qaddafi of Libya], Bouteflika [Abdelaziz Bouteflika of Algeria], who is here with us today, Jimmy Carter, the late James Grant, and OLS [Operation Lifeline Sudan], that has saved millions of lives since 1989, [U.S.] President Bush [George W. Bush] and his secretary of state Colin Powell and his special envoy Senator [John] Danforth and Andrew Natsios of USAID [United States Agency for International Development], both houses of the U.S. Congress, [British] Prime Minister Tony Blair and his envoys, ambassadors Allan Gulty and McFell, the UN secretary general [Kofi Annan] and his envoys, ambassadors [Mohamed] Sahnoun and [Jan] Pronk [of the Netherlands], who are here, and a special friend of the Sudan peace process, the Norwegian minister Hilder Johnson, and finally, last but not least, the leaders of this region, led by then President Daniel arap Moi [of Kenya] and now by President Mwai Kibaki, President [Yoweri] Museveni, [Ethiopian] Prime Minister Zenawi [Meles Zenawi], [Eritrean] President Afewerki [Issaias Afewerki] and the *wananchi* [citizens] of Kenya and east Africa *mzima* [as a whole].

And finally I pay tribute and thanks to my dear wife, Rebecca, and the wives of all my colleagues and comrades in the struggle, for their patience and contributions, for without their help the bush would not have been bearable. My sincere thanks to all these people. I pay tribute finally to all the Sudanese people, to whom this peace belongs, and I say to them: *mobruk ol lekum* [congratulations].

Thank you very much.

Source: "TEXT: Garang's Speech at the Signing Ceremony of S. Sudan Peace Deal." *Sudan Tribune.* January 9, 2005. Available at http://www .sudantribune.com/TEXT-Garang-s-speech-at -the,7476.

---

5. Excerpts from the United Nations Commission of Inquiry on Darfur (January 25, 2005)

The United Nations (UN) Commission of Inquiry on Darfur was established by UN Resolution 1564 to investigate reports of human rights violations in Darfur, Sudan. In October 2004, the UN secretary-general Kofi Annan appointed a five-person commission to complete this task and requested that they report their findings within three months. The commission began its work on October 25 and engaged in a regular dialogue with the government of Sudan throughout its process. The team conducted research in Darfur from November 2004 to January 2005. The report, cited in part here, details the establishment of the commission and its goals in greater detail, including its charge to determine the identity of the perpetrators and whether the crimes being committed in Darfur constituted genocide.

The original report is 176 pages long, so in order to highlight key aspects, we have subdivided excerpts of it according to the following topics:

A. *Establishment of the Commission*
B. *Do Crimes Perpetrated in Darfur Constitute Genocide?*
C. *Justice and Equality Movement*
D. *Sudan Liberation Movement/Army*
E. *The 'Janjaweed'*
F. *The Commission's Recommendations Concerning Measures Designed to Ensure that Those Responsible are Held Accountable.*

A. Establishment of the Commission

The following document outlines the role of the United Nations International Commission of Inquiry on Darfur.

1. The International Commission of Inquiry on Darfur (henceforth the Commission) was established pursuant to United Nations Security Council resolution 1564 (2004), adopted on 18 September 2004. The resolution, passed under Chapter VII of the United Nations Charter, requested the Secretary-General rapidly to set up the Commission. In October 2004 the Secretary-General appointed a five member body (Mr. Antonio Cassese, from Italy; Mr. Mohammed Fayek, from Egypt; Ms Hina Jilani, from Pakistan; Mr. Dumisa Ntsebeza, from South Africa, and Ms. Theresa Striggner-Scott, from Ghana), and designated Mr. Cassese as its Chairman. The Secretary-General decided that the Commission's staff should be provided by the Office of the High Commissioner for Human Rights. Ms Mona Rishmawi was appointed Executive Director of the Commission and head of its staff. The Commission assembled in Geneva and began its work on 25 October 2004. The Secretary-General requested the Commission to report to him within three months, i.e. by 25 January 2005.

2. TERMS OF REFERENCE

2. In § 12, resolution 1564 (2004) sets out the following tasks for the Commission: "to investigate reports of violations of international humanitarian law and human rights law in Darfur by all parties"; "to determine also whether or not acts of genocide have occurred"; and "to identify the perpetrators of such violations"; "with a view to ensuring that those responsible are held accountable". Under the resolution, these tasks must be discharged "immediately".

3. The first of the above tasks implies that the Commission, rather than investigating alleged violations, must investigate "reports" of such violations committed by "all parties". This means that it is mandated to establish facts relating to possible violations of international human rights and humanitarian law committed in Darfur.. [ibid.] In this respect the Commission must act as a fact-finding body, beginning with an assessment of information contained in the various reports made by other bodies including Governments, United Nations bodies, organs of other intergovernmental organizations, as well as NGOs [non-governmental organization].

4. It also falls to the Commission to characterize, from the viewpoint of international criminal law, the violations of international human rights law and humanitarian law it may establish. This legal characterization is implicitly required by the further tasks of the Commission set out by the Security Council, namely (i) to establish whether those violations amount to genocide, and (ii) to identify the perpetrators. Clearly,

the Commission may not be in a position to fulfil these tasks if it has not previously established (a) whether the violations amount to international crimes, and, if so, (b) under what categories of crimes they fall (war crimes, crimes against humanity, genocide, or other crimes). This classification is required not only for the purpose of determining whether those crimes amount to genocide, but also for the process of identifying the perpetrators. In order to name particular persons as suspected perpetrators, it is necessary to define the international crimes for which they might be held responsible.

5. The second task with which the Security Council entrusted the Commission is that of legally characterizing the reported violations with a view to ascertaining whether they amount to genocide.

6. The third task is that of "identifying the perpetrators of violations" "with a view to ensuring that those responsible are held accountable". This requires the Commission not only to identify the perpetrators, but also to suggest possible mechanisms for holding those perpetrators accountable. The Commission therefore must collect a reliable body of material that indicate which individuals may be responsible for violations committed in Darfur and who should therefore be brought to trial with a view to determining their liability. The Commission has not been endowed with the powers proper to a prosecutor (in particular, it may not subpoena witnesses, or order searches or seizures, nor may it request a judge to issue arrest warrants against suspects). It may rely only upon the obligation of the Government of the Sudan and the rebels to cooperate. Its powers are therefore limited by the manner in which the Government and the rebels fulfil this obligation.

7. In order to discharge its mandate in conformity with the international law that it is bound to apply, the Commission has to interpret the word "perpetrators" as covering the executioners or material authors of international crimes, as well as those who may have participated in the commission of such crimes under the notion of joint criminal enterprise, or ordered their perpetration, or aided or abetted the crimes, or in any other manner taken part in their perpetration. The Commission has included in this inquiry those who may be held responsible for international crimes, under the notion of superior responsibility, because they failed to prevent or repress the commission of such crimes although they a) had (or should have had) knowledge of their commission, and b) wielded control over the persons who perpetrated them. This interpretation is justified by basic principles of international criminal law, which provide that individual criminal responsibility arises when a person materially commits a crime, as well as when he or she engages in other forms or modalities of criminal conduct.

8. Furthermore, the language of the Security Council resolution makes it clear that the request to "identify perpetrators" is "with a view to ensuring that those responsible are held accountable". In § 7 the resolution reiterates its request to the Government of the Sudan "to end the climate of impunity in Darfur" and to bring to justice "all those responsible, including members of popular defence [ibid.] forces and Janjaweed militias" for violations of human rights law and international humanitarian law (emphasis added). Furthermore, the tasks of the

Commission include that of "ensuring that those responsible are held accountable". Thus, the Security Council has made it clear that it intends for the Commission to identify all those responsible for alleged international crimes in Darfur. This is corroborated by an analysis of the objective of the Security Council: if this body aimed at putting an end to atrocities, why should the Commission confine itself to the material perpetrators, given that those who bear the greatest responsibility normally are the persons who are in command, and who either plan or order crimes, or knowingly condone or acquiesce in their perpetration?

9. This interpretation is also in keeping with the wording of the same paragraph in other official languages (for instance, the French text speaks of "*auteurs de ces violations*" and the Spanish text of "*los autores de tales transgresiones*"). It is true that in many cases a superior may not be held to have taken part in the crimes of his or her subordinates, in which case he or she would not be regarded as a perpetrator or author of those crimes. In those instances where criminal actions by subordinates are isolated episodes, the superior may be responsible only for failing to "submit the matter to the competent authorities for investigation and prosecution". In such instances, unquestionably the superior may not be considered as the author of the crime perpetrated by his or her subordinates. However, when crimes are committed regularly and on a large scale, as part of a pattern of criminal conduct, the responsibility of the superior is more serious. By failing to stop the crimes and to punish the perpetrators, he or she in a way takes part in their commission.

10. The fourth task assigned to the Commission therefore is linked to the third and is aimed at ensuring that "those responsible are held accountable". To this effect, the Commission intends to propose measures for ensuring that those responsible for international crimes in Darfur are brought to justice.

11. As is clear from the relevant Security Council resolution, the Commission is mandated to consider only the situation in the Darfur region of the Sudan. With regard to the time-frame, the Commission's mandate is inferred by the resolution. While the Commission considered all events relevant to the current conflict in Darfur, it focused in particular on incidents that occurred between February 2003, when the magnitude, intensity and consistency of incidents noticeably increased, until mid-January 2005 just before the Commission was required to submit its report.

3. WORKING METHODS

12. As stated above, the Commission started its work in Geneva on 25 October 2004. It immediately discussed and agreed upon its terms of reference and methods of work. On 28 October 2004 it sent a Note Verbale [French for "verbal note," it is a piece of diplomatic correspondence prepared in the third person and is unsigned] to Member States and intergovernmental organizations, and on 2 November 2004 it sent a letter to non-governmental organizations, providing information about its mandate and seeking relevant information. It also posted information on its mandate, composition and contact details on the web-site of the

Office of the High Commissioner for Human Rights (www.ohchr.org).

13. The Commission agreed at the outset that it would discharge its mission in strict confidentiality. In particular, it would limit its contacts with the media to providing factual information about its visits to the Sudan. The Commission also agreed that its working methods should be devised to suit each of its different tasks.

14. Thus, with regard to its first and second tasks, the Commission decided to examine existing reports on violations of international human rights and humanitarian law in Darfur, and to verify the veracity of these reports through its own findings, as well as to establish further facts. Although clearly it is not a judicial body, in classifying the facts according to international criminal law, the Commission adopted an approach proper to a judicial body. It therefore collected all material necessary for such a legal analysis.

15. The third task, that of "identifying perpetrators", posed the greatest challenge. The Commission discussed the question of the standard of proof that it would apply in its investigations. In view of the limitations inherent in its powers, the Commission decided that it could not comply with the standards normally adopted by criminal courts (proof of facts beyond a reasonable doubt), or with that used by international prosecutors and judges for the purpose of confirming indictments (that there must be a prima facie case). It concluded that the most appropriate standard was that requiring a reliable body of material consistent with other verified circumstances, which tends to show that a person may reasonably be suspected of being involved in the commission of a crime. The Commission would obviously not make final judgments as to criminal guilt; rather, it would make an assessment of possible suspects that would pave the way for future investigations, and possible indictments, by a prosecutor.

16. The Commission also agreed that, for the purpose of "identifying the perpetrators", it would interview witnesses, officials and other persons occupying positions of authority, as well as persons in police custody or detained in prison; examine documents; and visit places (in particular, villages or camps for IDPs, as well as mass grave sites) where reportedly crimes were perpetrated.

17. For the fulfilment of the fourth task the Commission deemed it necessary to make a preliminary assessment of the degree to which the Sudanese criminal justice system has been able and willing to prosecute and bring to trial alleged authors of international crimes perpetrated in Darfur, and then consider the various existing international mechanisms available. It is in the light of these evaluations that it has made recommendations on the most suitable measures.

4. PRINCIPAL CONSTRAINTS UNDER WHICH THE COMMISSION HAS OPERATED

18. There is no denying that while the various tasks assigned to the Commission are complex and unique, the Commission was called upon to discharge them under difficult conditions. First of all, it operated under serious time constraints. As pointed out above, given that the Security Council had decided that the

Commission must act urgently, the Secretary-General requested that the Commission report to him within three months of its establishment. The fulfillment of its complex tasks, in particular those concerning the finding of serious violations and the identification of perpetrators, required the Commission to work intensely and under heavy time pressure.

19. Furthermore, both its fact-finding mission and its task of identifying perpetrators would have benefited from the assistance of a great number of investigators, lawyers, military analysts and forensic experts. Given the scale and magnitude of incidents related to the conflict in Darfur, the establishment of facts and the collection of credible probative elements for the identification of suspected perpetrators are difficult tasks, which are not to be taken lightly. The Commission's budget did not allow for more than thirteen such experts. Having said this, the Commission nevertheless was able to gather a reliable and consistent body of material with respect to both the violations that occurred and the persons who might be suspected of bearing criminal responsibility for their perpetration. The Commission thus considers that it has been able to take a first step towards accountability.

B. Do Crimes Perpetrated in Darfur Constitute Genocide?

The report, quoted in part here, answers the question: Do the crimes perpetrated in Darfur constitute acts of genocide? Unlike the U.S. government, the UN Commission of Inquiry on Darfur found the answer to be no. In coming to this conclusion, the Commission determines protected group status and weighs genocidal intent. Though the Commission does not deem the crimes in Darfur to be genocide, it reaffirms that the atrocities occurring on a large scale in Darfur are serious offenses for which the perpetrators should be held accountable.

II. DO THE CRIMES PERPETRATED IN DARFUR CONSTITUTE ACTS OF GENOCIDE?

507. General. There is no doubt that some of the objective elements of genocide materialized in Darfur. As discussed above, the Commission has collected substantial and reliable material which tends to show the occurrence of systematic killing of civilians belonging to particular tribes, of large-scale causing of serious bodily or mental harm to members of the population belonging to certain tribes, and of massive and deliberate infliction on those tribes of conditions of life bringing about their physical destruction in whole or in part (for example by systematically destroying their villages and crops, by expelling them from their homes, and by looting their cattle). However, two other constitutive elements of genocide require a more in depth analysis, namely whether (a) the target groups amount to one of the group protected by international law, and if so (b) whether the crimes were committed with a genocidal intent. These elements are considered separately below.

508. *Do members of the tribes victims of attacks and killing make up objectively a protected group?* The various tribes that have been the object of attacks and killings (chiefly the Fur, Massalit and Zaghawa tribes) do not appear to make up ethnic groups distinct from the ethnic group to which persons or militias that attack them belong. They speak the same language (Arabic) and embrace the same religion

(Muslim). In addition, also due to the high measure of intermarriage, they can hardly be distinguished in their outward physical appearance from the members of tribes that allegedly attacked them. Furthermore, intermarriage and coexistence in both social and economic terms, have over the years tended to blur the distinction between the groups. Apparently, the sedentary and nomadic character of the groups constitutes one of the main distinctions between them. It is also notable that members of the African tribes speak their own dialect in addition to Arabic, while members of Arab tribes only speak Arabic.

509. *If not, may one hold that they subjectively make up distinct groups?* If objectively the two sets of persons at issue do not make up two distinct protected groups, the question arises as to whether they may nevertheless be regarded as such subjectively, in that they perceive each other and themselves as constituting distinct groups.

510. As noted above, in recent years the perception of differences has heightened and has extended to distinctions that were earlier not the predominant basis for identity. The rift between tribes, and the political polarization around the rebel opposition to the central authorities, has extended itself to issues of identity. Those tribes in Darfur who support rebels have increasingly come to be identified as "African" and those supporting the government as the "Arabs". A good example to illustrate this is that of the Gimmer, a pro-government African tribe and how it is seen by the African tribes opposed to the government as having been "Arabized". Clearly, not all "African" tribes support the rebels and not all "Arab" tribes support the Government. Some "Arab" tribes appear to be either neutral or even support the rebels. Other measures contributing to a

polarization of the two groups include the 1987–1989 conflict over access to grazing lands and water sources between nomads of Arab origin and the sedentary Fur. The Arab-African divide has also been fanned by the growing insistence on such divide in some circles and in the media. All this has contributed to the consolidation of the contrast and gradually created a marked polarization [ibid.] in the perception and self-perception of the groups concerned. At least those most affected by the conditions explained above, including those directly affected by the conflict, have come to perceive themselves as either "African" or "Arab".

511. There are other elements that tend to show a self-perception of two distinct groups. In many cases militias attacking "African" villages tend to use derogatory epithets, such as "slaves", "blacks", ["]*Nuba*", or "*Zurga*" that might imply a perception of the victims as members of a distinct group. However, in numerous other instances they use derogatory language that is not linked to ethnicity or race. As for the victims, they often refer to their attackers as *Janjaweed*, a derogatory term that normally designates "a man (a devil) with a gun on a horse." However, in this case the term Janjaweed clearly refers to "militias of Arab tribes on horseback or on camelback." In other words, the victims perceive the attackers as persons belonging to another and hostile group.

512. For these reasons it may be considered that the tribes who were victims of attacks and killings subjectively make up a protected group.

513. *Was there a genocidal intent?* Some elements emerging from the facts including the scale of atrocities and the systematic nature of the attacks, killing, displacement

and rape, as well as racially motivated statements by perpetrators that have targeted members of the African tribes only, could be indicative of the genocidal intent. However, there are other more indicative elements that show the lack of genocidal intent. The fact that in a number of villages attacked and burned by both militias and Government forces the attackers refrained from exterminating the whole population that had not fled, but instead selectively killed groups of young men, is an important element. A telling example is the attack of 22 January 2004 on Wadi Saleh, a group of 25 villages inhabited by about 11 000 Fur. According to credible accounts of eye witnesses questioned by the Commission, after occupying the villages the Government Commissioner and the leader of the Arab militias that had participated in the attack and burning, gathered all those who had survived or had not managed to escape into a large area. Using a microphone they selected 15 persons (whose name they read from a written list), as well as 7 *omdas* [leaders], and executed them on the spot. They then sent all elderly men, all boys, many men and all women to a nearby village, where they held them for some time, whereas they executed 205 young villagers, who they asserted were rebels (*Torabora*). According to male witnesses interviewed by the Commission and who were among the survivors, about 800 persons were not killed (most young men of those spared by the attackers were detained for some time in the Mukjar prison).

514. This case clearly shows that the intent of the attackers was not to destroy an ethnic group as such, or part of the group. Instead, the intention was to murder all those men they considered as rebels, as well as forcibly expel the whole population so as to vacate the villages and prevent rebels from hiding among, or getting support from, the local population.

515. Another element that tends to show the Sudanese Government's lack of genocidal intent can be seen in the fact that persons forcibly dislodged from their villages are collected in IDP camps. In other words, the populations surviving attacks on villages are not killed outright, so as to eradicate the group; they are rather forced to abandon their homes and live together in areas selected by the Government. While this attitude of the Sudanese Government may be held to be in breach of international legal standards on human rights and international criminal law rules, it is not indicative of any intent to annihilate the group. This is all the more true because the living conditions in those camps, although open to strong criticism on many grounds, do not seem to be calculated to bring about the extinction of the ethnic group to which the IDPs belong. Suffice it to note that the Government of Sudan generally allows humanitarian organizations to help the population in camps by providing food, clean water, medicines and logistical assistance (construction of hospitals, cooking facilities, latrines, etc.)

516. Another element that tends to show the lack of genocidal intent is the fact that in contrast with other instances described above, in a number of instances villages with a mixed composition (African and Arab tribes) have not been attacked. This for instance holds true for the village of Abaata (north-east of Zelingei, in Western Darfur), consisting of Zaghawa and members of Arab tribes.

517. Furthermore, it has been reported by a reliable source that one inhabitant of the Jabir Village (situated about 150 km from Abu Shouk Camp) was among the victims of

an attack carried out by Janjaweed on 16 March 2004 on the village. He stated that he did not resist when the attackers took 200 camels from him, although they beat him up with the butt of their guns. Instead, prior to his beating, his young brother, who possessed only one camel, had resisted when the attackers had tried to take his camel, and had been shot dead. Clearly, in this instance the special intent to kill a member of a group to *destroy the group as such* was lacking, the murder being only motivated by the desire to appropriate cattle belonging to the inhabitants of the village. Irrespective of the motive, had the attackers' intent been to annihilate the group, they would not have spared one of the brothers.

518. *Conclusion.* On the basis of the above observations, the Commission concludes that the Government of Sudan has not pursued a policy of genocide. Arguably, two elements of genocide might be deduced from the gross violations of human rights perpetrated by Government forces and the militias under their control. These two elements are: first, the *actus reus* consisting of killing, or causing serious bodily or mental harm, or deliberately inflicting conditions of life likely to bring about physical destruction; and, second, on the basis of a subjective standard, the existence of a protected group being targeted by the authors of criminal conduct. Recent developments have led to the perception and self- perception of members of African tribes and members of Arab tribes as making up two distinct ethnic groups. However, one crucial element appears to be missing, at least as far as the central Government authorities are concerned: genocidal intent. Generally speaking the policy of attacking, killing and forcibly displacing members of some tribes does not evince a specific intent to

annihilate, in whole or in part, a group distinguished on racial, ethnic, national or religious grounds. Rather, it would seem that those who planned and organized attacks on villages pursued the intent to drive the victims from their homes, primarily for purposes of counter-insurgency warfare.

519. However, as pointed out above, the Government also entertained the intent to drive a particular group out of an area on persecutory and discriminatory grounds for political reasons. In the case of Darfur this discriminatory and persecutory intent may be found, on many occasions, in some Arab militias, as well as in the central Government: the systematic attacks on villages inhabited by civilians (or mostly by civilians) belonging to some "African" tribes (Fur, Masaalit and Zaghawa), the systematic destruction and burning down of these villages, as well as the forced displacement of civilians from those villages attest to a manifestly persecutory intent. In this respect, in addition to murder as a crime against humanity, the Government may be held responsible for persecution as a crime against humanity. *This would not affect the conclusion of the Commission that the Government of Sudan has not pursued the policy of genocide in Darfur.*

520. One should not rule out the possibility that in some instances single individuals, including Government officials, may entertain a genocidal intent, or in other words, attack the victims with the specific intent of annihilating, in part, a group perceived as a hostile ethnic group. If any single individual, including Governmental officials, has such intent, it would be for a competent court to make such a determination on a case by case basis. Should the competent court determine that in some instances certain individuals pursued the genocidal intent, the question

would arise of establishing any possible criminal responsibility of senior officials either for complicity in genocide or for failure to investigate, or repress and punish such possible acts of genocide.

521. Similarly, it would be for a competent court to determine whether some individual members of the militias supported by the Government, or even single Government officials, pursued a policy of extermination as a crime against humanity, or whether murder of civilians was so widespread and systematic as to acquire the legal features proper to *extermination* as a crime against humanity.

522. The above conclusion that no genocidal policy has been pursued and implemented in Darfur by the Government authorities, directly or though [ibid.] the militias under their control, should not be taken as in any way detracting from, or belittling, the gravity of the crimes perpetrated in that region. As stated above genocide is not necessarily the most serious international crime. Depending upon the circumstances, *such international offences as crimes against humanity or large scale war crimes may be no less serious and heinous than genocide.* This is exactly what happened in Darfur, where massive atrocities were perpetrated on a very large scale, and have so far gone unpunished.

C. Justice and Equality Movement

The following excerpt consists of the description of the Justice and Equality Movement (JEM). Emerging in 2001, JEM, alongside the Sudan People's Liberation Movement/ Army (SLM/A), is one of the principal groups rebelling against the Sudanese government.

3. Rebel movement groups

(ii) The Justice and Equality Movement (JEM)

133. Like the [Sudan Liberation Movement/ Army or] SLM/A, the Justice and Equality Movement (JEM) is a Darfur-based rebel movement, which emerged in 2001, and formed part of the armed rebellion against the Government [of Sudan] launched in early 2003. In the field, it is difficult to make a distinction between JEM and SLM/A, as most often reports on actions by rebels do not distinguish between the two. It has been reported that members of the JEM have yellow turbans. It also appears that while SLM/A is the larger military actor of the two, the JEM is more political and has a limited military capacity, in particular following the reported split of the group and the ensuing emergence of the [National Movement for Reform and Development or] NMRD (see below).

134. The JEM is led by Dr. Khalil Ibrahim, a former State Minister who sided with Hassan El Turabi [a leading politician in the Sudanese government who was instrumental in institutionalizing Sharia law in Sudan] when the latter formed the Popular National Congress in 2000. Various sources of information have stated that the JEM have been backed by Turabi. While Turabi's role in and influence on the JEM remains unclear, after an initial release following two years' detention in October 2003, he reportedly admitted that his party has links with JEM. However during a meeting with the members of the Commission, Dr. Khalil Ibrahim denied such a link, and stated that in fact Turabi was the main reason for the atrocities committed in the Darfur.

135. The "Black Book" appears to be the main ideological base of the JEM. This manifesto, which appeared in 2001, seeks to prove that there has been a total marginalization of Darfur and other regions of the Sudan, in terms of economic and social

development, but also of political influence. It presents facts that aim to show, "the imbalance of power and wealth in Sudan". It was meant to be an anatomy of Sudan that revealed the gaps and discrimination in contrast to the positive picture promoted by the Government. The Black Book seeks to show in a meticulous fashion how the Sudan's post-independence administrations have been dominated by three tribes all from the Nile valley north of Khartoum, which only represent about five per cent of the Sudan's population according to the official census. Despite this, the Black Book argues, these three tribes have held between 47 and 70 per cent of cabinet positions since 1956, and the presidency up until today. Persons from the North are also reportedly overwhelmingly dominant in the military hierarchy, the judiciary and the provincial administration. According to the Black Book, those leaders have attempted to impose a uniform Arab and Islamic culture on one of the continent's most heterogeneous societies41. The message is designed to appeal to all marginalized Sudanese—whether of Arab, Afro-Arab or African identity, Christian or Muslim. Based on this ideology, the JEM is not only fighting against the marginalization, but also for political change in the country, and has a national agenda directed against the present Government of the Sudan.

136. The Commission obtained very little information about the size and geographic location of JEM forces in Darfur. Most of its members appear to belong to the Zaghawa tribe, and most JEM activity is reported in the northern parts of West Darfur. The Commission did find information about a number of incidents in which the JEM had been involved in attacks on civilians (see below).

137. In early May 2004, the JEM split into two factions: one group under the leadership of Dr. Khalil, while the other group comprises commanders in the field led by Colonel Gibril. The split reportedly occurred after the field commanders called a conference in Karo, near the Chadian border in North Darfur State, on 23 May 2004. The conference was organized by the commanders to discuss directly with the political leaders the future of the movement and their ideological differences.

D. Sudan Liberation Movement/Army

In this excerpt, the commission describes the makeup and nature of the SLM/A. It provides an overview of the history, agenda, and leadership of the rebel organization that has played a key role in fighting Janjaweed and government troops in Darfur.

(i.) The Sudan Liberation Movement/Army (SLM/A)

127. The Sudan Liberation Movement/Army (SLM/A) is one of the two main rebel organizations in Darfur. By all accounts, it appears to be the largest in terms of membership and geographical activity. It is composed mainly of Zaghawa, Fur and Masaalit, as well as some members of Arab tribes. The SLM/A initially called itself the Darfur Liberation Front, and at the time was defending a secessionist agenda for Darfur. In a statement released on 14 March 2003, the Darfur Liberation Front changed its name to the Sudan Liberation Movement and the Sudan Liberation Army (SLM/A), and called for a "united democratic Sudan" and for separation between State and religion.

128. The SLM/A claims that all post-independence Governments of the Sudan

have pursued policies of marginalization, racial discrimination, exclusion, exploitation and divisiveness, which in Darfur have disrupted the peaceful coexistence between the region's African and Arab communities. As indicated in its policy statement released in March 2003, "the SLM/A is a national movement that aims along with other like-minded political groups to address and solve the fundamental problems of all of the Sudan. The objective of SLM/A is to create a united democratic Sudan on a new basis of equality, complete restructuring and devolution of power, even development, cultural and political pluralism and moral and material prosperity for all Sudanese". It called upon tribes of "Arab background" to join its struggle for democracy. At various occasion it has stated that it was seeking an equitable share for Darfur in the country's distribution of wealth and political power.

129. The SLM/A emphasizes that it has a national agenda and does not argue its case from a tribal perspective, and underlines that its cause is directed against the Khartoum Government, and not the Arab tribes in Darfur: "The Arab tribes and groups are an integral and indivisible component of Darfur social fabric that have been equally marginalized and deprived of their rights to development and genuine political participation. SLM/A firmly opposes and struggles against the Khartoum government's policies of using some Arab tribes and organization such as the Arab Alliance and Quresh [a mercantile Arab tribe] to achieve its hegemonic devices that are detrimental both to Arabs and non-Arabs."

130. In addition, it should also be noted that the SLM/A is part of the Sudanese opposition umbrella group, the National Democratic Alliance (NDA), which also includes the Sudan People's Liberation Movement /

Army (SPLM/A), the Umma party and other Sudanese opposition parties.

131. The SLM/A, as indicated by its name, is influenced in terms of agenda and structure by its southern counterpart, the SPLM/A. During the Commission's meetings with the SLM/A leadership in Asmara, Eritrea, it was made clear that the group is divided into a political arm, the "Movement", and a military arm, the "Army". At the oustset [ibid.] of the conflict, the structure of the SLM/A remained unclear. In October 2003, the SLM/A reportedly held a conference in North Darfur State during which changes in their structure were discussed and a clear division of work proposed between the military and the political wings. Nowadays, and following the discussion members of the Commission had with SLM/A representatives in Eritrea, it appears that the movement's non-military chairman is Abdel Wahid Mohamad al Nur and that the main military leader and the group's Secretary-General is Minnie Arkawi Minawi. The negotiation team in the peace talks with the Government is headed by Dr. Sherif Harir. Little is known about the detailed structure, or about the actual size of the military arm. According to information obtained by the Commission, the SLM/A has acquired most of its weapons through the looting of Government installations, in particular police stations as well as army barracks. Other sources claim that foreign support has also played an important role in the build-up of the SLM/A forces. The Commission, however, was not in a position to confirm this.

132. The Commission obtained little information about the areas controlled by the SLM/A in Darfur. While certain rural areas are said to be under the group's control, given its operation as a mobile guerilla

group, these areas of control are not fixed. In the beginning of the conflict most of the fighting seems to have taken place in North and northern West Darfur, while it gradually moved southward into South Darfur during the last months of 2004.

E. The 'Janjaweed'

The following excerpt discusses the organization of the Janjaweed and links the militias to the Sudanese government. The document also details the potential legal responsibility of government officials for acts perpetrated by Janjaweed militias.

2. Government supported and/or controlled militias—the 'Janjaweed'

(iii.) Organization and structure of Janjaweed

106. The Janjaweed are not organized in one single coherent structure, and the Commission identified three main categories of Janjaweed actor[s], determined according to their type of affiliation with the Government of Sudan. The first category includes militias which are only loosely affiliated with the Government and which have received weapons and other supplies from the State. These militias are thought to operate primarily under a tribal management structure. They are thought to undertake attacks at the request of State authorities, but are suspected by the Commission of sometimes also acting on their own initiative to undertake small scale actions to loot property for personal gain.

107. A second category includes militias which are organized in paramilitary structures and in parallel to regular forces, including groups known as "the Strike Force", the Mujahedeen [the plural form of

mujahid, one who is engaged in Jihad] or the Fursan (the horsemen). Some of these may be headed by officers in the regular army while also controlled by senior tribal leaders. While militias in this category are thought to operate within a defined command structure they do not have any legal basis.

108. A third category of militia includes members of the [Popular Defense force or] PDF and Border Intelligence which have a legislative basis under Sudanese law. The PDF fight alongside the regular armed forces.

109. There are links between all three categories. For example, the Commission has received independent testimony that the PDF has supplied uniforms, weapons, ammunition and payments to Arab tribal militia from the first category. The leaders of these tribes meet regularly with the PDF Civilian Coordinator, who takes their concerns to the Security Committee of the locality.

110. The Commission has gathered substantial material attesting to the participation of militia from all three categories in committing violations of international human rights and humanitarian law. The Commission has determined, further, that attackers from all 3 categories have been identified by victims and other witnesses as Janjaweed.

(iv) Links between the militias and the State

111. The Commission has established that clear links exist between the State and militias from all three categories. The close relationship between the militias and the PDF, a State institution established by law, demonstrates the strong link between these militias and the State as a whole. In addition, militias from all three categories have received weapons, and regular supplies of ammunition which have been distributed to the militias by the army, by senior civilian authorities

at the locality level or, in some instances, by the PDF to the other militias.

112. The PDF take their orders from the army and conduct their attacks on villages under the direct leadership of an army officer with the rank of Captain or Lieutenant. Testimonies of victims consistently depict close coordination in raids between government armed forces and militia men who they have described as Janjaweed and the Commission has very substantial material attesting to the participation of all categories of militia in attacks on villages in coordination with attacks or surveillance by Sudanese military aircraft. Numerous sources have reported that Government of Sudan aircraft have been used to supply the Janjaweed with arms.

113. Members of the PDF receive a monthly salary from the State which is paid through the army. The Commission has reports of the tribal militia members, or their leaders, receiving payments for their attacks and one senior Government official involved in the recruitment of militia informed the Commission that tribal leaders were paid in terms of grants and gifts according to the success of their recruitment efforts. In addition, the Commission has substantial testimony that this category of militia has the tacit agreement of the State authorities to loot any property they find and to gain compensation for their attacks in this way. A consistent feature of attacks is the systematic looting of the possessions of villagers, including cash, personal valuable items and, above all, livestock. Indeed, all of these militias operate with almost complete impunity for attacks on villages and related human rights violations. For example, the Commission has substantial testimony indicating that police officers in one locality

received orders not to register or investigate complaints made by victims against Janjaweed.

114. A Report of the Secretary-General, pursuant to paragraphs 6 and 13 to 16 of Security Council resolution 1556 (2004) of 30 August 2004, mentions that "the Government also accepted that the militias under its influence were not limited to those previously incorporated into the Popular Defence [ibid.] Forces, but also included militias that were outside and later linked with or mobilized to join those forces. This means that the commitment to disarm refers both to the Popular Defence [ibid.] Forces and to militias that have operated in association with them".

115. Confidential documents made available to the Commission further support the above conclusions on links between the militias and the Government, and identify some individuals within the governmental structure who would have had a role in the recruitment of the militias.

116. The Commission does not have exact figures of the numbers of active Janjaweed, however, most sources indicate that in each of Darfur's three states there is at least one large Janjaweed group as well as several smaller ones. One report identified at least 16 Janjaweed camps still active throughout Darfur with names of Janjaweed commanders. According to information obtained by the Commission, Misteria, in North Darfur, is one Janjaweed camp which continues to be used today and which incorporates a militia known as the Border Guards. It was set up as a base for Janjaweed from which they receive training, weapons, ammunition and can eventually be recruited into the PDF structure, into the police, or into the army. The Commission received evidence that

civilians have been abducted by leaders of this camp and detained within the camp where they were tortured and used for labour. These civilians were taken out of the camp and hidden during 3 pre-arranged monitoring visits by AU forces. In the first half of 2004 the Misteria camp was populated by approximately 7,000 Janjaweed. By the end of 2004 most of these men had been registered as PDF or police and army regular forces. An army officer with the rank of Colonel was stationed in the camp throughout the year and was responsible for training, ammunition stores and paying salaries to the Janjaweed. Two military helicopters visited the camp roughly once a month bringing additional weapons and ammunition. On at least one occasion the camp was visited by an army Brigadier.

(v.) The position of the Government

117. Especially since the international community has become aware of the impact of the Janjaweed actions, responses of the Government of the Sudan to the use of the term seems to have been aimed at denying the existence of any links between the State and the Janjaweed; and most officials routinely attribute actions of the Janjaweed to "armed bandits", "uncontrolled elements", or even the [Sudan Liberation Army or] SLA and [Justice and Equality Movement or] JEM. The Government position has nevertheless been inconsistent, with different officials, both at national and Darfur levels, giving different accounts of the status of the Janjaweed and their links with the State.

118. The Minister of Defence [ibid.] during a press conference on 28 January 2004 invited the media to differentiate between the "rebels", the "Janjaweed", the "Popular Defence Forces (PDF)" and "tribal militias", such as the "militias" of the Fur tribe, and the "Nahayein" of the Zaghawa. He said the

PDF are volunteers who aid the armed forces but the Janjaweed are "gangs of armed bandits" with which the government has no relations whatsoever. President Bashir intended his pledge on 19 June 2004 to "disarm the Janjaweed" to apply only to the bandits, not the Popular Defence Forces, Popular Police or other tribesmen armed by the state to fight the rebels.

119. Contrasting with the above, some official statements confirm the relationship between the government and the militias. In a widely publicized comment addressed to the citizens of Kulbus, a town the rebels had failed to overrun in December 2003, the President said: "Our priority from now on is to eliminate the rebellion, and any outlaw element is our target . . . We will use the army, the police, the mujahedeen, the horsemen to get rid of the rebellion". The Minister of Justice told the ad hoc delegation of the Committee on Development and Cooperation of the European Parliament during its visit in February 2004 that "the Government made a sort of relationship with the Janjaweed. Now the Janjaweed abuse it. I am sure that the Government is regretting very much any sort of commitments between them and the Government. We now treat them as outlaws. The devastation they are doing cannot be tolerated at all".

On 24 April 2004, the Foreign Minister stated: "The government may have turned a blind eye toward the militias," he said. "This is true. Because those militias are targeting the rebellion." The Commission has formally requested the Minister on three occasions to provide it with the above statement or any other statement related to the militias, but has not received it.

120. Despite Government statements regretting the actions of the Janjaweed, the various militias' attacks on villages have continued

throughout 2004, with continued Government support.

(vi.) The question of legal responsibility for acts committed by the Janjaweed

121. The "Janjaweed" to whom most victims refer in the current conflict are Arab militias that raid the villages of those victims, mounted on horses or camels, and kill, loot, burn and rape. These militias frequently operate with, or are supported by, the Government, as evidenced both by consistent witness testimonies describing Government forces' support during attacks, the clear patterns in attacks conducted across Darfur over a period of a year, and by the material gathered by the Commission concerning the recruitment, arming and training of militias by the Government. Some militias may, as the Government alleges, sometimes act independently of the Government and take advantage of the general climate of chaos and impunity to attack, loot, burn, destroy, rape, and kill.

122. A major legal question arises with regard to the militias referred to above: who (in addition to the individual perpetrators) is criminally responsible for crimes allegedly committed by Janjaweed?

123. When militias attack jointly with the armed forces, it can be held that they act under the effective control of the Government, consistently with the notion of control set out in 1999 in *Tadić (Appeal)*, at §§ 98–145. Thus they are acting as *de facto* State officials of the Government of Sudan. It follows that, if it may be proved that all the requisite elements of effective control were fulfilled in each individual case, responsibility for their crimes is incurred not only by the individual perpetrators but also by the relevant officials of the army for ordering or planning, those crimes, or for failing to prevent or repress them, under the notion of superior responsibility.

124. When militias are incorporated in the PDF and wear uniforms, they acquire, from the viewpoint of international law the status of organs of the Sudan. Their actions and their crimes could be legally attributed to the Government. Hence, as in the preceding class, any crime committed by them involved not only the criminal liability of the perpetrator, but also the responsibility of their superior authorities of the Sudan if they ordered or planned those crimes or failed to prevent or repress such crimes (superior responsibility).

125. On the basis of its investigations, the Commission is confident that the large majority of attacks on villages conducted by the militia have been undertaken with the acquiesecence [ibid.] of State officials. The Commission considers that in some limited instances militias have sometimes taken action outside of the direct control of the Government of Sudan and without receiving orders from State officials to conduct such acts. In these circumstances, only individual perpetrators of crimes bear responsibility for such crimes. However, whenever it can be proved that it was the Government that instigated those militias to attack certain tribes, or that the Government provided them with weapons and financial and logistical support, it may be held that (i) the Government incurs international responsibility (vis-à-vis all other member States of the international community) for any violation of international human rights law committed by the militias, and in addition (ii) the relevant officials in the Government may be held criminally accountable, depending on the specific circumstances of each case, for instigating or for aiding and abetting the

violations of humanitarian law committed by militias.

126. The Commission wishes to emphasize that, if it is established that the Government used the militias as a "tactic of war", even in instances where the Janjaweed may have acted without evidence of Government support, Government officials may incur criminal responsibility for joint criminal enterprise to engage in indiscriminate attacks against civilians and murder of civilians. Criminal responsibility may arise because although the Government may have intended to kill rebels and destroy villages for counter- insurgency purposes, it was foreseeable, especially considering the history of conflicts between the tribes and the record of criminality of the Janjaweed, that giving them authorization, or encouragement, to attack their long-term enemies, and creating a climate of total impunity, would lead to the perpetration of serious crimes. The Government of Sudan willingly took that risk.

F. The Commission's Recommendations Concerning Measures Designed to Ensure that Those Responsible are Held Accountable

Here, we see the recommendations of the investigation team, which include referring the situation to the International Criminal Court (ICC) and strengthening the independence of the Sudanese judiciary. The ICC is an intergovernmental organization and international tribunal located in The Hague, in the Netherlands, with jurisdiction to prosecute individuals for international crimes of genocide, crimes against humanity, war crimes, and crimes of aggression.

IV. THE COMMISSION'S RECOMMENDATIONS CONCERNING MEASURES DESIGNED TO ENSURE THAT THOSE RESPONSIBLE ARE HELD ACCOUNTABLE

1. Measures that should be taken by the Security Council

647. With regard to the judicial accountability mechanism, the Commission strongly recommends that the Security Council should refer the situation in Darfur to the International Criminal Court, pursuant to Article 13(b) of the Statute of the Court. Many of the alleged crimes documented in Darfur have been widespread and systematic. They meet all the thresholds of the Rome Statute for the International Criminal Court [ICC]. The Sudanese justice system has demonstrated its inability and unwillingness to investigate and prosecute the perpetrators of these crimes.

648. The Commission holds the view that resorting to the ICC would have at least six major merits. First, the International Court was established with an eye to crimes likely to threaten peace and security. This is the main reason why the Security Council may trigger the Court's jurisdiction under Article 13 (b). The investigation and prosecution of crimes perpetrated in Darfur would have an impact on peace and security. More particularly, it would be conducive, or contribute to, peace and stability in Darfur, by removing serious obstacles to national reconciliation and the restoration of peaceful relations. Second, as the investigation and prosecution in the Sudan of persons enjoying authority and prestige in the country and wielding control over the State apparatus, is difficult or even impossible, resort to the ICC, the only truly international institution of criminal justice, which would ensure that justice be done. The fact that trials proceedings would be conducted in

The Hague, the seat of the ICC, far away from the community over which those persons still wield authority and where their followers live, might ensure a neutral atmosphere and prevent the trials from stirring up political, ideological or other passions. Third, only the authority of the ICC, backed up by that of the United Nations Security Council, might impel both leading personalities in the Sudanese Government and the heads of rebels to submit to investigation and possibly criminal proceedings. Fourth, the Court, with an entirely international composition and a set of well-defined rules of procedure and evidence, is the best suited organ for ensuring a veritably fair trial of those indicted by the Court Prosecutor. Fifth, the ICC could be activated immediately, without any delay (which would be the case if one were to establish ad hoc tribunals or so called mixed or internationalized courts). Sixth, the institution of criminal proceedings before the ICC, at the request of the Security Council, would not necessarily involve a significant financial burden for the international community.

649. The Security Council should, however, act not only against the perpetrators but also on behalf of victims. In this respect, the Commission also proposes the establishment an International Compensation Commission, consisting of fifteen (15) members, ten (10) appointed by the United Nations Secretary- General and five (5) by an independent Sudanese body.

2. Action that should be taken by the Sudanese authorities

650. Government of the Sudan was put on notice concerning the alleged serious crimes that are taking place in Darfur. It was requested not only by the international community, but more importantly by its own people, to put an end to the violations and to bring the perpetrators to justice. It must take serious measures to address these violations. The Commission of Inquiry therefore recommends the Government of the Sudan to:

(i) end the impunity for the war crimes and crimes against humanity committed in Darfur. A number of measures must be taken in this respect. It is essential that Sudanese laws be brought in conformity with human rights standards through *inter alia* [among other things] abolishing the provisions that permit the detention of individuals without judicial review, the provisions granting officials immunity from prosecution as well as the provisions on specialized courts;

(ii) respect the rights of [internally displaced persons or] IDPs and fully implement the Guiding Principles on Internal Displacement, particularly with regard to facilitating their voluntary return in safety and dignity;

(iii) strengthen the independence and impartiality of the judiciary and to confer on courts adequate powers to address human rights violations;

(iv) grant the International Committee of the Red Cross and the United Nations human rights monitors full and unimpeded access to all those detained in relation to the situation in Darfur;

(v) ensure the protection of all the victims and witnesses of human rights violations, particularly those who were in contact with the Commission of Inquiry and ensure the protection of all human rights defenders;

(vi) with the help of international community, enhance the capacity of the Sudanese judiciary through the training of judges, prosecutors and lawyers. Emphasis should be laid on human rights law, humanitarian law, as well as international criminal law;

(vii) fully cooperate with the relevant human rights bodies and mechanisms of the United Nations and the African Union, particularly, the special representative of the United Nations Secretary-General on human rights defenders; and

(viii) create through a broad consultative process, including civil society and victim groups, a truth and reconciliation commission once peace is established in Darfur.

3. Measures That Could be Taken by Other Bodies

651. The Commission also recommends that measures designed to break the cycle of impunity should include the exercise by other States of universal jurisdiction, as outlined elsewhere in this report.

652. Given the seriousness of the human rights situation in Darfur and its impact on the human rights situation in the Sudan, the Commission recommends that the Commission on Human Rights consider the re-establishment of the mandate of the Special Rapporteur on human rights in the Sudan.

653. The Commission recommends that the High Commissioner for Human Rights should issue public and periodic reports on the human rights situation in Darfur.

Source: United Nations. 2005. *Report of the International Commission of Inquiry on Darfur to the United Nations Secretary-General.* January 25.

Available at http://www.iccnow.org/documents/UN%20commission_inquiry_report_darfur.pdf.

6. "Sudan: Accountability for War Crimes," U.S. Department of State Press Guidance (January 28, 2005)

On January 28, 2005, the U.S. Department of State issued a confidential press guide to selected staff that repeated the U.S. opposition to the use of the International Criminal Court (ICC) to resolve the conflict in Darfur and explains that the United States was working with African nations to create a hybrid African Union (AU) and United Nations (UN) court as an alternative to the ICC. As a permanent member of the UN Security Council, the United States wanted to avoid being confronted with a decision on whether to veto an ICC resolution. This document elucidates that even before the genocide concluded, the United States and its partner nations were discussing how to achieve some measure of justice when the time finally came to hold perpetrators accountable.

[S/WCI Input for AF Press Guidance]
January 28, 2005

SUDAN: ACCOUNTABILITY FOR WAR CRIMES

Q: Is the U.S. asking governments on the UN Security Council to create a court to prosecute individuals for war crimes in Sudan?

• We are appalled by the atrocities that have occurred in Darfur and believe that those responsible must be held accountable. We sponsored a UN resolution that produced a UN commission that's been looking into the atrocities there, and as you all know from the UN and from press reports, that commission is nearing the end of the work.

- We have begun now to consult with our partners, especially African countries which have been so active in trying to stop the violence in Sudan, to find the best possible mechanism for achieving accountability.
- **(If pressed)** We do not discuss the details of diplomatic discussions.
- **(If asked)** We understand that some countries support the International Criminal Court as the appropriate mechanism. Our position regarding the ICC is well known. WE believe there are better options for accountability and are examining them.

Background:

S/WCI [Ambassador] Prosper met in New York yesterday with representatives of Gabon, Tanzania, Nigeria, Benin, and the U.K. to discuss our proposal for a "hybrid" court administered by the African Union and UN. We have approached, via demarche, six other African countries and the AU [African Union]. This proposal, which remains confidential, would serve as an alternative to the ICC. We do not want to be confronted with a decision on whether to veto an ICC resolution in the Security Council.

The UN's Darfur Commission of Inquiry has delivered its report to the Secretary General; however, the report will not be released to the public until sometime next week. We have not seen the full text, but understand the report will lay out details of serious violations of human rights and of international humanitarian law. However, the Commission apparently will not draw a conclusion as to whether genocide has taken place. We

understand the Commission will recommend that the issue be referred to the ICC as the only workable solution for justice.

Source: U.S. State Department. 2005. "Sudan: Accountability for War Crimes." January 28. Available at the National Security Archive, https://nsarchive2.gwu.edu//NSAEBB/NSAEBB335/Document5.PDF.

7. John Garang: Speech on "Social Contract" for Sudan (March 5, 2005)

John Garang led the Sudan People's Liberation Movement/Army (SPLM/A), which fought for the self-rule of southern Sudan for more than twenty years and now dominates the politics of autonomous South Sudan. An economist educated in the United States at Cornell University and Iowa State University, Garang became the first vice president of Sudan following the landmark peace agreement of January 2005. Tragically, he died in a helicopter crash in July of that year. Prior to his death he delivered the speech, as excerpted here, at the invitation of the Belgian government at the Third Conference on Federalism in the Belgian capital, Brussels, on March 5, 2005. In the speech, he called for a "social contract" to hold all of Sudan—including South Sudan and Darfur—together.

. . . In the literature on federalism, analysts identify two processes of federalism: so-called "coming-together" federations formed by independent states for the sake of common goods otherwise unattainable, and "holding-together" federations, which develop from unitary states as governments respond to mitigate threats of secession. In the Sudanese situation, both processes are involved, as the Sudanese seek to "come together," perhaps for the first time, and as they try to "hold together" to preserve a union that was imposed on them by colonialism . . .

I am not here bemoaning the colonial experience . . . [but the colonial encounter and the historical movement of peoples are] some of the historical events that have contributed to the making of the present country called Sudan. The real task facing the Sudanese is therefore to build a Sudanese "nation-state" out of these circumstances, a Sudanese political dispensation that belongs equally to all its citizens irrespective of race, ethnicity, religion, or gender, something which we have not done before and which lies at the root of the wars we are now seeing afflicting our country all over—in southern Sudan, Nuba Mountains, Blue Nile, eastern Sudan, and Darfur.

What we really need to do, which we should have done 50 years ago at independence but which I am happy we are doing now in Sudan, is to go back to appreciate the classical justification of the state as based on a "social contract" between the people and the state. . . .

The question then is whether the present Sudanese state would be the object of an agreement if the Sudanese people were asked? The conventional wisdom is that northern Sudanese would answer the question in the affirmative, that the present Sudanese state is the object of an agreement and that Sudan exercised the right of self-determination at independence in 1956. Southern Sudanese, on the other hand, would answer in the negative and instead argue that they have never been part of any agreement on the present Sudanese state before, at, or after independence and therefore demand the right of self-determination. To compound things even more, the legitimacy of the present Sudanese state is not only being challenged by southern Sudanese, it is also being questioned by the people of Darfur, eastern Sudan, Nuba Mountains, Blue Nile, the far North, and other parts of the country. Many Sudanese are asking a serious question, whether the present Sudanese state as inherited from 1956 at independence represents their interests in their various groupings and regions. The present crisis and wars in the Sudan spring from the fact that many Sudanese do not associate with the present Sudanese state, although many identify with a Sudanese entity or homeland.

In fact, the present Sudanese state was originally contrived as a result of the colonial encounter, and its initial objective was to achieve interests that were particular to colonialism. It was therefore not based on any social contract or agreement by the Sudanese people. It can even be argued that the colonial encounter shifted and distorted the trajectory of indigenous nation-state formation and that this continues to haunt Africa today.

It is this type of state that Sudanese elites in Khartoum and the adjacent riverian areas of central Sudan took over at independence. Sadly, there was no conscious attempt by these elites to recast the state, to base its legitimacy on a social contract and consensus of the people. These elites took over the colonial state and looked at it as if it were a magical tree that perpetually bears and gives to them fruits of all kinds. In Africa, the colonially inherited state became like the proverbial goose that lays golden eggs. Unfortunately for them as the elites fought and continue to fight over custody of the goose, they killed the goose along with millions of innocent people. . . .

With the collapse of the colonially inherited state, or the threat of its collapse, this may or should sufficiently challenge Africa to conceptualize a correct and sustainable form of state that is based on the notion of a social contract that represents the interests of all the people in that state. This approach could result in a possible redrawing of the colonially inherited boundaries in Africa so as to be better able to face the realities and challenges of the 21st century and beyond, to forestall unnecessary and costly wars, and to promote development and prosperity for the peoples of Africa and the world using Africa's vast natural resources. . . .

The Sudan has over 500 different ethnic groups, speaking more than 130 distinct languages. These ethnic groups fall into two broad categories: indigenous African Sudanese, those whose mother tongue is some African language other than Arabic, constituted 69% of the population at independence in 1956; [and] Arab Sudanese, those who have Arabic as their community language, were 31% of the population. Ethnicity is thus one major form of contemporary diversity. The other form of contemporary diversity is religion. The Muslims are mostly in the north and constitute about 65% of the total population, while Christians and followers of traditional African religions constitute the remaining 35%. Sudan also has a rich and long historical heritage. Civilizations and various forms of the state have flourished and perished in the geographical area that constitutes the present, modern Sudan, from ancient Cush of the Biblical days to Christian Nubia and Merowe, to the Islamic states of Sennar and [the Kingdom of] Darfur, to the Turko-Egyptian and Anglo-Egyptian regimes of recent years.

Yet and despite the richness of Sudan's historical and contemporary diversity, the current and previous rulers of Khartoum present a false picture of the country. They based the Sudanese state on a poor mixture of a dysfunctional, colonially inherited state

and two exclusionist ideologies of Arabism and Islamism. They insisted that Islamic Sharia must be the supreme law of the land and even waged Jihad to impose it. This poor vision of Sudan by the present and previous regimes has been the fundamental problem of Sudan responsible for the many wars.

Source: Garang, John. 2005. "Sudan's Comprehensive Peace Agreement and Federalism." Address on the Occasion of the Third Conference on Federalism in Brussels, Belgium, March 5. Available online at https://paanluelwel.com/2011/08/08/dr-john-garangs-speech-on-the-conclusion-of-the-cpa-january-9-2005.

8. Darfur Peace and Accountability Act (2006)

The Darfur Peace and Accountability Act (H.R. 3127) is a thirteen-page bill from 2006 that reaffirms the position of the U.S. Congress that Sudanese government–sponsored violence in the region of Darfur constitutes genocide, and introduces a number of measures aimed at ending the conflict. Furthermore, it authorizes the president of the United States to impose asset freezes and travel restrictions against those suspected of responsibility for crimes taking place in Darfur, as well as against their associates and family members. The act also authorizes the sitting U.S. president to provide various forms of support to the African Union (AU) peacekeeping force in Darfur and introduces measures meant to disrupt the flow of oil revenues to the Sudanese government.

The bill was introduced on June 30, 2005, to Congress and was sponsored by Henry Hyde, the representative for Illinois's sixth congressional district. On April 5, 2006, it passed the House, and on September 21, it passed the Senate with an amendment (approved again by the House on September 25) by unanimous consent. The bill was later signed and enacted by President George W. Bush on October 13, 2006. Excerpts from the bill appear here.

An Act

To impose sanctions against individuals responsible for genocide, war crimes, and crimes against humanity, to support measures for the protection of civilians and humanitarian operations, and to support peace efforts in the Darfur region of Sudan, and for other purposes. [. . .]

SEC. 3. FINDINGS.

Congress makes the following findings:

(1) On July 23, 2004, Congress declared, 'the atrocities unfolding in Darfur, Sudan, are genocide.'

(2) On September 9, 2004, Secretary of State Colin L. Powell stated before the Committee on Foreign Relations of the Senate, 'genocide has occurred and may still be occurring in Darfur,' and 'the Government of Sudan and the Janjaweed bear responsibility.'

(3) On September 21, 2004, in an address before the United Nations General Assembly, President George W. Bush affirmed the Secretary of State's finding and stated, '[a]t this hour, the world is witnessing terrible suffering and horrible crimes in the Darfur region of Sudan, crimes my government has concluded are genocide.' [. . .]

SEC. 4. SENSE OF CONGRESS.

It is the sense of Congress that—

(1) the genocide unfolding in the Darfur region of Sudan is characterized by acts of terrorism and atrocities directed against civilians, including mass murder, rape, and sexual violence committed by the Janjaweed and associated militias with the complicity and support of the National Congress Party–led faction of the Government of Sudan;

(2) all parties to the conflict in the Darfur region have continued to violate the N'Djamena Ceasefire Agreement of April 8, 2004, and the Abuja Protocols of November 9, 2004, and violence against civilians, humanitarian aid workers, and personnel of AMIS [African Union Mission in Sudan] is increasing;

(3) the African Union should immediately make all necessary preparations for an orderly transition to a United Nations peacekeeping operation, which will maintain an appropriate level of African participation, with a mandate to protect civilians and humanitarian operations, assist in the implementation of the Darfur Peace Agreement, and deter violence in the Darfur region;

(4) the international community, including the United States and the European Union, should immediately act to mobilize sufficient political, military, and financial resources through the United Nations and the North Atlantic Treaty Organization, to support the transition of AMIS to a United Nations peacekeeping operation with the size, strength, and capacity necessary to protect civilians and humanitarian operations, to assist with the implementation of the Darfur Peace Agreement, and to end the continued violence in the Darfur region;

(5) if an expanded and reinforced AMIS or subsequent United Nations peacekeeping operation fails to stop genocide in the Darfur region, the international

community should take additional measures to prevent and suppress acts of genocide in the Darfur region;

(6) acting under article 5 of the Charter of the United Nations, the United Nations Security Council should call for suspension of the Government of Sudan's rights and privileges of membership by the General Assembly until such time as the Government of Sudan has honored pledges to cease attacks upon civilians, demobilize and demilitarize the Janjaweed and associated militias, and grant free and unfettered access for deliveries of humanitarian assistance in the Darfur region;

(7) the President should use all necessary and appropriate diplomatic means to ensure the full discharge of the responsibilities of the Committee of the United Nations Security Council and the panel of experts established pursuant to section 3(a) of Security Council Resolution 1591 (2005);

(8) the President should direct the United States Permanent Representative to the United Nations to use the voice, vote, and influence of the United States to urge the adoption of a resolution by the United Nations Security Council that—

   (A) extends the military embargo established by United Nations Security Resolutions 1556 (2004) and 1591 (2005) to include a total ban on the sale or supply of offensive military equipment to the Government of Sudan, except for use in an internationally recognized demobilization program or for nonlethal assistance necessary to carry out elements of the Comprehensive Peace Agreement for Sudan or the Darfur Peace Agreement; and

   (B) calls upon those member states of the United Nations that continue to undermine efforts to foster peace in Sudan by providing military assistance to the Government of Sudan, government supported militias, or any rebel group operating in Darfur in violation of the embargo on such assistance and equipment, as called for in United Nations Security Council Resolutions 1556 (2004) and 1591 (2005), to immediately cease and desist.

(9) the United States should not provide assistance to the Government of Sudan, other than assistance necessary for the implementation of the Comprehensive Peace Agreement for Sudan and the Darfur Peace Agreement, the support of the regional Government of Southern Sudan, the Transitional Darfur Regional Authority, and marginalized areas in Northern Sudan (including the Nuba Mountains, Southern Blue Nile, Abyei, Eastern Sudan (Beja), Darfur, and Nubia), or for humanitarian purposes in Sudan, until the Government of Sudan has honored pledges to cease attacks upon civilians, demobilize and demilitarize the Janjaweed and associated militias, grant free and unfettered access for deliveries of humanitarian assistance in the Darfur region, and allow for the safe and voluntary return of refugees and internally displaced persons; [. . .]

SEC. 5. SANCTIONS IN SUPPORT OF PEACE IN DARFUR. [. . .]

'(1) BLOCKING OF ASSETS—Beginning on the date that is 30 days after the date of the enactment of the Darfur Peace and Accountability Act of 2006, and in the interest of contributing to peace in Sudan, the

President shall, consistent with the authorities granted under the International Emergency Economic Powers Act (50 U.S.C. 1701 et seq.), block the assets of any individual who the President determines is complicit in, or responsible for, acts of genocide, war crimes, or crimes against humanity in Darfur, including the family members or any associates of such individual to whom assets or property of such individual was transferred on or after July 1, 2002.

'(2) RESTRICTION ON VISAS— Beginning on the date that is 30 days after the date of the enactment of the Darfur Peace and Accountability Act of 2006, and in the interest of contributing to peace in Sudan, the President shall deny a visa and entry to any individual who the President determines to be complicit in, or responsible for, acts of genocide, war crimes, or crimes against humanity in Darfur, including the family members or any associates of such individual to whom assets or property of such individual was transferred on or after July 1, 2002.' [. . .]

(c) Sanctions Against Janjaweed Commanders and Coordinators or Other Individuals- It is the sense of Congress, that the President should immediately impose the sanctions described in section 6(c) of the Comprehensive Peace in Sudan Act of 2004, as added by subsection (a), against any individual, including the Janjaweed commanders and coordinators, identified as those who, among other acts, 'impede the peace process, constitute a threat to stability in Darfur and the region, commit violations of international humanitarian or human rights law or other atrocities.'

SEC. 6. ADDITIONAL AUTHORITIES TO DETER AND SUPPRESS GENOCIDE IN DARFUR.

(a) Presidential Assistance To Support AMIS- Subject to subsection (b) and notwithstanding any other provision of law, the President is authorized to provide AMIS with—

(1) assistance for any expansion of the mandate, size, strength, and capacity to protect civilians and humanitarian operations in order to help stabilize the Darfur region of Sudan and dissuade and deter air attacks directed against civilians and humanitarian workers; and

(2) assistance in the areas of logistics, transport, communications, material support, technical assistance, training, command and control, aerial surveillance, and intelligence.

(b) Conditions-

(1) IN GENERAL- Assistance provided under subsection (a)—

(A) shall be used only in the Darfur region; and

(B) shall not be provided until AMIS has agreed not to transfer title to, or possession of, any such assistance to anyone not an officer, employee or agent of AMIS (or subsequent United Nations peacekeeping operation), and not to use or to permit the use of such assistance for any purposes other than those for which such assistance was furnished, unless the consent of the President has first been obtained, and written assurances reflecting all of the forgoing have been obtained from AMIS by the President.

(2) CONSENT- If the President consents to the transfer of such assistance to anyone not an officer, employee, or agent of AMIS (or subsequent United Nations peacekeeping operation), or agrees to permit the use of such assistance for any purposes other than those for which

such assistance was furnished, the President shall immediately notify the Committee on Foreign Relations of the Senate and the Committee on International Relations of the House of Representatives in accordance with the procedures applicable to reprogramming notifications under section 634A of the Foreign Assistance Act of 1961 (22 U.S.C. 2394–1). [. . .]

(e) Denial of Entry at United States Ports to Certain Cargo Ships or Oil Tankers-

(1) IN GENERAL- The President should take all necessary and appropriate steps to deny the Government of Sudan access to oil revenues, including by prohibiting entry at United States ports to cargo ships or oil tankers engaged in business or trade activities in the oil sector of Sudan or involved in the shipment of goods for use by the armed forces of Sudan until such time as the Government of Sudan has honored its commitments to cease attacks on civilians, demobilize and demilitarize the Janjaweed and associated militias, grant free and unfettered access for deliveries of humanitarian assistance, and allow for the safe and voluntary return of refugees and internally displaced persons.

(2) EXCEPTION- Paragraph (1) shall not apply with respect to cargo ships or oil tankers involved in—

(A) an internationally-recognized demobilization program;

(B) the shipment of non-lethal assistance necessary to carry out elements of the Comprehensive Peace Agreement for Sudan or the Darfur Peace Agreement; or

(C) the shipment of military assistance necessary to carry out elements of an agreement referred to in subparagraph (B) [. . .]

(f) Prohibition on Assistance to Countries in Violation of United Nations Security Council Resolutions 1556 and 1591-

(1) PROHIBITION- Amounts made available to carry out the Foreign Assistance Act of 1961 (22 U.S.C. 2151 et seq.) may not be used to provide assistance (other than humanitarian assistance) to the government of a country that is in violation of the embargo on military assistance with respect to Sudan imposed pursuant to United Nations Security Council Resolutions 1556 (2004) and 1591 (2005).

(2) WAIVER- The President may waive the application of paragraph (1) if the President determines, and certifies to the appropriate congressional committees, that such waiver is in the national interests of the United States

SEC. 7. CONTINUATION OF RESTRICTIONS.

(a) In General- Restrictions against the Government of Sudan that were imposed pursuant to Executive Order No. 13067 of November 3, 1997 (62 Federal Register 59989), title III and sections 508, 512, 527, and 569 of the Foreign Operations, Export Financing, and Related Programs Appropriations Act, 2006 (Public Law 109–102), or any other similar provision of law, shall remain in effect, and shall not be lifted pursuant to such provisions of law, until the President certifies to the appropriate congressional committees that the Government of Sudan is acting in good faith to—

(1) implement the Darfur Peace Agreement;

(2) disarm, demobilize, and demilitarize the Janjaweed and all militias allied with the Government of Sudan;

(3) adhere to all associated United Nations Security Council Resolutions, including Security Council Resolutions 1556 (2004), 1564 (2004), 1591 (2005), 1593 (2005), 1663 (2006), 1665 (2006), and 1706 (2006);

(4) negotiate a peaceful resolution to the crisis in eastern Sudan;

(5) fully cooperate with efforts to disarm, demobilize, and deny safe haven to members of the Lord's Resistance Army in Sudan; and

(6) fully implement the Comprehensive Peace Agreement for Sudan without manipulation or delay, by—

    (A) implementing the recommendations of the Abyei Boundaries Commission Report;

    (B) establishing other appropriate commissions and implementing and adhering to the recommendations of such commissions consistent with the terms of the Comprehensive Peace Agreement for Sudan;

    (C) adhering to the terms of the Wealth Sharing Agreement; and

    (D) withdrawing government forces from Southern Sudan consistent with the terms of the Comprehensive Peace Agreement for Sudan.

(b) Waiver- The President may waive the application of subsection (a) if the President determines, and certifies to the appropriate congressional committees, that such waiver is in the national interests of the United States.

SEC. 8. ASSISTANCE EFFORTS IN SUDAN.

(a) Assistance for International Malaria Control Act- Section 501 of the Assistance for International Malaria Control Act (Public Law 106-570; 50 U.S.C. 1701 note) is repealed.

(b) Comprehensive Peace in Sudan Act- Section 7 of the Comprehensive Peace in Sudan Act of 2004 (Public Law 108-497; 50 U.S.C. 1701 note) is repealed.

(c) Economic Assistance-

(1) IN GENERAL- Notwithstanding any other provision of law, the President is authorized to provide economic assistance for Southern Sudan, Southern Kordofan/Nuba Mountains State, Blue Nile State, Abyei, Darfur, and marginalized areas in and around Khartoum, in an effort to provide emergency relief, to promote economic self-sufficiency, to build civil authority, to provide education, to enhance rule of law and the development of judicial and legal frameworks, and to support people to people reconciliation efforts, or to implement any nonmilitary program in support of any viable peace agreement in Sudan, including the Comprehensive Peace Agreement for Sudan and the Darfur Peace Agreement. [. . .]

Source: Darfur Peace and Accountability. 2006. H.R. 3127/S. 1462. October 13. Available at https://www.govinfo.gov/app/details/BILLS-109hr3127enr.

Perspective Essays

What Was the Primary Cause of the Darfur Genocide?

The 2004 genocide in Darfur was shaped primarily by the violent targeting of the black non-Arab population by the Sudanese government. Through the use of government troops and Arab militias, Sudanese president Omar Hassan Ahmed al-Bashir sought to displace the black African population from the region through military force. Using the pretext of rebellion and the cover of war, the Bashir regime attacked non-Arab civilians in Darfur, who were either killed or fled to internally displaced persons (IDP) camps within Sudan or neighboring Chad. Amid the poor living conditions of these IDP camps, many of those who fled the violence succumbed to disease. While much of the blame for the events in Darfur in 2004 can be placed on the Bashir regime, Arab militias, known collectively as Janjaweed, also participated in the killing and displacement of the black population of Darfur. The violence was fueled by fervent racism and animus on the part of the Sudanese Arabs against the black population of Darfur. Moreover, the inability of the international community to come to any sort of coordinated preventative measures, outside of sanctions, allowed the violence to continue unabated.

In his Perspective Essay, John Hubbel Weiss states that the role of Omar Hassan Ahmed al-Bashir and racist notions of Arab supremacy contributed to the actions undertaken by the Sudanese regime against the black population of Darfur. The rebellion in the province gave Bashir the ideal pretext to ruthlessly act against the black population of Darfur, with the cooperation of Arab elites, government forces, and Janjaweed militias. In his Perspective Essay, while Hannibal Travis also places responsibility on the Bashir regime and the prevalence of Arab supremacy in the region, he considers other factors that shaped the violence in Darfur. Among these were Janjaweed cooperation with the regime and the economic context shaped by competition over scarce water resources by Arab and non-Arab populations in Darfur.

Background Essay

From 2003 to 2004, the regime of President Omar Hassan Ahmed al-Bashir in Sudan sought to destroy the black African population in the province of Darfur. As the international community took notice and failed to take action, Bashir's Government of Sudan (GOS) troops and Janjaweed militias initiated a campaign that led to the deaths of an estimated range of 250,000 to 400,000 people.

In the 1990s, lingering tensions between Sudan's Arab and black African populations, created by land and water rights disputes, led to a series of armed clashes. The outbreak of violence between these two groups intensified mostly in the Darfur region. Amid this chaos, black Africans in Darfur faced discrimination when seeking redress by the courts. In contrast, the Arab population was treated far more favorably by government institutions, contributing to the growing resentment of the black African population. This resentment led to the establishment of the Sudan Liberation Army (SLA) in 2003, a rebel militia that attacked government and military installations in Darfur. In response, Bashir contracted mercenaries, mostly Arab nomads, to assist GOS forces in fighting the rebel SLA. These militias, known as Janjaweed, launched a series of scorched-earth attacks against the black African population in Darfur.

Both government forces and Janjaweed militias groups were responsible for the murder of men, women, and children during their campaigns in Darfur. Moreover, they also raped young girls and women, as they destroyed and pillaged black African villages. In the midst of the destruction, hundreds of thousands of black Africans fled their homelands, seeking refuge from the path of GOS and Janjaweed forces. In late 2004, an estimated 2 million refugees were living in internally displaced persons (IDP) camps within Sudan. Another 200,000 refugees relocated to camps in neighboring Chad.

The main victims of the Darfur genocide were three non-Arab tribal groups: the Fur, the Zaghawa, and the Masaliet. Once these groups were displaced, having fled after scores of their populations were murdered, Arab settlers moved into the region. Much of the resentment against these groups was driven by racist animus and the concept of Arabism, which held Arab culture as superior to that of other people, particularly black Africans. In this manner, the institutional discrimination by the Sudanese government prior to the genocide had escalated to mass murder after the violent resistance to the government by rebel forces had provided an excuse.

As the conflict unfolded, the international community observed, seeking a way to end the violence through diplomatic or military action. The U.S. State Department initiative, the Darfur Atrocities Documentation Project, conducted a series of interviews from July to August 2004 to understand the nature of the violence committed against the black African population of Darfur. The U.S.-sanctioned Atrocities Documentation Team (ADT) collected these interviews from refugees within Sudan and in Chad. In addition to the violence they witnessed, the ADT found that many of these individuals were now under threat of hunger and disease amid the poor conditions of life in IDP camps. These findings led U.S. secretary of state Colin Powell, on September 4, 2004, to refer to the events in Sudan as genocide.

The United States referred the matter to the United Nations (UN) in order to orchestrate an international solution to end the slaughter. While the UN Security Council had voted on resolutions proposing sanctions against the GOS in an effort to quell the violence, specific members of the council hindered any real solutions. In particular, Russia, with oil interests and arms deals with the GOS, was reluctant to vote for sanctions. China, who had sizable oil interests in Sudan as well, also refused to vote for sanctions. While the United States tentatively supported sanctions against Sudan, it was also hesitant to do so, given that Sudan was an ally on the international war on terror. Thus, the international community, led by the United Nations, which was tied up by the economic and diplomatic national interests of the Security Council, failed to act. As a result, the violence continued in Darfur.

Despite the lack of international initiative to intervene, the United Nations conducted its own investigation of events in Darfur. From December 2004 to January 2005, the UN Commission of Inquiry (COI) went to IDP camps in Darfur and Chad. In contrast to the U.S. position on the events as genocide, the UN report argued that while crimes against humanity had been committed by Bashir's GOS forces and Janjaweed militias, this set of events did not constitute genocide. However, it did maintain that further analysis of events was necessary to conclude if genocide was committed, leaving the door open for further investigations. As a result of the COI's findings, the UN Security Council placed several key individuals from GOS under sanctions, including Bashir. The matter was then referred to the International Criminal Court (ICC), which began a series of investigations into actions committed by GOS forces and Janjaweed militias. They also collected information from IDP camps in Sudan and Chad as the prior U.S. and UN investigations had. Despite the condemnations over the years against the Bashir regime, the United Nations was only able to place an African Union (AU) force in Darfur for peacekeeping purposes.

In May 2006, the Darfur Peace Agreement was agreed upon between the Sudan People's Liberation Army (SPLA) and the Sudanese government. This arrangement lasted until December 2010, when the SPLA withdrew from it. In 2010, Bashir was reelected as president of Sudan and has remained a popular figure in the northern region of the country, despite the events of the last decade. Sudanese government troops

and Janjaweed militias have remained in the region and have continued to engage in violence. While the UN-led AU force has remained in place in Darfur, clashes have continued into the present.

Abraham O. Mendoza

Essay I: Omar al-Bashir, Arabism, and the International Community

The thickest thread woven into the narrative of the Darfur genocide is the determination of the regime of President Omar Hassan Ahmed al-Bashir to concentrate the political power, economic wealth, and cultural institutions of the country in the hands of the Arab ruling elite in the riverine valley of the Nile where the capital, Khartoum, is located. Accompanying this extreme centralization of resources and control was the marginalization of the periphery of the country whose residents became the oppressed colonial populations of a predatory internal empire.

An Islamist political agenda became the ideological underpinning of the National Islamic Front (NIF) regime that seized power in 1989. But the Islamist theme encountered difficulties as a rallying cry in Darfur because, like the NIF, the population was almost entirely Muslim. A more effective mobilizing option was the ideology of Arab supremacy, promoted by the semi-secret Arab Gathering. Arab racism provided the controlling elite in Khartoum with its targeted group, an essential element in distinguishing genocide from mass murder: the non-Arab Africans.

The Khartoum regime's use of an Arab supremacist ideology, however, should not be allowed to obscure the fact that ethnic identities in Darfur were considerably more fluid than in other regions. It is incorrect to view the Darfur genocide as a war of all Arabs against all non-Arabs. Nevertheless, in recruiting the groups who constituted the

Janjaweed militias, the ideology of Arab supremacy combined well with cash payments, remission of jail sentences, and promises of land and booty.

In 2003, faced with an armed insurgency, the Government of Sudan (GOS) launched a scorched-earth campaign against the non-Arab population in which the violence reached a scope and intensity far beyond that of previous encounters. In the most common pattern, bombs dropped by Government planes would set houses on fire. Militias trained and supplied with weapons by Khartoum would then attack the village, killing either its males or as many of its population as a whole who remained, raping many of its female population, looting, and rustling most of its livestock, the repository of much of a rural village's wealth. By the end of 2005, more than 2000 villages had been destroyed; at the end of 2009, the total was 3,300. Estimates of the number who have died as a result of the attacks range between 200,000 and 500,000; estimates for the number expelled to become displaced persons inside or outside Darfur range between 1.7 million and 2.5 million.

The report of a commission of inquiry contracted by the U.S. State Department in the summer of 2004 formed the basis of the conclusion of the George W. Bush administration that genocide was being committed in Darfur. The responses of international actors to the atrocities in Darfur, however, have proved to be hesitant, slow, uncertain, confused, and ineffective. Part of the explanation for the international failure lies with the varying ways international actors defined the mass atrocity. The United Nations' (UN) own investigating commission reported in early 2005 that since it did not find evidence of intent as described in international law, it was constrained to limit its findings to crimes against humanity. President Bashir's

attendance at a May 2004 Janjaweed victory parade in Nyala convinced most observers, however, that he was aware of, could have stopped, but instead approved of the ongoing genocidal destruction.

Despite its initial finding that genocide was occurring, the U.S. government took no action that had a serious chance of stopping the genocide. Some of the considerations that guided policy were:

- A harsher line toward the GOS might prompt it to pull back from the Naivasha, Kenya, peace treaty negotiations with the Sudan People's Liberation Army (SPLA) that were thought to be in their final stages. After South Sudan became independent, the same argument was employed to avoid putting teeth in any GOS policy for fear this might rekindle the war with the South.
- Since 2001, the Sudanese government had been providing the U.S. Central Intelligence Agency with intelligence concerning terrorist activities.
- As the wisdom of the American unilateralist policy that drove the invasion of Iraq in spite of UN Security Council opposition became increasingly under challenge, the possibility of anymore U.S. actions lacking Security Council approval became increasingly remote.

Faced with accusations of genocide and crimes against humanity, Bashir's regime responded with flexibility, skill, and brutality. Favored by the remote location of Darfur and the primitive state of its transportation network, the GOS did everything it could to block access to the region by investigators and journalists. The bureaucratic techniques that had already served as critically important methods for controlling its internal colonies were ramped up into a deadly arsenal of permits, fees, blocking regulations, arrests, harassments, and delays. The GOS combined its policies of "divide and conquer" with a solid knowledge of how to sign and make best use of proposals that it knew would never be accepted by all its adversaries, contracts that it never intended to enforce, and agreements that it never intended to keep.

The United Nations encountered great difficulty in stopping the genocide in Darfur or even in bringing a significant measure of justice, peace, or stabilization to the region. Russia, who found in the GOS a customer for its military aircraft and its other weapons in Sudan, and China, who became a major importer of Sudan's oil, both opposed measures such as economic sanctions or mandates that empowered intervening troops to use force to protect civilians.

In the fall of 2004, the observers and their African Union (AU) military escort known as AMIS began their work in Darfur, encountering a level of obstruction and deception from the GOS that would only increase as observation missions were replaced by peacekeeping missions. AMIS was replaced in 2007 by a hybrid force called UN-AU Hybrid Operation in Darfur (UNAMID). It was authorized to reach a level of some 23,000 troops, police, and civilian personnel. In 2009, Mandate Darfur, an important initiative that would have brought together 300 representatives from the different regions of the civil society, was blocked by the GOS, who refused safe passage to the Darfurian delegates. A second attempt at an overall peace agreement for Darfur, held in Doha, Qatar, between 2010 and 2013, also failed to bring any kind of agreement between the opposition groups and the GOS, who refused to concede points concerning major issues affecting their monopoly of power at the center.

Darfur thus remains the twenty-first century's best example of a successfully executed genocide. The GOS has constructed a political atmosphere of near-total impunity, enabling it to calibrate with some care its bombing, attacking, starving, and harassing attacks on people in refugee camps and in villages in regions considered to be possible strongholds of the resistance. The indictment of President Bashir for genocide actually gained him support from some African Union members and from influential Arab League countries. UNAMID reports upticks in violence at times, but "Forgotten Darfur" remains a low priority for international actors who could influence the situation and, especially, provide opportunities for victims to restore their capability to seek justice. Hope for change rests pretty much entirely with the beginnings of a unification of opposition groups behind a plan for a transition to democracy and redress of human rights abuses.

John Hubbel Weiss

Essay 2: Role of Government of Sudan

In light of the allegations of the International Criminal Court (ICC) and the findings of the African Commission on Human and Peoples' Rights (ACHPR), it seems clear that the Sudanese government is primarily responsible for the Darfur genocide. Other explanations do not tell us why the genocide occurred in Darfur as opposed to in other parts of the world.

According to the Pre-Trial Chamber I of the ICC, there were reasonable grounds to believe in 2009 that the government of Sudan mobilized the Janjaweed militia in response to rebel activity in Darfur, and that thousands of civilians belonging to Darfur's Far, Massalit, and Zaghawa groups were exterminated by the Janjaweed and government forces. The Office of the Prosecutor at the

ICC theorized that one aspect of the Darfur Genocide was the decision by the government to destroy the very means of survival of African tribes. These actions included stealing or destroying food, poisoning wells and breaking pumping machines, burning crops and homes, and killing livestock. This decision was probably the main cause of the genocide in the Darfur region of Sudan. However, there may be other causes, such as climate change's contribution to conflicts over land and water resources in an environment of worsening scarcity, the international arms trade including massive flows of weaponry into Sudan, and the policy of the United Nations (UN) to adopt a double standard on Sudan versus Bosnia, Rwanda, or Libya.

Moreover, the prosecutor wrote that the government planned discriminatory violence including murder and rape against "other, smaller ethnic groups, such as the Tunjur, Erenga, Birgid, Misseriya Jebel, Meidob, Dajo and Birgo." Similarly, the African Union (AU) concluded that the "Janjawid was commonly identified as the Arab militia which has been fighting on the side of government against the rebels, and is associated with massive human rights violation[s]," including "the looting of property and cattle, burning of villages, rape, abduction of women, and wanton killing of defenseless civilian population in the Darfur region." National and international humanitarian aid agencies' workers told the AU mission that "men who are commonly identified as [Janjaweed] militia can be seen roaming streets of the three Darfur states, with impunity, wearing military uniforms, with guns on their backs riding donkeys, horses or camels, suggesting that they were known, and tolerated by the government."

Similarly, the ICC prosecutor said that President Bashir's genocidal plan for Darfur featured impunity for the Janjaweed and other progovernment militia (and their incorporation into state security structures). The policy of impunity for Janjaweed crimes included: the termination of government employees who were opposed to crimes against non-Arabs, the failure to hand over Minister of State for the Interior Ahmed Harun after an ICC warrant for genocide had been issued against him, a propaganda campaign to conceal the crimes in Darfur, and purposeful interference with humanitarian aid efforts. The blockade of international humanitarian aid exacerbated the plight of more than 2.4 million displaced persons, many of whom lacked access to sufficient food and medicine to survive. The ICC prosecutor quoted Harun, speaking in reference to powers delegated to him by President Bashir, stating that, "for the sake of Darfur, they were ready to kill three quarters of the people in Darfur, so that one quarter could live."

Both the ICC prosecutor and the African Union believed that a political conflict existed in Sudan between tribes aligned with the government and known as Arab tribes, and economically and socially marginalized tribes known as black (Nuba or Zurga). According to Sudan expert Robert O. Collins, President Bashir's government made an "Arab supremacist" the governor of North Darfur State in 2000, a governor who disarmed non-Arabs and armed the Janjaweed forces.

The UN secretary-general, Kofi Annan, and the ACPHR have suggested that a cause of the Darfur conflict may have been the scarcity of water resources in western Sudan, exacerbated by climate change. But as Al Gore pointed out in his "Inconvenient Truth" lectures, climate change has caused desertification and the drying up of freshwater lakes and rivers around the world, including in the United States, the Russian Federation and other countries in Asia, and various countries in Latin America and Africa. Based on average temperature increases from 1950 through 2008, which are used to project warming through 2050, many countries experienced temperature rises worse than those in Sudan's region, including Brazil, China, Colombia, India, Indonesia, and Venezuela. In high-income countries, climate change is not even linked with a breakout of civil war, let alone genocide, due in part to rich countries' relative independence of climactic conditions.

Another cause of the genocide was the rebellion of the Sudan Liberation Movement/Army and the Justice and Equality Movement. Had the tribes of Darfur remained peaceful, they would still have experienced structural violence bringing about tens or hundreds of thousands of excess deaths from hunger and disease, but they may have been spared the massacres, destruction of villages, and mass rapes that occurred from 2004 through 2006 and beyond. The ICC prosecutor alleged that the intent to destroy the Fur, Massalit, and Zaghawa groups arose after some members of these groups rose in rebellion against the government in 2003, and that President Bashir's "orders giving 'carte blanche' to his subordinates to quell the rebellion and take no prisoners triggered a series of brutal attacks against the Fur, Massalit and Zaghawa groups" (International Criminal Court 2008). Without these orders, the rebellion would not have caused a genocide, although it would have caused a civil war, and no doubt a number of war crimes, as we have seen in other countries.

The international arms trade and the policy of the United Nations on Sudan represent other causes that were not sufficient to bring about a genocide, but may have contributed to causing its scale to be larger than it would have been had the government of Sudan

been cut off from arms, or had the Darfur region been declared eligible for a United Nations safe area or a large peacekeeping force. The ACHPR identified a flood of arms into the Darfur region from other conflict zones in the region as a factor in causing the conflict, but not the genocide. As the U.S. Government Accountability Office concluded (in a report endorsed by the State Department and prepared by studying reports from the United Nations, African Union, U.S. military observers, and nongovernmental organizations), the money and troops given to the UN and AU peacekeepers in Darfur were insufficient to protect the population from its widespread destruction. Had the peacekeepers been backed by air power or Western armies, as in Bosnia, Rwanda, and Libya, the Sudanese government could have been removed from the Darfur region.

Hannibal Travis

Bibliography

Collins, Robert O. 2008. *A Short History of Modern Sudan.* Cambridge: Cambridge University Press.

Hsiang, Solomon, Marshall Burke, and Edward Miguel. 2013. "Quantifying the Influence of Climate on Human Conflict," *Science* 5, no. 5, 17. Available at http://sciencemag.org/content/early/recent.

International Criminal Court. 2008. "Situation in Darfur, The Sudan: Prosecutor's Application for Warrant of Arrest Under Article 58 Against Omar Hassan Ahmad Al Bashir." July 14. https://www.icc-cpi.int/NR/rdonlyres/64FA6B33-05C3-4E9C-A672-3FA2B58CB2C9/277758/ICCOTPSummary20081704ENG.pdf.

U.S. Government Accountability Office. 2006. *Darfur Crisis: Progress in Aid and Peace Monitoring Threatened by Ongoing Violence and Operational Challenges,* Report No. GAO-07-9. November 9.

Is the Conflict in Darfur an Example of a Just Case for Intervention?

On February 26, 2003, rebels demanding greater regional autonomy and economic opportunity captured Gulu, a town in the heart of Sudan's western region of Darfur. This revolt, a seemingly minor event in a nation then mired in a decades-long civil war, set in motion a crackdown that rapidly created a catastrophic humanitarian crisis. More than sixteen years since the conflict first erupted, more than 2 million people remain displaced in Darfur and violence continues, though on a lesser scale than during the conflict's peak from 2003 to 2006, and despite a tenuous peace accord signed in May 2011. In July 2010, the International Criminal Court (ICC) in The Hague issued a second arrest warrant for Sudanese president Omar Hassan Ahmed al-Bashir on three counts of genocide, for actions intended to "bring about the physical destruction" of the Fur, Masaliet, and Zaghawa peoples. Previously, the ICC had charged Bashir and other Sudanese officials with war crimes and crimes against humanity related to actions in Darfur.

The situation in Darfur, Sudan, is an ongoing concern for the international community. A year after the conflict began, the United States labeled the situation genocide, but stopped short of committing to military action to intervene. When the United Nations (UN) Security Council decided to send a force of 26,000 troops to end the violence in 2007, the Sudanese government agreed to cooperate with the peacekeeping mission, but has required the United Nations–African Union Mission in Darfur (UNAMID) to seek approval to deploy non-African troops and to inform the government of troop movements. Many human rights groups have questioned the effectiveness of UNAMID and its ability to protect civilians under a weakened mandate. Despite the unquestionable gravity of the situation in Darfur, the issue of international intervention in Sudan became entangled with recent memories of colonial oppression, and arrest warrants against Bashir and other Sudanese government officials sparked worldwide debate over just how far the arm of international law should be permitted to reach.

Our first Perspective Essay author, Dr. Robert O. Collins, makes the argument that regardless of whether the situation in Darfur is called genocide, foreign intervention is strongly called for. The difference between the crisis in Darfur and other recognized genocides, he observes, is the lack of proof regarding organization and planning by the ruling government. Dr. Paulos Milkias argues further, questioning how effective intervention to date has been. Citing the example of the ICC declaring war crimes suspects in Darfur and the ineffectiveness of this action, Dr. Milkias points out that in Sudan, the criminal chain of command may stretch up to the president himself. Finally, in the third perspective, Jennifer Christian argues that despite having enough legal justifications for intervention—specifically the 1948 United Nations Convention on the Prevention and Punishment of the Crime of Genocide and the responsibility to protect doctrine (R2P)—the international community refused to involve itself, thus allowing the slaughter of thousands.

Background Essay

The Rome Statute is a multilateral treaty that came into force on July 1, 2002, and in so doing established the International Criminal Court (ICC) to try crimes of genocide, crimes against humanity, war crimes, crimes of aggression, and offences against the administration of justice. The investigation into war crimes committed in Darfur, Sudan, began in 2005 when the United Nations (UN) Security Council voted to refer the situation in Darfur to the ICC. In February 2007, the ICC issued arrest warrants for two suspects: Sudanese minister of humanitarian affairs Ahmad Harun and Janjaweed militia leader Ali Kushayb. ICC chief prosecutor Luis Moreno-Ocampo had compiled overwhelming evidence pointing to the two men's involvement in fifty-one counts of war crimes and crimes against humanity, including charges of murder, rape, pillage, torture, destruction of property, and forced transfer of people. In 2009, the ICC took further action by issuing an arrest warrant for Sudanese president Omar Hassan Ahmed al-Bashir on charges of war crimes and crimes against humanity. In response, Bashir rejected the authority of the ICC and in retaliation ordered many humanitarian groups to cease work or leave the country.

The seeming futility and failure of the court to enforce the arrest warrant, combined with Bashir's devastating response, has inspired some to question the international community and the ICC's decision to pursue trials in the first place. Sudan—like China and the United States—has not become party to the Rome Statute of the ICC and thus is not obligated to comply with it.

China and the United States both abstained from voting on the Security Council resolution referring the situation in Darfur to the court. Under President George W. Bush (2001–2009), the United States was among the institution's fiercest opponents, arguing that the ICC's authority could be abused to initiate prosecution against U.S. citizens for political reasons. China's Foreign Ministry, meanwhile, has taken issue with the very premise of the court on the grounds that respect for the independence of nations,

including their judicial systems, should be "the basic principle of foreign policy." Still, both countries chose to abstain rather than to veto the case's referral to the ICC, signaling that whatever objections they may harbor about an international court empowered to charge suspects against the will of their governments, they also acknowledge the failure of the Sudanese justice system and the need for some form of intervention.

Not surprisingly, Sudan's government has responded to the released warrants by refusing to extradite the suspects to face trial. (In addition to Bashir, Harun, and Kushayb, nine more high-ranking Sudanese government officials are known to be among the fifty-one individuals that may ultimately be charged by the ICC, though their names have been kept confidential.) This government resistance shows that whether or not the ICC will ultimately be the body to hold these suspects accountable, the power of international law is limited so long as those responsible for the war crimes remain in the highest echelons of Sudanese politics. This dilemma has left many in the international community scrambling to find alternative means of pressure.

In the United States, most of these strategies involve indirect pressure exerted against Sudan via China, its top export market and foreign investor. Oil exports, mostly to China, brought the Sudanese government $5.25 billion in 2006, accounting for 70 percent of export earnings and constituting the primary source of funding for the ongoing atrocities in Darfur. Those funds have often found their way back to China in the form of Sudanese purchases of Chinese-made military aircraft, tanks, and weaponry.

Strongly criticized by some while cautiously commended by others, China's policy in Sudan, which supplies China with

7 percent of its oil imports, is clearly at the center of the conflict. One think tank, the International Crisis Group, has gone so far as to accuse the Chinese of desiring a continued low-level conflict in Sudan to discourage less risk-taking foreign investors from competing. In contrast, however, the U.S. special envoy to Darfur under Bush, Andrew Natsios, has pointed to Chinese diplomacy as the "critical factor" in some of the small steps toward resolution that have been made. He notes the value of the leverage that China's unique relationship with Sudan provides. "I think they may be the crucial actors," Natsios told a U.S. Senate hearing in April 2007. "I think there has been a lot of China bashing in the West, and I'm not sure, to be very frank with you, right now it's very helpful."

Still, for those U.S. citizens who are not diplomats or international prosecutors, actions discouraging China's financial complicity in the conflict may be among the most effective courses to take. One such tactic involved using the 2008 Beijing Summer Olympics as an opportunity to force China to take a harder stance against Sudan, thus avoiding negative publicity during the event. Not since the coordinated popular demonstrations against South Africa's apartheid system in the 1980s has the current of activism in the United States been so strong.

As with the antiapartheid movement, one of the most effective tools being used by people to bring about change in Darfur is divestment, the organized sell-off of stocks in companies that support a morally objectionable political regime with their business. Such a program of action is documented in the documentary, *Darfur Now*, which profiles University of California, Los Angeles, student Adam Sterling in his successful quest to get a bill passed that orders the state

of California to divest its interests in companies that do business with Sudan.

Such efforts as the Divest for Darfur campaign spearheaded by Save Darfur, a coalition of more than 180 organizations, target Chinese petroleum giants Petrochina and Sinopec. These firms are generally given the dubious distinction of being the major corporate facilitators of the Darfur conflict. The primary goal of such campaigns in the U.S. is to force divestment from these companies by the mutual fund groups that are the major U.S. shareholders (namely, Capital Group, Fidelity, Franklin Templeton, JP Morgan Chase, and Vanguard). By 2009, more than twenty-five states, as well as sixty-one colleges and universities—from the University of Southern California in the west to Maine's Colby College in the east—had responded to citizen and student activism and pursued targeted divestment from such companies.

David Paige

Essay I: Moral and Legal Obligations May Be Contradictory

By February 2004, the ethnic devastation caused by Janjaweed raids had become so widespread and methodical that humanitarian agencies began to declare genocide in Darfur. Much of the dialogue about genocide soon became focused on the sterile and legal definitions as to what actually constitutes "genocide." The 1948 United Nations (UN) Convention on the Prevention and Punishment of the Crimes of Genocide is clear that there is a moral obligation by its signatories to intervene if the Security Council determines that genocide is taking place.

By summer 2004, the issue of genocide had to be addressed, and after the visit of then-U.S. secretary of state Colin Powell to Darfur at the end of June, an Atrocities Documentation Team (ADT) from the U.S.

Department of State was, rather belatedly, organized. In late July and early August, the ADT conducted more than a thousand interviews with Sudanese refugees who had crossed the border into Chad. Despite the rising demands from humanitarian agencies for the U.S. government to declare genocide, particularly after the U.S. Congress passed a unanimous resolution in July confirming the carnage in Darfur as "genocide," officials in the George W. Bush administration, the United Nations, the European Union, and the African Union (AU) were more restrained.

After their visit to the internally displaced persons (IDPs) camps in Darfur at the end of June 2004, Powell and UN secretary-general Kofi Annan had different opinions about the situation in Darfur. Having assessed the work of the ADT, which worked closely with the American Bar Association and the International Coalition for Justice, and the massive reports from the field by a wide variety of agencies, Powell concluded in testimony before the Senate Foreign Affairs Committee on September 9, 2004, that "genocide has been committed in Darfur and that the government of Sudan and the Janjaweed bear responsibility—and genocide may still be occurring." The personal representative of Kofi Annan in Sudan, Jan Egeland, used the more sanitary term "ethnic cleansing," which soon became fashionable among diplomats and the media. The reaction of the Sudanese government was complete denial. Unlike crimes against humanity, genocide, and war crimes—all of which are legally defined crimes according to the Rome Statute—ethnic cleansing has not been recognized as an independent crime under international law. In July, the heads of the African Union concluded there was no genocide in Darfur. Not

surprisingly, the Arab League and the influential Organization of the Islamic Conference, both of which supported the government of the Sudan, reached the same conclusion.

Powell was very careful in his declaration, however, to invoke Article VIII of the Genocide Convention, which enables its signatories to refer the matter to the United Nations to take whatever action it considers appropriate "to prevent genocide." Having done that, the relevant signatories, and in this instance the United States, would have fulfilled their obligations "to prevent genocide" without having to intervene militarily. A new U.S. resolution was consequently sent to the Security Council, but "in fact, no new action [by the United States] is dictated by this determination [of genocide]." This was the first time in history that a single state had declared that a conflict in progress was called "genocide," which both President Bush and Secretary of State Condoleezza Rice publicly reaffirmed in their comments concerning the affairs in Darfur.

Was the crisis in Darfur, in fact, genocide? Shortly after Powell's statement before the U.S. Senate in 2004, the European Parliament passed a resolution by a vote of 566–6 that "realities in Darfur were tantamount to genocide," which relieved the European Union, like the United States, from taking any action for "realities" that were almost, but not quite, genocide. An array of European politicians followed with similar rhetoric that Darfur was "the site of genocide" but not genocide. These legalistic sophistries plunged the European Union into months of acrimonious debate over the definition of genocide, during which the spiral of violence continued unabated in Darfur.

There were, however, other realities in Sudan and on the ground in Darfur that blurred the definition of genocide. The two most famous acts of genocide in world history, the Nazi Holocaust against European Jews during World War II (1939–1945) and the slaughter of the Tutsi by the Hutu of Rwanda (April–May 1994), were methodically planned by the ruling government to exterminate a single ethnic group. This does not appear to be the case in Sudan. The government of Sudan had never established its control, governance, or administration in Darfur, unlike the Nazi regime in Europe or Hutus in Rwanda. Moreover, the ruling Arab clique in Khartoum has never been sufficiently disciplined to devise a policy to methodically exterminate the non-Arab peoples of Darfur.

The government's policy to impose the Arabic language, Arab culture, and fundamental Islam and to drive the non-Arab Africans off the land to make way for Arabs was certainly ethnic cleansing but not extermination—that would have required the slaughter of the displaced seeking sanctuary in the massive IDP camps. With the government having seized the land after compelling the non-Arabs to flee, the violence in Darfur soon shifted to fighting among rival Arab tribes to consolidate their control over vacant African lands, a conflict which can hardly be described as genocide.

In February 2010, the Appeals Chamber of the International Criminal Court (ICC) in The Hague, Netherlands, reversed an earlier ICC decision not to include charges of genocide in a 2009 arrest warrant for Sudan's president Omar Hassan Ahmed al-Bashir. In July, the ICC issued a second arrest warrant stating there were reasonable grounds to accuse Bashir of directing Sudanese forces to attempt genocide against three tribal groups in Darfur, the Fur, Masaliet, and Zaghawa. To date, none of those accused by the ICC have been tried in court, and the tribunal does not try defendants in absentia.

Robert O. Collins

Essay 2: People's Welfare Outweighs States' Sovereignty

Darfur is not the only case of international intervention in an African human rights dilemma. During the last three decades, Africa had several crises that needed international attention. The conflicts in Somalia, Uganda, Ethiopia, Eritrea, Côte d'Ivoire, Sierra Leone, and Liberia devastated entire communities. Of particular concern to the international community was the widening conflict in the Democratic Republic of Congo, which spilled over into the neighboring countries of the Central African Republic, the Republic of Congo, Rwanda, Burundi, Uganda, Tanzania, and Zambia—several of which were already experiencing humanitarian emergencies of their own. Even after a shaky peace accord was signed between the Democratic Republic of Congo and Rwanda (2002), humanitarian conditions did not improve significantly, and the International Criminal Court (ICC) had to deal with known human rights abusers.

While humanitarian emergencies continue to proliferate in Africa, a question with far-reaching implications arises: what is to be done regarding Darfur? Are there justifications for the Sudanese government's position that international organization cannot interfere in its internal affairs? And if intercession is contemplated, what constitutes a sufficiently just cause to warrant intervention? All these depend on several factors: the intentions of the interveners, whether interventions are a last resort, who and what might be a legitimate target of intervention, reasonable prospects for success, and proper authorization.

The issue of just cause requires that severe suffering warranting help has arisen. These include such threats to vital interests as indiscriminate killings, torture, rape, and displacement of people. These would count as significant threats to human dignity and normal life. When such activities are widespread, and the state either perpetrates the injustices or does nothing appropriate to end the suffering of people, it would be reasonable to suggest that the just cause threshold has been reached. These were undoubtedly present in the ICC's Darfur case.

Sudan has vehemently opposed what it considers intervention in its domestic affairs by the ICC. The Sudanese government has rejected the ICC's request that war crimes suspects Ahmad Harun and Ali Kushayb be arrested and handed over to them. They consider the action an intrusion into their national affairs. But they could not stop the International Criminal Police Organization (INTERPOL) from publishing a notice for the arrest of Harun. Sudan's justice minister, Ali al-Mardi, said that any attempts to arrest Harun and Kushayb through INTERPOL would be treated as tantamount to kidnapping.

This opposition to the ICC's adjudication represents both practical and fundamental hurdles. On one level, there is no possibility for an international tribunal to operate without a state's cooperation in turning over defendants and evidence and permitting investigation within its own territorial boundary. If the government of President Omar Hassan Ahmed al-Bashir shields its citizens from the ICC, the court would be hard pressed to carry out its prosecution.

On another level, criminal proceedings by international tribunals have rarely fulfilled victims' expectations of universal justice. The international criminal tribunals for Rwanda and Yugoslavia were both severely criticized as being too remote, too sluggish, and biased in their choice of defendants. The prosecutions were accused of sparing the most senior defendants from the local courts where they might be tried in accordance with local standards and within view of the local population that had witnessed the atrocities, and where, just like their subordinates, they could face the death penalty if convicted. This of course could not be expected in Sudan, where the chain of command in the crime may stretch up to President Bashir himself.

The International Commission on Intervention and State Sovereignty, after a thorough study of international law and conventions, determined that it may be appropriate for supranational bodies to intervene in what are normally considered the domestic affairs of a state for the purpose of protecting people who are at risk. The commission's report pinpointed principles on which its prominent jurists reached consensus and which it believes to be "politically achievable in the world as we know it today." The cardinal principles the commission considered legitimate were stated in the following words:

> State sovereignty implies responsibility, and the primary responsibility for the protection of its people lies with the state itself. . . . However, where a population is suffering serious harm, as a result of internal war, insurgency, repression, or state failure, and the state in question is unwilling or unable to halt or avert it, the principle of nonintervention yields to the international responsibility to protect.

The report does not deny that sovereignty is important, but it calls attention to what sovereignty entails. For the jurists, sovereignty is not best conceived of in terms of control but rather in terms of responsibility. Government officials are responsible for assuring the safety of citizens and for advancing their welfare. The commission did not find genuine support for a view that sovereignty necessitates unlimited state power over its own citizens, but instead acknowledged that "sovereignty implies a dual responsibility: externally—to respect the sovereignty of other states—and internally—to respect the dignity and basic rights of all the people within the state." The report noted in its conclusion that "sovereignty as responsibility has become the minimum content of good international citizenship."

The general responsibility to safeguard peoples' welfare requires the implementation of three specific tasks. In the first instance, it entails a responsibility to prevent or to contend with the root causes of conflict that puts people at risk of requiring humanitarian intervention. Contending with the root causes can mean putting to an end political repression. In the second instance, it entails a responsibility to respond aptly when there is a pressing human need. A fitting response may call for sanctions, international prosecutions, or military interventions. And last but not least, the responsibility to protect people in distress demands a responsibility to rebuild by providing the right kind of help with recovering, reconstructing, and setting in motion a process of national reconciliation.

Regarding the issue of proper type of authorization for interventions, there is no better or more appropriate body than the United Nations Security Council that charged the ICC to take up the Darfur crisis. By its very design, the Security Council bears a primary obligation to deal with all requests for emergency authorizations and it has to do that within an appropriate time period, particularly when they entail urgent, large-scale crises like Darfur. There is clear tension between the goals of nations shielding themselves from outside interference and international goals of responding to victims who suffer in humanitarian crises; but when it comes to respecting sovereignty and respecting the welfare of individuals who are in distress, the matter should definitely be resolved in favor of protecting the vulnerable individuals who suffer in humanitarian crises.

Paulos Milkias

Essay 3: Does the Conflict in Darfur Provide a Just Reason for International Intervention?

In late February 2003, conflict erupted in Sudan's western region of Darfur when two Darfurian rebel groups attacked government military installations. In response, Sudan's armed forces and government-backed Arab militias, the Janjaweed, launched a brutal campaign targeting non-Arab Darfuri tribes suspected of supporting the rebels. During the ensuing years, the Sudanese government and Arab militias committed gross human rights violations and crimes against humanity in Darfur.

Some, including the U.S. government, asserted that the Sudanese government committed genocide. While the international community made efforts to pressure the Sudanese government to cease its attacks against non-Arab Darfurians, no state or international organization undertook an international intervention to protect civilian populations in Darfur. This raises the question of whether the conflict in Darfur provided a just reason for international intervention. A review of applicable international conventions and legal principles reveals that, during the height of the conflict in Darfur, from 2003 to 2006, the crimes that the Sudanese government and its forces committed against civilians did provide a just reason for an international intervention. Specifically, under the 1948 United Nations Convention on the Prevention and Punishment of the Crime of Genocide and the responsibility to protect doctrine (R2P), the conflict in Darfur provided a just reason for an international intervention to protect civilians in the region. Today, while conflict continues in Darfur, the level of violence does not warrant an international intervention.

Over a year into the Darfur conflict, on September 9, 2004, then-U.S. Secretary of State Colin Powell declared that the Sudanese government had committed genocide in Darfur, and that genocide may be ongoing in the region. In doing so, Powell became the first member of the U.S. government to ever use the term "genocide" to describe an ongoing conflict. The prior reluctance of the United States to deem ongoing conflicts "genocides" was, in part, motivated by the U.S.'s obligation to prevent genocide under the UN Genocide Convention, to which it is a party. In total, 142 states are party to the UN Genocide Convention, including Sudan.

The International Court of Justice (ICJ) has recognized that the prohibition against the commission of genocide contained in the UN Genocide Convention is a peremptory norm under international law. A peremptory norm under international law is a rule that no state may violate. Moreover, all states have an obligation to bring to an end another state's violation of a peremptory norm.

In the case of Darfur, this means that the government of Sudan was under an obligation to not commit genocide. As well, all other states in the world had an obligation to stop the government of Sudan's commission of genocide. Therefore, if the Sudanese government indeed committed genocide in Darfur, the conflict in the region would have provided a just reason for an international intervention to prevent the Sudanese government's ongoing commission of genocide. Notably, the U.S. government was one of the few international actors to characterize the Sudanese government's actions as genocide. Another, the International Criminal Court (ICC), issued an arrest warrant for Sudanese president Omar Hassan Ahmed al-Bashir for the crime of genocide in 2010. The ICC has not yet been able to arrest President Bashir and bring him to trial, which means that no international court ruling exists today confirming or denying whether the Sudanese government committed genocide in Darfur. Since genocide in Darfur is not ongoing today, the conflict in the region does not currently provide a just reason for an international intervention under the UN Genocide Convention.

Even if it is determined that the Sudanese government did not commit genocide in Darfur, the conflict, nonetheless, provided a just reason for an international intervention under R2P. A 2009 report from UN secretary-general Ban Ki-moon outlined the following "three pillars" of R2P:

(1) A state holds the primarily responsibility to protect individuals within its territory from genocide, war crimes, and crimes against humanity;

(2) The international community must assist states in realizing this responsibility; and

(3) The international community has the responsibility to employ appropriate diplomatic, humanitarian, and other means to protect populations from the crimes listed in (1). Should a state fail to realize its responsibility to protect, the international community has an obligation to take collective action, in accordance with the UN Charter, to protect the affected populations.

In the case of Darfur, not only did the government of Sudan fail to protect civilians within its territory from genocide, war crimes, and crimes against humanity, the government was actively committing some or all of these crimes against its own people. Under R2P, the obligation to protect civilians in Sudan from these crimes then shifted to the international community.

When the burden shifts to the international community to protect civilians within a state, there is a hierarchy of actions that the international community may take to realize its responsibility. First, the international community must explore diplomatic and peaceful means to ensure protection, such as negotiation, public advocacy and diplomacy, mediation, judicial settlement, and fact-finding missions.

Should a state, in this case Sudan, not respond to these diplomatic overtures, the international community, with a mandate from the UN Security Council, may take collective measures under Chapter VII of the UN Charter. Chapter VII provides for the imposition of sanctions against a state or individual regime members as well as the use of force to establish safe zones, impose no-fly zones, or deploy a protection or deterrence force. The international community may only undertake an international intervention under Chapter VII if:

(1) A just cause exists, meaning that large scale loss of life or ethnic cleansing is occurring or is likely to occur;
(2) The purpose of the intervention is to prevent human suffering;
(3) The intervention is the last resort, is undertaken by proportional means, and has a reasonable prospect of halting or averting human suffering; and
(4) The right authority, namely the UN Security Council, authorizes the intervention.

An examination of the international community's reaction to the Darfur conflict indicates that the international community undertook diplomatic and peaceful means in an effort to prevent further human suffering. These included negotiations, public advocacy, and diplomacy. Next, the international community enacted economic sanctions and travel restrictions against the government of Sudan and certain regime officials for their roles in the conflict. The UN Security Council referred the situation in Darfur to the ICC for investigation. The United Nations and the African Union also deployed two successive peace keeping missions to Darfur in an effort to address the conflict. None of these actions deterred the government of Sudan and its forces from continuing to perpetrate large-scale atrocities against the people of Darfur.

Under R2P, the international community was therefore permitted to initiate an international intervention designed to prevent human suffering. The situation certainly provided the requisite just cause. By 2008, the United Nations estimated that between 200,000 and 300,000 people had died in Darfur, and 2.7 million more were displaced. So long as the intervention met with the other criteria, identified previously, it would have been a lawful intervention under R2P.

Similar to the justification for intervention under the UN Genocide Convention, an international intervention justified under R2P would not be appropriate today, because the current conflict in Darfur does not create a just cause.

Notably, R2P remains controversial among some in the international community. Many international commentators assert that R2P is not yet a peremptory norm under international law. The UN Security Council most recently used the doctrine as justification for the 2011 intervention in Libya, undertaken by the North Atlantic Treaty Organization (NATO). Some have criticized NATO's intervention as an abuse of R2P designed to cause the downfall of Libyan president Muammar Gaddafi's government. Future attempts to use the doctrine as justification for a military intervention on humanitarian grounds will, no doubt, have to overcome the negative stigma that the doctrine now enjoys.

During the height of conflict in Darfur, from 2003 to 2006, the international community would have been justified in launching an intervention designed to stop the Sudanese government's attacks against civilians in the region. Two separate international legal doctrines—UN Genocide Convention, and the associated peremptory norm related to the prohibition against genocide, and R2P—provided justification for an intervention. Importantly, the UN Genocide Convention would only have applied if genocide were committed in Darfur. On the other hand, R2P applied regardless. Despite these legal justifications for an intervention, the international community did not intervene in the Darfur conflict militarily. Today, hundreds of thousands of civilians remain displaced and are at constant risk of further attacks from government and government-backed militia

forces who continue to commit human rights abuses in the region.

Jennifer Christian

Bibliography

Bedi, Shiv R. S. 2007. *The Development of Human Rights Law by the Judges of the International Court of Justice.* Portland, OR: Hart.

Beyrer, C., and H. Pizer. 2007. *Public Health and Human Rights: Evidence-Based Approaches.* Baltimore: Johns Hopkins University Press.

Burr, J. Millard, and Robert O. Collins. 2006. *Darfur: The Long Road to Disaster.* Princeton, NJ: Markus Wiener.

Daalder, I. H. 2007. *Beyond Preemption: Force and Legitimacy in a Changing World.* Washington, DC: Brookings Institution Press.

Daly, Martin. 2007. *Darfur's Sorrow: A History of Destruction and Genocide.* New York: Cambridge University Press.

Donage, Ted. 2011. "Sudan: The Crisis in Darfur and the Status of the North-South Peace Agreement," Congressional Research Service. June 15. Available at https://fas.org/sgp/crs/row/RL33574.pdf.

Flint, Julie, and Alex de Waal. 2006. *Darfur: A Short History of a Long War.* London: Zed Books.

Henham, R. J., and P. Behrens. 2007. *The Criminal Law of Genocide: International, Comparative, and Contextual Aspects.* Burlington, VT: Ashgate Publishing Company.

Human Rights Watch. 2019. "World Report." Available at https://www.hrw.org/world-report/2019.

Kindiki, Kithure. 2003. *Humanitarian Intervention and State Sovereignty in Africa: The Changing Paradigms in International Law.* Eldoret, Kenya: Moi University Press.

Kindiki, Kithure, and Institute for Security Studies (South Africa). 2007. *Intervention to Protect Civilians in Darfur: Legal*

Dilemmas and Policy Imperatives. Tshwane, South Africa: Institute for Security Studies.

Nardin, T., and M. S. Williams. 2006. *Humanitarian Intervention.* New York: New York University Press.

Prunier, Gerard. 2005. *Darfur: The Ambiguous Genocide.* Ithaca, NY: Cornell University Press.

Totten, S., and E. Markusen. 2006. *Genocide in Darfur: Investigating the Atrocities in the Sudan.* New York: Routledge.

Chronology

1603
Start of the 271-year rule of the sultanate of Darfur.

1821
The Ottoman Turkish viceroy of Egypt sends his armies to conquer the Sudanese Nile region.

1874
The sultanate of Darfur falls to the Sudanese warlord Rabih az-Zubayr.

1881–1885
A Sudanese Islamic mystic known as the *Mahdi* leads a rebellion against Ottoman-Egyptian rule of the region and defeats them. He declares Sudan an Islamic state.

1899
British and Egyptian forces defeat the Mahdist state and establish the Anglo-Egyptian Condominium (i.e., joint colonial rule) to govern Sudan.

1913–1914
Darfur is plagued by a devastating famine known as the *Julu* ("wandering").

1916
Anglo-Egyptian forces kill the last ruling sultan of the Fur, Ali Dinar, and incorporate Darfur into Sudan.

1922
Anglo-Egyptian forces incorporate Dar Masalit into Sudan.

1948
On December 11, the United Nations (UN) Convention on the Prevention and Punishment of the Crime of Genocide is enacted by the UN General Assembly.

1955
Civil war ignites in Sudan between the north and south.

1956
Sudan becomes an independent nation, free of the rule of Britain and Egypt.

1958
General Ibrahim Abboud overthrows the civilian government that had been elected earlier that year.

1964
Abboud is swept from power in a popular uprising in the so-called October Revolution. For the next two years, the Democratic Unionist Party (DUP) and Umma Party form an uneasy coalition government.

1969
In a coup, General Gaafar Muhammad an-Nimeiry becomes president of Sudan.

1971

Joseph Lagu becomes the president of the Southern Sudan Liberation Movement (SSLM).

1972

The Addis Ababa Peace Accords are signed between the government of Sudan and the Anya Nya (southern Sudan separatist army), granting the southern region of Sudan autonomy under the umbrella of the Sudanese government. A cease-fire between the north and south begins.

1978

Oil is discovered in the town of Bentiu, in southern Sudan.

1983

President Nimeiry rescinds the southern region's autonomy. He passes the September Laws, which privilege Muslims and oppress Christians, and north and south Sudan again become locked in violent civil war.

1984

The year of the so-called Great Drought sharpens the ongoing violent confrontation over resources in the Darfur region, bringing about a devastating famine that kills some 240,000 Darfurians and displaces 2.3 percent of the population.

1985

President Nimeiry is overthrown by the Sudanese army. Lieutenant General Abd al-Rahman Siwar adh Dhahab heads the transitional government and proposes that free elections be held the following year.

1989

General Omar Hassan Ahmed al-Bashir and Hassan al-Turabi overthrow the government.

Sharia punishments are reinstated, and political parties and unions are banned.

1990

Al-Turabi forms the Popular Arab Islamic Conference.

1991

The Islamic Penal Code is introduced in Sudan, which sanctions amputations, floggings, and other violent punishments for so-called infidels.

1992

The war against the southern region of Sudan is declared a jihad.

1994

The government of Sudan divides the region of Darfur into three administrative districts or states; in so doing, it diminishes the power of the Fur, the largest ethnic group in the region.

1997

Musa Hilal is arrested for killing seventeen black Africans. He is released shortly thereafter.

1998

Hilal is accused of and imprisoned for armed robbery and the killing of a police officer.

1999

The National Islamic Front is renamed the National Congress Party. The ban on political parties is lifted. Sudan starts exporting oil.

2000

President Bashir is elected to a second five-year term in what is considered a rigged election.

2001

The Justice and Equality Movement (JEM) is established by Khalil Ibrahim. U.S. senator John Danforth is appointed as special envoy for peace in Sudan. Bashir places al-Turabi under house arrest. The Darfur Liberation Front (DLF) is formed by Abdel-Wahid Mohammad Ahmad al-Nur and his associates.

2002

On January 19, a cease-fire agreement between north and south Sudan is brokered by the United States and Switzerland.

In October, the Sudanese government and the rebels of southern Sudan agree to participate in peace talks in Kenya.

2003

On February 26, the DLF and JEM attack Sudanese military forces in Gulu.

In March, the DLF announces that it is changing its name to Sudan Liberation Army (SLA).

In April, the Sudan Liberation Army (SLA), with assistance from JEM, take over the airport at el-Fasher.

The next month, Ahmad Muhammad Harun is appointed Sudan's minister of the interior.

In August, Harun gives a speech in Mukjar declaring that members of the Fur are rebels and their property may be looted.

2004

In January, Minni Minawi becomes SLA chief of staff.

In February, the town of Tweila is attacked by the Sudanese army and Janjaweed militias, who kill at least sixty-seven, rape and brand girls and women, and displace 5,000 people. Bashir announces an end to government military operations and partially opens the Sudanese border to foreign aid.

The next month, al-Turabi is arrested by the government of Sudan on allegations of planning to overthrow the government.

On April 11, a cease-fire agreement (signed three days earlier by the SLA, the JEM, and the government of Sudan) comes into effect, but it will quickly unravel.

On April 25, the United Nations finds that Sudanese police in Kailek are holding internally displaced persons, with the intent of starving them to death.

An agreement is reached in May to end the civil war over southern Sudan.

In June, the African Union Mission in Sudan (AMIS) is up and running in Darfur.

The next month, the U.S. House and Senate pass measures stating that the atrocities in Darfur constitute genocide. The United Nations imposes an embargo on arms transfers to Darfur with the passage of Security Council Resolution 1556.

On September 9, U.S. secretary of state Colin Powell declares that the Sudanese government has committed genocide against non-Arab groups in Darfur.

On September 18, the UN International Commission of Inquiry on Darfur is established.

In October, some 3,500 additional African Union troops enter Sudan in a force known as AMIS II.

On November 18, political asylum is granted to the first group of Sudanese refugees entering Chad.

On December 19, Labado is attacked by government helicopters and burned.

On December 31, a permanent cease-fire is established between the government of Sudan and the southern rebels.

2005

On January 9, John Garang and Sudan's first vice president, Ali Osman Muhammed Taha, sign the Comprehensive Peace Agreement

(CPA), which establishes southern Sudan as a semiautonomous region. A referendum for full independence is to be held six years later.

On January 14, an attack on Hamada, Darfur, leaves 100, including many women and children, dead.

On January 25, the UN International Commission of Inquiry issues a report stating government actions in Sudan are not genocide, but instead constitute crimes against humanity.

On February 1, the UN Commission of Inquiry publishes a report on Darfur stating that, despite other serious violations of international humanitarian and human rights law, the violence in Darfur does not represent a policy of genocide.

In March, United Nations adopts Resolution 1593 and refers the situation in the Darfur region to the International Criminal Court (ICC). The UN Security Council adopts Resolution 1591 to strengthen the arms embargo in Darfur. The ICC charges Ahmad Muhammad Harun, Sudan's minister of humanitarian affairs, of having committed war crimes and crimes against humanity in Darfur.

In May, SLA forces under Minni Minawi (known as the SLA-MM) attack JEM at Gerieda and Jughana.

On June 6, the ICC opens an investigation into the perpetrators of the Darfur genocide.

In July, SLA-MM and JEM attempt to unify their resistance but are unsuccessful.

On June 29–30, U.S. secretary of state Colin Powell travels to Sudan to meet with President Bashir and visit a refugee camp in the Darfur region.

On July 9, Garang is sworn in as vice president of Sudan; he would be killed in a helicopter crash less than three weeks into his term.

On July 13, President Bashir asks the United States to lift economic sanctions that had been in place since 1997.

In August, Garang dies and is succeeded by Salva Kiir as the first vice president of Sudan.

The SLA divides into two factions in November: one led by Nur and the other by Minawi.

2006

In May, the government of Sudan and the Sudan Liberation Movement (SLM) faction led by Minawi sign a peace accord, but it is quickly broken.

U.S. president George W. Bush signs the Darfur Peace and Accountability Act in October.

2007

On April 27, the ICC issues arrest warrants for Ali Kushayb and Ahmad Harun.

On July 31, AMIS is replaced by the African Union–United Nations Hybrid Operation in Darfur (UNAMID) after the United Nations passes Resolution 1769.

2008

In May, JEM forces attack Omdurman, a city across the White Nile from the national capital of Khartoum. The Sudanese government accuses Chad of having supported the JEM rebels and breaks off diplomatic relations.

The ICC indicts Sudanese president Bashir in July for war crimes, crimes against humanity, and genocide.

2009

On March 4, the ICC issues an arrest warrant for Bashir.

In October, U.S. president Barack Obama unveils a new comprehensive policy toward

Sudan that opens up the possibility of lifting sanctions and removing the country from the State Department's list of state sponsors of terrorism.

In December, leaders from north and south Sudan agree to the terms of a referendum on independence, to be voted on in the south by 2011.

2010

In February, JEM and the government sign a preliminary agreement, by which JEM would attain seats in the government and become a recognized political party. However, within two months, the agreement disintegrates amid mutual accusations of violating the cease-fire and stalling the peace process.

In April, President Bashir is elected in a highly contested and suspect election.

On July 12, the ICC issues its second arrest warrant for President Bashir.

In August, despite the ICC arrest warrant, Bashir travels to Kenya, a signatory of the ICC. Kenya refuses to enforce the warrant.

In October, the UN Security Council adopts Resolution 1945, which strengthened the arms embargo in Darfur.

2011

Fighting breaks out in February in the Abyei region, which is claimed by both the north and south of Sudan.

On March 7, the ICC confirms charges of war crimes against the military leader Abdallah Banda.

In July, South Sudan votes overwhelming for independence in January and gains its statehood.

JEM joins the newly formed Sudanese Revolutionary Front (SRF) in November.

The next month, government forces kill Khalil Ibrahim, a key Darfur rebel leader.

2012

On March 1, the ICC issues an arrest warrant for Abdel Raheem Muhammad Hussein, Sudan's defense minister.

2013

The Sudanese government launches the Rapid Support Forces (RSF), which is composed of many former members of the Janjaweed.

2014

In February, President Bashir launches Operation Decisive Summer, a military campaign against Darfur rebel groups led by the RSF.

On September 11, the ICC issues an arrest warrant for Banda.

In October and November, the government of Sudan blocks UNAMID from accessing the Jebel Marra region in North Darfur to investigate allegations of mass rape by government forces. At least 200 women were reportedly raped in a thirty-six-hour period.

In December, the chief prosecutor of the ICC stops investigations into crimes committed in Darfur owing to lack of support from the UN Security Council.

2015

RSF soldiers rape scores of girls and women around the town of Golo in January.

In April, Bashir is elected for another five-year term. The election has a low turnout and is boycotted by nearly all the opposition parties.

2016

In October, the Sudanese Professionals Association (SPA) drafts a charter that is approved by three of Sudan's largest professional groups: the Central Committee of

Sudanese Doctors, the Sudanese Journalist Network, and the Democratic Lawyers Association.

2017

On October 12, the United States lifted some sanctions in relation to the conflict in Darfur.

2018

In January, the government of Sudan removes food subsidies, leading to escalating prices for bread. Protests ensue.

Government forces, including the RSF, attack more than a dozen villages in the Jebel Mara region of Darfur from March to May, killing at least twenty-three civilians, destroying and looting civilian property, and causing thousands to flee.

In December, *The New York Times* reports that since 2016, Saudi Arabia has recruited Darfurian children to fight Houthi rebels in Yemen.

2019

Protests over rising bread costs reach a peak in February. President Bashir declares a state of emergency and fires his cabinet and regional governors. Forty people are killed.

In a military coup on April 11, Bashir is arrested. The military refuses to work with civilian leaders represented by the SPA to create a coalition government, and violence breaks out.

On June 12, UN Security Council condemns the military violence against the protestors. The next day, the United States names a special envoy to Sudan to help support a solution between the military and protestors.

Abbreviations

AASG
American Anti-Slavery Group

ACHPR
African Commission on Human and
Peoples' Rights

ADT
Atrocities Documentation Team

AMIS
African Union Mission in Sudan

AU
African Union

CPA
Comprehensive Peace Agreement

DDF
Darfur Development Front

DDPD
Doha Document for Peace in Darfur

DLF
Darfur Liberation Front

EU
European Union

GNPOC
Greater Nile Petroleum Operating
Company

GOS
Government of Sudan

ICC
International Criminal Court

IDP
Internally displaced person

IGAD
International Authority on Development

JEM
Justice and Equality Movement

LJM
Liberty and Justice Movement

NCP
National Congress Party

NIF
National Islamic Front

OAU
Organization of African Unity

PDF
Popular Defense Force

R2P
Responsibility to protect

RSF
Rapid Support Forces

SFDA
Sudan Federal Democratic Alliance

SLA
Sudan Liberation Army

SLA-AW
Abdel Wahid al Nur faction of the Sudan
Liberation Army

SLA-MM
Minni Minawi faction of the Sudan
Liberation Army

SLM
Sudan Liberation Movement

SPLA
Sudan People's Liberation Army

SPLM
Sudan People's Liberation Movement

SSLM
Southern Sudan Liberation Movement

SSP
Satellite Sentinel Project

UN
United Nations

UNAMID
United Nations–African Union Mission in
Darfur

UNEP
United Nations Environment Programme

UNHCR
United Nations High Commission on
Refugees

U.S.
United States

USAID
United States Agency for International
Development

WHO
World Health Organization

Bibliography

Altman, Sheryl, and Sheryl Berk. 1998. *Matt Damon and Ben Affleck: On and Off Screen*. New York: HarperCollins Publishers.

Amnesty International. 2004. *Sudan, Darfur: Rape as a Weapon of War: Sexual Violence and Its Consequences*. Available at: https://www.refworld.org/docid/4152885b4.html.

Anderson, Scott. 2004. "How Did Darfur Happen?" *The New York Times*. October 17.

Annan, Kofi. *Interventions: A Life in War and Peace*. New York: Penguin Books, 2012.

Anyidoho, Henry Kwami. *Guns over Kigali: The Rwandese Civil War*. Accra, Ghana: Sub-Saharan Publishers, 2012.

Bedi, Shiv R. S. *The Development of Human Rights Law by the Judges of the International Court of Justice*. Portland, OR: Hart, 2007.

Beyrer, C., and H. Pizer. 2007. *Public Health and Human Rights: Evidence-Based Approaches*. Baltimore: Johns Hopkins University Press.

Brockman, Norbert C. *An African Biographical Dictionary*. Santa Barbara, CA: ABC-CLIO, 1994.

Brosché, Johan, and Daniel Rothbart. *Violent Conflict and Peacebuilding: The Continuing Crisis in Darfur*. New York: Routledge, 2013.

Burr, J. Millard, and Robert O. Collins. 2006. *Darfur: The Long Road to Disaster*. Princeton, NJ: Markus Weiner.

Burr, J. Millard, and Robert O. Collins. 2003. *Revolutionary Sudan: Hasan al-Turabi and the Islamist State, 1989–2000*. Boston: Brill Academic Publishers.

Cheadle, Don, and John Prendergast. 2007. *Not on Our Watch: The Mission to End Genocide in Darfur and Beyond*. New York: Hyperion.

Cheadle, Don, and John Prendergast. 2010. *The Enough Moment: Fighting to End Africa's Worst Human Rights Crimes*. New York: Three Rivers Press.

Cheadle, Don, and John Prendergast. 2013. "Cheadle/Prendergast: Lessons from Darfur, 10 Years Later." *USA Today*. March 19.

CNN. 2006. "Egeland: 'Meltdown' in Darfur." November 22. Available at http://www.cnn.com/2006/WORLD/africa/11/22/un.darfur/index.html.

Coalition for the International Criminal Court. n.d. "Abdallah Banda Abakaer Nourain." Available at http://www.coalitionforthe-icc.org/cases/abdallah-banda-abakaer-nourain.

Cockett, Richard. 2010. *Sudan: Darfur and the Failure of an African State*. New Haven, CT: Yale University Press.

Collins, Robert O. *A History of Modern Sudan*. Cambridge: Cambridge University Press, 2008.

Daalder, I. H. 2007. *Beyond Preemption: Force and Legitimacy in a Changing World*. Washington, DC: Brookings Institution Press.

Deng, Francis Mading. 1995. *War of Visions: Conflict of Identities in the Sudan*. Washington, DC: Brookings Institution Press.

De Waal, Alex. 2005. *Famine That Kills: Darfur, Sudan*. Oxford: Oxford University Press.

De Waal, Alex. 2019. "Sudan Crisis: The Ruthless Mercenaries Who Run the Country for Gold." BBC. July 20. Available at https://www.bbc.com/news/world-africa-48987901.

Doctors Without Borders/Médecins Sans Frontières. 2005. "The Crushing Burden of Rape, Sexual Violence in Darfur." Briefing Paper, March 8.

Donage, Ted. 2011. "Sudan: The Crisis in Darfur and the Status of the North-South Peace Agreement." Congressional Research Service. June 15. Available at https://fas.org/sgp/crs/row/RL33574.pdf.

Eggers, David. 2006. *What Is the What: The Autobiography of Valentino Achak Deng*. New York: Random House.

Ekengard, Arvid. 2008. *The African Union Mission in Sudan (AMIS): Experiences and Lessons Learned*. Stockholm: FOI, Swedish Defense Research Agency.

Elass, Mateen. 2004. *Understanding the Koran: A Quick Christian Guide to the Muslim Holy Book*. Grand Rapids, MI: Zondervan, 2004.

Evans, Glynne. 1997. *Responding to Crises in the African Great Lakes*. Oxford: Oxford University Press.

Flint, Julie. 2005. "Meet Salva Kiir, an SPLA Democrat." *The Daily Star*, August 9.

Flint, Julie, and Alex de Waal. 2006. *Darfur: A Short History of a Long War*. London: Zed Books.

Flint, Julie, and Alex de Waal. 2008. *Darfur: A New History of a Long War*. New York: Zed Books.

Fowler, Jerry. 2006. "A New Chapter of Irony: The Legal Definition of Genocide and the Implications of Powell's Determination." In Samuel Totten and Eric Markusen, eds., *Genocide in Darfur: Investigating the Atrocities in the Sudan*. New York: Routledge, 127–138.

"A Guide to the Coalition for International Justice Records." University of Connecticut Archives and Special Collections. Accessed November 18, 2018, from. https://archives.lib.uconn.edu/islandora/object/20002%3A860116155#accessAndUse.

Hagan, John, and Wenona Rymond-Richmond. 2009. *Darfur and the Crime of Genocide*. New York: Cambridge University Press.

Hamilton, Rebecca. 2011. *Fighting for Darfur: Public Action and the Struggle to Stop Genocide*. London: Palgrave Macmillan.

Henham, R. J., and P. Behrens. 2007. *The Criminal Law of Genocide: International, Comparative, and Contextual Aspects*. Burlington, VT: Ashgate Publishing Company.

Holt, P. M., and Martin Daly. 2000. *The History of the Sudan, from the Coming of Islam to the Present Day*. New York: Longman.

Hsiang, Solomon, Marshall Burke, and Edward Miguel. 2013. "Quantifying the Influence of Climate on Human Conflict," *Science* 5, no. 5, 17. Available at http://sciencemag.org/content/early/recent.

Human Rights Watch. 2006. "Sudan: Imperatives for Immediate Change. The African Mission in Sudan." January 19. Available at https://www.hrw.org/report/2006/01/19/sudan-imperatives-immediate-change/african-union-mission-sudan.

Human Rights Watch. 2019. "World Report." Available at https://www.hrw.org/world-report/2019.

International Crisis Group. 2004. "Darfur Rising: Sudan's New Crisis." *Africa Report* 76. March 25.

International Crisis Group. 2007. "Darfur: Revitalizing the Peace Process." *Africa Report* 125. April 30.

Johnson, Hilde F. 2016. *South Sudan: The Untold Story from Independence to Civil War*. New York: I. B. Tauris.

Jolie, Angelina. 2003. *Notes from My Travels*. New York: Pocket Books.

Jolie, Angelina. 2007. "Justice for Darfur." *The Washington Post*. February 28.

Kelsay, John. 2015. "Jihad." In Gerhard Bowering, ed., *Islamic Political Thought: An Introduction*. Princeton, NJ: Princeton University Press, 86–104.

Kiernan, Ben. 2007. *Blood and Soil: A World History of Genocide and Extermination from Sparta to Darfur*. New Haven, CT: Yale University Press.

Kindiki, Kithure. 2003. *Humanitarian Intervention and State Sovereignty in Africa: The Changing Paradigms in International Law*. Eldoret, Kenya: Moi University Press.

Kindiki, Kithure, and Institute for Security Studies (South Africa). 2007. *Intervention to Protect Civilians in Darfur: Legal Dilemmas and Policy Imperatives*. Tshwane, South Africa: Institute for Security Studies.

Kobrin, Stephen J. 2004. "Oil and Politics: Talisman Energy and Sudan." *NYU Journal of Law and Politics*. 36, nos. 2–3: 425–456.

Kostas, Stephen A. 2006. "Making the Determination of Genocide in Darfur." In Eric Markusen and Samuel Totten, eds., *Genocide in Darfur: Investigating Atrocities in the Sudan*. New York: Routledge, 111–126.

Kristof, Nicholas. 2019. "In a Career of Reporting, These Are the Stories That Still Touch Me." *The New York Times*. October 1. Available at https://www.nytimes.com/2019/10/01/opinion/kristof-new-york-times.html.

Lacey, Marc. 2005. "Sudan and Southern Rebels Sign Pact to End Civil War." *The New York Times*. January 1.

LeBor, Adam. 2008. *"Complicity with Evil": The United Nations in the Age of Modern Genocide*. New Haven, CT: Yale University Press.

Lippman, Matthew. 2007. "Darfur: The Politics of Genocide Denial Syndrome." *Journal of Genocide Research* 9, 193–213.

Makinda, Samuel M. 2007. *The African Union: Challenges of Globalization, Security, and Governance*. New York: Routledge.

Meisler, Stanley. 2008. *Kofi Annan: A Man of Peace in a World of War*. New York: Wiley.

Mills, Kurt. 2015. *International Responses to Mass Atrocities in Africa: Responsibility to Protect, Prosecute, and Palliate*. Philadelphia: University of Pennsylvania Press.

Moore, Jina. 2017. "U.S. Is Open to Removing Sudan from Terrorism List, Diplomat Says." *The New York Times*. November 16.

Nardin, T., and M. S. Williams. 2006. *Humanitarian Intervention*. New York: New York University Press.

Natsiosis, Andrew S. 2012. *Sudan, South Sudan, and Darfur: What Everyone Needs to Know*. Oxford: Oxford University Press.

Olson, James S. 1996. *The Peoples of Africa: An Ethnohistorical Dictionary*. Westport, CT: Greenwood Press.

Park, Linda Sue. 2010. *A Long Walk to Remember*. New York: Houghton Mifflin.

Powell, Colin. 2004. "The Crisis in Darfur." U.S. Department of State Archives. September 9. Available at https://2001-2009.state.gov/secretary/former/powell/remarks/36042.htm.

Power, Samantha. 2007. *"A Problem from Hell": America and the Age of Genocide*. New York: Harper Perennial.

Power, Samantha. 2008. *Chasing the Flame: Sergio Vieira de Mello and the Fight to Save the World*. New York: Penguin.

Power, Samantha. 2019. *The Education of an Idealist: A Memoir*. New York: HarperCollins.

Prunier, Gerard. 2005. *Darfur: The Ambiguous Genocide*. Ithaca, NY: Cornell University Press.

Prunier, Gerard. 2008. *Darfur: A 21st-Century Genocide*. 3rd ed. Ithica, NY: Cornell University Press.

Reeves, Eric. 2005. "The Failure of the African Union in Darfur: A Global Failure to Protect Civilian Populations Facing Genocide." Global Policy Forum. September 7.

Reeves, Eric. 2007. *A Long Day's Dying: Critical Moments in the Darfur Genocide*. Toronto: Key Publishing House.

Rolandsen, Øystein H., and M. W. Daly. 2007. *Darfur's Sorrow: A History of*

Destruction and Genocide. Cambridge: Cambridge University Press.

Rolandsen, Øystein H., and M. W. Daly. 2016. *A History of South Sudan: From Slavery to Independence.* Cambridge: Cambridge University Press.

Schabas, William. 2016. *The International Criminal Court: A Commentary on the Rome Statute.* Oxford: Oxford University Press.

Scherrer, P. Christian. 2002. *Genocide and Crisis in Central Africa: Conflict Roots, Mass Violence, and Regional War.* Westport, CT: Praeger.

Seekers of Truth and Justice. 2004. *The Black Book: Imbalance of Power and Wealth in Sudan.* Trans. Abdullahi Osman El-Tom. Self-published; available online at http://www.sudanjem.com/sudan-alt/english/books/blackbook_part1/book_part1.asp.htm.

Seri-Hersch, Iris. 2017. "Education in Colonial Sudan, 1900–1957." In *Oxford Research Encyclopedia of African History.* February. Accessed November 12, 2018, from http://africanhistory.oxfordre.com/view/10.1093/acrefore/9780190277734.001.0001/acrefore-9780190277734-e-12?print=pdf.

Slim, Hugo. 2004. "Dithering over Darfur? A Preliminary Review of the International Response." *International Affairs* 80: 811–828.

Sørbø, Grunnar M., and Abdel Ghaffar M. Ahmed, eds. 2013. *Sudan Divided: Continuing Conflict in a Contested State.* New York: Palgrave Macmillan.

Steib, Aspen. 2007. "Cheadle Acts to Stop Darfur Genocide." CNN. May 4. Available at https://www.cnn.com/2007/SHOWBIZ/books/05/04/darfur.book/index.html.

Steidle, Brian, and Gretchen Steidle Wallace. 2008. *The Devil Came on Horseback: Bearing Witness to the Genocide in Darfur.* New York: PublicAffairs Books.

Straus, Scott. 2016. *Fundamentals of Genocide and Mass Atrocity Prevention.* United States Holocaust Memorial Museum.

Totten, Samuel. 2010. *An Oral and Documentary History of the Darfur Genocide.* 2 vols. Santa Barbara, CA: Praeger Security International.

Totten, Samuel, and Eric Markusen, eds. 2006. *Genocide in Darfur: Investigating the Atrocities in the Sudan.* New York: Routledge.

Tubiana, Jérôme. 2019. "The Man Who Terrorized Darfur Is Leading Sudan's Supposed Transition." *Foreign Policy.* May 14. Available at https://foreignpolicy.com/2019/05/14/man-who-terrorized-darfur-is-leading-sudans-supposed-transition-hemeti-rsf-janjaweed-bashir-khartoum/.

Turse, Nick. 2016. *Next Time They'll Come to Count the Dead: War and Survival in South Sudan.* Chicago, Illinois: Haymarket Books.

United Kingdom House of Commons International Development Committee. 2005. "Darfur, Sudan: The Responsibility to Protect." In *Fifth Report of Session 2004–2005, Volume I.* Available at https://publications.parliament.uk/pa/cm200405/cmselect/cmintdev/67/67i.pdf.

United Nations. 1999. "Kofi Annan Emphasizes Commitment to Enabling UN Never Again to Fail in Protecting Civilian Population from Genocide or Mass Slaughter." Press Release SG/SM/7263 AFR/196. December 16. Available at https://www.un.org/press/en/1999/19991216.sgsm7263.doc.html.

United Nations. 2005. "Report of the International Commission of Inquiry on Darfur to the United Nations Secretary-General." January 25. Available at http://www.iccnow.org/documents/UN%20commission_inquiry_report_darfur.pdf.

United Nations. 2008. *Atrocities and International Accountability: Beyond Transitional Justice.* New York: United Nations.

United Nations. 2019. *Conflict-Related Sexual Violence: Report of the United Nations Secretary-General.* March 29,

S/2019/280. Available at https://www .un.org/sexualviolenceinconflict/wp -content/uploads/2019/04/report/s-2019 -280/Annual-report-2018.pdf.

United Nations Security Council. 2005. "Sudan Peace Agreement Signed 9 January Historic Opportunity, Security Council Told." Press Release SC/8306. February 8. Available at https://www.un .org/press/en/2005/sc8306.doc.htm.

U.S. Government Accountability Office. 2006. "Darfur Crisis: Progress in Aid and Peace Monitoring Threatened by Ongoing Violence and Operational Challenges." Report No. GAO-07-9. November 9.

Walzer, Craig, ed. 2008. *Out of Exile: Narratives from the Abducted and Displaced People of Sudan.* San Francisco: Voice of Witness.

World Health Organization. 2009. "Healing Child Soldiers." *Bulletin of the World Health Organization* 87, no. 5, 325–404. Available at http://www.who.int/bulletin /volumes/87/5/09-020509/en/.

Young, Helen, Abdul Monim Osman, Yacob Aklilu, Rebecca Dale, Babiker Badri, and Abdul Jabbar Abdullah Fuddle. 2005. *Darfur—Livelihood Under Siege.* Medford, MA: Feinstein International Famine Center. Available at http://fic.tufts .edu/assets/Young-Darfur-Livelihoods -Under-Seige.pdf.

List of Contributors

Dr. Alexis Herr

Lecturer

San Francisco State University and
University of San Francisco

CONTRIBUTORS

Dr. Paul R. Bartrop

Professor of History

Director of the Center for Judaic,
Holocaust, and Human
Rights Studies

Florida Gulf Coast University

Evan Brown

University of Washington

Jennifer Christian

Policy Analyst

Enough Project

Dr. Robert O. Collins

Professor of History, Emeritus

University of California,
Santa Barbara

Abraham O. Mendoza

Independent Scholar

Jane Messah

Independent Scholar

Dr. Paulos Milkias

Professor of Humanities and Political
Science

Marianopolis College/Concordia
University

Montreal, Canada

Dennis Moran

Independent Scholar

Terri Nichols

Independent Scholar

Dr. James S. Olson

Distinguished Professor of History

Sam Houston State University

David Paige

Independent Scholar

Dr. Paul G. Pierpaoli Jr.

Fellow

Military History, ABC-CLIO, Inc.

Dr. David L. Porter

Louis Tuttle Shangle Professor of History

William Penn University

Regina Rainwater

Independent Scholar

Melissa Stallings

Independent Scholar

Elinor O. Stevenson

Attorney

Public International Law and Policy Group

Hannibal Travis

Professor of Law

Florida International University College of Law

Dr. Andrew J. L. Waskey

Professor of Social Science

Dalton State College

Dr. John Hubbel Weiss

Professor of History

Cornell University

Dr. Karl A. Yambert

Editor

The Contemporary Middle East: A Westview Reader

Index

Note: Page numbers in **boldface** type indicate main entries.

Abakir, Abadallah, 105

Abboud, Ibrahim, 132, 144

Abdallah, Mohamed Ahmed ibn ("al Mahdi"), 25, 53, 122

Abdel Shafi, Ahmad, **1–2**, 139

Addis Ababa Peace Agreement, 92, 133, 136, 139, 151

ADT. *See* Atrocities Documentation Team

Affleck, Ben, 56

African Belt, xxi

African Commission on Human and Peoples' Rights (ACHPR), 215, 217

African Mission in Burundi (AMIB), 4

African Union (AU), xviii–xix, **2–4**, 215
goal of, 3
headquarters (Addis Ababa), 3
peacekeeping force in Darfur, 39–40, 213, 215
response to Darfur situation, xxxii–xxxiii, 4
on use of genocide terminology, 44–45

African Union Mission in Sudan (AMIS), xviii–xix, xxxiii, **4–6**
AMIS II and IIE, 5

African Union–United Nations Mission in Darfur (UNAMID), xviii–xix, xxix, xxxiii, **6–7**, 215

AIDS, 37, 156–157

Alliance for Direct Action Against Rape in Conflicts and Crises, 90–91

al Qaeda, 19, 75, 145, 151–152

American Anti-Slavery Group (AASG), 143

AMIS. *See* African Union Mission in Sudan

Amnesty International, **7–9**
Egeland, Jan, and, 51

Anglo-Egyptian Condominium, 25–26, 54, 136

Annan, Kofi, **9–13**
Darfur Genocide and, 12–13
early life and career, 9–10
genocide, term use/non-use, 12, 44, 221
phone call to Bashir, 12
Rwandan Genocide and, 10–11
as secretary-general of UN, 11–12

Anyanya movement, 133, 136

Anyidoho, Henry Kwami, **13–15**

Arab, as category, xvii, xx, xxvii, 81, 91, 204
interpreted as Muslim, xxvii
misleading characterizations, xvii, xxvii, 38, 91
vs. "non-Arab" and "black Africans," xvii, xx, xxvii, 19, 25, 38, 54, 81, 133, 134, 211, 213

Arab Gathering, xx–xxi, 213

Arab militias. *See* Janjaweed

Arabs
Arab settlers of Khartoum, 91–92
arming by Sudanese government, xx–xxi
intermarriage of, xvii, xx, xxvii, 38

Arabs (*cont.*)
  as nomadic herders, xvii, xx, xxvii
  preferential treatment by government,
    92, 212
  resettlement of lands vacated by conflict,
    xviii, xxvii, 212, 222
  tribal affiliation through male line,
    xxviii
Arab supremacism, xxi–xxii, 134, 211, 212,
  213–214, 216, 222
Armenian Genocide, 162
Arrest warrants (ICC) for Sudan officials,
  xx, xxv, xxviii, xxxiv, 44, 219, 222,
  225
  ignored by Sudan government, 219, 222,
    223, 225
  INTERPOL and, 223
As We Forgive (film), 61
Atrocities Documentation Team (ADT),
  40–41, 212, 220–221

Baez, Joan, 8
Baldo, Suliman, 56
Banda, Abdallah, **17–18**, 87–88
  arrest warrant for, xxxiv, 17, 148
  JEM and, 17, 87
  war crimes accusations, 17, 87–88
Ban Ki-Moon, 12, 51
  on three pillars on R2P, 225–226
Bashir, Omar Hassan Ahmed el-, **18–22**,
  92, 128–129, 213–215
  arrest warrants for, xx, xxiii, xxv, xxxii,
    xxxiv, 20, 44, 61, 134, 148, 219, 222,
    225
  coup to take power, 18, 107, 128–129,
    133, 151
  current status of, xxxiv, 21, 135
  Darfur Genocide and, 1, 19–21, 211,
    213–217
  dissolution of parliament, 19
  early life, 18
  Egypt and, 54, 134
  genocide charged by ICC, 20, 44, 134,
    222, 225

Islamic (Sharia) law and, 18–19, 67–68
Janjaweed and, 19–20, 82, 134,
  212, 214
jihad issuance by, 83–84
Muslim Brotherhood and, 107, 133
National Islamic Front and, 18, 92, 107,
  108
peace and power-sharing agreement
  (2004), 19
popularity of, 20–21, 213, 215
removal from office (2019), 8, 21, 135,
  156
South Sudan and, 21
Turabi and, 19, 144, 145
U.S. relationship with, 150–152
Bassolé, Djibril, **22–23**
Benenson, Peter, 8
Beyond Borders (film), 85
Billion Lives, A (Egeland), 52
bin Laden, Osama, 75, 151
  Sudan as safe haven for, 19, 68, 133, 145,
    151
"Black Africans," xvii, xx, xxvii, 19, 25,
  38, 54, 81, 133, 134, 211, 213
Black Book, The, xxi, **23–24**, 86–87,
  192–193
  Ibrahim, Khalil, and, 77
  Part Two, 24
Blood diamonds, 61
Bor mutiny, 139–140
Bosnian Genocide, 161
British involvement in Darfur, **24–27**, 41,
  127
  Anglo-Egyptian Condominium, 25–26,
    54, 136
  colonial period, 25–26, 53–54, 122–123,
    127, 135–136
  response to genocide, 26
Burkina Faso, 22, 23
Bush, George W., xix, 20, 117, 152, 205
  Minawi, Minni, 105
Bystanders, Darfur Genocide, xxix
  bystanderism, 112
  Upstanders vs., 30–31

Cambodia, 86

Carter, Jimmy, 44

Causes of Darfur Genocide, xx–xxii, 134, 211–217
  about (overview), xx–xxii, 211–213
  Arab supremacy, rise of, xxi–xxii, 134, 211, 212, 213–214, 216, 222
  arms transfer over porous borders, xxii, 135, 216
  conflict over resources, xvii, xx–xxi, 1, 59, 134, 212, 216–217
  marginalization of Sudanese borderlands, xxi, 19, 24
  Sudanese Civil War, impact of, xxii, 135–137

Celebrities, 8, 29
  Affleck, Ben, 56
  Cheadle, Don, 29–31
  Clooney, George, 32–34, 56
  Damon, Matt, 37–38, 56
  Enough Project and, 56
  Farrow, Mia, 56, 60–62
  Jolie, Angelina, 84–86
  Pitt, Brad, 29, 56, 85, 86
  Spielberg, Steven, 61

Center for American Progress (CAP), 55

Central Emergency Response Fund (CERF), 52

CERF. See Central Emergency Response Fund

Chad
  Itno as president, xviii, xxx–xxxi, 163
  proxy war with Sudan, xxiv, 107–108
  refugee camps in, xix, xxii, 212
  See also Itno, Idriss Déby

Cheadle, Don, **29–31**, 152
  China, trip to, 30, 33
  Darfur Now (film), 30
  Enough Moment, The (film), 30, 115
  honors, 30
  Hotel Rwanda (film), 29
  Not on Our Watch, 29–30, 33, 114, 115
  Prendergast, John, and, 29, 56, 114
  Summit Peace Award, 30

Child soldiers, **31–32**, 114

China, 219–220
  Beijing Olympics, 60, 220
  Cheadle and Clooney trip to, 30, 33
  funding and arms for Sudanese government, xviii, xxx, 215
  oil purchases from Sudan, xviii, xxx, 212, 219–220
  Olympic Dream for Darfur campaign, 60–61, 220
  opposition to UN sanctions for Sudan, 219

Christianity, 122–123
  in South Sudan, xxii, 25, 122–123, 132

CIJ. See Coalition for International Justice

Civil Wars. See Sudanese Civil Wars

Climate/climate change, 216–217
  droughts, xvii, xx, xxi, 59
  Famine of 1984–1985 and, 59–60

Clinton, Bill, 111, 113, 117, 143, 151, 161

Clooney, George, **32–34**, 56, 162
  China trip of, 30, 33
  Darfur Now (film), 33
  humanitarian work of, 32–33
  Journey to Darfur, A (film), 33
  Not on Our Watch, 29, 33–34, 115
  Sand and Sorrow (film), 33
  Satellite Sentinel Project and, 56, 125
  Sentry, The, and, 125
  Summit Peace Award, 33

Coalition for International Justice (CIJ), **34–35**

Colonial period, 25–26, 53–54, 122–123, 135–136
  in South Sudan, 127–128

Commission of Inquiry on Darfur. See United Nations Commission of Inquiry on Darfur

Comprehensive Peace Agreement (CPA), xxii, **35–36**, 68, 129, 137, 140
  Garang, John, and, 35–36, 68, 140
  implementation of, 149–150
  John Garang's speech at signing of, 173–183
  politics of, xxiii

Consequences of Darfur Genocide,
    xxii–xxiv
  human consequences, xxii–xxiii
  ongoing consequences, xxiv
  political consequences, xxiii–xxiv
  regional dynamics and proxy wars, xxiv,
    107–108
CPA. *See* Comprehensive Peace Agreement

Dagolo, Mohamed Hamdan "Hemeti"
    ("Little Mohamed"), 82
Dallaire, Roméo, 10, 14
Damon, Matt, **37–38**, 56
  Not on Our Watch, 29, 33, 37–38, 115
Darfur, **38–40**, 133
  British involvement in, 24–27, 41, 127
  continued violence in, 40
  data and statistics on, 23–24, 53–54
  distance from Khartoum (remoteness),
    xxi, 91, 214
  early rulers of, 38–39
  Egyptian involvement in, 25, 41, 53–55,
    122–123, 127
  ethnic groups/tribes in, xvii, xxvii, 38,
    122, 213
  ethnic tensions/conflict in, xvii, xx,
    xxvii, 19, 25, 38–39, 133
  history of conflict in, xviii, 39
  location in Africa, xvii
  maps, xxxv–xxxvi
  new states in (Central and East Darfur),
    38, 135
  population of, xvii
  religion in, 39, 122–123, 213
  states and capitals within, 38
  U.S. involvement in, xxxii, 150–153, 212
  village self-defense committees, xxvi, 1
Darfur Atrocities Documentation Project,
    40–41, 212
Darfur Development Front (DDF), **41–42**
  Diraige, Ahmed, and, 42, 47
Darfur Dream Team, 115
Darfur Genocide, 42–45, 133–134
  about (overview), xvii–xxxiv, 211–213

Bashir and Sudan government role in,
    213–217
  causes of, xx–xxii, 134, 211–217
  current/continuing status of, xix
  denial of, 42–45
  eyewitness accounts, xviii, xxviii, 71, 81,
    97, 100, 119
  funding and arms for, xviii, xxx, 135,
    215, 216
  government/Janjaweed tactics in, xxii,
    xxv, 73, 81, 100, 119, 121, 133–134,
    138, 212, 216
  lifestyles and (nomadic herders vs.
    farmers), xvii, xx–xxi, xxvii, 38, 59,
    212
  major battles (map), xxxvi
  maps, xxxv–xxxvi
  perspective essays on, 211–228
  resettlement of vacated lands, xviii,
    xxvii, 212, 222
  scorched-earth campaign, xix, xxiv, 81,
    100, 138, 214
  tribal/ethnic labeling as "Arabs" vs.
    "non-Arab" and "black Africans," xvii,
    xx, xxvii, 19, 25, 38, 81, 133, 211, 213
  U.S. declaration of genocide, xix, xxxii,
    41, 43–44, 150–151, 152, 212
  U.S. Department of State Memo on
    (June 2004), 167–169
  See also Genocide
Darfurian rebel groups, xvii–xviii, xxvi–
    xxvii, 43, 163, 211–214
  about (overview), xxvi–xxvii, 211–213
  attacks on government installations, xxi,
    43, 87, 212, 214
  child soldiers used by, 31–32
  Darfur Liberation Front (DLF), xxvi, 1
  funding for, xxx–xxxi
  Fur, Zaghawa, and Massalit in, xxvi, 43,
    163
  internal struggles and splits, xxvi, 1–2,
    99, 138–139
  Justice and Equality Movement (JEM),
    xxvi, 86–88, 105, 192–193

Liberation and Justice Movement (LJM), 99–100

rebellion as cause of/intensifier of genocide, 214, 217

role in perpetuating conflict, xxv

Sudan Liberation Army (SLA), xxvi, 105, 137–139, 193–195

United Nations Commission of Inquiry statement on, 192–195

See also specific groups

Darfur in Flames with Janjaweed's Return (SSP Report, 2014), 125

Darfur Liberation Front (DLF), xxvi, 1, 137–138

attacks on government installations, xxi, 1

renamed as SLA, xxvi, 1, 137–138

See also Sudan Liberation Army (SLA)

Darfur Now (film), 30, 33, 220

Darfur Peace and Accountability Act (U.S., 2006), 204–209

Darfur Peace and Agreement (DPA, 2006), xxiii, 105, 134, 213

SLA-MM signing of, 105, 155, 213

DDPD. *See* Doha Document for Peace in Darfur

Déby, Itno. *See* Itno, Idriss Déby

Deng, Valentino Achak, 159–160

Denial of the Darfur Genocide, **42–45**

Devil Came on Horseback, The, 130–131, 158

Dinar, Sultan Ali, 25

Dinka, **45–47**, 129–130

Garang, John, and, 66

Kiir, Salva, and, 92

Lost Boys and Lost Girls of Sudan, 46, 100

oil on land of, 46

war with Nuer, 94

"What Is the What?" legend, 159–160

Diraige, Ahmed Ibrahim, **47–48**

Darfur Development Front and, 42, 47

warnings of drought effects, 59

Divest for Darfur, 220

Doctors Without Borders, 86, 95

rape statistics from, xxviii

Doha Document for Peace in Darfur (DDPD), xxiv, xxxiii, 40, **48–49**, 134

Doha Peace Agreement (DPA)

Bassolé, Djibril, and, 22

implementation of, 49, 99–100

monitoring of, 56

signed by LJM and government, 1, 23, 40, 47, 139

withdrawal of JEM, 47, 87, 88

Doha peace talks, 22–23, 48

DPA. *See* Darfur Peace and Agreement

Drought, xvii, xx, xxi

Famine of 1984–1985 and, 59–60

Great Drought of 1984–1985, 59

Economics of Ethnic Cleansing, The (SSP Report), 125

Education of an Idealist, The (Power), 113

Egeland, Jan, **51–53**

A Billion Lives, 52

Eggers, David, 159–160

Egyptian involvement in Darfur, 25, 41, **53–55**, 122–123, 127

Anglo-Egyptian Condominium, 25–26, 54, 136

Bashir trips to Egypt, 54, 134

Mubarak, Hosni, 54

Muslim Brotherhood in Egypt, 107

response to Darfur Genocide, 54

Enough Moment, The (film), 30, 115

Enough Project, xix, xxxii, **55–57**, 114

celebrity supporters, 56

Ethiopia, 68

Ethnic tensions/racism, xvii, xx, xxvii, 19, 25, 38, 54, 81, 133, 134, 211, 213

ethnic cleansing, term use, 221

other smaller ethnic groups, 216

targeted groups (Fur, Zaghawa, and Massalit), xxvii–xxviii, 211, 215, 217

European Union (EU), 26, 221

"Sudan Demarche: Crisis in Darfur Requires EU Pressure and Resources" (June 2004), 169–173

Famine
  Famine of 1913–1914 (*Julu*), 59
  Famine of 1984–1985, **59–60**
Farmers, xvii, xxvii, 38
  conflict over resources, xvii, xx–xxi, 1, 59, 212
  fencing of lands, xx
Farrow, Mia, 56, **60–62**
  As We Forgive (film), 61
  Olympic Dream for Darfur, 60–61
Female victims, xxviii–xxix, 119–120, 212
Free Lions, 87
Free Officers Movement, 133
Funding
  for Darfur rebel factions, xxx–xxxi
  for government troops and militias, xviii, xxx, 135, 215
Fur, xxvii–xxviii, **62–63**, 217
  Abdel Shafi and, 1, 139
  African Belt, xxi
  attacks by Minawi troops, 105
  Diraige, Ahmed, and, 42
  early rulers, 62
  eyewitness accounts of attacks on, xviii, xxviii
  as farmers, xx, xxvii, 63
  as largest ethnic group in Darfur, 38, 42, 62
  in Sudan Liberation Army (SLA), xxvi, 137
  Wahid, Abdel, and, 63, 105
Fur-Arab War of 1987–1989, 63

Gaddafi, Muammar, 3, 227
Galukoma, Haydar, 99–100
Gambari, Ibrahim, **65–66**
Garang, John, xxxi, **66–69**, 128, 139–140, 173–183, 202
  Comprehensive Peace Agreement and, 35–36, 68, 140
  death of, 36, 68, 93, 129, 140
  Kiir, Salva, and, 93
  Nimeiry and, 67, 128, 139–140
  as president of South Sudan, 140

  Speech at Signing of Comprehensive Peace Agreement (2005), 173–183
  Speech on "Social Contract" for Sudan (2005), 202–205
  as vice president of Sudan, 35, 68, 129, 140
Garda, Bahar Abu, xx, xxxiv, 148
Genocide, 42–45, 160–162, 220–222
  agreement on mass murder and atrocities, xix, 43–44, 188, 213, 221
  definition of, xix, 41, 42–43, 148, 168, 221
  ethical questions of recognition/response, 42–45, 168–169, 220–222
  genocidal intent, xxxiii, 13, 43, 168, 189–190, 214
  International Association of Genocide Scholars, 44
  perspective essay on, 220–222
  requirement to intervene, xxxii, 43, 44–45, 220–222
  responsibility to protect (R2P), 223–224, 225–227
  United Nations Commission of Inquiry on Darfur and, xxxiii, 147–148, 188–192, 213
  United Nations Convention on the Prevention and Punishment of the Crime of Genocide (Genocide Convention), xix, 41, 43, 44–45, 116, 148–149, 220–221
  U.S. declaration of genocide, xix, xxxii, 41, 43–44, 150–151, 152, 212, 221
  U.S. Memo on Genocide in Darfur (June 2004), 167–169
  See also Darfur Genocide
Global Grassroots, 157
Good Lie, The (film), 101–102
Goodwill ambassadors. *See* United Nations goodwill ambassadors
Gordon, Charles, 25, 53
Gore, Al, 216
Gosh, Salah Abdallah, **69–70**

Habré, Hissène, xxx, 78
The Hague, Netherlands, xix, 17, 34, 61
Harun, Ahmad, **71–72**
    arrest warrant for, xx, xxv, xxxiv, 71,
        134, 148, 219
    as "butcher of Nuba," 71
    current status and suspected activities,
        xxxiv, 72
Herders, xvii, xxvii, 38
    characterization as "Arabs," xvii, xxvii
    vs. "non-Arab" and "black Africans,"
        xvii, 38
    promise of lands vacated, xxi, xxvii
    tensions over resources, xx–xxi,
        59, 212
    Zaghawa (non-Arabs) as, xvii, xxvii
Hilal, Musa, **72–75**, 82
    U.S. sanctions against, 74
Holocaust, 41, 149, 160–162, 222
    UN Genocide Convention after, 41
    U.S. Holocaust Memorial Museum, 43,
        62, 114, 126
Humanitarian aid, xxxi, 222–224
    blocked by Bashir/Sudan government,
        xxiii, xxxii, 40, 214–215
    humanitarian workers killed, xxiii
    Kapila, Mukesh, and, 89
    UNAMID, 6–7, 215
    U.S. call for, 169–173
Hussein, Abdel Raheem Muhammad,
    75–76
    arrest warrant for, xx, xxxiv, 75, 82,
        148
    bin Laden and, 75
    current status and suspected activities,
        xxxiv
    ICC charges against, 75
Hyde, Henry, 204

Ibrahim, Fatima, 18
Ibrahim, Jibril, 88
Ibrahim, Khalil, **77–78**, 192
    Black Book and, 77
    JEM and, xxvi, 77–78, 86

ICC. *See* International Criminal Court
IGAD. *See* Intergovernmental Authority on
    Development
Iman al-Hadi, 42
Intergovernmental Authority on
    Development (IGAD), xxix, xxx, 26
Internally Displaced Persons (IDP), xix,
    xxii, 119, 212
    camps, map of locations, xxxv
    numbers of, xxii, xxviii, 212
    See also Refugees
International Commission. *See* United
    Nations Commission of Inquiry on
    Darfur
International Commission on Intervention
    and State Sovereignty, 223–224
International Criminal Court (ICC),
    xix–xx, xxxiii–xxxiv, 44, 134, 148,
    213, 218–219
    arrest warrants issued, xx, xxv, xxxiv,
        20, 134, 148, 219, 225
    referral by United Nations Commission
        of Inquiry on Darfur to, 199–201, 213
International Criminal Tribunal for
    Rwanda (ICTR), 115–117
International Crisis Group, 220
International Partners Forum, 26
International Reaction to Darfur Genocide,
    xviii, xxxi–xxiv, 211, 218–228
    about (overview), xxxi–xxiv, 212–213
    African Union, xxxii–xxxiii, 2–7
    Britain (UK), 26
    cable from Colin Powell calling for
        international action (June 2004),
        169–173
    delayed response, xviii, 26
    humanitarian response, xxxi–xxxii, 6–7,
        169–173
    intervention, issues concerning, 218–228
    just cause concept, 223–224, 226
    peace overtures of UN and AU, xxxii–
        xxxiii, 39–40, 218
    perspective essays on intervention,
        218–228

International Reaction to Darfur Genocide (*cont.*)
responsibility to protect (R2P) doctrine, 223–224, 225–227
sanctions against Sudan, xix, 20, 21, 151, 152, 212
Sudanese Civil Wars, foreign policy objectives in, xxix–xxx, 212–213, 214
United Nations, xxxii–xxxiii, 6–7, 147–150
U.S. call for international action, 169–173
U.S. reactions, xxxii, 150–153, 165–173, 212
See also Peace; Peacekeeping missions in Darfur; United Nations
INTERPOL, 223
Intervention, issues concerning, 218–228
background, 218–220
just cause, 223–224, 226
just reason for international intervention, 224–228
moral and legal obligations, 220–222
peremptory norm under international law, 225, 227
responsibility to protect (R2P), 223–224, 225–227
sovereignty, vs. people's welfare, 222–224
Islam, 122
majority Muslim population in Darfur, 39, 122, 213
Islamic (Sharia) law, 18–19, 83, 107, 122, 139, 144, 151
Islamic Charter Front (ICF), 107, 144
Islamists, 122–123, 144–145, 213–215
Islamization of north Sudan, xxi–xxii, 18–19, 132–133, 134, 213–214
National Islamic Front (NIF), 107–108
Sunni sect, 122
Itno, Idriss Déby, xxx, **78–79**, 163, 164
Abuja Peace Talks and, 4
ethnic identity, xxx
plot to unseat Habré, xxx

relationship to Darfur Genocide, xxx–xxxi
support for Darfurian rebel groups, xviii, xxx

Jamus, Saleh Mohammed Jerbo, xx
Janjaweed, xxv, 39, **81–83**, 121, 133–134, 138, 195–199, 215–217
about (overview), xviii, xxv
as Arab militia, xxv, 39, 81
Bashir and, 19–20, 82, 134, 212, 214
brutality of attacks, 39, 73
categories within, 82
Darfur in Flames with Janjaweed's Return (SSP Report, 2014), 125
Devil Came on Horseback, The, 130–131, 158
eyewitness accounts of attacks by, xviii, xxviii, 71, 81, 97, 100, 119
Hilal and, 72–75, 82
Hussein and, 82
impunity policy for Janjaweed crimes, 216
Kushayb and, 82, 96–97
leaders of, 72, 82
meaning of term, xviii, xxv, 81
origins of, 81
as perpetrators in Darfur Genocide, xxv, xxviii, 81–83
Popular Defense Force (PDF) and, 82
popular support for, 138
rape and, 119–120, 121, 212
Rapid Support Forces (RSF), 82
scorched-earth campaign, xix, xxiv, 81, 138, 214
tactics of, 73, 81, 119, 121, 133–134, 138, 216
United Nations Commission of Inquiry statement on, 195–199
U.S. Department of State description of (March 2004), 165–167
JEM. *See* Justice and Equality Movement
Jihad, **83–84**
Kushayb and, 96–97
meanings and types of, 83

Jolie, Angelina, **84–86**, 113
    Beyond Borders (film), 85
    honors and awards, 86
    Jolie-Pitt Foundation, 86
    Notes from My Travels, 85
Journey to Darfur, A (film), 33
Just cause, 223–224, 226
Justice and Equality Movement (JEM),
    xvii–xviii, xxvi, 43, **86–88**,
    105, 138
    attacks on government installations,
        xxi, 43
    Banda, Abdallah, and, 87–88
    Black Book and, xxi, 86–87, 192–193
    child soldiers used by, 31–32
    distinction from SLA, 86
    Doha Document for Peace in Darfur,
        refusal to sign, 47, 87, 88
    establishment of, xxvi, 77, 86
    Ibrahim, Jibril, and, 88
    Ibrahim, Khalil, and, xxvi, 77–78,
        86, 192
    Islamists and, xxvi, 86
    JEM-Eastern Command, 87
    rifts and fracturing, 87
    Turabi and, 86–87, 192
    United Nations Commission of Inquiry
        statement on, 192–193
    Zaghawa affiliation of, 86

Kapila, Mukesh, **89–91**
Khartoum, xxi, **91–92**
    Arab settlers of, 91–92
    bin Laden residing in, 151
    as capital of Sudan government, 91
    distance from Darfur, xxi, 91
    Gordon, Charles, in, 25, 53
    location (map), xxxv
    public protests in, 135
Kiir, Salva, **92–94**, 129, 140–141
    Garang, John, and, 93
Kony, Joseph, 52
    After Kony (film), 114
Kristof, Nicholas, 43, **94–96**, 109

Kushayb, Ali, 82, **96–97**
    arrest warrant for, xx, xxviii, xxxiv, 82,
        96, 134, 148, 219

Legal principles, 218–228
    just cause, 223–224, 226
    peremptory norm under international
        law, 225, 227
    responsibility to protect (R2P), 223–224,
        225–227
    sovereignty, 222–224
    See also Genocide
Lemkin, Raphael, 148–149
Liberation and Justice Movement (LJM),
    99–100
    Abdel Shafi and, 2
    Doha Document for Peace signing, xxiv,
        1, 2, 22, 40, 139
    Gambari, Ibrahim, and, 65
    SLA factions and, 2
    splits within, 99
Libya, 3, 107–108
LJM. *See* Liberation and Justice
    Movement
Long Day's Dying, A (Reeves), 121
Lost Boys and Girls of Sudan, 46, **100–
    102**, 129, 133
    Lost Boys of Sudan (film), 101
    What Is the What (book), 159–160

Machakos Protocol, 140
Machar, Riek, 94, 129
Mahdi, the, 25, 53, 122
Mahdist War (1885–1898), 127
Marginalization of Sudanese borderlands,
    xxi, 19, 24
Mariam, Mengistu Haile, 68
Massalit, xxvii–xxviii, **103**, 217
    eyewitness accounts of attacks on, xviii,
        xxviii
    as farmers, xx, xxvii
    in Sudan Liberation Army (SLA), xxvi
Mbeki, Thabo, 22
McGrady, Tracy, **103–104**, 115

Minawi, Minni, **104–106**, 138–139
  Bashir and, 105
  Bush, George W., and, 105
  SLA-Minni Minawi (SLA-MM), xxvi,
    xxvii, 104–105, 139, 155
Mubarak, Hosni, 54
Mugabe, Robert, 3
Muslim Brotherhood, 75, 107, 133
  NIF and, 71, 107
  in Sudan, 69, 75, 107

Naivasha Agreement. *See* Comprehensive
    Peace Agreement (CPA)
National Congress Party (NCP), xxiii, 86,
    92, 107, 129, 145, 175
  CPA and, xxiii
National Islamic Front (NIF), xxv, 38, 92,
    107–108, 144
  Bashir and, 18, 92, 107, 108
  Ibrahim, Khalil, and, xxvi
  Turabi and, 18, 144
National Redemption Front, 77, 155
NATO (North Atlantic Treaty
    Organization), 155, 227
Natsios, Andrew, 220
NCP. *See* National Congress Party
New York Times, 94–96
NIF. *See* National Islamic Front
Nile River, xxxv, 132, 213
Nilotic peoples, 46, 163
Nimeiry, Gaafar Muhammad an-, 67,
    92–93, 107, 139
  Second Sudanese Civil War and, 128,
    133
  Sharia law and, 144, 151
  Turabi and, 144–145
  United States and, 151
Nomadic herders. *See* Herders
North Atlantic Treaty Organization
    (NATO), 155, 227
Notes from My Travels (Jolie), 85
Not on Our Watch (book), 29, 114
Not on Our Watch (organization), 29–30,
    33–34, 37–38, 115, 159

Nuba, xx, xxxiv, **108–110**, 137
  Harun, Ahmad, and, 71
Nuer, 94, 120–130
  Lost Boys of Sudan and, 100
Nur, Abel Wahid Mohammad Ahmad al-.
    See Wahid, Abdel

OAU. *See* Organization of African Unity
Obama, Barack, 29, 112, 152
Oil interests
  China and, xviii, xxx, 212, 215, 219–220
  Greater Nile Petroleum Operating
    Company (GNPOC), 143
  oil on Dinka land, 46
  oil-producing regions, 139, 143–144
  Second Sudanese Civil War and, 133
  Talisman Energy Corporation, 143–144
Olympic Dream for Darfur, 60–61, 220
Omdurman, 77
Omidyar Network, 121
ONE Campaign, 32
Organization of African Unity (OAU), 2
Ottoman Empire, 39, 53, 62

Pastoralists. *See* Herders
PDF. *See* Popular Defense Force
Peace
  ceasefires, xxxii–xxxiii, 87, 138, 172–
    173, 205
  Comprehensive Peace Agreement
    (2005), xxiii, 35–36, 129, 137, 140,
    173–183
  Darfur Peace Agreement (2006), xxiii,
    105, 134, 213
  Darfur Peace and Accountability Act
    (U.S., 2006), 204–209
  Doha Document for Peace in Darfur
    (2011), xxiv, xxxiii, 40, 48–49, 134
  Doha Peace Agreement (DPA), 1, 23, 49,
    56, 99–100, 139
  United Nations and African Union
    efforts toward, xxxii–xxxiii, 39–40,
    213, 215
  See also specific acts and documents

Peacekeeping missions in Darfur
  African Union Mission in Sudan
    (AMIS), xviii–xix, 4–6, 213
  United Nations-African Union
    (UNAMID), xviii–xix, xxxiii, 6–7,
    39–40, 215
Peremptory norm under international law,
    225, 227
Perpetrators of Darfur Genocide, xxiv–
    xxvii, 147, 211–217
  about (overview), xxiv–xxvii, 211–213
  accountability for, 199–209
  Bashir, xxv, 1, 19–21, 211, 213–215,
    213–217
  funding and arms for, xviii, xxx, 135,
    216
  identification as Muslims, xxv, xxvii
  Janjaweed, xxv, 81–83, 133–134,
    195–199, 215–217
  policy of impunity for Janjaweed crimes,
    216
  Popular Defense Force (PDF),
    xxiv–xxv
  scorched-earth campaign, xix, xxiv, 81,
    100, 138, 214
  strategy to remove "non-Arabs," xxv,
    211
  Sudan's government forces, xvii–xviii,
    xxv, 211–217
  Sudan's intelligence services, xxv
Perspective essays
  Bashir, Arabism, and international
    community, 213–215
  cause of Darfur Genocide, 211–217
  Darfur conflict as just case for
    intervention, 218–228
  Sudan government, role of, 215–217
Pitt, Brad, 29, 56, 85, 86, 115
Popular Congress Party (PCP), 86–87, 145
Popular Defense Force (PDF), xvii–xviii,
    xxiv–xxv, 82, 108
  campaign against the Nuba, 109
  jihad and, 84
  Kushayb and, 96–97

Powell, Colin, xxxii, 12, 41, 117, 150–151,
    152, 169–170, 212, 220
  ADT report cited by, 41
  call for international action on Darfur
    Genocide (June 2004), 169–173
  Education of an Idealist, The, 113
  genocide declared for Darfur, 12, 26, 41,
    150–151, 152, 212
  Problem from Hell, A, 111
Power, Samantha, **111–113**
Prendergast, John, **113–115**, 152
  Cheadle, Don, and, 29, 56, 114
  Enough Project, 55–57, 114
  Not on Our Watch (Cheadle and
    Prendergast), 29, 114
  organizations cofounded by, xix, xxxii,
    29, 37–38, 114–115
  Satellite Sentinel Project, 125
  Sentry, The, and, 125
Pressman, David, 29, 33
Problem from Hell, A (Power), 111
Prosper, Pierre-Richard, **115–118**
Proxy wars, xxiv, 107–108

R2P (responsibility to protect) doctrine,
    223–224, 225–227
Rahman, Ali Muhammad Ali Abd-Al-.
    See Kushayb, Ali
Rape, xxviii–xxix, **119–120**, 212
  Alliance for Direct Action Against Rape
    in Conflicts and Crises, 90–91
  children of, xxviii, xxix
  numbers of rapes, xxviii, 119, 120
  perpetrators, 119, 120
  refugee/IDP camps and, 119–120
  survivor accounts of, xxviii,
    119–120
  torture and, xxviii, 119
  tribal affiliation through male line,
    xxviii
Rapid Support Forces (RSF), 82, 120
Rashaida, 87
Reagan, Ronald, 128, 145, 149
Rebel groups. See Darfurian rebel groups

Reeves, Eric, 74, **120–122**
  on African Union, 4
  Long Day's Dying, A, 121
Refugees, xix, xxii–xxiii, 170, 212
  child soldiers recruited from, 31–32
  cost of repatriating/resettlement, xxiii
  difficulties of returning home, xxiii
  due to drought and famine, 60
  Internally Displaced Persons, xix,
      xxii, 119, 212
  Internally Displaced Persons camps,
      map, xxxv
  Lost Boys and Girls of Sudan, 100–102
  numbers of refugees, xxii, xxviii, 39,
      100, 119, 212, 214
  rape, vulnerability to, 119–120
  refugee camps in Chad, xix, xxii, 212
  from Sudanese Civil Wars, xxix, 137
  United Nations High Commission for
      Refugees (UNHCR), xxiii
  unwillingness to return home, xxiii
  See also Humanitarian aid
Religion, **122–123**, 144
Resources, conflicts over, xvii, xx–xxi, 1,
    59, 134, 212, 216–217
Responsibility to protect (R2P), 223–224,
    225–227
Revolutionary Awakening Council, 72–73
Rice, Condoleezza, 117
Rice, Susan, 112, 113
Rome Statute, xxv, 148, 218
  states not party to, 219
RSF. *See* Rapid Support Forces
Russia, xviii, xxx, 212, 215
Rwanda
  As We Forgive (film), 61
  genocide in, 10–11, 222
  Hotel Rwanda (film), 29
  International Criminal Tribunal for
      Rwanda (ICTR), 115–117, 223
  Kapila, Mukesh, and, 89
  Prosper, Pierre-Richard, and, 115–117
  UN Assistance Mission for Rwanda,
      10, 14

Sadiq al-Mahdi, 42, 107
Sanctions against Sudan, xix, 20, 21, 151,
    152
  opposed in United Nations, 212–213, 215
Sand and Sorrow (film), 33, 114
Satellite Sentinel Project (SSP), 56,
    125–126
Save Darfur Coalition, xix, xxxii, **126–127**
Scheffer, David, 117
Scorched-earth campaign, xix, xxiv, 81,
    100, 138, 214
Sentry, The, 115, 125
September laws (1983), 145, 151
Sharia law, 18–19, 83, 107, 122, 139, 144,
    151
Sierra Leone, 61
Sikha, 107, 108
Sisi, Tijani, 99
SLA. *See* Sudan Liberation Army
Slaves/slavery, 53, 91, 92, 122
  American Anti-Slavery Group (AASG),
      143
  females and, 100, 119
  sex slavery, 100, 119, 134
  Sudanese Civil Wars and, 133
Small arms, xxii, 135, 216
  funding and sourcing of, xviii, xxx,
      xxx–xxxi, 215
Smith, Gayle, 55, 114
Social Contract for Sudan (John Garang's
    speech, 2005), 202–205
South Sudan, 21, **127–130**
  British involvement and, 25, 136
  Christianity in, xxii, 25, 122–123, 128,
      136
  civil wars, 94, 128–129
  colonial period, 127–128
  Comprehensive Peace Agreement (CPA)
      and, xxii, 35–36, 68, 129, 137, 173–183
  conflicts in, xviii, xxii
  Dinka in, 45–47, 129–130
  Garang, John, and, 66, 93, 140
  independence for, 21, 35, 69, 94, 127,
      129, 137, 141

Kiir, Salva, as president, 92, 93–94, 129, 140–141
  as "non-Arab" and Christian, xxii, 25, 122–123, 136
  Nuer in, 129–130
  population of, 130
  present-day conflicts, 129–130
  size of, 94
  Sudan People's Liberation Movement/ Army (SPLM/A), xviii
Sovereignty, vs. people's welfare, 222–224
Spielberg, Steven, 61
SPLA. *See* Sudanese People's Liberation Army
SPLM/A. *See* Sudan People's Liberation Movement/Army
SSP. *See* Satellite Sentinel Project
Steidle, Brian, **130–132**, 157
  Devil Came on Horseback, The, 130–131, 158
Sudan, **132–135**
  civil wars in, xviii, xxii, 132–133, 135–137
  Darfur conflict in, xvii–xxxiv, 38–40, 133–134
  data and statistics on, 23–24, 53–54
  Egyptian involvement in, 25, 41, 53–55, 122–123, 127
  Government of Unity, 129
  government role in Darfur Genocide, 213–217
  intelligence services, xvii–xviii, xxv
  northern half, xxii, 132–133
  power imbalance in (*Black Book*), 23–24, 86–87, 192–193
  size and location, xxxv, 132
  "Social Contract" (Garang), 202–205
  southern half, 127–130, 132
Sudan, government forces, xvii–xviii, xxv, 211–217
  air force, xxv
  Bashir as commander-in-chief, xxv, 213–217

Popular Defense Force (PDF), xvii–xviii, xxiv–xxv
  rapes reported for, xxix, 212
  role in Darfur Genocide, 213–217
  security and intelligence services, xxv
Sudanese borderlands, marginalization of, xxi, 19, 24
Sudanese Civil Wars, xviii, xxix–xxx, 128–129, 132–133, **135–137**
  Addis Ababa Peace Agreement, 92, 133, 136, 139, 151
  Comprehensive Peace Agreement (CPA), xxii, 35–36, 129, 137, 173–183
  First Civil War (1955–1972), 128, 132–133, 135–136
  Garang, John, and, 66–69
  impact on Darfur, xxii
  international community, policy objectives in, xxix–xxx, 212–213, 214
  interwar period (1972–1983), 128, 136
  Lost Boys and Girls of Sudan, 100–102, 129, 133
  north vs. south in, xxii, 132–133
  numbers displaced, xxix, 35, 129
  numbers killed, xxix, 35, 129
  Second Civil War (1983–2005), 109, 128, 133, 136–137
  sources of conflict, xxii
  SPLM/A and, xviii
Sudanese People's Liberation Army (SPLA), 108–109, 133, 139–140
  Comprehensive Peace Agreement and, 175–182
  Garang, John, and, 128, 140, 175
  SPLA-North, 109
  SPLA-United, 140
  See also Sudan People's Liberation Movement/Army (SPLM/A)
Sudanese Professional Association, 135
Sudan Federal Democratic Alliance (SFDA), 47
Sudan Liberation Army (SLA), xvii–xviii, xxvi, 43, 121, **137–139**, 193–195
  Abdel Shafi and, 1–2, 139

Sudan Liberation Army (*cont.*)
  about (overview), xxvi, 137
  attacks on government installations, xxi,
    43, 212
  child soldier use, 69
  creation of, 1, 212
  Fur, Zaghawa, and Massalit in, xxvi,
    137, 138
  leaders of, xxvi, 104–105
  rapes by, 120
  SLA-Abdel Wahid (SLA-AW), xxvi, 1,
    105, 120, 139, 155–156
  SLA-Field Leadership, 99
  SLA-Juba, 1, 139
  SLA-Justice, 99
  SLA-Minni Minawi (SLA-MM), xxvi,
    xxvii, 1, 104–105, 139, 155
  splits within, xxvi, 1–2, 138–139
  United Nations Commission of Inquiry
    statement on, 193–195
  village self-defense committees, xxvi
Sudan Liberation Movement (SLM), 1–2
  SLM-Juba Unity, 2
Sudan Muslim Brotherhood, 75, 107
Sudan People's Liberation Movement/
  Army (SPLM/A), xviii, xxxi, 136,
  139–141
  about (background), xviii, xxxi, 139
  Comprehensive Peace Agreement and,
    xxiii, 140, 175–182
  factions and splits, 140
  Garang, John, and, xxxi, 66–68, 128,
    139–140, 175
  SLPM-North, 105
  union with JEM and SLA, xxvii, 87
  United Nations Commission of Inquiry
    statement on, 193–195
Sudan Revolutionary Front (SRF), xx,
  xxvii, xxxiv, 105, 156

Taha, Ali Osman Muhammad, 100
Talisman Energy Corporation, **143–144**
Taylor, Charles, 61
Tiger Division, 129

Trump, Donald, 21, 152
Turabi, Dr. Hassan al-, 67–68, **144–145**
  arrest and imprisonment of, 19, 145
  Bashir and, 19, 144, 145
  JEM and, 86–87, 192
  National Islamic Front (NIF) and, 18
  NIF and, 107
  Nimeiry and, 144–145

Uganda
  Kony, Joseph, in, 52, 114
  Night Commuters of, 114
Umma Party, 42, 107, 144
UNAMID (United Nations–African
  Mission in Darfur), xviii–xix, xxix,
  xxxiii, 6–7, 215
UNCG. *See* United Nations Convention on
  the Prevention and Punishment of the
  Crime of Genocide
UNHCR. *See* United Nations High
  Commission for Refugees
United Kingdom. *See* British involvement
  in Darfur
United Nations
  Central Emergency Response Fund
    (CERF), 52
  Millennium Development goals, 12
  response to Darfur situation,
    xxxii–xxxiii
  sanctions opposed in, 212–213, 215,
    219
  Security Council, 212–213, 224, 226
  Universal Declaration of Human Rights,
    8
  See also United Nations Security
    Council resolutions
United Nations–African Union Mission in
  Darfur (UNAMID), xviii–xix, xxix,
  xxxiii, 6–7, 215
  current day operations of, xxxiii
United Nations Commission of Inquiry on
  Darfur, xxxiii, **147–148**, 183–201, 213
  accountability, recommendations on,
    199–201

establishment of, xxxiii, 184–188
excerpts (primary document), 183–201
final report (2005), 147–148, 183, 188–201
on genocide, 188–192
on the Janjaweed, 195–199
on Justice and Equality Movement, 192–193
referral to ICC, 199–201, 213
on Sudan Liberation Movement/Army, 193–195
United Nations Convention on the Prevention and Punishment of the Crime of Genocide (UNCG), xix, xxxii, 41, 43, 44–45, 116, **148–149**, 220–221
Article VIII, 221
responsibility to protect doctrine, 223–224, 225–227
United Nations Darfur Task Force, xxviii
United Nations goodwill ambassadors
Cheadle, Don, 30
Farrow, Mia, 60
Jolie, Angelina, 84–85
United Nations High Commission for Refugees (UNHCR), xxiii
United Nations Mission in the Sudan (UNMIS), **149–150**
United Nations Security Council
resolutions, xix
Resolution 1556 (2004), xxxiii, 6
Resolution 1564 (2004), xxxiii, 26, 44, 147
Resolution 1590 (2005), 149
Resolution 1591 (2005), xxxiii
Resolution 1593 (2005), xix
Resolution 1769 (2007), xxxiii, 12
Resolution 1945 (2010), xxxiii
Resolution 2046 (2012), 21
Resolution 2363 (2017), xix, 7
United Nations World Food Programme, 30, 34
United States involvement in Darfur, xxxii, **150–153**, 212

cable from Colin Powell calling for international action on Darfur Genocide (June 2004), 169–173
Darfur Atrocities Documentation Project, 40–41, 212, 220–221
Darfur Peace and Accountability Act (2006), 204–209
Department of State Describes the Janjaweed Militia (March 2004), 165–167
Department of State Memo on Genocide in Darfur (June 2004), 167–169
Department of State Press Guidance: "Sudan: Accountability for War Crimes" (2005), 201–202
genocide in Darfur, declaration of, xix, xxxii, 41, 43–44, 150–151, 152, 212, 221
sanctions against Sudan, xix, 20, 21, 151, 152
Universal Declaration of Human Rights, 8
UNMIS. *See* United Nations Mission in the Sudan
Upstanders, 30–31

Victims of Darfur Genocide, xxvii–xxix
about (overview), xxvii–xxix, 212
burning and razing of villages, xxii–xxiii
characterized as "non-Arab" and "black Africans," xvii, xx, xxvii, 19, 25, 38, 81, 133, 211, 213
female victims, xxviii–xxix, 119–120, 212
identification as Muslims, xxvii
numbers displaced, xix, xxii, xxviii, 20, 39, 214
numbers killed, xix, xxii, xxviii, 20, 39, 211, 214
numbers of rapes, xxviii
scorched-earth campaign, xix, xxiv, 81, 100, 138, 214
tribal groups targeted (Fur, Zaghawa, and Massalit), xxvii–xxviii, 211, 215, 217

Wahid, Abdel, 1, 138–139, **155–156**
  self-exile in Paris, 105, 155–156
  SLA-Abdel Wahid (SLA-AW), xxvi, 105, 139, 155–156
  as SLA leader, xxvi, 63, 105, 138
Wallace, Gretchen Steidle, **156–158**
Water resources. *See* Resources, conflicts over
Weapons. *See* Small arms
Weintraub, Jerry, **158–159**
  Not on Our Watch, 29, 33, 159
What Is the What, **159–160**
Wiesel, Elie, 29, 33, 114, 126, **160–162**
Women, xxviii–xxix, 18–19, 119–120
  khimar or burka, wearing of, 19
  rape of, xxviii–xxix, 119–120, 212

Sharia dress code and punishments, 19
  Sharia law and, 18–19
World Health Organization (WHO), 90

Zaghawa, xxvii–xxviii, **163–164**, 217
  attacks on Fur, 105
  in Chad, xxxi, 163
  eyewitness accounts of Janjaweed attacks on, xviii, xxviii
  Itno, Idriss Déby, and, 78, 163, 164
  Justice and Equality Movement (JEM) and, 86
  Minawi, Minni, and, 104–106, 163
  as non-Arab herders, xvii, xx, xxvii, 163
  SLA-Minni Minawi (SLA-MM), xxvi, 105, 139, 155
  in Sudan Liberation Army (SLA), xxvi

About the Editor

Dr. Alexis Herr has dedicated her life to combating genocide and atrocities through education and advocacy. In addition to holding academic positions at California State University, Berkeley, San Francisco State University, University of San Francisco, Keene State College, and Northeastern University, she has worked for nonprofit organizations focusing on Holocaust, genocide, and refugee education and advocacy, including the Holocaust Center, a division of Jewish Family and Children's Services, Refuge-Point, and Jewish World Watch. She is the author of *The Holocaust and Compensated Compliance in Italy: Fossoli di Carpi, 1942–1952,* and the editor of *Rwandan Genocide: The Essential Reference Guide.* Herr earned her doctorate in Holocaust History from the Strassler Center for Holocaust and Genocide Studies at Clark University in 2014.